VUNAMAMI

VUNAMAMI

Economic Transformation in a
Traditional Society
by
Richard F. Salisbury

UNIVERSITY OF CALIFORNIA PRESS

BERKELEY AND LOS ANGELES 1970

University of California Press
Berkeley and Los Angeles, California
University of California Press, Ltd.
London, England
Copyright © 1970, by
The Regents of the University of California
Standard Book Number: 520-01647-5
Library of Congress Catalog Card Number: 70-79062
Printed in the United States of America

pire ToMas, Tion, ma IaGaak
upi ra warmari kai Kalou
na wardone diat
ma ra tarai Vunamami.

Acknowledgements

Financial support for this study has been provided, at various stages, by the University of California (by the Committee on Research, and by the Institute of International Studies), the U.S.P.H.S. (Grants M 4427 and MH-4912), McGill University, and the Canada Council. This support is gratefully acknowledged, although responsibility for any findings of the study must rest with the author.

Additional facilities were accorded to the author by the Sacred Heart Mission (in Münster, Westfalen, at Vunapope, and at Geneva, Illinois), by the Museum für Völkerkunde in Hamburg, by the Australian National University, the University of Papua and New Guinea, the Methodist Overseas Mission (in Sydney and Rabaul), the Mitchell Library, and the Department of Territories in Canberra. Permission to quote from unpublished sources has been granted by the three last-named bodies. Any worker in New Guinea must be grateful for the assistance unfailingly given by the Administration of the Territory, in the present case chiefly through Messrs John Foldi, William Kelly, and Sidney Smith and their staffs.

In New Guinea the ideas emerged partly from discussions with, among Europeans, David Fenbury, Harry Gaywood, Ken Gorringe, David Hope, William Kelly, Father Krümpel, Rev. Wesley Lutton, J. K. McCarthy, Tony Monaghan, Max Orken, Ian Purvis, Don Preston, Charles Rowley, Bishop Scharmach, Rev. J. Sharp, John Walsh, and, above all, Sid Smith. Collaboration with him facilitated this study to an extent beyond even the calls of friendship. The text indicates my debt to many New Guineans for providing all the material, and to the people of Vunamami for the hospitality shown to me and my family. I have used personal names throughout as a recognition of this. But the argument of the present

vii

work developed also from discussions with Vin ToBaining, Enos Teve, John ToMarangrang, ToLungen, Dale ToPin, Beniona ToKarai, and Darius ToMamua.

In anthropological circles I have had most fruitful discussions over the years with Gunder Frank and Peter Lawrence. An S.S.R.C. Workshop in Economic Anthropology in 1959 brought constructive comment from Raymond Firth, Bert Hoselitz, Manning Nash, Ed LeClair, Stanley Udy, and Sidney Mintz. Interdisciplinary seminars of the McGill Centre for Developing-Area Studies have provided a continual challenge to relate my material to studies in other areas and other disciplines than anthropology. But the main challenge has come from the discussion of ideas with students, too numerous to be listed individually. Those who have helped in specific ways in data analysis have been Henry Lewis, Klaus Koch, Helgi Osterreich, Katherine Roback, and Gillian Sankoff. Typing help was provided by Wera VanEschen, Laraine Ryder, and Kathy Morris.

This manuscript includes in the text Tolai material up to 1963. Later Tolai material and references to literature up to 1965 have been included where possible in the text, but otherwise in footnotes. References to materials later than 1965 have been included only sporadically in the course of manuscript revision.

R.F.S.

Waigani, Papua
November 1967

Contents

TABLES

MAPS

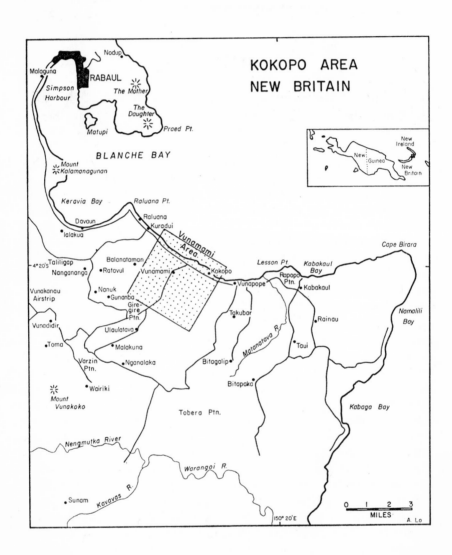

KOKOPO AREA
NEW BRITAIN

Nodup

Malaguna

RABAUL

Simpson
Harbour

The Mother

The
Daughter

Matupi

Praed Pt.

BLANCHE BAY

Mount
Kalamanagunan

Keravia Bay

Raluana Pt.

Davaun

Raluana

Kuradui

Ialakua

Vunamami
Area.

4°20'S Taliligap

Balanataman

Lesson Pt.

Kabakaul
Bay

Cape Birara

Nangananga

Ratavul

Vunamami

Kokopo

Vunapope

Rapopo
Ptn.

Kabakaul

Vunakanau
Airstrip

Nanuk

Gunanba

Gire-
gire
Ptn.

Tokubar

Namalili
Bay

Vunadidir

Ulaulatava

Matanatava R.

Rainau

Toma

Malakuna

Bitagalip

Taui

Varzin
Ptn.

Nganalaka

Bitapaka

Wairiki

Kabaga Bay

Mount
Vunakoko

Tobera Ptn.

Nengmutka River

Warangoi R.

Sunam

Kavavas R.

0 1 2 3
MILES

150°20'E

A. Lo

New
Guinea

New
Ireland

New
Britain

Introduction

Can the non-industrial countries achieve sustained economic development using their own resources alone? This book's answer is "Yes, given adequate resources, and given the right social changes during development." The answer is based on a detailed study of ninety years of development in a small society in New Guinea. A succession of technological changes, each one associated with a political change, has led the society to the threshold of sustained development—a net capital investment of from 10 to 23 percent of income, almost 100 percent literacy, and rapidly rising incomes. Although much of the study does describe the economics and history of the society, the focus is on the nature of the internal political changes, which, it is argued, have been the crucial factors, turning pre-existing conditions conducive to development, and available technological knowledge, into the reality of development.

The focus on internal factors producing growth does not deny the importance of external factors—overseas finance, technical know-how, and advice and personnel to create an infrastructure of social services. Technological knowledge indeed is fundamental to growth, but the other factors only facilitate it, though the assumption is often made that they are the causes for it. They are the factors most often stressed by economic advisers and planners from overseas—largely because they are the factors that can be most easily contributed from overseas. Yet too many people in the developing countries themselves—administrators and expatriates in particular—tend to make the jump to assuming that they are the *only* important factors. What is needed internally, such people argue, is to remove barriers which prevent the external inputs from being effective—local disincentives to saving, political instability discouraging foreign investment, low levels of skill or productivity in labour, rigid social barriers which discourage efficiency, or corruption which diverts investment into private gains. For such people the volume of external aid is of first importance, with the readiness of the recipients to learn how to use it "properly" a second need.

Such a formulation presents a gloomy prospect to the people of low-income countries. Rich countries are increasing their per capita income faster, both absolutely and proportionately, than the poor countries. Aid would need to increase beyond any contemplated present level if it were to counteract this process. Nor does income from imports promise to increase greatly. Prices for exports from low-income countries have declined, virtually as productivity has increased, while the prices of machinery from high-income countries have risen. At the same time repayment and interest due for loans already incurred take an increasing amount of earnings. Further borrowing and further debts seem to indicate a future of bondage. Since most low-income countries have high birth rates, it is as much as many of them can do to sustain present per capita incomes. Self-help, though desired by many, seems to offer little; it means reducing barriers, but not providing positive growth.

This pessimistic view, the present study argues, is not necessarily justified. On the one hand, pessimism is based on a false view that "traditional society" was inherently unchanging and economically stagnant. The speed of change in societies before they were contacted by literary cultures is hard to document, even in New Guinea, where Europeans were making first contacts in the interior even into the 1950's. Yet it is clear that crops like tobacco and sweet potatoes had spread rapidly across the country well before Europeans arrived (Riesenfeld 1951, Watson 1965), dramatically altering the economies of many areas. Cult movements were endemic long before European contact (Salisbury 1958), and groups prided themselves on their cultural borrowings from elsewhere (Mead 1938). What was seen by the first European explorers was not "age-old traditions persisting for centuries," but the current versions of rapidly changing sets of behaviours. If the adoption of manioc in Africa (Jones 1959) and the American adoption of the horse (Ewers 1955) are guides, similar rapid changes within traditional non-industrial societies were common in other parts of the world too. Unreasoning conservatism was not characteristic of "traditional society." Experimentation was (and is) constant, but it is necessarily on a small scale when a crop failure can mean starvation. Innovations must be clearly successful before they are widely accepted, yet once they are widely accepted the outside observer without historical records has difficulty in realizing that they have not always been part of the local scene.

Nor are traditional societies internally homogeneous. True, almost every adult male may be a farmer, and so a village appears homogeneous to an external and superficial observer. Yet every farmer is different, and the differences in the size of his family, in area of land owned, in political aspirations, in technical knowledge, or in energy profoundly affect his farming. Each subsistence farmer's running of his farm is much more significantly different from every other farmer's than is the running of different machines by operatives in a factory. The farmer must make highly complex decisions: he must, in a subsistence society, visualize how much land must be planted to feed his household until the next-harvest-but-one is ready; he must make allowances for contingencies of weather, or social needs like weddings or funerals throughout that period; he must evaluate crop possibilities in terms of land types available to him; if he practices bush fallow, he must think of how the cultivating of a particular piece of land now will affect his children twenty years hence; he must plan his work so that the necessary weeding of one crop does not coincide with the time needed for planting a second or harvesting a third; he must think ahead to how he can get additional labour over and above that of his household for major tasks like fencing or harvesting; he must anticipate capital needs by months or years so that scarce imported requirements are on hand when needed; to accumulate pigs for a wedding feast he must begin breeding years ahead. Even if all farmers had the same level of technical knowledge, their plans would be expected to differ, as their labour and land resources, as their consumption needs, and as the risks they are willing to run also differ. In fact vast differences in technical knowledge abound. Much technical knowledge is embodied in rules which, to the city dweller, seem part of an immutable cultural heritage, known to everyone—everyone knows you make hay when the sun shines. But much of the total corpus of knowledge in a village is not known to everyone, nor is it universally available. Particular lineages own particular varieties of seed yam; different families swear by different herbs to be used for blessing gardens; good fishing and hunting sites are jealously kept secrets; fathers pass on knowledge of soil types to their sons alone, in the course of cultivating familial land. No theory of economic development is adequate if it ignores the calculating abilities, the entrepreneurial tendencies, or the range of individual variation found among traditional farmers.

The false view of "traditional society" as necessarily conservative, unchanging, and homogeneous has indeed been fostered by many anthropologists even as they have gone beyond the point of view of the superficial outside observer. In trying to show the wealth of knowledge, the cultural richness, and the intricate interconnectedness of activities in other societies they have often generalized their descriptions of diversity and talked about uniform "cultures," organized bodies of "rules of behaviour" verbalized by informants, or "norms" abstracted from the observation of diverse behaviour. They analyse the rules as being logically consistent, so that any other behaviour is seen as deviant or illogical. They treat the "rules" not as statistical central tendencies or technical precepts but as moral norms, enforced by social control mechanisms and conformed to by everyone but deviants. The compelling force of "tradition" is assumed, when the "rules" may often be little more than practical suggestions which leave the choice of actual behaviour open to the individual. Other tasks than haying may take precedence even in sunshine.

A different picture emerges, however, when field anthropologists initially assume that the behaviour they observe is the result of a choice by the actor among other alternatives.[1] The assumption is supported, since actors can always, when properly questioned, give coherent reasons *in their own terms* for their behaviour. In their own terms they can outline the calculations that they made in choosing. Three main tasks confront the economic anthropologist who has data of this kind. He must first properly translate the terms that the informants use to describe their economic calculations, and must never assume that the terms have exactly the same connotations as those used in the intellectual discipline of economics. But he must be aware that his translation is being made for people versed in the terminology of "economics"

[1] Within the terminology current in economic anthropology in 1965, I clearly espouse what has been called a "formalist position." I do not see any "controversy" between my position and what has been called the "substantivist position." It is merely a matter of substantivists having used antiquated field data, which ignored the role of individual rational choice in non-Western economies. Given these inadequate data, "substantivists" have made important contributions describing the institutional framework of choice. It is on the basis of such knowledge that more modern formalistic, quantitative studies are possible.

and so must relate the two terminologies. His second task is to relate local economical terminology to its background in the local society and culture—to show, for example, how different categories of land or land tenure are associated with different types of social grouping, or with different religious concepts. His third task is to record in quantitative terms the decisions that people make, and to determine how the decisions are in fact related to the various decision criteria listed earlier. The economic anthropologist expects the final answer to be that the decisions are "rational" given the uncertainties involved, the variable resources of different farmers, or the extremely high costs of alternative courses of action. They may turn out, unexpectedly, to be empirically "irrational" and the reasons for irrationality must be sought.

Much of the present study, particularly in the second part, is a documentation of the economic calculations, the economic terminology, the social background, and the quantitative implications of such calculations among a group of Tolai villagers in New Britain. No argument is explicitly made against anthropologists or economists who assume that people living in "traditional societies" are "bound by custom" or are "inherently conservative." An exposition of the facts is enough to show the falsity of the assumptions on which such theories are based. The reader should bear in mind during the exposition of Tolai economic concepts, with which each chapter starts, that the aim is to demonstrate quantitatively how these concepts underlie the decisions that are made. This demonstration is, I feel, the main contribution of the study to economic anthropology.

But if simple societies show such diversity and such internal rationality, how can the present study be reconciled with studies of economic development such as those of Rostow (1960), Hagen (1961), and McClelland (1961), in which a stagnant, unchanging, traditional society forms an integral part of the theory? Before concluding that the theories themselves are incorrect, one must examine several alternatives. It may well be that the sort of society called "traditional" by such theorists is a stereotype, based on stagnant agricultural societies of Latin America and South and East Asia (usually of "peasant" type), which is inapplicable to the subsistence-based societies found in the Pacific, Africa, or North America. If this is true, and I shall later discuss evidence supporting this answer, then the present study should be viewed as complementing theories about stagnant traditional societies with one analysing the development process in "dynamic traditional societies."

The second alternative is that such theorists have postulated stagnant unchanging society in the pre-change situation merely in order to construct a hypothetical model, and not with the intention of generalizing about real societies. With this single assumption about the internal conditions of a society, the way is open for discussing only inputs into the system from outside and for relating changes in the total system only to those exogenous forces. But such a procedure deals only with exogenous forces; it assumes that endogenous forces are either negligible, or are randomly related to the exogenous forces and so cancel out in a study of the latter. Again, the present work, in discussing mainly endogenous developmental forces, complements studies dealing only with exogenous development. But at the same time it should be noted that to the extent that the presence of developmental forces within traditional societies facilitates or reinforces the working of exogenous forces, to that extent the amount of variation apparently explained by theories of the latter type must be reduced by the amount due to interaction between endogenous and exogenous forces.

Finally, theorists may have assumed that "traditional societies" are stagnant simply because they were working from faulty primary descriptions. The present study suggests that for historical materials, as well as for old-style anthropological reports, this may very likely be true. Reports of a small-scale society written by external observers, knowing the society for only a short period, will describe it as unchanging during that period. The reports tend to be of topics that interest the outside observer—the way of life of plantation owners for the tourist attracted to gracious living, the administration of law and order for the government official. Histories are usually compiled from just such written accounts. The historian reads each observer's report, and can place it in terms of the history of the country from which the observer came; he can place it in terms of the innovations of expatriates reported by earlier observers. The result inevitably focuses on the way in which foreigners, or events in the outside world, bring local change out of stagnation. An equally intensive study of local (oral) sources is needed to place the events in a local historical sequence of dynamic events.

Historians are not unaware of the biases of their sources. A modern social historian, by cross-checking differing accounts, by critically appraising the influence of differing viewpoints on the testimony of missionaries, traders, government officials, or visiting travellers, and by compiling statistics, can often disprove the accuracy of particular documents. He can give a plausible approximation of the truth. But he still gives a version in which the local people—"the natives"—appear as puppets, moved by the actions of foreigners, or, where the observer could see no reasons for what the locals did, as "irrational savages swayed by impulse, emotion, and tradition."

Part One is an attempt to review the history of the Tolai people of Vunamami village as it might be written by a social historian with access only to written records.[2] To some extent its purpose is that of illustrating how different would be a history written by the people themselves, as attempted in Part Two. But it also highlights the merits of such a historian's account. Such an account is easily understood by the foreigner—he knows about the voyages of discovery, missionaries, traders, and colonial administrators, and can gradually be introduced to the exotica of New Britain. One can more easily remember a sequence of local events if they are presented within a wider chronology of German imperial expansion, the First World War, the Depression, and the Second World War. And most important, on particular topics —the dating of events in absolute chronology, the identities of

[2] Research for this part of the study was conducted between 1958 and April 1961 with support from the University of California Committee on Research, the U.S.P.H.S. (Grant No. M-4427), and the University of California Institute of International Studies. Current newspapers were reviewed, and all issues of the *Pacific Island Monthly* (which began in 1931). Libraries in the United States (particularly that at Harvard) were consulted for German colonial publications; the library of the Sacred Heart Mission (M.S.C.) in Münster, Westfalen, was searched, together with the Richard Parkinson collection and colonial materials at the Museum für Völkerkunde in Hamburg; in Australia the Methodist Overseas Mission collection at the Mitchell Library was made available to me, as were the archives of the Department of Territories in Canberra. The only major source not consulted, owing to lack of permission, was the German official archives in Potsdam. I should like to express my gratitude for permission to view the other records, and to cite manuscript sources in the case of the Methodist Overseas Mission and the Australian Department of Territories. Neither, of course, should be considered responsible for any views expressed in this study. Mr. Klaus Koch and Mrs. Helgi Osterreich assisted with the analysis of documentary materials. An early version of this analysis was published as Salisbury (1962*b*).

Europeans, and to a lesser extent statistical magnitudes—written accounts are reliable where local memories definitely are not.

The value of having compiled a documentary history became evident when collecting oral materials. Nearly every event that a foreign observer reported was remembered by local people (at second hand for most events before 1890), who would describe it with great circumstantial detail. Names mentioned briefly in written reports stimulated long discourses on where they lived, or what their clan was, and/or what events had occurred in their lives. This kind of detail (along with ethnographic information) indicated that in almost every case the foreign observer had misunderstood what the local people were doing, had misinterpreted the effects of his own actions, and was unaware of the local circumstances surrounding the events he observed. But though each event could be put into a local context, it would have been very hard to construct even a relative chronology for events that were not considered to have even a casual connection, and no suggestion of the complex motives of foreigners could be reconstructed from local accounts. Foreigners' descriptions here complemented local narrative.

Thus in the history of Part One, development appears to be entirely exogenous, as many theories of development assume it to be. The remainder of the book reconstructs the fuller history obtained by taking both the foreign "bird's eye view" of documents and the local "worm's eye view" of oral accounts. It shows how, although the bird's eye history may describe real events, it consistently misinterprets them. It omits almost all mention of development by self-help, of local people selectively utilizing knowledge made available to them and incorporating it into their own economic planning, of local people organizing themselves *against* foreigners as much as because of them, and following the creative leadership of their own big men. By contrast, the balanced history is one in which continuity is evident, where at all times the local people can be seen as trying to make rational choices in situations of great novelty, and in the face of tremendous ignorance of the long-term consequences of their actions.

Understanding the past in this way presupposes that one also understands the indigenous economic concepts, by an anthropological analysis of the kind already described. With minor exceptions, these economic *concepts* of the Vunamami people do not appear to have changed since the 1880's, when the first ethnologies of the area were written by Parkinson (1887) and Danks (1887). Marketing ideas of equivalence, and categories of payments for labour, or of title to land changed very little between the 1880's and the 1960's. But the decisions that individuals made at various times have changed dramatically as the types of goods entering the market changed, as populations rose and fell, as alternative demands for labour arose, and as new crops altered the balance of agriculture.

The plan of the second part of the book reflects the interplay between ethnohistory and economic anthropology. Each chapter considers a different aspect of the economic life of Vunamami village. It presents the relevant Tolai economic concepts first, and then relates those concepts to the situation as it was when Europeans first arrived in the area. It traces how in that particular aspect of economic life events succeeded one another until the present—specifically until 1961, but more generally until the period from about 1958 to 1963 for which detailed observations were available. Each chapter concludes by analysing the relevant economic activities of Vunamami, as they were observed during the ethnographic "present," as the results both of history and of local economic decisions.

As outlined thus far, the book is merely an analytical description of one history of successful economic development, dependent for its novelty on a combination of the methods of the oral historian and of the economic anthropologist concerned with formal microanalysis. Both of these techniques, it is maintained, give insights that are not available to workers relying on written history, on macro-economic analysis, or on descriptions utilizing only the concepts of the discipline of economics. Part Three shifts focus and tries to relate this pattern of successful economic development to the political events that accompanied each economic change, both empirically and in theoretical terms. Chapter 9 pulls together references to the most important economic innovators, and by tracing their life histories indicates how their innovations fitted within their political careers, and within the options of choice open to them at different ages. Chapter 10 sees their political innovations as changes within a total political *system*. It shows the interconnections between the changing political system and the institutionalization of economic innovations. The whole is presented as a formal model of development, in which progressively greater political consolidation is the dynamic force.[3]

Models of development based on micro-analysis of small societies are not common in the literature (see Hill 1966). The present model is most clearly derived from a model advanced earlier (Salisbury 1957, 1962a) to explain the effect of technological improvement in inducing social change. It was based on a study of the consequences of introducing steel axes into a prosperous Highland New Guinea society, the Siane, some twelve years before the area was brought under Australian administrative control. Briefly, the new tools at first produced no increase in production, for diet was (and is) adequate, and consumer goods were few; their efficiency meant that less time was used to produce the same amount of needed goods. The time set free was used for politicking, ceremonials, legal disputes, and fighting. Individuals who proved effective in this lively period consolidated control of larger groupings than had previously had a unified control. Australian administrators confirmed them in their new-found positions when they took over administrative control in 1945. They also found a ready supply of young underemployed men eager to earn the ceremonial valuables which the politicians had used so successfully in the previous decade. Indentured migrant labour was avidly adopted and consumer luxuries became widespread. Only in 1953 did increased capital investment occur with the building of roads and airstrips and the planting of coffee under the leadership of the big men. These new capital investments promised to yield sufficient income locally to supply the consumption demands which had by then arisen. All seemed set for the beginning of a new cycle of change, based on a new crop-processing technology.

The types of consumer demands found at different times were seen as the major indices of the phases in the cycle—demands for power-yielding valuables immediately after a labour-saving innovation; demands for consumer luxuries by many aspiring people after political consolidation; demands for capital goods and for

[3] It is interesting that macro-studies of national economic development have found (Moore 1966:36) that the single event that consistently has been followed by dramatic economic development, despite expected empirical difficulties, has been the granting of independence, or the emergence of a régime based on popular support. Though the present study only parallels the macro-study finding and cannot claim to deal with a national unit, it is hoped that the processes it analyses may be usefully applied for the understanding of the processes occurring at the national level.

mass consumption of what had formerly been "luxuries" in the final stage. The major dynamic forces of the model, however, were seen as the perfect elasticity of political activity by big men in the early phase: following Parkinson's law, it expands to fill whatever time is available for it. In the next phase came emulation of the leaders by the population at large, and an increased tolerance for individualism after political consolidation spread the demand for luxuries. In the final phase of capital investment (and possibly new innovation) two forces were active: economies of scale or organizational efficiency facilitated production, and affluence permitted the establishment of new inventions.

Although this micro-model could be applied to several other small case studies (e.g., Kwakiutl, Maori, Tiv, Chagga, Hawaii, Nupe, Lapps),[4] it clearly did not apply to others (Fiji, Truk, Samoa, Australian Aborigines, Mundurucu, Tzintzuntzan, Ojibwa). One important difference seemed to be that it applied in societies where significant political decisions were still taken at the local level; it did not apply when local decision-making was in the hands of outsiders such as traders, officials, or non-local bureaucrats. Banfield (1958) and Foster (1965) also see political apathy in villages as typical of town-dominated peasant societies.

A second limitation of the model is implied by the lack of increase in production following increased productivity (see Nash 1965). This would occur only if existing demand for food and subsistence requisites were already met—in other words, in a relatively affluent society. Overpopulation, pressure on land, or food shortage would mean that productivity increases would result directly in increased production; no time would be set free for political consolidation, organizational innovation, and the development of new consumer demands. It is to just such areas of south and southwest Asia, Latin America, and southern Europe, where land shortage and overpopulation are problems and where the solution appears to be to absorb the unemployed population by urbanization and industrialization, that most specialists in development have paid attention. In such countries wage levels are already low because of such unemployment, and labour-saving techniques depress wage levels further. In countries with available

---

[4] Some of these cases were analysed by myself (Salisbury 1962a); others were analysed by Leighton Hazlehurst, Helen Kreider Henderson, Allan Hoben, Stephen Holtzman, Grover Krantz, Henry Lewis, Leonard Plotnicov, and Zenon Pohorecky in seminar papers.

land, where wage rates are high (in real if not in money terms), so the model would maintain, technological innovation can provide for growth without any decline in wage levels. Labour needs to be absorbed in *either* manufacturing *or* service occupations at the same rate as it is freed from agricultural production; consumer demand must increase to absorb new manufactures or services. High wage rates make this possible, again provided that they are not used to purchase imports alone. Parallel explorations on the macro-model level of the significance for development of gains in agricultural productivity have been conducted by an increasing number of economists in recent years—by Boserup (1965) in Denmark, Colin Clark (1964) in England, Fisk in Australia, and by several workers in Latin America. The present study was designed to contribute further to this field, by improving the anthropological micro-model of the Siane.

Several considerations were involved in the design of the study. An area was sought showing the same end result of successful economic and social development with indigenous political involvement, but where development had continued for a much longer period. A larger historical study and an analysis of its phases would show first how general was the succession of phases isolated for the Siane, and second whether the process described was a single unique process—the emergence of a society from subsistence agriculture—or a cyclical repetitive process. In so far as only the end results of successful development were used as a criterion for selecting the new case, other similarities between it and the Siane would tend to be confirmed as related to successful development.

Personal knowledge of New Guinea[5] and a perusal of non-specialist journals suggested that the Tolai people of the Gazelle Peninsula of New Britain, who surrounded the town of Rabaul, fitted the first condition, of successful economic development combined with strengthened indigenous political organization. United Nations mission reports talked of "rapid progress" resulting from "communal enthusiasm" as "the local people set to with a will" (U.N. 1954). Newspapers cited successful "village councils" embracing thousands of individuals each, and receiving bank loans of over £50,000 to operate large-scale cocoa fermenteries. Inde-

[5] I should like to thank Dr. K. E. Read for first interesting me in the area in 1954, when he himself was planning a Tolai study. Mr. Ralph Craib rekindled my interest in 1958.

pendence of expatriate control was indicated by an anti-administration demonstration in one "village" of a thousand persons in 1953, during which the District Commissioner was hit on the head. Settler reports characterized the Tolais as "obstinate," "over-educated and cheeky," and "hard to get along with." A survey of readily available literature confirmed the suitability of the Tolai for study and led to the formulation of a detailed research proposal (Salisbury 1959) for a Tolai study.[6]

Documentary research in 1960 and 1961 (Salisbury 1962*b*) corrected many of the historical errors of this research proposal, and indicated clearly that the Tolai had indeed gone through several sequences of economic and social change, each one resembling the Siane sequence. One cycle had followed the introduction by traders in the 1870's of a market for surplus coconuts. Another had followed the deliberate planting by Tolai of coconuts for the market beginning in the 1890's. A third had begun with the introduction of hot-air copra driers in the late 1930's, but had not been completed until after the Second World War, and a fourth had involved the development of cocoa growing and mechanized processing in the late 1950's. Unfortunately, because contacts had gradually spread, documents did not enable each cycle to be clearly distinguished over the whole of the Tolai area. Villages near the coast had gone through all the cycles in succession, building their political organization as they went. Inland villages, which began later, had skipped phases, adopting several innovations simultaneously, and had developed less political unity.

The confirmation of the general hypothesis of the study thus opened the way to a more specific investigation in the field, in which it was hoped to develop the model—the way in which pre-existing local political organization contributed to economic development, or, to phrase it more dramatically, the way in which

[6] This hasty and often seriously erroneous document is closely parallelled by T. S. Epstein (1963). She adopts the same division into phases, though she sees the difference between them as being ones of, first, agricultural investment, second, consumption, next investment trial in secondary processing, and finally tertiary investment. Unfortunately my later research showed that the history I then cited was highly inaccurate, and the phases I then proposed are inappropriate. Salisbury (1962*b*) presents a better, though still inexact, survey of the early period, based on original research. In view of its historical inaccuracy, no further historical use will be made of Epstein's publication, based as it is on unreliable secondary or even tertiary sources.

"tradition" ensured successful change. Not only were all the economic data obtained in the Siane study to be collected—on land
ownership, land usage, yields, labour inputs, consumption, cash
incomes, capital ownership, investments, and ceremonial expenditures—but the changing political structure needed to be reconstructed, and the history of each technological innovation corre-
lated with it. For both purposes a file was kept on every Tolai
individual mentioned by name in any document, listing his village
or area, his probable birthdate, his significant actions, and the date
to which the reference applied. This file of about two hundred
names of individuals important in all Tolai areas before 1939, and
the dates of their activity, proved invaluable in later investigations
of oral history, although it did not in itself contain sufficient
information for statistical treatment.

It also served to focus interest on four villages, all of which had
gone through all four cycles of technological and social change,
and all of which had long and full historical records—Matupit,
Nodup, Raluana, and Vunamami (called Kinigunan in many
early records). Each could have served for detailed study, and
the final decision to study Vunamami was not taken until arrival
in the field. Three factors were decisive: reports of the 1950's
that Vunamami was the most progressive of all village councils,
having independently built its own post-primary school; the arrival of Dr. A. L. Epstein to study Matupit, which had developed
into a peri-urban satellite of Rabaul; and a meeting in Port
Moresby with Vin ToBaining, M.L.C., the president of Vunamami
Council.

Vunamami, it is true, is an exceptional "village," not only for
New Guinea as a whole but among the Tolai. It was one of the
first four villages in New Guinea contacted by missionaries and
traders in the early 1870's, and the first European plantation was
established on its borders in 1883 by the famous "Queen Emma"
Forsayth, and Richard Parkinson. The German administrative
centre for the area—Herbertshöhe, or Kokopo as it is now called
—was also next door, until 1910. The most extensive alienation of
land in all New Guinea occurred in Vunamami and the surrounding villages, and when the administrative capital moved across the
bay to the modern town of Rabaul, Kokopo remained as a main
centre of plantation and social life in the Territory of New
Guinea. Under Australian administration Vunamami had dynamic

local leaders between the late 1930's and the 1950's. It most quickly espoused Local Government (or Village) Councils when these were first officially established in 1950, and Vunamami Council, as the most progressive council in New Guinea, was awarded a mace by the Commonwealth Bank, and a presidential chair by the Sydney Town Council. Its president was elected to represent the New Guinea Islands constituency in the first Legislative Council elections of 1961.[7]

The village itself, the focus of the council to which it had given its name, included some five hundred persons in 1961. It was then a rich village, though by no means the richest in the Tolai area, with an average income per family of £150 and almost complete subsistence from local sources. Housing varied all the way from dwellings constructed entirely of native materials to three-bedroom houses of the Australian suburban type. The Council operated its own electric generator, though no private houses were wired to it, and it had its own medical aid posts, wells, laundry facilities, schools, brickmaking machinery, and a cocoa fermentery. The local Methodist church, with its own ordained Tolai minister, was attended by most of the population every Sunday in spotless, white, ironed clothes. Ninety-nine percent of the population was literate.

But though this aggregate of characteristics is unique, and makes Vunamami the most advanced village in New Guinea, there is no single characteristic that could not be parallelled in many other places in New Guinea and elsewhere in the Pacific. Council activity on a similar scale and with similar local enthusiasm is common in the Highlands; similar thoroughgoing involvement in cash cropping, while retaining a subsistence agriculture, prevails throughout Polynesia. Similar histories of enthusiastic adoption of Christianity in the nineteenth century, and of the emergence of locally run churches with universal church attendance and high literacy rates could again be cited throughout Polynesia and in much of Papua. Problems of land alienation and the co-existence of plantations and small farmers occur throughout the Pacific, and in New Guinea are acute around Madang and on Bougain-

[7] In the elections of 1964 he failed to secure re-election, owing to a divided constituency, when Vunamami was separated from other Tolai areas and grouped with a large majority of non-Tolai-speaking people. One of the latter secured election.

ville. Vunamami, in short, combines features from many histories of development; the lessons to be learned from it could be of considerably wider generality.

At the same time a caveat should be entered; the history of Vunamami is not representative of every Tolai area, nor has the development of all Tolai areas been the same. Separate studies of Matupit (a peri-urban satellite village of Rabaul in which "traditional" features were at a minimum) by A. L. Epstein, and of Rapitok (the most distant, and most land-rich Tolai village, but also one of the least organized villages politically) by T. S. Epstein, were conducted independently while the present study was in progress. No effort is made here to analyse the differences and similarities among the three areas, or to relate them to their different histories of relations with Europeans; such a comparison would require another book. But the reader should be warned in advance against assuming that the findings of any one of these studies can, without modification, be applied to any other Tolai area. As this entire study will show, the pattern of economic development and change in any one village is very much a function of its own internal social changes and their timing, and of the way in which economic choices appear in a given micro-situation. One should not expect contiguity and subordination to the same external administering authority to produce identical results.

Part One

The Outside View
of Development

Several histories of European influences in New Britain have already been written—of exploration (Wichmann 1917), of the Methodist and Sacred Heart missions (Danks 1899, Hüskes 1932), and of government (Hahl 1935, Mair 1948, Stanner 1953, Rowley 1958). These works discuss Tolai history in the context of the development of the entire Territory of New Guinea. Here, the over-all history is merely sketched in, as a background to the impact of Europeans on the people living in the area of Vunamami, and the account is purposely written as though by an "outside" historian with access only to written records. Interpretations of Vunamami reactions to European actions are based on documents only, and not on oral testimony, which is reserved for Part Two. This permits the history to capture the broad sweep of events and to discuss periods as wholes; on the other hand, detail is included both to give the history concreteness and to permit comparison with descriptions of the same detailed incidents contained in later chapters.

I

A European View
of Vunamami History

1787–1875: EARLY CONTACTS

The Gazelle Peninsula and the St. George's Channel first enter European history with Carteret's voyage of 1787. Until then the land masses of New Britain and New Ireland were thought to be joined, but Carteret discovered that it was possible to sail from the Coral Sea into the Bismarck Sea through the St. George's Channel, past the Gazelle Peninsula. During the next eighty-three years ships sailed through the channel at intervals. Several whaling ships stopped at the Duke of York Islands in mid-channel and at a few places on the New Ireland mainland or other small islands, but the only record of voyagers going ashore on the New Britain mainland seems to be that of Powell (1884), who in 1878 returned one of eight men kidnapped from Nodup, presumably by whalers. Some voyagers, like Duperrey in 1823, came close enough to the coast to meet New Britain canoes (1826:98). But for the most part Vunamami knowledge of Europeans and their goods remained indirect until about 1870.

With the growth of the German company of Godeffroy in Samoa, traders looking for shell, copra, or labourers penetrated into island Melanesia. Between 1870 and 1875 the most adventurous reached New Britain. On the Gazelle Peninsula and the offshore islands they found one of the densest populations of Melanesia—over one hundred per square mile even then. But the people seemed very uncivilized, despite the fertile volcanic soil and easy subsistence. Steel tools were almost unknown, both men and women went completely naked, head hunting and cannibalism were regularly practiced, and every man's hand seemed turned against his neighbour. People lived in small, scattered hamlets, fenced off to protect themselves against other hamlets. There was no semblance of political unity.

One pair of traders sent by Godeffroy, John Nash and W. T. Wawn, tried to establish a base or trading post on the mainland in 1873. Their houses were soon burned down and they barely escaped with their lives (Wawn 1893:169, 286 f). But the discovery by them and others that there were paying cargoes that could be obtained for next to nothing around New Britain—trepang, pearls, turtle and trochus shell—meant that commercial trading was to grow despite its dangers. Two or three ketches were constantly in local waters thereafter.

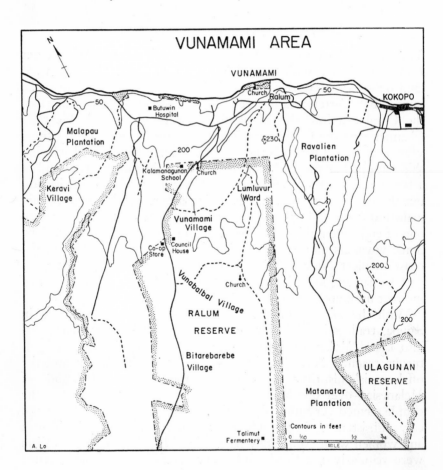

1875–1884: INDEPENDENT SETTLEMENT

On 15 August 1875 a Methodist missionary named Dr. George Brown landed at Molot in the Duke of York Islands and became the first permanent European resident. He had previously worked in Samoa and Fiji and he brought with him eight Fijian and Samoan mission teachers. The Fijian language is rather closely related to Tolai, and I myself found, when travelling in the reverse direction in 1962, that whole sentences of Tolai were understood in Fiji, and that the names for most useful plants were cognates. Dr. Brown immediately set about building his mission station and began to learn the language. To distinguish himself from the traders he refused to sell guns, or to buy shells or trepang (Brown Diary, 15 Oct. 1875).

Soon after his arrival he began his major task—getting to know the mainland and establishing relations there, so that the islanders would ask for mission teachers. Three coastal areas with large populations stood out—Nodup, Matupit, and "Kinigunan." Nodup and Matupit are on the curving hook of land where Rabaul now stands, the spine of which is formed by two active volcanoes called Mother and Daughter. Nodup faces north to the open sea; Matupit, a flat island connected to the mainland by a causeway, faces Blanche Bay, the huge bay enclosed by the hook of land.[1] "Kinigunan" is the area that I will call Vunamami. It lies on the semi-protected south shore of Blanche Bay, directly opposite the tip of the hook (Praed Point). The three "villages"[2] were then competing for the maritime supremacy of the whole

---

[1] Matupit is now practically a suburb of the town of Rabaul. Rabaul, "The Mangrove," was created in 1905 from a mangrove swamp which bordered Matupit to the west. As Dr. Alfred Hahl, the German governor, realized, it provided flat land of uncontested ownership in the most sheltered part of Simpson Harbour. Matupit has been studied by Dr. A. L. Epstein, and his discussions of how it has developed features of urban parasitism, along with a maintenance of many traditional practices (e.g., A. L. Epstein 1963), should be read as a complement to the present study. Discussions in the field with Dr. Epstein did much to sharpen my own appreciation of what factors were significant in the development of Vunamami as an independent, organized, and diversified society.

[2] The use of the term village is in accordance with Tolai and govern-

Tolai area, mainly by attempting to monopolize relations with traders. Emissaries from each reached Brown at Molot.

He visited them all, and by transporting representatives of each to the others, sought to make peace among them. Together they formed a reliable source of food supplies that were often unobtainable on the small Duke of York Islands. There were dangerous moments during his first visit to Vunamami, when only a warning and his own resolute action saved him from a massacre by the mob on the beach (1908:202). But when Nodup asked for the first resident Fijian missionary in October 1875, the other villages quickly asked for the same privilege. Before a teacher would come, the villagers had to sell land to build a house and had to promise support for the teacher. Vunamami obtained its teacher, Peni Raiwalui, in August 1876, and a mission site was established on the plot of land, also called Vunamami.

By the time Brown left for Sydney in 1876 on leave to collect his wife and family, peace had been established among the major coastal communities, and eight mission teachers had been posted on the mainland (Brown 1908:176). Brown notes in his diary for 29–30 August 1876 that he was "packing and giving beads to teachers [to pay] for their food, houses and boatbuilding" during his absence. A list also appears: "153 lbs. of beads @ 1/6 per lb., 6 dozen tomahawks @ 15/– per dozen, and 41 lbs. of hoop iron @ 7/6." This was in addition to the issues made to each teacher for his personal needs for clothing and tools, of thirty-two yards of cloth, four knives, two blankets, six handkerchiefs, two axes, and three bars of soap plus odds and ends of needles, thread, paper and pencils, and so on. If a teacher was married he received each year in addition the same amount of cloth, two more knives, and three more bars of soap (Brown Diary, 10 Oct. 1877). This indicates the impact of the teachers on the local economy, since tools and beads would be exchanged for food and labour, and the consumption itself was an example to be imitated.

By Brown's return in October 1877 other changes had occurred.

---

ment practice, though the Tolai word *vilis* actually means a collection of hamlets. Hogbin and Wedgwood (1953) suggested the word "parish" as a better term, but since this is a traditional political and residential unit, with no religious organization (which, like kinship organization, is on a different basis), it is appropriate to use the generally accepted term.

Trading had increased, as dried coconut meat, or copra, had become an alternative to shell. It was in great demand in the industrial world as the raw material for soap. As Brown noted in his diary in July 1878, "Copra is king." Two more Europeans were now permanent residents: a Mr. Blohm operated a depot for Godeffroy and Sons on Mioko in the Duke of Yorks, and Mr. Eduard Hernsheim traded independently out of Matupit. Other traders came and went, the number varying as some were killed in brawls among themselves or in attacks by natives. The safest place for a trading post was near a mission, and Brown's desire to make clear the difference between missionaries and traders was not helped by one trader who, in 1876, established himself next to Vunamami church.

Two dramatic events marked the period 1877–1880. The first was the volcanic eruption of the Daughter in January 1878, followed by the emergence of rocks in Simpson Harbour and of a small island near the west side of Blanche Bay. (The next eruption, in 1937, transformed this small island into a six-hundred-foot peak connected to the mainland.) The second event, an uprising among the northwestern Tolai, marked a stage in the rapid expansion of the copra trade. With the expansion of course came also increasing amounts of goods for which the coconuts were exchanged. The traders themselves were still, however, restricted to the coast, and the coastal villagers, especially their headmen, were now the middlemen who obtained the nuts from villagers living inland. It was customary for traders to leave a store of trade goods with a coastal "big man" and return later to collect the nuts. But as profits from the inland trade increased, the traders wanted to go inland themselves and do away with the middlemen. Naturally, the coastal villagers resisted.

Conflict came to a head in March 1878, when an important "big man" named Talili from the north coast region of Kabakada arranged an alliance among several coastal villages. The alliance included the village of Davaun, at the southwest corner of Blanche Bay, and other north coast villages, but did not include the missionized villages of Matupit, Nodup, and Vunamami. On 4 April 1878 a group of four Fijian teachers travelling across country from Kabakada to Blanche Bay were ambushed and murdered at the village of Ialakua near Davaun. Their bodies were cut up and sent far and wide for cannibal feasts, and Talili and his allies sent belligerent messages to Brown and the traders, threatening the same fate and demanding the monopoly of inland trade.

After a hasty evacuation of other Fijians, all the foreigners gathered in Matupit. The Fijians urged revenge and the recovery of the bodies; Matupit and Nodup offered support; the worried traders feared that their lives were in danger. Dr. Brown, realizing the urgency of the situation, and knowing that inaction would mean the failure of his entire mission, agreed to organize a punitive expedition. Working together, the settlers and the men from Nodup and Matupit executed a pincers movement across country and by sea and defeated Talili. They burned many villages and, following native custom, demanded heavy compensation in shell money (*tabu*)—small *nassa callosa* shells strung on lengths of rattan—for the deaths. As the villages paid, one by one, a teacher was established in turn. Talili himself was allowed to remain free, but the northwest confederacy was successfully broken and traders were free to move inland. Kabakada on the north coast, and Raluana on Blanche Bay near Davaun became the bases for inland expansion to the southwest.

In Vunamami to the east, however, the coastal monopoly was still unchallenged. The mission church under Peni Raiwalui was rebuilt in December 1878 (Brown Diary, 4 Dec. 1878). When the Rev. Benjamin Danks, Brown's assistant and eventual replacement, visited it in June 1879 he was met in style. The local "big man" was on the beach, "the most civilized native of New Britain [wearing] a clean white *malu* round his loins and a white shirt which seemed to have been made acquainted with soap and water pretty often" (Danks Diary, 16 June 1879). The two first mainland converts were baptized at Vunamami on 17 March 1880, and one of them, Elaita ToGimamara, became the first local preacher on 8 October 1880. Yet a trader named Powell, temporarily resident near Vunamami in December 1879, described the warfare between Vunamami and the next village, two miles inland (Powell 1884: 81). In travelling inland his coastal guides could only take him stealthily along a ravine bed, past the next hostile village, to one (Ngunguna) in which they had friends. The six-mile trip became one of thirty miles, and he never reached the mountain, eight miles inland, that was his goal. He saw cannibalism openly practised, and nudity everywhere. Powell's residence in his village was a major point of pride for the Vunamami guide.

The copra trade now dominated the islands. Danks (Letter to B. Chapman, 5 Sept. 1880) describes how the trade flourished: ". . . a great copra season. Native houses are full of trade. All they want is muskets, rifles, powder and shot. These are becoming as plentiful as spears and tomahawks were formerly. They are so fully supplied with every other article of trade that they want *tabu* only—we can't get food for the articles we brought down with us. We have to pay more for it [*tabu*] than we did twelve months ago. . . . Having obtained it, its market value seems to fall and we cannot purchase half the quantity of food a native can with the same amount." Competition was keen: there were five firms active (Danks 1933:151), and traders' profits averaged between £6 and £8 for each ton of copra (Danks, Letter to his cousins, 4 Feb. 1881). The rough-and-ready methods of the traders often made dealings risky, however, even when villages were peaceful. A trader in Matupit named Cook tried to give one and a half sticks of tobacco for fifty pounds of copra, though two sticks was usual. When the native objected, Cook shot him in the leg, but was then run out of Matupit, barely escaping with his life (Danks 1933:77). A trader was threatened at Vunamami (Brown 1908:391). Three traders who threatened natives were killed at Kabaira in October 1880 and H.M.S. *Beagle* came to investigate (Brown 1908:388). Patrols by British warships from Australia and Fiji, and by German ships from Samoa, appeared regularly to investigate (and punish) such murders, and to regulate the labour trade to Samoa and, for a time in 1883, to Queensland.

The most active large-scale traders at this period were still the firm of J. C. Godeffroy and Sons, based on Mioko in the Duke of Yorks, and two independent traders, Mr. Hernsheim, based on Matupit, and Thomas Farrell, operating also from Mioko. All employed other Europeans, Malays, Filipinos, and islanders as their boat captains and local traders. Farrell was always accompanied or "partnered" by his part-Samoan wife, the former Emma Coe, better known as Queen Emma, and after 1881 by his wife's younger sister Phoebe and her German-English husband, Richard Parkinson. In 1882, Queen Emma decided to establish a depot near Blanche Bay and chose the mainland site called Ralum, some three hundred yards east of Vunamami church. Here, fresh water, seeping down the course of a ravine, makes a break in the coral reef and gives a stretch of level ground. There is easy access to the beach and a gentle climb up to the pumice plateau. On the headland sheltering the harbor, Queen Emma built her house, looking across the bay to Matupit and the volcanoes. Mr. and Mrs. Parkinson joined the Farrells, but when Emma acquired more land at Malapau, a mile and a half to the west, the Parkinsons moved there as the managers.

Most copra at this time was sold by the natives as nuts. A main activity of the depots was to turn the nuts into copra by extracting and drying the meat. By 1884 Ralum employed one hundred and fifty workers at this—all Solomon Islanders from Buka, dependent on their employer in every way, and available to defend the depot from local attacks. Godeffroy and Sons, in bankruptcy, had become the Deutsche Handels- und Plantagengesellschaft der Südsee Inseln and concentrated on recruiting labor for the Samoan plantations. Farrell and Hernsheim had a virtual export monopoly. Guns, tobacco, clay pipes, beads, and cotton goods were the main commodities they traded with (Parkinson 1887:26).

But inland from Vunamami little had changed since Powell's visit. Coconuts were still traded down to the coast through native markets, the women bringing down coconuts, taro, and betel from the villages next inland to a market in Vunamami (Parkinson 1887:78). An occasional man came from as far away as six and a half miles, but there was always the risk of being attacked. The normal pattern was of a market site midway between villages, to which villagers, guarded by armed men, brought produce for barter (Weisser 1887:17). Guns were used in this area in native wars (Parkinson 1887:89), and the traders who supplied them were welcomed. But four miles inland in Tingenavudu only a few big men had them, and six miles inland in Malakun no one did. Prophetically, Parkinson saw the future for the inland villages on the crest of the plateau not in copra but in other tree crops such as coffee. Beyond this, the southern boundary of Tolai settlement, lay dense virgin forest, sparsely inhabited by the linguistically distinct (non-Melanesian-speaking) Baining people.

One other event of 1880–1881 indirectly affected Vunamami: the promotion of an abortive settlement scheme for New Ireland, by the Marquis de Rays in France. The settlement failed after three boatloads of unprepared and ill-equipped men were landed on a malarial coast of thick forest, without quinine. Dr. Brown and the traders came to their rescue and the majority of the survivors were repatriated, but a few of them stayed on in New Guinea. A Belgian named Mouton traded for a period, then obtained land two miles

east of Vunamami and subsequently became an important plantation owner. Another survivor, named Dupré, settled on land on the
north coast, at Volavolo. A third, Father Lanuzel of the Sacred
Heart Mission (M.S.C.), who had come to minister to the settlers,
stayed to work among the Tolai. He bought a small plot of land
near Nodup but his house was burned by the local people in late
1881. He was sheltered for a time by Dupré at Volavolo, but then
left for Sydney. Returning in April 1883 he was driven out again
within a month (Wawn 1893:287–305).

Father Lanuzel nevertheless laid the foundations for Roman
Catholic missionization. In September 1882[3] when two more French
M.S.C. priests, Fathers Navarre and Cramaille, arrived to start a
mission to the Tolai, they settled on his land at Nodup. Finding
the plot too small, they obtained a larger plot at Kokopo near
Mouton's trading post, a mile east of Vunamami. Here, too, the
local people burned the mission.[4] Father Navarre sailed to Sydney
for new supplies; Father Cramaille took shelter at Volavolo and
built a church there. In April 1884 Father Navarre returned with
three new priests and timber for permanent buildings at Volavolo,
but after establishing a new station at Malaguna he left with one
priest to start a new mission in Papua. By November 1884 the Sacred
Heart Mission owned land at Nodup, Volavolo, Kokopo, and
Malaguna, but the three resident priests and their lay-brother assistants lived close together in Volavolo and Malaguna. The other
sites were vacant.

By contrast, the Methodists in 1884 had divided their self-gov-
erning local mission into three "circuits" (Raluana being the one
including Vunamami), each supervised by a white missionary and
operating a small "school" for prospective teachers. Raluana circuit had seven churches staffed either by Fijian ministers or by
locally trained teachers and catechists, of which there were eleven
in 1885 (Methodist Minutes 1884, 1885). Probably several of these
were from Vunamami, yet Vunamami was only a mile from a

[3] In general, the account of mission history depends on Hüskes (1932)
for all names and dates not otherwise acknowledged. Contemporary sources
have been preferred, however, in interpreting the interconnections between events. Much important additional background material is given
by Hüskes.

[4] Sacred Heart records made veiled suggestions that this was done at the
instigation of Methodist teachers at Vunamami. The mission rivalry of the
time is evident, even if the accusation is false.

Catholic centre. Rivalry between the two missions was already evident.

1884–1892: GERMAN ADMINISTRATION BEGINS

International politics brought the next development to Vunamami, when the Germans, whose warships had already been active, hoisted their flag at Matupit on 3 November 1884 and declared it a German protectorate. The move was mainly commercial, closing the area to English (i.e., Australian) interests (Blum 1900:11), and no structure of government was at first created. In May 1885 commercial interests in Germany obtained letters patent setting up the Deutsche Neu-Guinea Compagnie, and to it was delegated governmental authority. The Compagnie concentrated its plans for development on the mainland, though a government judge (*Gerichtsassessor*), Herr Schmiele, took up evidence in Matupit in 1886.

In 1887 began a series of regulations designed to strengthen the position of the D.N-G. Compagnie.[5] Land acquisitions by Europeans could be made only through the D.N-G.C., and land acquired before November 1884 had to be registered; the sale of weapons, ammunition, and liquor to natives was prohibited; the export of labourers outside German territory was prohibited, and recruitment for German plantations was restricted; statistical returns and fees had to be sent by established businesses to the D.N-G.C., including a copra export duty of four marks per ton.

In many ways the regulations remained a dead letter in the absence of administrative power to enforce them. Few European claims of purchase of large areas of land before 1884, even if only for nominal amounts of trade goods, were refused by the D.N.-G.C., and as long as the D.N.-G.C. itself did not want it, private acquisition of new land does not seem to have been difficult. Judge Schmiele with a launch could police some of the recruiting and trading regulations, but his presence did not ensure peace. His report of inter-village fighting and of markets every two miles in the area he explored west of Raluana as far as Kabaira (*Nachrichten* 1888:154–160) is reminiscent of Powell's report of ten years earlier.

---

[5] R. Parkinson (Letter to Sir George Le Hunt, 20 March 1886) makes it clear how these regulations appeared as harassment to private businesses.

Queen Emma's plantations at Ralum and at Malapau grew slowly, with coconuts, cotton, and coffee being planted, but her traders were active and she gradually assumed supremacy in the copra trade. The D.H.P.G.S.I. mainly supplied labourers for Samoa, and Hernsheim concentrated on import trading and on the export of shell.

The prosperity of Ralum was in marked contrast to D.N-G.C. plantation experiments on the New Guinea mainland, and in 1889 the Compagnie bought some six to seven hundred hectares of land to the east of Ralum, adjoining Mouton's land. Beginning in January 1890 they set about establishing a station and a plantation there (*Nachrichten* 1890:16), which they called Herbertshöhe. The native name of the coastal part of the plantation was Kokopo (The Landslide), and this name is now universally used. I shall use the name Kokopo here, although German sources all refer to Herbertshöhe. By 1891 the station had fifteen buildings including residences for the Compagnie manager and the government judge. Obtaining labourers for the mainland was a major activity, 1,273 being recruited in 1890, though only 130 were from New Britain and the Duke of Yorks. Fifty Tolai, however, were working at Kokopo (*Nachrichten* 1891:15).

Neither the D.N-G.C. nor Queen Emma expanded entirely peacefully. "Inland Tribes" from Vunamami, Keravi, Bitarebarebe, and Tingenavudu villages attacked Ralum in March 1890 with success, until a combined force led by Parkinson and Judge Schmiele repelled them, killing three natives and burning Tingenavudu (*Nachrichten* 1890:75, *Monatshefte* 1890:134).

Methodist mission expansion proceeded steadily. There were fifteen churches in Raluana Circuit by 1886; a fourth missionary joined the others in 1891, and the number of converts grew rapidly, although most of these were from coastal villages (*Nachrichten* 1893:41). The first indication of changes being caused by the administration was the arrival of a German missionary named Fellman in February 1897 (Danks 1899).

For the Sacred Heart Mission, German administration brought no solution to the problems of manpower and local opposition. Two new priests from France, Fathers Verjus and Couppé, were both transferred to the Papuan mission. The priest at Malaguna fell ill with malaria and had to go to Sydney, and another priest died at Volavolo. Not until 1888 was the lonely survivor at Volavolo joined by others: Father Couppé and two other priests. The following year Father Couppé was appointed Bishop of New Britain. He returned to Europe for consecration, but in December 1891 he was back with men and money. There were now two more priests, six lay brothers, and five nuns of the mission in New Britain. The Bishop hurried to reoccupy the M.S.C. land at Kokopo, only to find the D.N-G.C. in possession. As compensation the D.N-G.C. gave him an equivalent site farther east, called by the natives Mioko.[6] The Bishop transferred his seat there and gave it the name Vunapope, "the base of the Roman Catholic Church."

The D.N.-G.C., fearful of the consequences for business, had already acted to suppress mission rivalry. On 20 June 1890 Judge Schmiele demarcated "spheres of influence" for each mission. Existing stations were to stand (including the Methodist Vunamami church in the M.S.C. sphere), but otherwise the Methodists were granted exclusive access to the main Tolai area west of Malapau and the Sacred Heart was granted the area east of Malapau and non-Tolai areas to the south and west. Bishop Couppé immediately agreed to the ruling, and after some protest the Methodists also agreed (German Foreign Office, Colonial Section, Letter to General Secretary, M.O.M., 13 June 1891). For the next seven years the large resources of the Roman Catholic mission were used to create a firm and impressive base for future expansion. At Vunapope were built a cathedral, houses for priests and brothers, a boarding school for boys, an iron-roofed house for the nuns, and a girls' boarding school for one hundred orphans.

The boarding schools were indeed a major part of the plan for the full conversion of local people. Slaves captured by the Tolai from the Baining were bought for twenty fathoms of shell money and given their freedom; the orphans were adopted by the mission (*Monatshefte* 1892:147). But there were other expressions of sympathy and interest. The Bishop himself defended the leader of the 1890 uprising, and when his defence failed and the leader was executed, the mission adopted his son (*Monatshefte* 1892:152, 168). A *laplap* (waistcloth) and tobacco were given to those who faithfully attended services for seventeen consecutive Sundays (*Monatshefte* 1891:39). Congregations were thus decently clad, and increased dramatically in size, while infant baptisms became common.

[6] This is the same name as the island in the Duke of Yorks. Place names recur throughout Tolai territory.

1893–1899: CONTROL ESTABLISHED

In 1893 an uprising against Ralum and the government marked a turning point in relations with the native population near Kokopo (*Monatshefte* 1894:6, 101–103, 133–137, 166–168; *Nachrichten* 1893:67, 1894:17–19). The uprising, which lasted from March until December, grew out of trouble at Queen Emma's plantation lands at Ralum, originally purchased in 1882. At the time, the native residents had been left undisturbed, as Ralum had not wished to plant immediately, but plantings expanded, and the natives resisted eviction. They were further antagonized by the attitudes of Buka labourers who used guns to make them sell produce at cheap rates. A "magician" selling medicine to repel bullets incited the rebellion, which was only brought to an end when the cruiser *Sperber* shelled the villages responsible. The D.N-G.C. resolved to create "effective and responsible chiefs" in place of those who had led the rebellion.

The Sacred Heart mission again tried to mitigate the hardship for the villages involved (Linckens 1921:16–19), especially Tingenavudu, which was burned again by the punitive expedition. The natives showed their gratitude: in September 1894 the graduates of the orphanage founded a church in Takabur, just inland from Vunapope, and Tingenavudu asked for a church, which was named Villa Maria. A Methodist catechist named Abraham attempted to stop the church-founding in Takabur but was brought to court by Bishop Couppé and fined forty fathoms of shell money or twenty-six days in jail (*Monatshefte* 1896:111).

By now the "spheres of influence" policy was intolerable to the Sacred Heart mission, and the matter was raised in the Reichstag by M.S.C. supporters in Germany (*N.A.Z.*, 15 Sept. 1895). The dispute between the mission and the D.N-G. Compagnie became a general criticism of the competence of the D.N.-G.C. to administer the area, culminating in the German government's announcing on 13 March 1896 that it would take over political control of the Territory from the D.N-G.C. It took three years to complete the negotiations for government control and for the withdrawal of the ban on mission expansion.

Public opinion notwithstanding, many improvements occurred during the final years of the D.N-G.C. administration. The job of station head at Kokopo was made separate from that of plantation

manager, although the latter still had three hundred workers under
him in 1895, and the former only eighty-five police, ship boys,
carriers, and so on (*Nachrichten* 1895:20). Wages for labourers
of eight marks a month were made payable in part each month, and
in part as a lump sum at the end of the three-year indenture
(*Nachrichten* 1895:4). Coins began to be introduced in 1894—
174,354 marks in the first year (*Nachrichten* 1895:47). Regular
shipping services began to Europe, via Singapore. And most important, Dr. Alfred Hahl arrived to take over as judge in January 1896.

Hahl was particularly concerned with the problems of claims
to have purchased land prior to 1884, but he also set about imple-
menting the decision to create responsible and effective chiefs,
and he began a program of road building. His investigations of
land claims generally found in favour of the planters, who were
judged to have purchased the land legally; at the same time, realizing that the natives had usually not understood what was involved
in the sale and would be unduly penalized if they were forced to
quit the land, Hahl confirmed the freehold title to the land for the
planters but established "reserves" which the local natives could
continue to occupy (see Miller Letter 1958). Vunamami land was
declared part of "Ralum Estate," but the villagers were permitted
to remain on a portion of the land. Stretching inland from the
original settlement at Ralum, and administered by Queen Emma
(now separated from Farrell, using her original married name of
Forsayth, and incorporated as Forsayth and Company) was Ravalien plantation. Stretching inland farther west was Malapau plantation, which the Parkinsons managed, but which was owned by
Forsayth and Company. Although the two plantations met for
three hundred yards near the shore and a road joined them along
this corridor, a mile-wide strip of Reserve separated them farther
inland. Another reserve lay to the southwest of Malapau.

Before creating local chiefs, Hahl learned the local language and
spent time listening to native complaints and native discussions of
their laws and customs (e.g., Hahl 1897). In 1897 he nominated
individuals from groups of villages to act as his agents in passing
out orders, and to bring him any native requests (Annual Report
1913:170). He gave them the indigenous title of *lualua*. The villages in Ralum Reserve were one group for this purpose.

For road building Hahl used teams of police to supervise native
workers; the villages were made responsible for road maintenance.

He began extending the Kokopo–Malapau road to Raluana, and built a new road, the Toma Road, to Mount Vunakoko.

With peace established the plantations flourished. Forsayth and Company had gradually switched from cotton and coffee to coconuts and had 43,000 palms planted by 1894; by 1897 it had expanded to 700 hectares or about 100,000 palms. The D.N.-G. Compagnie, starting with 114 hectares of cotton in 1894, had 431 hectares planted in 1897, but had begun a conversion to copra production. Mouton increased his plantings from 44 to 92 hectares. Altogether, the three plantations employed 1,229 workers. The non-indigenous population in the Bismarck Archipelago numbered 234 Europeans, 31 Chinese, and 67 Fijians and Samoans. Of the Europeans, 75 were missionaries, 5 were traders, 50 were craftsmen and sailors, 10 were planters, and 18 were officials, merchants, and doctors (*Nachrichten* 1898:45; Methodist Minutes 1899). Copra exports, after a slow but steady rise from 1878 on, now began to rise spectacularly as new plantings began to yield.

The development of the European economy was matched by growing prosperity for the native population. Although most coconuts were sold for tobacco (*Nachrichten* 1896:29), the list of trade goods demanded became more varied: "cloth, axes, knives, canned goods, jam, tobacco, false pearls, rings etc." (*Monatshefte* 1897:117). But as long as their material wants were satisfied, natives did not seem interested in participating more intensely in the money economy. They demanded higher prices for foodstuffs (*Monatshefte* 1894:292, 1897:373), but they sometimes refused casual work, such as ferrying Europeans from Kokopo to Matupit. The fines collected from them in 1897 amounted to 1,846 marks (though paid in the equivalent in shell money). Yet cash was in use and in 1897, £328 7s. 1d. was contributed on New Britain (probably over half of it from Raluana Circuit) towards Methodist mission expenses, estimated at £2,450 10s. for 1898. This included salaries for Fijian catechists of £1 to £1 13s. 4d. a month, and for indigenous "assistant teachers" of 7s. 6d. a month (Methodist Minutes 1897). Contributions rose by £20 a year until 1900, when they totalled £400 on New Britain alone.

Mission activities changed in nature, as conversion became a task for inland frontier stations, and coastal parishes needed routine care. In 1897 the M.S.C. began establishing local *Volksschulen* to provide village literacy (*Monatshefte* 1897:200) as well as the élite of displaced orphans trained at the boarding school. The Methodists already had one hundred seventy such schools in 1896, with two hundred pupils who could read, seventy of whom could also write (*Nachrichten* 1896:69); in 1898 they resolved to begin a college to give a higher standard of education to teachers (Methodist Minutes 1898). As a way of financing these expanded activities, first the M.S.C. began operating a plantation on land near Vunapope donated to the church by Mrs. Parkinson in 1895 (Webster 1898:102), and in 1897 the Methodists bought an uninhabited island in the Duke of Yorks called Ulu, for a plantation and for a college (Minutes 1897, 1898).

And to crown the growing acquaintanceship of the Tolai with the money economy, Mr. Parkinson arranged for a team of six dancers, headed by Pero ToKinkin, *lualua* of Raluana, to perform at the 1896 Berlin Colonial Exhibition.[7] They made a very good impression, especially when ToKinkin wrote a letter in Tolai, for the head of the D.N-G. Compagnie, which another member of the group read and translated into English. The group especially noted how much lower prices were in Berlin than they were in Kokopo.

1900–1914: GERMAN COLONIAL ADMINISTRATION

The takeover by the German government of administrative control began somewhat inauspiciously. There was a three-year delay between the decision and its execution. Then the first governor fell ill shortly after his arrival in Kokopo and had to be sent home. Fortunately, Dr. Hahl, who had been promoted to the post of Governor of German Micronesia, was able to assume the governorship in Kokopo, now the seat of government for the Bismarck Archipelago and the mainland, and from there, for the next decade, he supervised the development of the Territory in general and of Vunamami in particular.[8]

At the outset, the government took steps to involve the native

[7] One of the six dancers, Tinai, was still alive in 1961, some ninety years old. Though deaf, he was an excellent and invaluable informant. His village of Balanataman was not yet missionized in 1896, though next to Malapau, and he could remember the first establishment of Malapau. He remembered that Masai and Cameroonians danced in Berlin, and he could repeat the names of all the ports to Naples, and recalled the quality of German beer. In all checkable ways he seemed wholly accurate.

[8] Vunamami men who had worked for him asked for family news of "The Doctor" and his daughter in 1961; farther west the inquiries were for "Masta Pakitan."

population in the cash economy, passing a decree on 18 October 1900 that shell money, until then the main medium of exchange between natives as well as between Europeans and natives, could no longer be used in trade between Europeans and natives. Since a Chinese shipbuilder, named Ah Tam, had begun building bigger boats in 1899, large numbers of natives had begun travelling to the west where shells were to be found (*Monatshefte* 1900:103). According to the Annual Report of 1901 (p. 83), this had forced the natives "to remain in a state of unproductive activity for a comparatively long time." Furthermore, "it was often extremely difficult for European firms to obtain sufficient shell money to pay for copra. In this respect they were wholly dependent on the natives, and the rate for shell money was frequently increased." Prohibiting the use of shell money would force natives "to devote themselves to the production of really useful articles suitable for export, such as copra." This decree also included a prohibition on the sale of whole coconuts by the natives, a practice which had "encouraged native tendencies to do nothing, which is improper" (Annual Report 1901:80). Henceforth only copra could officially be bought by Europeans.

Dr. Hahl also made official the policy he had developed as judge, of appointing "native magistrates" as intermediaries between the government and the local people. Now he appointed one magistrate for each village, employing the vernacular term for a war chief, *luluai*. As he made clear, the *luluai* were the servants of the government, responsible to it to carry out such tasks as the supervision of road building or the reporting of crimes. He retained the *lualua* as his right-hand men but their positions remained unofficial. At the same time as a *luluai* was appointed, each village—often a collection of hamlets—was defined as a unit, called a union, and a census was taken. Unfortunately the details of the 1904 census are not reported, so that the 1909 figure of 229 in Vunamami is the first available, but on the basis of the increase in the total areal population it would seem likely that Vunamami had a population of about 200 in 1904.[9]

---

[9] The total population of Kokopo District in 1904 was 4,724; in 1909 it was 6,972. This remarkably high order of increase was probably due to an increase in the area controlled. Districts with definite demarcation increased as follows: Nanalar, 1,606 to 1,786; Watom, 974 to 1,170; Rabaul, 2,742 to 3,141. I take a 12 percent increase as average and assume a 15 percent increase for Vunamami.

Another policy that now became universal practice was the setting up of reserves (Hahl 1935:25–26), simultaneously with final demarcation of the boundaries of alienated land. This resulted in "increased native goodwill and fulfillment of work" (Annual Report 1904:89). Annual Reports list what this work was: the extension of the Kokopo–Raluana road eastward to the northeast tip of Birara, a new road cut directly inland through Matanatar plantation (the inland half of Ravalien) to join up with the Toma Road, and the extension of the Toma Road to the south and west to the limits of Tolai territory. Kokopo thus became the focus of the entire area, in fact as well as in theory.

The results of these measures can be seen in the economic statistics. Native copra production in the Bismarck Archipelago rose to 2,200 tons in 1902/1903, despite a drought in that year, and in 1909 the bulk of the 7,910 tons exported was still native trade copra. Plantation production in 1901 had been 280 tons of copra from Ralum and the D.N-G.C., with lesser amounts by Mouton and Vunapope (Annual Report 1901:243), but it had reached some 4,000 tons by 1912. New plantations developed throughout the area to the southeast of Kokopo, interspersed with native lands in general, but with a continuous strip claimed to be "unoccupied land" appropriated by the D.N-G.C. along the southern border of the Warangoi River. Although cotton as a crop had long since been abandoned, coffee and cocoa were being experimented with, and in 1903 Queen Emma planted several areas of ficus rubber, including one between her two plantations of Ravalien and Matanatar, and one farther west on Giregire plantation.

More money was available, while at the same time the price of tobacco dropped from between 2.50 and 3 marks a pound, to about 1.25 marks. The volume of twist tobacco imported rose from about 10 tons in 1903 to nearly 100 tons in 1913. Textile imports increased nearly fivefold in the same period, from a value of M. 146,000 to M. 765,000. Native demands for most kinds of European goods increased, although cooking utensils, as Burry points out, were not on the list (1909:178). Burry also reports that by 1907 some natives were earning 750 marks (p. 186), and the Annual Reports talk of some chiefs earning 300 marks a month from copra in 1910 (p. 171), and having stores of 10,000 silver marks.

Copra was not the only source of income. The sale of foodstuffs to Europeans living in Kokopo and to the plantations increased. All planters held "markets" and for standard numbers of sticks of tobacco bought eggs, chickens, taro, yams, and bananas (Burry 1909:94). In 1907 three eggs could be exchanged for two sticks of tobacco (26 sticks make one pound). Coconuts were the only commodity bought with coins. Yet trading profits could be made also, as coins slowly came into more general use.[10] One native regularly sold four chickens to the Methodists at Raluana for one mark, yet made a profit of four sticks of tobacco over the price at which he bought them from other natives. Three chickens for ten sticks of tobacco was the regular price (A. S. Booth Letter to Gen. Sec. M.O.M., 13 Dec. 1910).

Some of the Vunamami money was passed on in contributions to the church. Contributions in Raluana Circuit in 1903 were £480, and the rate rose 70 percent by 1909, when total New Britain collections reached £1,700. Collections were started for the construction of permanent metal-roofed churches, though Vunamami church was not finally built until 1920. An estimate of the size of annual building fund collections is provided by reports for Roman Catholic churches: Ratogor, M. 500; Vunavavar, M. 200 (*Monatshefte* 1908:162, 254); Gunanba, M. 200 (1909:111); Birara, M. 500 (1910:153). Cash also went to the government, which in 1905 instituted a head tax of five marks for males in rich villages. In 1909, with the extension of the tax to backward villages, rates for Vunamami and most of Raluana Circuit were increased to ten marks. This caused a temporary drop in church contributions (H. Fellman Letter to Gen. Sec. M.O.M., 1 July 1910). The pressing native demand for cash to pay taxes was exploited by traders, who began paying only half as much for nuts as they had done previously (*Monatshefte* 1909:207, 535).

The demand for European goods was changing in nature also. By 1909 at Malaguna "trousers, jacket, hat and even raincoat" (*Monatshefte* 1909:535) were being worn; there were requests for sewing machines (*Monatshefte* 1910:308); houses were built by progressive villagers with hinged doors of planks (Kleintitschen 1906:48) and assisting a carpenter was a preferred occupation, since it enabled one to "secrete a nail or tools here and there" (Kleintitschen 1906:57).

Education seems to have been a key to these changes. By 1901 Raluana School had fifteen pupils from the circuit studying at a

[10] This was true especially for the Methodist mission, which had long had moral misgivings about its use of tobacco for exchange and in 1910 seriously tried to abandon the custom.

level higher than the village school; the Methodist seminary on Ulu
Island had forty-five pupils, twelve of whom graduated to teach in
villages. Half of these probably came from Raluana Circuit, two
of whom would likely have come from Vunamami. German teaching began in 1902 under Mr. Fellman (Annual Reports 1901:233;
1902:260). By 1910 there were almost one hundred students at Ulu
Seminary, which was renamed George Brown College (Methodist
Minutes 1910). Attendance from the circuit at Raluana Training
Institute averaged about twenty-five, and about seven each year
went on to Ulu. As a result, and even though the number of mission stations increased, Fijian teachers began to be replaced by
Tolai teachers. As against 37 Fijians for approximately 95 churches
in 1898, there were in 1911 only 26 for about 186 churches. A
large proportion of the Tolai who replaced the Fijians as "assistant
teachers"—some of whom were promoted to "teachers" or even
"catechists"—were from Vunamami and Raluana villages. Salaries
of assistant teachers were still just £6 a year, but promotion was
possible to a salary level of £13 10s. for a senior catechist. With
a house provided, offerings from his congregation, and land near
his church for a vegetable garden, the "teacher" was an affluent
figure in the Methodist village. The church was the main avenue of
social mobility for Vunamami people.

It took over in this respect from the German government. When
Kokopo became the seat of government in 1899, many of the
sophisticated local Tolai obtained employment there as policemen
or servants for government officials. But as shipping connections
became more regular and larger ships were employed, Kokopo,
with only shallow anchorage, became unsuitable as the Territory
capital. The Norddeutsche Lloyd Company had begun a deep-
water dock across Blanche Bay at Rabaul in 1903 and Dr. Hahl
decided to remove the capital to a nearby site, drained from an uninhabited mangrove swamp (Ra baul means "the mangrove").
Buildings were gradually erected there, one of the first being a government school, which was opened on 16 September 1907 (Annual
Report 1908). After two years of instruction in Tolai, pupils
switched to German as the language of instruction. The curriculum
had a bias towards training artisans, and the pupils printed the Government Gazette. On the other hand, there do not seem to have been
many pupils at this school from across the bay. Kokopo remained
the focus for an area of prosperous planters, both European and
native, with both the Catholic mission centre of Vunapope and the

Methodist centre of Raluana nearby. The bustle of transient businessmen, sailors and government servants was removed to Rabaul. Kokopo was still the area of social importance.

In the world of the settlers there also were some changes. Queen Emma married a German civil servant named Kolbe; Mr. and Mrs. Parkinson developed another small plantation of their own, named Kuradui, between Malapau and Raluana. In 1907 Queen Emma sold Ralum Estate for £175,000 to Herr Wahlen of the Hamburger Südsee A.G., and not long after that she died in Monte Carlo. Richard Parkinson died in 1907 just before the final appearance of his massive and authoritative ethnography, *Dreissig Jahre in der Südsee*. Mrs. Parkinson, now living at Kuradui, carried on her sister's tradition, entertaining the Governor, the captains of warships, and any visitors to the area.[11] The Samoan family of Queen Emma and Mrs. Parkinson, their nephews and nieces, and their German and Australian spouses, were the nucleus of the settlers. They continued to work for Forsayth and Company as traders; they ran the Kokopo Hotel; and they developed new plantations in distant areas. Vunapope school taught their children, and Vunapope Cathedral, under Bishop Couppé, was their spiritual home.

1914–1921: AUSTRALIAN MILITARY OCCUPATION

For Kokopo the change of régime in 1914 meant surprisingly little, even though the only local casualties of the war occurred when an Australian Expeditionary Force met resistance after landing at Kabakaul on 11 September 1914 to capture the inland radio station at Bitapaka. In Rabaul the German officials were interned, shipped to Australia, and replaced by completely untrained Australians.[12] As civilians, the Kokopo plantation owners were left undisturbed, so long as they observed an oath of neutrality. Since

[11] Mead (1960) gives an evocative picture of the life of Mrs. Parkinson, as told by herself in 1929. This picture is strikingly confirmed by all contemporary European accounts, except for a few dates and some small changes in the sequence of events. Native informants are often less flattering to Mrs. Parkinson, however, though agreeing on significant events.

[12] Rowley's (1958) account is invaluable. It has been followed here without specific acknowledgement. Perusal of primary sources indicates there is little to add, except to point out that what Rowley says was a general policy for the whole Territory was in most cases specifically one designed for the Kokopo area. Then, as now, this area has provided much of the revenue for support of the rest of the Territory.

no peace treaty with Germany existed, the Territory continued to be operated under German laws (or those "not repugnant" to Australian sensibilities), with the intention of maintaining the civil status quo of 1914 until the peace treaty permitted a change.

Unfortunately, all the officials who knew what the status quo was, and who were familiar with the projected liberalizing policies of Dr. Hahl, were interned, and for advice on how to administer the Territory the newcomers had to rely on the experienced German planters, and on the big Australian shipping interests that had tried unsuccessfully to compete with the N-D Lloyd before the war. The result was predictable: a series of regulations ensuring the planters' absolute control over workers and trade, against which German officials had so far resisted.

The indentured labour system was tightened by making it a criminal offence for any labourer to break his contract in any way. Government gaols became the supporters of plantation labour discipline. True, the power of a plantation owner to administer corporate punishment, subject to review of his actions by an administrative officer, was withdrawn in October 1914, fulfilling Dr. Hahl's proposals. But wages were fixed statutorily at five marks (or shillings) per month—less than in 1895—even though Papuan experience suggested that the rate of ten shillings was an economic one that encouraged workers to engage. Employers could now sell the contracts of their labourers to other employers, without their workers' consent. These regulations affected Vunamami only indirectly by keeping wage rates low and thereby discouraging local participation in wage labour.

Regulations governing trading were more significant. Numbers of Chinese artisans had been brought to New Britain when Rabaul was built, and had stayed on. In 1914, with the N-D Lloyd shipping connections to China cut, artisans whose contracts had expired could not be repatriated and were allowed to remain in New Britain. Many of them turned to trade, not merely as agents for the large companies but as independent operators. This might have stimulated vigourous competition in the copra trade, with higher prices paid and correspondingly lower prices for trade goods. But this would have disrupted the pre-war situation, it was argued, and a series of regulations ensued. The first, forbidding the Chinese to engage in wholesale trade, caused such an outcry that it was withdrawn. Others, on 20 February and 14 April 1917, fixed the price to be paid for copra, first at twelve pounds (or 36 nuts or 24 lbs.

wet meat) for one shilling, and then at thirteen pounds (or equiv-
alents) for one shilling. Regulations were also issued for the
licensing of new trading stations, no new ones being permitted
to open within two miles of an existing station. If an existing station
was on a plantation, the two-mile zone was to be counted from the
boundaries of the plantation. For the Kokopo area, the regulations
meant that no Chinese could set up a trade store except in the most
distant bush, and that Vunamami village could sell its copra only
to Ravalien plantation for a fixed price—and this at a time when
copra prices were finally rising after earlier wartime uncertainties.

To complete the economic stranglehold, the regulations fixed
prices for trade goods—four sticks of tobacco for one shilling, and
a woman's *laplap* for three shillings. For copra purchases made
with sticks of tobacco, five sticks were to be treated as equivalent
to a shilling, to give natives an incentive to accept tobacco rather
than cash. It will be recalled that traders bought tobacco wholesale
at about fifteen to twenty sticks for a shilling.

A further discouragement to natives asking for cash was the
regulations fixing the exchange rates for German and Australian
currency. Marks and shilling pieces were used interchangeably; but
when Australian paper money was introduced the value of a pound
note was established at twenty shillings, or twenty-one marks.
Natives were convinced that premium prices had to be paid for
notes, and they did not take to their use.[13] The effect of this has
been reported by observers. Plantation labourers were given the
monthly part of their pay in the form of tobacco. Much of this they
smoked, but some they set aside to exchange for trade goods at
stores, or for fresh foodstuffs (and betel) from Tolai. Trade stores
were obliged to accept tobacco in payment for goods or to go out
of business, but whereas they demanded five sticks for one shilling's
worth of goods, they sold at the rate of four sticks per shilling. Tobacco displaced shillings in currency, as Gresham's Law would suggest.

But though the military occupation strengthened plantocracy
control over the native economy, prosperity did not decline.
Planters could not send their earnings back to Germany or import quantities of consumer goods. They could only invest money
in further plantings, and hope to sell their plantations after the
war and recoup their investments. Between 1914 and 1918 the

[13] Cf. Epstein (1964:59). She, however, attributes the payment of pre-
miums for notes to the rapacity of Chinese traders.

acreage planted in the Territory increased from 84,000 to 134,000;
the number of indentured labourers rose from 17,500 in 1914 to
31,000 in 1921 (Annual Reports 1921:14); the volume of copra
exported rose from 14,000 tons in 1913 to nearly 30,000 tons in
1921, and its value from £309,000 to £807,000. From paying for
only three-quarters of the Territory imports in 1913, exports returned one-third *more* than the total imports of 1921 (*ibid.*, p. 18).
As an index of native prosperity one can take the figures of contributions to churches. Raluana Circuit subscribed £447 in 1916,
almost the same as in 1903, the last year before government taxes;
in 1917 the subscription rose to £620, and in 1921 it amounted to
£860 (Methodist Minutes 1917, 1922).

The military government abdicated government control over
education by closing the Rabaul (Namanula) school. The Methodists began an Industrial Department in Rabaul to fill the gap and
to absorb graduates from Raluana Circuit Training Institute who
did not want to go on to the mission teacher training college at
Ulu.

The George Brown College, though no longer actively expanding, was operating on a stable basis, but the shortage of European
staff kept the educational standards low (Methodist Minutes 1917).
Nevertheless, the first products of the college began to complete
the long sequence of "trials" necessary before acceptance as full
ministers in the Methodist Church. Between 1918 and 1922 three
Tolai were received as ministers: Peni ToPitmur of Vunamami,
ToQuere of Kabakada, and Ismael ToPuipui of Vunamami. Their
salaries were increased to between £19 and £24 per annum. A
fourth Tolai became a minister shortly afterwards, Kuila ToGoru,
also a Vunamami man. These figures provide one index of Vunamami's close connection with the Methodist Church. Another was
the building of Vunamami church, an impressive structure with
a metal roof and concrete footings, paid for by local subscriptions
(except for a £9 overdraft remaining in 1922), and rivalled only
by the churches built in Raluana and Matupit.

1922–1930: THE MANDATE

Prior to the mandating by the League of Nations, Australian policy
for New Guinea was set by a Royal Commission (Australia 1920).
One member of the Commission, Sir Hubert Murray, Governor
of Papua, advocated a liberal, native-oriented policy; the majority

supported the business-oriented policy advocated by Walter Lucas. Lucas had been an officer of the major Australian trading company in the Pacific—Burns Philip—before the war and had organized Territory exporting during the occupation. The status quo, as it had evolved during the occupation, was continued, except that all German businesses and plantations were expropriated so that the places of Germans, who might be "disloyal," could be taken by "loyal" Australians, especially returned servicemen (Australia 1920:23).

When the Mandate was finally accepted in 1921 the appropriate sentiments were expressed regarding development of the country in the interests of the natives. The Report on the military occupation mentioned how native coconut plantings had increased "after encouragement by administrative officers" (Annual Reports 1921:15); it mentioned changes in the labour regulations, especially regarding corporal punishment, the hospital service provided by Rabaul, and ambitious plans for technical schooling. Annual Reports thereafter talk of "proposals for encouraging native agriculture".

In practice, most of the measures were ignored. After some delay to consider which plantation owners were German, those so classified were in due course expropriated. Mrs. Parkinson at Kuradui was not, but she lost her estate when it was foreclosed upon, over a debt; Ravalien and Matanatar were sold and purchased first by S. S. Mackenzie and later by two brothers, named Rowe.[14] But private purchasers for most plantations did not come forward, as had been hoped. By June 1924 in Rabaul District only 14,550 of 38,000 available acres had been bought. The majority were left in the hands of the official Custodian of Expropriated Property,[15] who ran plantations through managers. Many others were bought by big companies, using "dummies" who nominally had title. The efficiency of plantation operations may be judged by comparing the profitability of their wartime operation with the approximately £1,000,000 that was lost on them by the middle

---

[14] The Hamburger Südsee Aktien Gesellschaft which owned Ralum Estate also had properties in Samoa. The New Zealand occupation of Samoa followed a different procedure and expropriated H.S.A.G. during the war. For accounting ease, the Australians did likewise with the New Guinea assets of the company. I did not determine how Ralum was administered between the wartime takeover and its purchase by Mackenzie.

[15] Mr. Lucas of the Parliamentary Commission of 1920.

of 1924 (Lyng 1925:240). The number of labourers employed
in Rabaul District, which had risen to 8,260 by 1921, dropped to
6,561 in 1923 and did not get back to 1921 levels until 1927. The
truth was that Australians had no experience in tropical agriculture of this type,[16] and having driven out the Germans who had
painfully acquired it, they were in no position to encourage either
plantation or native agriculture.

The government administrative organization was in a similarly
awkward position. During the war, personnel had often changed
rapidly, with sometimes alarming consequences, such as those described in the memoirs of one who, overnight, was made the District Officer at Madang (Lyng 1925). Even with the best of goodwill, nothing constructive could be done, and legal judgements
were capricious, based on the opinions of other Europeans who
had been in the Territory a little longer, rather than on first-hand
knowledge of problems. Colonel J. Ainsworth (1924), the Administrator of Kenya, was asked to advise on Territory problems
in 1924. He cited that there had already been six different District
Officers in Rabaul in three years and that the current D.O.,
Colonel John Walstab, was away in the Sepik because of disturbances there. Too many white officials resided in Rabaul, and
too few went out to encourage the development of resources
(p. 39). Village officials were too numerous, and with the lack
of supervision were too despotic in their control. In Rabaul District they settled cases by imposing fines, half of which went to
the plaintiff and half to the official (p. 18). Ainsworth recalls a
case from Kokopo District in which the District Officer sentenced
a man to two weeks of hard labour "for disobeying the order of
a *luluai*." The *luluai* had told the man to stop beating his wife,
though the wife had not complained, but the man had persisted.
On the *luluai*'s suggestion, the D.O. divorced the wife and gave
her into custody of her brother (p. 26). This case appears, from
the native names quoted, to refer to the Bainings and not to
Vunamami, but the pattern seems clear. *Luluai* who had held office
under the Germans were dismissed and new ones appointed. At
each change of European officials, the newcomer felt dissatisfied
with the appointees of his predecessor and made new and addi-

---

[16] Queensland experience was of cane fields employing large gangs of
labourers; here, the agriculture was slow-growing tree crops requiring
dispersed workers.

tional appointments.[17] Each *luluai* was a despot so long as his patron remained at Kokopo. Overell (1923:159) reports how Jonah, the new *luluai* of Raluana, tried to control the egg supply to Europeans, urging natives not to sell eggs at two for one stick of tobacco but to hold out for one stick each. "Women have a hard time evading him."

In education, however, where a few trained personnel were available, the intentions of the Mandate were carried out. In 1923 a government school was opened at Kokopo, W. C. Groves being first principal. After a year it was moved to new buildings at Malaguna, near Rabaul, where it came under the long-term control of J. H. L. Waterhouse. As Malaguna Technical School it is still one of the most important educational centres of the Territory. It taught in English, and its graduates, virtually alone in New Guinea, knew English before 1950. In its early days, however, it was fought by traders and plantation owners, who thought it discouraged recruitment for indentured labour and provoked rebelliousness and wage demands from workers (Annual Reports 1929–30, Appendix C). When they complained to the League Mandate Commission, the Australian government defended giving *any* post-primary education on the grounds that the Technical School made water tanks, guttering, and office furniture for the administration. This saved money for tax-paying employers and also saved them the expense of training drivers and mechanics.

Mission education also was encouraged, though the Rabaul Industrial School closed when its prospective pupils went to Malaguna. The Methodists obtained a lay headmaster for George Brown College, and considered how to strengthen their whole post-village school system so as to permit a higher level of theological training for the native ministry (Methodist Minutes 1922). They obtained a large coastal site in the western Tolai area, called Vunairima. Beginning in 1927 classes for the 453 students of George Brown College were gradually transferred to the new site, together with a concentration of the teaching of the various circuit training institutions (Methodist Minutes 1927). As early as 1922 it had been reported that some students of the College "felt superior and wished to do only book work, not food growing," but the new site of

[17] The same thing happened in the New Guinea Highlands when transient military administrators arrived in the closing years of the Second World War.

Vunairima involved all students in manual labour. Dormitory building, planting of food gardens, and decorative tree planting were all possible on the new site, and were all required to keep going what was now a large, self-sustaining boarding school. The mission press also operated on the site. In support of the mission expenses Raluana Circuit in 1927 contributed £1,119; since the actual expenses of the mission, other than expatriate salaries provided by Australian congregations, were only £849, Raluana had almost become what the Synod of 1922 decided should be the goal of the mission—"a Native Church progressing to self-support and self-government."

There were still, however, too few native ministers to make self-government possible in a complete system of sub-circuits, run by natives, operating under the supervision of the Australian circuit heads. In 1927, for the first time, a new minister, Isimel Taqaqau, was posted to Vunamami. The Minutes for that year report that "For years, work in Vunamami has been hard." One of the difficulties was the number of indentured labourers from Ralum who played on the beach by Vunamami church on Sundays. Even so, Vunamami had built a new European-style church and gladly paid the salary of their catechist, as well as making their annual contributions, which were "excellent." The improvement when the fully trained minister was posted there was marked. To pay for the minister's salary, coconuts had been planted on church land. Yet in the same year, men from Vunamami village were ministers in Matupit, Nodup, and Rapitok.

Nearly all the Annual Reports note that native agriculture was "encouraged," but what the encouragement was is not clear, although the Australian government continually asked for details (Australia 1923). In February 1923 the Administrator's notion of encouragement was to compel each village to plant a quota of coconuts and to urge the opening of savings bank accounts, though he admitted that little progress had been made. When the quota provision was incorporated in Native Regulations (Part Va, Para. 79, 1924), the League of Nations objected and it was withdrawn. The major goal was apparently to do away with "shifting cultivation, practiced by natives here along with other uncivilized races" (Annual Report 1927), although just what would replace it was not determined. Suggestions were made of potential crops, but little was done to exploit the work begun by the Germans at Rabaul Botanical Station. The Germans had planned to institute an agricultural experimental station and in 1913 had appropriated land for it at Kerevat on the western boundary of the Tolai area beyond Vunairima, but it was not until May 1930 that the Australians began work at Kerevat. Difficulties in obtaining a superintendent were blamed for the delay.

The major item noted with pride in Annual Reports was the increased sale of market garden produce in Rabaul and Kokopo. It is hard to see how the government could claim credit for this. A market had grown up in Rabaul during the war to serve the rapidly expanding Chinese community, for the Chinese, unlike the European settlers, demanded fresh vegetables, fruit, eggs, and fowls, rather than imported canned goods.[18] On the edge of Chinatown, under a spreading tree, sat native women with "baskets of pawpaws, green oranges, bananas, grenadillas, pineapples, and coconuts" (Overell 1923:9). To the native markets—and internal evidence suggests she was talking about the traditional market behind Vunakabi fishing beach in front of Malapau plantation—Overell (p. 92) saw the following brought—copra (by men only), "cooked food, taro, corn, tapioca, sugar, nuts, yams, spinach, coconuts, betel, pepper, bananas, pawpaw, pineapple, oranges, limes, breadfruit, mangoes, eggs," as well as ochre, lime, and fish by the canoeload. This would seem to have been what the Annual Report for 1927–1928 described as the "steadily increasing practice of selling vegetables and fruit on the Kokopo road to the public. Fish is frequently included. The practice was encouraged and reasonable prices were maintained." Overell also describes the purchasing of native copra and food for labourers by plantations. Tobacco and shillings only were used, and the pattern of the preceding forty years continued.

What did clearly encourage both native and plantation agriculture was that the price of copra, after a slump immediately after the war ended, steadily rose until it reached £22 3s. 6d. a ton

[18] This was still true in 1961. I never saw a European buy an egg in a native market (price 4d.), though they complained about no supplies when the ship from New Zealand was delayed (price 5d.). The Chinese bought eggs by the dozen. My experience was that few were bad, and that it was easy to tell the bad ones. Fresh green beans were always available in the markets at about sixpence a pound, yet canned green beans at two shillings a tin were the staple vegetable in Australian homes. Chinese buyers regularly visited native villages to buy live pigs or fresh fish. Europeans never did so, fresh fish being used only when a fish and chip shop opened near Rabaul cinema in 1961.

in 1926. This was followed by a steady decline, but for a few years at least the increasing volume of exports from the wartime plantings made it possible to regard the decline as unimportant and temporary.

It was at just this time that there emerged upon the Territory scene a figure whose career matched that of Dr. Hahl—the Chief Justice, Judge (later Sir) Beaumont Phillips. In his task of re-registering all European land titles in accordance with Australian law, he did not simply accept documentary evidence but reviewed each case *de novo*. Beginning in 1928 he collected evidence regarding Ralum Estate, and on 17 March 1930 he issued a judgement that formed the basis for the operation of Ralum Reserve for the next thirty years. This judgement, which is extant, apparently clarified and expanded the decisions of Dr. Hahl, but unfortunately the grounds for the judgement appear to have been lost (New Guinea 1956a).

1930–1941: PROGRESS DESPITE THE DEPRESSION

In the 1930's, while the world at large was preoccupied with the Depression and with preparations for a world war, the Tolai area benefited from increasingly enlightened local administration and an expanded educational program, made possible by the Administration's revenues from gold-mining. Enrollment at Malaguna Technical school, which had graduated about ten students a year in the 1920's, increased to 66 in 1933 and to 92 in 1937. Eighteen of the 22 in the first advanced class were graduated from the Methodist training institution in 1932, and there were 32 new students. In 1933 the Sacred Heart Mission—which of course did not touch Vunamami—also began a boarding school at Vunapope for post-village-school education. It went beyond the Methodists, who retained Tolai as the language of higher education, and taught in English. In 1939 a minor seminary was inaugurated with five pupils, four of them Tolai.[19] With the graduates of Malaguna

[19] The war interrupted this seminary class, but two students, Hermann ToPaivu and George ToBata, were ordained as the first New Guinean Roman Catholic priests in 1954. The other three have been active in Territorial politics. ToMatthias, a schoolteacher, was elected to the Territorial House of Assembly in 1964 and became Under-secretary to the Department of the Administrator. His younger brother, Stanis ToBoramilat, was an unsuccessful candidate at the Territorial elections both in 1961 and 1964 but has been a councillor in local government for many years. Anton

Tech, an élite core of English speakers was emerging by 1942.

In local administration the policy of appointing Paramount Lulais, adopted in 1929, proved successful, and in 1932 there were twelve in Rabaul District. These covered the Tolai area with a three-level administrative hierarchy. The District Officer in Rabaul (or the Assistant D.O. in Kokopo Sub-district) was in charge. Each Paramount reported directly to him and co-ordinated the activities of about ten *luluai*. Each of these (assisted usually by a *tultul*) had charge of a village of about three hundred people. Vunamami village was one of twenty in Vunamami Paramountcy. Paramounts had no powers granted by ordinance, and no salaries, but in Kokopo Sub-district they were allowed to accept payments for mediating or judging civil disputes. They were usually former *luluai* who had been "progressive" (i.e., receptive to D.O.'s suggestions) and effective in controlling their villages. They had considerable power, being frequently consulted by D.O.s, although in villages other than their own they were often regarded as upstart rivals and not as superiors.

A policy statement to the League of Nations on 5 April 1932 that village councils would be created as a more democratic way to hear cases formerly heard by *luluai* was followed in 1936 by the establishment of experimental councils. Their decisions could be appealed to the D.O., and they were supervised by a Tolai-speaking officer, W. B. Ball. The volcanic eruption of 1937 and later a shortage of supervisory staff prevented their extension to Kokopo Sub-district, but councils became known in Kokopo, together with their achievements, such as the building at Nodup in December 1940 of a thatched-roof timber council chamber with a concrete floor, paid for by contributed funds (*Rabaul Times*, 13 Dec. 1940).

The new Kerevat Agricultural Station actively encouraged development. In its first year thirteen of sixteen trainees completed the course, six going to work on plantations, six returning to their villages, and one staying for further training. The three crops proposed since 1927—rice, maize, and peanuts—were developed as a rotation cycle which was actively taught in villages. Extension Officers worked on the north coast and near Toma. In 1932 rice was generally a failure except at low levels, but peanuts proved

---

Kiari of Bougainville was also unsuccessful in the 1961 elections, but like ToBoramilat he served on several governmental missions and committees as training in administrative techniques.

a good crop. Local Chinese bought them readily at twopence a pound, and the Agriculture Department began further marketing arrangements. Even where good rice crops resulted, husking the grain proved difficult (New Guinea 1932). Fifty acres of hill rice were planted in 1933, producing 35 tons (Annual Report 1933), but the 1936 Report finally acknowledged the failure of the rice experiment. Peanuts, on the other hand, are still a cash crop, the cultivation of which was spread by empowering Paramounts to recruit teams of ten workers from each village. These workers cultivated "village gardens," and the cash returns were used for "communal village purposes" (*Rabaul Times*, 16 June 1933). Thirty villages near Rabaul, on the north coast, and behind Raluana made gardens.

Despite these efforts at diversification, copra remained the economic mainstay of Europeans and natives, although the Depression was reflected in lower copra prices. In 1934 the price received by European growers was only £4 11s. per ton as compared with £22 3s. 6d. in 1926; natives received probably half that price from trade stores. During the period of prosperity the 1917 regulations against opening new trade stores and buying undried coconut meat had not been strictly applied, but as traders cut prices, they were invoked to eliminate competition. "The village [trade] store disappeared when the two-mile limit was enforced" (Australia 1933). Inside trading limits one shilling was paid for 120 nuts, whereas outside it bought only 60. Traders found it uneconomical to visit outlying areas; Toma and Varzin plantations became inactive, yet no trader could buy there, and many villages were forced out of the cash economy. Vunamami was lucky, for the Rowes continued to operate trade stores and buy copra.

At the same time, however, agricultural innovations were making possible better returns for natives. At Malaguna Tech a low-cost hot-air drier was designed using corrugated iron and oil drums. By 1935 these driers were much used in Malaguna, but they spread only gradually to outlying areas. The first drier in Toma, constructed by the Paramount ToLiman, was not erected until 1938 (P. Krümpel, personal communication).[20] By 1936 driers

[20] T. S. Epstein (1963) reports that ToManoa of Navuneram owned a drier in 1931. Native informants generally agreed, however, that driers

were coming into use near Kokopo, and "with the increase in the drying of native copra, the cultivation of . . . other crops has diminished considerably" (Annual Report 1936–1937). The other crops were mainly those that had been adopted only during the Depression. Copra prices fell again on the outbreak of war in 1939, but copra drier use increased, and Vunamami prosperity continued.

By 1942 increased income was also coming from wage labour in the gold-mining centres of the mainland. The amount can be judged from the employment figures. In 1925 only 253 New Britain natives were employed outside the island, and though 707 were so employed in 1930, 428 were from newly controlled areas farther west who worked on plantations in New Ireland. After 1930 plantation employment dropped markedly, but employment in Morobe District—the gold-fields, and the town of Salamaua—increased even more. In 1936, of 963 New Britain migrant workers—almost all Tolai—837 were in Morobe, and numbers rose higher by 1940.

Rabaul as the capital felt the economic activity of the gold-fields in other ways also. Stevedoring became a source of employment for Tolai. They began to buy trucks to transport copra and foodstuffs to Rabaul instead of the horses and carts of 1914. The 1938 Report felt that too many trucks had been bought. For Vunamami, rising plantation activity meant more sales of foodstuffs for the workers. Employment on plantations had shrunk from a 1930 level of 11,319 to 8,307 in 1934. It passed the 1930 figure in 1938 and was still climbing.

This picture of slowly increasing and diversifying Vunamami income and of increasing involvement in migrant wage labour, while the missions were the only avenue of social mobility at home, must not be thought of as implying a declining rural population. The Tolai population[21] rose from 24,366 in 1924 to 29,629 in 1930, or

---

came into use only in 1934–1935. An explanation of this may be that ToManoa was the protégé of an "eccentric" (i.e., liberal) plantation owner who tried to assist native development near her plantation. She may have supplied ToManoa with a drier at the earlier date.

[21] Annual Reports list these figures by subdivisions variously as "Rabaul," "Kokopo," "North Tolai," "South Tolai." Because subdivision boundaries changed in 1930 and 1937, comparisons cannot be made for subdivisions. New Guinea census figures are compiled from "village books" listing persons born or regularly resident there, even if temporarily absent for work elsewhere. Migrant workers are counted in their home villages.

about 3.3 percent a year. It rose more slowly during the Depression, to 30,600 in 1936, the year before the volcanic eruption killed over 1,000 Tolai and reduced the population to 29,843. In 1938 the population was back up to 30,018, as a result mainly of a higher birth rate (or lower infant mortality). Adults formed 62 percent of the population in 1924, but only 56 percent in 1929. With the Depression and low birth rate the proportion rose slightly, to 57 percent, in 1936, but since most of the casualties of the volcanic eruption were adults the proportion fell dramatically to 50 percent in 1938. In numbers the adult population stayed constant, but as indentured workers were counted with their home villages, this means that resident adults fell in number slightly. But the number of children under sixteen increased by over 60 percent between 1924 and 1938.

THE WAR, 1941–1946

War with Germany and threats of war with Japan did not interrupt Vunamami prosperity. Though Rabaul was isolated and nearly indefensible, Australian troops were sent there, to build coastal gun batteries and an excellent airfield on the plateau at Vunakanau, as a supplement to Rabaul's small airfield of Rakunai. The European population grew, and it spent money more freely than before.

The Japanese invasion of 22 January 1942 was overwhelming. The 2/22nd Battalion fought gallantly for one day, especially near Raluana, but was dispersed by the huge Japanese forces, to straggle back the length of New Britain or to be captured and shot. The Japanese began a massive build-up in Rabaul of a supreme headquarters for their Southwest Pacific operations. Two more airstrips were built near Kokopo, one on coastal plantation land at Rapopo near Kabakaul, and another inland at Tobera. The track up the crater wall between Rabaul and Vunakanau was made into a graded highway, known to Japanese as Mount Tana Road, and to later Australians as "the Burma Road." Six thousand Indian prisoners were brought from Singapore and all Tolai males were conscripted for the work. After a few objectors were publicly beheaded, construction was rapid, but many Tolai died of incessant work, poor food, and lack of medical attention.

Village officials had been told not to resist, and to continue normal village administration. Again after some public beheadings, they speedily learned obedience and continued as agents for conscripting labour, collecting food, and communicating orders. Japanese administrators, without local family ties or other commitments, often formed close ties with village officials, teaching them skills and listening to their comments. For many élite Tolai the Japanese occupation meant hardship, but also comradeship with the foreign rulers.

For the ordinary Tolais there was no fraternization, but only rigid discipline. They were made to carry identification passes, and if found away from home without reason were liable to imprisonment or death. House searches for stolen Japanese goods were frequent. But misconduct by troops was punished equally severely, and soldiers found guilty of assault or theft of Tolai goods were publicly beaten. The 100,000 Japanese troops appear to have fathered no half-caste children, and occasional bartering of *sake* for fresh food seems to have been the only contact between villagers and Japanese troops. Thoroughly cowed by constant forced labour, inadequate food, and summary punishments, the natives saw any resistance as a threat to survival. Tolai saboteurs working with the Coastwatchers, the Australian force operating behind Japanese lines, and sent in to blow up arms dumps, for example, were not welcomed, but they were not betrayed.

The most hated action of the Japanese was their creation of a native police force, or *kempe tai*, using both Tolais and non-local indentured labourers who had been stranded by the war. These police were as adept as the Japanese themselves in forms of militarism and violence, with the additional brutality of being against their kinsmen, often in pursuit of personal vengeance. Many intervillage hatreds of the 1950's date from executions resulting from *kempe tai* actions.

The worst Tolai hardships occurred when the Allied leapfrogging campaign of 1943–1944 cut Rabaul off from contact with Japan. The size of the stronghold—some 100,000 troops—made a landing unfeasible (Morison 1950:408), but the troops were immobilized by constant air attacks and left to "wither on the vine" (Odgers 1957:328). All Japanese fighter planes were shot down, and daily Allied raids dropped thousands of tons of bombs. Even in 1964 concrete shelters were still being uncovered in Rabaul, and tunnels, trenches, and bomb craters everywhere bear witness to this period. The Kokopo area, with its airstrips, storage depots, and military camps, was a major target, and Vunamami was often hit. Digging trenches and shelters for themselves and the military kept all men fully employed.

Food supplies, always a problem, became desperate. Exactions by the Japanese were continuous. Both the Japanese and their Indian prisoners encouraged rice growing, and by 1945 rice covered much of the available plantation land. The Japanese also set up plants for the hand manufacture of such articles as cigarette paper, or for the reworking of aluminium salvaged from wrecked planes. Relief came when Allied bombers swept over early on 15 August 1945 and dropped leaflets saying that the war was over.

Allied forces reached Rabaul on 10 September 1945, but Vunamami life did not immediately return to normal. The population itself was unbalanced: one-quarter of the pre-war Vunamami population was dead, from sickness and hunger or as a result of bombings, and very few babies had been born for five years. Workers absent in 1942 were still away, and there had been little formal education for years. Nearly half of all the coconut palms had been destroyed in badly bombed areas like Vunamami. There was an immediate need for camps and hospitals for Indians and Japanese awaiting repatriation, and also for natives in need of housing, food, and medical care.[22] The Kokopo area became one huge staging depot, with Vunamami people housed nearby, at the beach site of the Methodist church.

The resumption of plantation and trade store activity and of shipping services had to await the return of Australian personnel and the rehiring of labour. But the Australian New Guinea Administrative Unit (A.N.G.A.U.) tried to supply local services as best it could, using the still effective structure of *luluai* and Paramounts. The Production Control Board, the wartime organization covering all territory free of the Japanese, made the first economic moves by opening a buying and shipping depot at Kabakaul, east of Kokopo. At first they bought mainly native copra, but when they found that to obtain it they also had to provide goods for purchase, they opened a trade store with the limited supplies available. Missions were allowed to resume work early in 1946, although the few missionaries who had survived the hardships of Japanese prison camps needed home leave and inexperienced staff took over. By June 1946, when A.N.G.A.U. transferred control to civil ad-

[22] A meningitis epidemic was barely averted and anti-malarial measures were urgently required.

ministration, no Tolais were still receiving rations, but the major tasks of reconstruction still lay ahead.

POST-WAR RECOVERY, 1946–1951

The military administration had attended to problems of survival with urgency and financial abundance. Civil administration brought budget stringency and a priority scale in which the rehabilitation of New Guinea ranked below that of Australia. And the administration was also affected by policy changes in Australia. When the new Labour government reduced all indentured labour contracts from three years to eighteen months, a third of the labour force of plantations struggling to get started again immediately quit work. Such necessary commodities as sacks for bagging copra were unavailable, although surplus American military supplies of huts, corrugated iron, Jeeps, and trucks were cheap and plentiful. Despite its efforts the plantation economy stagnated from 1946 to 1951. The hastily erected buildings of A.N.G.A.U. days rusted, and grass and bush invaded plantings.

The government also decided to administer Papua and New Guinea jointly, even though Papua was an integral Territory of Australia and New Guinea was a United Nations Trust Territory. And most of the new Australian subsidy for New Guinea (pre-war New Guinea had been self-supporting) was put into the building up of Port Moresby in Papua as a single capital, housing Australian civil servants in Australian-style suburbs in a sparsely populated semi-desert. Little money went to help outlying areas: in Rabaul administrators still used A.N.G.A.U. huts for offices in 1961, and roads constantly used by plantation trucks were not improved. The government paid War Damage Compensation amounting to some £2,500,000 to natives in the Rabaul area alone (Stanner 1953:119), but the unavailability of goods or of avenues for productive investment resulted in price inflation and much foolish buying.

The greatest economic benefits came through the Production Control Board, later renamed the Copra Marketing Board. The P.C.B.'s wartime contract with the United Kingdom Ministry of Food guaranteed a market at stable prices for any copra production above Australian needs. This contract expired in 1948, but the P.C.B. renegotiated price-supported markets in the U.K. until 1957. Sellers with accounts at the P.C.B. received a first payment on delivery, well below market prices, and a second payment at year's end based on prices realized by the P.C.B. in the U.K. All plantations had accounts, but few native growers had sufficient production to meet P.C.B. requirements for the size of minimum shipments until 1948, and most still sold their copra to traders and plantations. In 1948, the District Commissioner, C. D. Bates, estimated that Tolai copra production had again reached 6,000 tons, but even by 1950 only 2,029 of the total Territory production of 50,669 tons was delivered by native account holders (Australia 1953a:7). By 1952, however, natives delivered 3,816 of the 25,476 tons produced in New Britain (Australia 1953b:17).

But if policy in Canberra did little to help Vunamami in the years immediately following the war, local administrative officers were active. Many pre-war officials had served in New Guinea with A.N.G.A.U. or the Coastwatchers, and many ex-servicemen returned to an area familiar from wartime days. They supported the trend towards greater local participation in administration by means of improved village councils. As the Rabaul D.C. said, "If the Administration didn't assist people, they themselves would take the first steps." But drafting legislation in Canberra took time, and it was passed in 1950 only. In the interval in many areas, such as Madang and Manus, people took the first steps through cult movements. Around Kokopo local "Committees" were formed (see Mead 1956:22–23), each one grouping three or more villages and having eight or nine members, termed *Komiti*. Some were village officials but others were unofficial representatives. Liaison between advising officials and the committees was good, and confidence was inspired for the same officials to later introduce Local Government Councils in 1950 and 1951.

The Education and Agriculture departments, though active, were unable to help Vunamami during this period, for they were too busy restoring their own organizations. Kerevat Agricultural Station was quickly brought back into operation, trying out cocoa as a crop to supplement copra. But since cocoa takes three or more years to bear, it was not until 1949 that beans became available for planting, and Extension Officers, led by Mr. Ryan could introduce the crop widely. The Education Department under W. C. Groves decided on the bold policy of giving all government schooling after the first few years in English, but it first had to train teachers. Concentrating on the Rabaul area, a teacher training centre was carved from virgin forest at Kerevat in 1948; Malaguna Tech was revived, and mission schools also were persuaded to use English.

But few English speakers were available except pre-war graduates of Malaguna Tech or the Catholic school, and after 179 teachers had been trained by this emergency programme there were almost no new trainees until post-war pupils became available in the mid 1950's. A programme to train Australian Cadet Education Officers attracted four people in 1950, and it was further delayed by budget cuts for two more years.

BREAKTHROUGH: THE 1950'S

The passing of the Village Councils Ordinance in 1950, and the rapid decision by five Tolai groups to form councils provides a clear date for the beginning of change. Most councils perpetuated Paramountcies of the 1930's or amalgamated several of them. Vunadidir Council amalgamated Vunadidir, Toma, and Nangananga Paramountcies; Vunamami Council, gazetted in September 1950, added a few isolated villages to Vunamami Paramountcy. The legislation was especially written so that the president of a council did not necessarily have to stand for election in a village, to permit the respected Vunamami Paramount, Enos Teve, to be acclaimed as its first council president (Public Service Institute 1955:103). Otherwise councils were all elected biennially, and administered about 5,000 people, with one representative for every 300 individuals.

Councils had taxation powers, and under the close guidance of the Native Affairs Officers—G. C. O'Donnell for Vunamami and D. M. Fenbury for Rabaul—they began learning how to budget their funds to carry out public works, mainly the construction and operation of medical aid posts, wells, and council offices, the acquisition of council trucks, the development of market sites, and the building of water-storage tanks. Officers discouraged ambitious proposals for large tax increases and encouraged practical innovations like the installation of electric generators, rice-hulling equipment, or power saws. Coronation festivities, funds for overseas scholarships, school sports days, and district agricultural shows needed organizing, and Vunamami soon gained a reputation as being the most active and progressive New Guinea council, receiving awards from Australia as already mentioned.

One of its progressive actions was at its first meeting when it put aside money to plan for a post-primary school (New Guinea 1954). The District Education Officer tried to assist the Vunamami plans, and while the Council selected ground and built classrooms, dormitories, and teachers' houses out of native materials, he tried to obtain teachers to operate the school. He was not successful until 1952, when Darius ToMamua, a Raluana man who had taught at the Kundiawa English-language school in Chimbu before the war, took charge of 87 pupils coming from villages within a range of ten miles. This original Village Higher School of Standards 2–5 made a virtue of the necessity for boarding pupils. In addition to regular classroom work, pupils made gardens, and the school became self-supporting in food; pupils also learned about new crops including cocoa, and built academic programmes around agricultural interests.

In September 1953 a European teacher, V. McNamara, arrived and carried the work further, introducing a two-year Central School programme up to Standard 6. For this, too, the prospective students were the labour force for building. By May 1954 it was possible to institute the compulsory use of English at all times, with marked success. By 1955 the agriculturally biased curriculum of the school had been further developed, and the school fully established as Nganalaka School (New Guinea 1955). Although the school subsequently adopted the curriculum that was worked out for the Territory at large, it retains a high degree of local Council involvement and agricultural interest from its pupils.

In the field of agriculture, Vunamami Council was also actively involved. The enthusiasm of the Agricultural Officers at Kerevat for cocoa growing has already been described, and they early used influential Council members as local leaders in cocoa adoption. They recognized that only a high quality and reliable product would enable New Guinea to enter the competitive world cocoa market. If a high grade of cocoa were to be produced, its processing from wet beans in their pod to dried flavorful beans would have to be centrally controlled. The process is one of heaping the mucus-covered wet beans in boxes, and controlling the temperature of the fermenting mass by turning and aerating it for about three days. The fermentation induces the flavour in the bean, but it must be stopped when peak flavour has been reached. The now-soluble mucus is then washed off, and the beans are dried and polished.

Councils, which had been sending youths to Kerevat to learn cocoa techniques, were approached about organizing the fermenteries needed. Vunamami Council, with supervision, formed a Cocoa

Growers Association and lent the money to build a small fermentery at a village called Ngatur. The crop grew and another fermentery was built in 1954, again with £259 6s. 6d. of Vunamami
Council money, at Talimut, three miles inland from Vunamami
village. Both fermenteries were operated by the Vunamami Council as Vunamami Cocoa Marketing Account. Small government
loans financed extensions, but the Agricultural Department fore-
saw the need for a network of fermenteries of larger, modern
types to handle the larger crops anticipated from new plantings.
They managed in 1955 to arrange a loan of £50,000 from the Bank
of New South Wales to a new organization called the Tolai Cocoa
Project, with the four Tolai councils guaranteeing the loan with
their tax revenues.

The operation of the Tolai Cocoa Project has been fully described elsewhere (Australia 1958, Williamson 1958, etc.), at
least from the point of view of management of the Project. Only
an outline will be given here. Three Europeans were employed by
the Project central office in Rabaul, which kept all central accounts
and arranged for the marketing of the cocoa. It was responsible to
a board of directors, representing the Department of District
Administration, the Agriculture Department, and representatives of
the Councils. It held monthly meetings which were attended by the
Tolai managers of the fourteen fermenteries and certain outside
representatives. Each fermentery was accounted for separately,[23]
and its products were distinctively marked and sold as such. The
Project acted only as the middleman, accepting wet beans from
growers and advancing a "first payment" in exchange, pending the
ultimate sale of the dry beans, when the realized price (less operating costs and first payments) would be paid to the growers. In
theory, growers remained the owners of beans until the ultimate
sale.

Additional finance was required and the bank loan was increased
to £227,020 by 1961. The terms of the loan required the close
supervision indicated, and also amortisation of the loan by a fixed
sum from each ton of cocoa shipped—a very high rate of amortisation as it turned out. By 1961 £175,000 of the original loan had
been spent; Vunamami Council, guaranteeing four fermenteries,
had an allocation of £69,620. It had spent £60,000 of this, but
had already repaid £21,000.

[23] The implications of this separate accounting will be considered in
Chapter 7.

Problems were encountered as the Project developed. During the early years, when cocoa prices were near their peak of £467 per ton in 1954, a first payment of 6d. per pound wet beans, and a second payment of 9d. had masked the 1½d. per pound paid for loan amortisation. By 1957 world cocoa prices had dropped to £202 per ton; first payments were now 4d. per pound, second payments 2¼d., and the amortisation component of 1½d. was worrisome. Some feared that plantations and trading concerns were beginning to buy beans, thus reducing the tonnage sold to the Project. Outsiders, gambling on a gross return of 7¾d. per pound, could afford to pay up to 6d. per pound for wet beans, an attractive price for growers wanting cash when the Project offered only 4d. By 1961 world prices had fallen to £150 per ton. A first payment by the Project of 3d. per pound, with an amortisation contribution reduced to 1.2d. per pound, left virtually no margin for second payments or further price drops. Large outside concerns, in need of huge supplies to operate efficiently, were offering 4d. for native beans. Although Project tonnages were still rising rapidly, worries about low prices were aggravated by the blatant patronizing of plantation and other fermenteries in a few discontented areas, and a major crisis seemed in the offing.

Hoping to avert trouble, the Administration managed to secure more favourable amortisation terms from the bank of New South Wales, which lowered the amount paid by growers to the equivalent of 0.7d. per pound. Although the Crown Law Department felt that legislation establishing the Project as the sole buyer for Tolai cocoa would be discriminatory on racial grounds against establishing Chinese and European fermentery owners, an ordinance was finally passed in 1962 to make licensing of new fermenteries mandatory. Thus an Agriculture Department introduction of a new crop had soon involved Councils as extension agencies, for all practical purposes, had then turned them into important agencies for obtaining bank finance and controlling the operation of an enterprise with a million pound annual turnover, and had finally become an important national political issue in the Legislative Council. Vunamami Council had been in the forefront at each stage, and through its president, Vin ToBaining, elected in 1961 as member for New Britain, had brought it to a political head.

Two other governmental fields also impinged on Vunamami economic life—land and co-operatives. All alienated land titles had been lost during the Second World War, and the Land Titles

Restoration Ordinance had set up a commission to investigate claims to title and if they were satisfactorily proved, to restore them as they had been before the war. This proved difficult, because Judge Phillips' decisions were also lost. The prospect of re-investigating every case, as Judge Phillips had done, emerged when problems arose over the boundaries of land on Giregire and Varzin plantations (the first in connection with the original founding of Nganalaka school on what was subsequently judged to be plantation land), and when natives realized that new evidence, not considered by Judge Phillips, might be introduced and might lead to a new decision.

The Department of District Services, as trustee over the Reserves, also became involved. In particular, it hoped for clarification of the anomalous nature of Ralum Reserve land, owned in freehold by the owners of Ralum but unusable by them owing to the fact that natives had permanent rights of use and occupancy. If Ralum would sell these worthless freehold rights to the government, it could relinquish its trusteeship and return the land to native ownership. But without clear title no plantation could sell freely. The situation was deadlocked, and was further complicated when the Rowe brothers sold Ravalien and Matanatar to a company called Plantation Holdings, Ltd., which proposed to develop much of the coastal land as a residential extension of Kokopo.

These official and interdepartmental discussions stimulated native interest in land questions, especially around Rabaul, where the government's attempts to acquire land for town and airport extensions had already provoked discussion. Questions were asked in the District Advisory Council in 1958, and the urgency of obtaining new lands for resettlement of the rapidly increasing and land-short Tolai became apparent. Although a scheme for Rabual Council to resettle people at Vudal, near Kerevat, had failed in 1952, the government acquired land in the Baining area south of the Warangoi River, and in 1958 began a resettlement scheme, leasing some of the land to European planters and some to the Councils. In succeeding years it changed its policy to leasing to individual native planters on ten- or fifteen-acre blocks, and resettlement became a recognized part of the government's economic development programme.

Native concern about Reserve lands and land shortage was also stimulated by the arrival in Kokopo in 1956 of a Native Lands Commissioner, S. S. Smith, to investigate and record indigenous land titles. His investigations aroused, after initial hesitations, great interest. After investigating the few, but acrimonious, disputes that occurred and recording inter-native land sales he embarked on a compilation of clan titles to named land areas, and the membership of clan groups. By 1961 he had almost completed a compilation for Kokopo Sub-district; his jurisdiction did not apply to alienated lands, so his activities made even more prominent to natives the anomalous status of the reserves.

In 1948 the D.C. had declared that the Tolai area was not yet ready for co-operatives. Only in 1953 was a Co-operative Officer posted to Rabaul. With great enthusiasm (and no doubt aided by the surplus cash available from War Damage Payments and high copra prices) he obtained the formation of nineteen co-operative societies in the area, including two very close to Kokopo—Bitatali in Vunamami village, and Bitaulagumgum next to Vunapope Mission. Society members subscribed £56,595, of which £29,498 was used to found the New Britain Association, as a central wholesaling agency for buying bulk copra from societies and selling goods to them in return. The Co-operatives Officer, whose salary is paid by the Administration, supervises the operations of all societies in his area, ensuring that each society meets the standards laid down by the central registry in Port Moresby for annual accounts, reserves, and distributions. He also gives advice, organizes the training of storekeepers and clerks, and in the early stages can effectively run local societies.

The early years of co-operatives in New Britain were ones of enthusiasm and high hopes, but by 1955 most of the societies were struggling, partly because officers could not keep up with the supervision that was needed. Not until 1958 was the tide turned, but by then half the societies were bankrupt. Those that remained were ones that had always been effective, including, as the best, the two near Kokopo. By 1961 the co-operative movement in New Britain was the most active in the Territory, with an annual turnover of £160,000. Again, Vunamami was in the lead.

In Methodist Mission matters, too, Vunamami (and the wider area of Raluana Circuit) was still a leader, although the spread of education meant that it was no longer dominant—of the thirteen natives received as ministers between 1939 and 1961, only five were from Raluana Circuit, and none from Vunamami village itself. Fifty youths from Raluana Circuit were graduated from George Brown College between 1946 and 1960 to become teachers. A respected native minister, Elias ToVutnalom, was in charge of Vunamami Church in 1961, and supervising teachers in other outlying churches.

Financially, Raluana Circuit was more than paying its way; by 1961 it was contributing a large proportion of the £587 that went from New Britain to support mission activities in the Southern Highlands. Besides payments made to local teachers and ministers the circuit contributed for general Mission funds the amounts of £360 in 1946 (a time of poverty), £1,241 in 1950, £2,547 in 1955, and £5,043 in 1960. In 1950 this had been less than a third of the total of New Britain contributions; in 1960 it was nearly half. The largest villages of Raluana, Davaun, and Ratavul contributed the largest amounts in the circuit, but in 1960 Vunamami Church collected £360, and Bitapabek Church, which included some Vunamami residents, collected another £208 (Methodist Minutes, 1946–1960).

SUMMARY

The foregoing brief history, compiled from published sources or from records, gives a clear picture of the general lines of Vunamami development. It is a history of gradual, if not always continuous, growth by a small village, originally at war with its neighbours and having a largely subsistence economy, into a large village predominantly concerned with cash cropping of tree crops and their processing. It participates actively in its own local government and by means of an elected representative, in national politics also, and it contributes a significant number of the technicians, clerks, and bureaucrats to run not only its own internal economy but also to staff other parts of the Territory. As of 1961, apart from concern over world prices for cocoa and copra, the future seemed rosy. In every sphere developments fostered by expatriate administrators and missions had been adopted, had successfully weathered adversity, and were increasingly being taken over by local people. Incomes were high, and so were the possibilities for the future.

Succeeding chapters will re-examine this picture, viewing the developments not merely as introductions by outsiders but looking from the inside at the local contributions and initiatives. A somewhat different picture will emerge. But as a framework of dates, and an exposition of the European organizations with which natives have to deal, the preceding account is important for understanding the local picture.

It also enables us to divide the period into over-all phases. The dates for these, from a European point of view, are most easily given by political events. The first phase was the arrival of resident Europeans in 1875, the final pacification of the Vunamami area in 1893 and the steady development up to 1921, followed by the Australian Mandate and a period of stagnation until about 1937, when village councils were experimentally begun; the war interrupted a period of slow growth which lasted until 1950 when a village council was proclaimed. The 1950's were a period of rapid growth.

In subsequent chapters we shall see that these dates are not as precise as they appear. Decisive political events preceded some official actions by several years. At roughly the same time as the political changes, there occurred economic changes: around 1875 the arrival of traders, around 1893 the beginning of coconut planting by natives, after 1921 an increase in wage employment, around 1937 the adoption of copra driers, and around 1950 the adoption of cocoa as a crop, along with large-scale processing of it. A main task of this work will be to elucidate the connections between the political events and the economic events. This will mean some revision of the dating of the phases, but the framework will stand.

Part Two

The Inside View
of Development

Presenting an "inside view" of Vunamami development for an "outside" audience raises problems. The historical framework is identical with the one already given in the "European" history, which describes events, and analyses the reasons for them, as they appeared to missionaries, administrators, and businessmen; but without some knowledge of indigenous economic thinking, the Tolai actions in those events often appear irrational or capricious. Each chapter in this section therefore analyses Vunamami concepts applying to a single sphere of economic activity, such as agriculture or marketing. The events since 1875 relating to that sphere of activity are then re-analysed in terms of those concepts, which Vunamami people themselves use in discussing their history. Each chapter then concludes with a description of how the Vunamami economy actually functioned in 1961. Such a presentation, it is hoped, will serve both to make the "inside view" of history a comprehensible one and to show how the present and its problems are an outgrowth of that history.

The order in which spheres of activity are analysed is related partly to their importance in the local economy and partly also to their historical development. Basic activities, and those in which there were the earliest changes, come first; activities like co-operatives which emerged after the Second World War come last. The order is occasionally altered, in later chapters, to permit the logical exposition of theoretical points.

II
Land

Land, as any Vunamami inhabitant will say, is the most basic element of life. Every plot of land (*pakana pia:* "piece of land"), large or small, from beach landing place to uncultivated virgin forest, has its own name, and without a knowledge of these names one is lost. They are used to refer not merely to a specific plot but to the settlements near the plot, the group of people living on that plot or descended from an owner of the plot, the village of which the plot is a part, or the activity generally performed there. Thus, no native (unless he is talking to a European) will say that he is "going to the Rabaul market"; he goes to Vunamai, the plot of land on which the market, the Rabaul Local Government Offices, and a cemetery are situated. So too, he goes to "Mioko," the plot of land settled by the Sacred Heart Mission, and he rarely refers to the Mission, to the name Vunapope which Bishop Couppé gave to the vast area now owned by the Mission, or to the Mission Hospital, which is his usual destination. The name Kokopo, used by Europeans for the whole area around the government offices, is used by natives to refer strictly to the site of those offices, and one will be corrected if, say, one refers to "Chinatown in Kokopo," for Chinatown is on the land called Vunatali.

Most names refer to some natural feature of the land, or to an event that occurred there. Kokopo, for example, means "landslide," Matanakalivurvur means "head of the (dog named) Whirlwind" that was buried there. Commonly names are compounds of Vuna- (the base of), Bita- (underneath), or Tingena- (a clump of) and the name of a tree, for example, Vunalama "the base of the coconut," Bitakoai "under the mango tree," Tingenavudu "the clump of bananas." It will be appreciated that the same names occur in many different Tolai areas.

There is also a great chance of confusion over the exact referent

67

of a name. Vunabalbal, for example, is the name of a plot of land just south of Vunamami village and of the hamlet located there. More generally it refers to the collection of houses on plots neighbouring Vunabalbal which forms a "ward." The political unit or "village" in which this ward is located has been called Vunabalbal by the government since German days, although the mission prefers the name Bitapabek, the plot (and ward) where the church is located. Vunabalbal is even more widely known as the name of a clan, the founding ancestor of which lived on its eponymous plot (its *madapai*). The clan is now large and has segments living in all the villages of the area. If a man says "Vunabalbal gave birth to me" (*ga kava iau*) he may mean that his father was of Vunabalbal clan, or that he lived during his youth in Vunabalbal village, hamlet, or plot of land. He may mean all these things or only one of them; only the context can indicate. But in any case, it is probably unnecessary to make distinctions, since a man would make such a comment to justify his attending a ceremony given on Vunabalbal land and it is immaterial whether his tie is close or distant, one of locality or of kinship; the tie is one that brings him to Vunabalbal land.

A similar confusion applies to the word *gunan* or "place." It strictly means "an inhabited place" in contrast to the term *pui* or "the bush." Thus it may refer to an inhabited plot of ground or hamlet, to a group of plots or a ward, or to the group of wards that make up a village. In reply to a question "Where is your *gunan?*" the most frequent answer is the name of a village. If one really wanted to know the ward, one might then ask "What *pakana gunan?*"—What piece of a *gunan?* To know the piece of land on which a person's house was situated, one could then specify "What is your *pakana* [your piece of land]?" Alternatively, if one were told first the name of a plot of land and wanted to know specifically the ward or village name, one could ask "What is your *papar a gunan?*"—What area of a *gunan?* Again, the degree of specificity required is usually evident from the context, as it is when an English-speaker asks one what "place" one comes from.

Further confusion is possible over the ownership of any particular plot of land. There are two kinds of rights involved: those of the man who cultivates the plot (*i papalum tana*), and those of people who control (*kure*) it. Most land is "clan land" (*a pia na vunatarai*), meaning that a clan may be named as the ultimate "controller," represented by its senior member or *lualua* (lit. "first man"), and that inheritance of rights to the land is normally within the clan. But even in such cases, more immediate rights of control are exercised by individuals who may have cultivated the land in the past, or by the successors of such people. Any of these categories of person may equally well say "the land is mine." To understand what their rights—of cultivators, or *lualua*, and of various levels of "controllers"—involve it will be helpful first to explain some other less common types of land ownership.

Some land, until the early 1950's at least, had never been systematically cultivated and was either virgin forest or *kunai* (*imperata*) grass. But these areas were all within the territorial boundaries of one village or another, and were therefore controlled by one clan *lualua*. The jurisdiction of each *lualua* was limited to initiating action against outsiders who trespassed on the land by hunting or collecting wild produce, and to a right to veto any actions by members of the village that he thought were undesirable. Customarily, villagers could clear forest on such uncultivated land, or make gardens on kunai land, and could expect the veto to be exercised only in special circumstances[1]—if, for example, there was unused garden land already available, or if the villager wished to plant a "permanent" crop of coconuts on kunai land and so withdraw the land from common use for hunting, pig pasture, or temporary garden sites. Such land might be simply described as land, owned in common by the village, with the *lualua* of a particular clan acting as trustee.

By legitimately clearing common forest land, an individual could make the land his own personal property as "family land" (*a pia na bartamana*). He would usually clear only a portion of a larger area, and would give a new name to his own plot. He could give the plot to whomever he wished on his death or retirement,

---

[1] A case heard before the Native Lands Commissioner Kokopo (N.L.C.K. 5–14, dated April 1960) suggests that it was normal for a small present to be given to the *lualua* before requesting his approval for using such land. This was a token acknowledgement of his jurisdiction rather than a purchase of rights or a payment of rent. In the present case the "controller" vetoed the planting of coconuts and demanded £100 and 100 fathoms of *tabu* for a 33-acre plot on which plantings had already been made illegally. This sum was eventually paid in order to save the palms from being cut down. Title was registered in the names of the 29 purchasers. Another village (Mokurapau) sold its common lands to individuals in about 1954 and deposited the proceeds in a collectively held village bank account.

without consideration of clan rules of matrilineal inheritance.[2] The group that then came to live with him on the family land and received the new land from its original owner would form the nucleus of a new clan, or clan segment, called by the name of the plot. The plot from which a clan takes its name is called its *madapai*. After the land has been once transferred through matrilineal inheritance it is "clan land." Clearing new land, attracting dependents, and so founding a new clan were the ways of achieving fame and immortality; one was remembered not by one's name in a genealogy but by the name of the land one cleared, developed as "family land," and then converted into the clan estate.

In more recent times, as uncleared land has become scarce, "family land" has more commonly been created by the purchase of cleared land (*a kunukul*), though such purchases, despite the payment of large sums of *tabu*, or shell money, do not make the land into "family land" in perpetuity. During the buyer's lifetime, if the original owners return the payment in full, the land is supposed to revert to the original clan. If the owner has not designated an heir before his death, the land is transferred according to normal matrilineal rules, and it becomes clan land. It should also be noted that until recently the distinction between clan and family land was of little practical importance. The man who was most likely to clear an area of forest was the man who could command a large work force to assist him, namely a *lualua*. The *lualua*'s dependents were mainly his own clansmen, and when the new land was transferred to them, it went mostly in accordance with matrilineal rules. He controlled and acted as trustee for clan land and for most family land. In the rare cases when land was captured by a village expelling or annihilating the former occupants, it also went into the hands of the *lualua* of the village, and again it was largely immaterial whether they were acting as the controllers of clan land or as the owners of family land. The distinction was primarily important

---

[2] The possibility that an individual would clear and enclose common land and then immediately sell it does not seem to have arisen in the past. I should guess that such an action would have provoked a reaction from the *lualua* and the villagers, indicating that their rights were not immediately abrogated, but I have no evidence for this. The point is somewhat academic in view of the disappearance of such land, the absence of written contracts, and the somewhat despotic powers of *lualua*, although an analogous case arose in 1966 under the Land Tenure (Conversion) Ordinance. The individual involved migrated to New Ireland.

when there were rivals for the position of *lualua*, or when clans were segmenting.

Certain rights are inherent in clan land. In Tolai thinking it is, as we have seen, always identified with the original occupier who made it the clan's estate. All his clan, both present and future, have the right to use the land; the present *lualua* who controls the land is merely the trustee for the original ancestor and for succeeding generations. A clansman need only ask a *lualua* for land on which to grow his own food and the *lualua* is bound, as the person who looks after (*balaure*) the living members of the clan, to give him land to cultivate. The rights to cultivate are then permanently transferred to the user, so long as he cultivates continuously, subject to the possible intervention by the *lualua* if the intended use of the land will affect future generations—if, that is, tree crops are contemplated, or if the user is threatening to sell the land to outsiders.

In practice, however, matters are more complex. After a plot has been used by one segment of a clan for several generations, a *lualua* has in fact very little control. A senior member of the clan segment will undoubtedly have allocated some land to junior members (or dependants) of the segment, and will himself be acting as a "controller." And there may be allocations within sub-segments, so that there is a hierarchy of controllers nominally concerned with a plot. Effectively the persons who make most decisions about any plot are the actual user and the particular controller who allocated him the plot, though these may be the same person if the user inherited his use rights. On 98 of 129 plots in Vunamami, user and controller were the same.

This allocation of control does not result in too rapid a decrease in the size of holdings or proliferation of claimants. Thus, an individual may assign plots to the three sons of his sister in one generation; the heirs of the sister's sons are not their own children but the children of their sisters. One child may be equally the chief heir of them all, may arrogate the right to allocate all the land, and may become the single successor of his mother's-mother's brother. The splitting of estates does not automatically occur in each generation, since under matrilineal regulation of inheritance there is little tendency for "lines of descent" to achieve unity and separate identity. At the same time there are, of course, many individuals with no land who live as dependants.

Other controllers and the *lualua* usually remain inactive, stressing their claims in two circumstances: to stop a controller from
selling his plot, or allocating use rights over the plot to a person
who is not a member of the clan. Even in pre-contact times, before 1875, plots of land were sometimes sold, usually to a member
of the owning clan, who paid *tabu* to the clan *lualua* so as to make
the land his own family land, which he could then give to his son.
Alienation to non-members was also possible, however. The phi-
losophy seems to be that a sale merely exchanges land for *tabu*,
and that the *tabu* remains as the selling clan's estate for future
generations. If the *lualua* approves, the sum received is put in the
clan treasury. The sale by ToAitak of Tetegete clan of some
eight acres of land to the Vunamami Council as a site for the
council chambers in 1950 followed this pattern, a small amount
of the proceeds (300 fathoms of *tabu*, listed for European eyes
as £30) being distributed, but most being kept by ToAitak as a
clan fund. The claims of a senior *lualua* to the proceeds are as
important as his potential veto of the transaction.

On the other hand, the *lualua* of a clan may act in a very arbi-
trary way—and many of them did in the early years of European
contact—selling lands that have previously been allocated and
are in use. But by doing so, and by dispossessing fellow-clansmen,
he runs the risk of losing support and even of being killed, although he may distribute the goods received and thereby gain
support from those not dispossessed. The assumption is that he is
acting in good faith as a trustee of the clan and believes that the
clan will ultimately benefit by his actions.

The allocation of rights to a user is also a controversial issue.
In theory, any member of any segment of a clan who has no land
to cultivate or to build a house on may request the use of a plot
from any controller of land belonging to the clan. In fact such
requests are most commonly made by members of a controller's
own clan segment, but there are exceptions—outsiders who are
given house sites and land for cultivation when they indicate they
wish to live in the village, merely on the basis of their having a
distant clan tie with a land controller. Before 1875 a complete outsider, with no clan ties at all, could request such use rights by
presenting the controller with a gift of a basket of food, a fathom
of *tabu*, and a spear (*a rumu*). These gifts were termed *a totokom*.
They were made once for each continuous period of use regardless of duration. It seems appropriate to regard the *totokom* as a

token payment to obtain temporary admission as a clan member rather than as a rent for the land itself.

This is in line with the attitude to the third major group of applicants for use rights—children of men of the clan. A child customarily leaves the land of his father's clan at marriage, if not before, or at the death of the father. But he still has a personal right to expect "food"—interpreted widely as the necessities of subsistence—from his father's clan. This right does not extend to his wife or children—hence the departure from the father's house at marriage—and at the father's death payments are made to the child's own clan, that is, to the clan of the dead man's wife, which formally absolves the father's clan of further obligations to support. Nevertheless, any offspring without land may request use rights simply by saying "I live by the blood of my father" (*lau laun tara gapu kai tamagu*). It is demeaning for a controller to refuse such a request, since it is tantamount to saying he cannot afford to live up to his moral obligations. A child making such a request could not give a *totokom* to the controller, as "the clan give him *tabu* in any case, and would be ashamed to accept *tabu* from him."

But before replying to any particular request for use rights, the controller of a plot must consider whether it is feasible to give the applicant those rights, or whether he will displace some more qualified future applicant. Even more care must be exercised in granting permission for a user to plant a tree crop. Not only are the potential claims of the controller's clan segment to be considered, but the *lualua* of other segments will voice their claims as being more pressing than those of the applicant—assuming that the other *lualua* hear of the request before it is a *fait accompli*. What usually happens is that a controller takes an applicant to live with him on his own house site; the applicant helps him plant the land, as if he were merely an assistant or hired worker. In the course of time the newcomer gradually comes to be recognized as the possessor of use rights, and by then it is too late for other *lualua* to intervene.

In short, although the balance of rights between the user, the controller, and the corporate clan is theoretically clear, and although the names of the three parties may be universally agreed upon, the extent to which those rights are exercised is a matter of convenience. It depends on the relative political power of individual controllers, on the length of time use has been under way,

on the size and compactness of the clan group, on the land pressures on other segments of the clan, and on the general willing-
ness of individuals to dispute the actions of clansmen. Vunamami
village provides a good example of how these land tenure concepts
have adapted in changing historical situations.

LAND IN VUNAMAMI

(a) The Background

The name Vunamami itself primarily refers to a small plot of
land on the coast, where a landing place and hamlet were located
in 1875. The Methodist Mission "bought" the site, and, except for
a brief period during the Japanese occupation, a church has existed
there ever since. According to the Government Land Registry
this land is the freehold property of the Methodist Mission, but the
local inhabitants have never moved away from the site (except
temporarily) and the Mission regards itself as holding the land in
trust for the people, and defending their rights against the en-
croachments of plantations.

The settlement, or hamlet, of Vunamami[3] was only one—the

---

[3] The word *Kinigunan* is frequently found in early literature. I could
obtain no recognition of it by Vunamami informants. It is first mentioned
as one of a list of coastal village names (Brown Diary, 27 Jan. 1876) co-
ordinate with Kabakaul (see Brown 1908:147). Internal evidence indicates
that the village was Vunamami, and it is in this sense that "Kinigunan"
appears in Brown (e.g., 1908:292), Danks (1933:20), and most Methodist
Mission writings. Elsewhere, however (e.g., p. 146), Brown uses it for a
general area all along the coast. Parkinson (1887:60, 74) apparently uses
it in much the same general sense, but Powell (1884:79) is explicit in
using Kinigunan to refer to the whole area between Cape Gazelle and
Raluana Point, and "Kinigunan proper" when he means one of the three
sub-districts of this area, the others being Kabakaul (Abercole) and
Raluana. But Powell is generally unreliable on native terms, having apparently depended on local European informants. In other places (1887:
104, 114) Parkinson contrasts it with Raluana and Birara *"Distrikte."* The
Sacred Heart Mission called their first station on the coast in 1883 by this
name, although it was situated at Kokopo in Kinabot territory. They kept
the name when they relinquished this plot to the Neu-Guinea Compagnie
and received land at Mioko in 1890 (now Vunapope). The term Kinigunan
was retained, however, for their plantation farther to the east in Takubar
and Kabakaul territories. Their usage would seem to have originated in a
belief that the whole coast was called Kinigunan. Against this, Bishop
Couppé in his 1894 report to the Neu-Guinea Compagnie refers to "the
three Wesleyan stations of Ravalien, Kinigunan and Kabakaul" (*Monats-*

fishermen's hamlet—of a group of hamlets having control of an area extending along the coast for half a mile on each side of Vunamami and just over a mile inland. The names of the seven or eight inhabited plots at this time need not concern us, but they were grouped into two almost independent wards. The name Lumluvur was (and is) applied to the easterly group along the ridge that borders the present Ravalien plantation; the westerly hamlets, more scattered over a plateau and separated from Lumluvur by a deep ravine, were known as Kunakunai. This term, meaning "Just Kunai Grass," was strictly the name of the uncultivated no man's land separating these hamlets from the neighbouring village of Keravi, but by extension was used for the westerly ward, and even for the entire village. In a ruling dated March 1930, Judge Phillips uses it rather than the term Vunamami. However, the Methodist Mission used the name of the church site for the village, and the German administration followed suit. They appointed a headman, or *luluai*, with jurisdiction over the village area and it has been known as Vunamami ever since. Later, when the Australian government appointed a Paramount Luluai with jurisdiction over Vunamami and nineteen other villages, his area was called Vunamami Paramountcy. In 1950 most villages of Vunamami Paramountcy and one village of another paramountcy requested that they be constituted as Vunamami Village Council and elect their own council. Following the 1953 ordinance the title became Vunamami Native Local Government Council, and by 1961 other villages had asked to join the council to make a total of thirty. In the ensuing analysis, in which I shall be primarily concerned with Vunamami village, I shall use the term Vunamami to mean the village. When I wish to refer to the plot of land, the Paramountcy, or the Council—and I shall discuss several other villages within the council area—I shall make my meaning clear.

In 1875 the western boundary of Vunamami village with Keravi village was a somewhat indefinite one running from the open kunai plain near the present boundary of Malapau plantation as far as the coast, where the present Butuwin Hospital is situated. To the

---

hefte 1895:132), using it as a specific village or locality name. I interpret the confusion thus: the native usage was that Kinigunan was originally a locality name; Brown used it both correctly and to refer to a village and the nearby area; all later Europeans have followed the second looser usage, with progressively less regard for native usage.

east were first the village of Tokokok and next the village of
Kinabot. The boundary of Vunamami and Tokokok ran roughly
along the bottom of a ravine which is the present eastern boundary
of Ravalien plantation but then cut across the flat land where,
since 1883, the plantation buildings have stood. Inland from Vunamami was the village of Vunabalbal, and beyond it lay the
villages of Bitarebarebe and Tingenavudu. Vunamami, Tokokok,
Vunabalbal, Keravi, and Bitarebarebe, though often at odds, inter-
married and formed a virtually endogamous entity, as they still
largely do to this day. Balanataman, the western neighbours of
Keravi, did not intermarry with them, and were in a relationship
of permanent hostility. Kinabot and Tingenavudu were also outside the intermarrying "district." Population figures for this period
are, of course, not available, but a guess, based on the German
census of 1910 and recognizing comments on population increases
since 1895, and taking into account the incidence of wars, migrations, and epidemic diseases, would be that Vunamami had just
under two hundred members. For this population the village had
land area of about seven hundred acres. Three clans, Toalave,
Tetegete, and Timel, had *madapai* in the area, though they were
actually segments of the widespread clans of Takaptar, Turlom,
and Matupit. Several other clans including Vunabalbal, Davara,
and Vunaibu owned one or more plots.

(b) Relations with Europeans

The first alienation of land, to the Methodist Mission, would
seem to have been acceptable within the indigenous ideas of land
tenure. The Vunamami people, having heard of teachers being
placed in Nodup and Matupit, wanted one to settle among them.
When George Brown visited them in late 1876, one of the important men of the village, Ilaita ToGimamara (Brown 1908:378;
Danks Diary, 8 Oct. 1880), invited a Fijian teacher to settle, and
a church and house were built close to the hamlet. No doubt
Brown gave presents to the people at this time, but his diary contains no record of how much he "paid for the land." In 1879, however, Danks records in his diary for 16 June that he gave three
axes, two knives, one pound of beads, and three fathoms of cloth
for an area at Birara, or roughly three times the traditional *totokom*.
I should expect that presents had become inflated since 1876,
possibly increasing threefold. If this is the case, then it is likely
that smaller payments in 1876 may well have merely equalled the

traditional *totokom* payment instead of being three times as large. The mission, in short, was accepted as village members of Vunamami with permanent rights of residence, through the payment of *totokom*.

Direct confirmation of this is given in comments by the old man Tinai regarding the first settlement about 1884 of Queen Emma and the Parkinsons at Tomarongrong (Malapau). Muzzle loaders were given, one each, to four clan *lualua* in the villages of Raluana, Ratavul, Nanuk, and Balanataman. "These were," said Tinai, "for coconuts and not for the land. Then Mr. and Mrs. Parkinson showed people how to plant coconuts, clear bush and plant bananas, and also sweet potatoes. We helped them and planted coconuts for them." I inquired about "markets" at which produce was bought. "They did not *buy* [*kul*] food; they told the *lualua* to bring in bananas, sweet potatoes, and so on, and the *lualua* presented them [*tabatabar*] to the Parkinsons. Then the Parkinsons would give a pig feast [*lukara*] for all the people. The people obeyed them [*ave ga toromia*]." The newcomers were received into the village, on payment of a *totokom*, and then, like a *lualua*, they were supported and fed for as long as they met their obligations to act as important people, giving occasional feasts and dances, and providing trade goods for coconuts.

Not all traders or missionaries in the early days were on such good terms with the local population as were the Methodists and the Parkinsons. Many, after a good initial reception (and presumably after the payment of *totokom* gifts to a *lualua*), failed to live up to their obligations and were driven out; usually the villagers simply set fire to their thatched houses. In Vunamami by 1880 any trader was regarded with disfavour, and the only one tolerated was a survivor of the Marquis de Rays' expedition, a man called Champion, located near the Mission church, who was apparently a trader for Farrell, Queen Emma's husband, Toti,[4] a

---

[4] This account reconciles conflicting native and published accounts. Danks (1933:127) says Toti was from "Guvalien near Raluana," yet in a letter to his wife (28 Oct. 1880) he says "Champion was threatened at Kinigunan." Vunamami informants say Toti lived in Lumluvur. Brown (1908:389–391) gives the impression that the trader who shot was a different person from Champion, who is identified as the captain of a passing boat. Brown's diary, however, has no entry for this period, whereas Danks's contemporary letters and the book based on them say that Champion did the shooting. I infer that Brown purposely kept his account unclear so as not to risk a defamation suit from Champion, who was still alive.

rich man, was at Champion's store in September 1880 and while Champion's back was turned several youths present began to laugh. Champion thought they were laughing at him and turned round in a rage, yelling at them to clear out. Toti stood up for the boys, but Champion turned on him, shouting that if he said three more words, he would shoot him. Toti spoke up again and was shot dead. A crowd attacked Champion and he barely escaped to sea with his life. The villagers plundered his store, but the Methodist Mission teacher intervened, and four-fifths of the trade goods were recovered; an axe and a knife were given by Champion "as compensation" for the shooting (Brown 1908:390, Danks 1933:127). Local informants say that in addition "the Government" (presumably the gunboat H.M.S. *Beagle*) came; there was no fighting, but Toti's house was destroyed and because a bolt of cloth from the store was not recovered some land was taken. The stretch of coast east of Vunamami, where the buildings of Ravalien plantation now stand, was given to the trader to compensate him (*ure ra balbali*).

Thereafter life continued fairly peaceably in Vunamami. The land on the shore at Ravalien nominally became Ralum Depot, owned by the Farrells in 1882. The Parkinsons settled at Malapau as agents for Farrell. Neither settlement took up much land or did much planting, because the limited labour available (imported from Bougainville) was almost entirely occupied processing the coconuts brought in for trade by the local people. By 1890, however, the "plantations" were on a sounder footing, and the Deutsch Neu-Guinea Compagnie, the Sacred Heart Mission, and Mouton (a survivor of the ill-fated expedition of the Marquis de Rays) had stations at Kokopo and farther east. Trouble arose when Queen Emma decided to build a road connecting the outstation of Malapau to the centre of the European settlement. A party under a Filipino named Moses began marking out the route. A Vunamami sacred men's place (*taraiu*) stood in the direct line, near the present Butuwin hospital site, but Moses, heedless of warnings, cut right through the sacred place.

A conspiracy vowed revenge, and ToRuruk of Vunaibu clan, who had land in Ulaulatava and Tingenavudu villages, caught Moses and killed him by biting his jugular vein. Moses was eaten and on 28 March 1890 Vunamami, Keravi, Bitarebarebe, Tingenavudu, and, presumably, Vunabalbal and Ulaulatava (*Monatshefte* 1890:134, *Nachrichten* 1890:75) joined forces to attack Ralum.

The Europeans under Parkinson beat them off, and aided by a naval party commanded by the head government official, Judge Schmiele, they conducted a punitive expedition to Tingenavudu. One Vunamami man was shot by the expedition, and another was shot by nervous native police when he was collecting coral on the reef. ToRuruk went into hiding and was not captured until a year later when his clan brother, ToInia, betrayed him. ToRuruk was executed, and at least three men of other villages were killed.

Vunamami informants consider that the death of Moses was adequately "compensated for" (*bali*) by the death of the man on the reef. They feel that they should have received compensation for the additional deaths they suffered. Instead, the government decreed that all the land between Malapau and Ralum, stretching from the coast inland for some four hundred yards (or about one hundred yards inland of the road), was to be given to Queen Emma and vacated, "to seal the peacemaking" (*ure ra vinivi*).

In 1893 the resentment over encroachment by the plantations reached a peak. The settlers were eager for more copra, but the natives, whose land was mainly covered with kunai, with clumps of coconuts near each scattered hamlet, showed no inclination to plant new palms. The settlers' solution was to import labourers from Bougainville and New Ireland and to plant cotton and coconuts on land to which they laid claim because of their initial *totokom*. The imported labourers acted arrogantly when dealing with local people who brought food or coconuts to trade at the plantations, and when they began clearing and planting inland from Ralum they used guns to keep local people away (*Monatshefte* 1894:101). In early July the labourers wantonly destroyed some gardens belonging to Tokokok village; the villagers fought back. Police from Kokopo were quickly called and the local people fled. Order, if not harmony, returned when Tokokok and Kinabot villages paid one hundred fathoms of *tabu* each to "seal the peace" (*Monatshefte* 1894:135).

Farther inland, however, at Ulagunan a magician (*a tena malira*) was claiming to have discovered an ointment of lime that would repel bullets. Men from Tokokok, Vunabalbal, and several other villages (though informants deny that Vunamami participated), greatly excited, went together to pay the one thousand fathoms of *tabu* required for the magic ointment. In September a force drawn from five villages, estimated at two thousand by missionaries and at three hundred by officials (*Nachrichten* 1893:67), many armed with muskets, attacked Ralum and the Neu-Guinea Compagnie residency in Kokopo. The attack was barely beaten off, and an attempted punitive expedition with a naval landing party got lost in the bush and ended in fiasco (*Monatshefte* 1894:137, 166). The settlers were confined to their stations.

Help appeared when a Vunabalbal man, who was an enthusiastic convert to Methodism, obtained some of the magic ointment and took it to the government forces. The police and labourers smeared themselves with it and in December when they sallied forth they proved invulnerable and the local people sued for peace. Official sources attribute the change of heart to shelling and an assault by sixty men from the cruiser *Sperber*, but since this party also got lost in the bush (*Nachrichten* 1894:18), the native account seems more likely.

Following this war all Tokokok land was given to Queen Emma. It was at roughly this time also—when Tinai was about fifteen—that Malapau plantation expanded inland, taking land to "seal the peace" after a labourer was killed by a man of Balanataman village. By June 1893 Queen Emma had roughly 580 acres of cotton and 860 acres of coconuts planted at Ralum and Malapau (*Nachrichten* 1894:20); by April 1895 she had 900 acres of cotton and 1,600 of coconuts, and by April 1896 she had an additional 300 acres of cotton and 550 acres of coconuts (*Nachrichten* 1896:16). The Neu-Guinea Compagnie in June 1893 had about 250 acres of cotton and 150 of coconuts (*Nachrichten* 1893:24, 1894:16). By April 1894 it had planted an additional 170 acres of cotton and 70 of coconuts, and by July 1896, some 750 more acres of cotton and 740 of coconuts.

The Tokokok and Kinabot people dispersed to Vunamami, Vunabalbal, and Ulagunan. Men of Ineinau, ToMomoi, Vunagigi, Vunakua, and Bitagunan clans were given plots to work within Vunamami by allied clans. Still other men took up residence on the land of their wives' clans, thereby taking care of their own children's future but leaving their sisters' children and clan heirs to be cared for otherwise. Of the seven cases appearing in my genealogies of the formally prohibited marriage between a man and a woman of his father's clan, four involve the sons of fathers who lived uxorilocally after the expulsion of Tokokok. They can be seen as attempts to provide land for both sons and a sister's sons at the same time.

The settler pressure on Vunamami did not cease with the taking over of Tokokok. Queen Emma still maintained that her payments of *totokom* had purchased all of Vunamami and Vunabalbal, and the residents of those villages lived with the threat that she would plant their land as soon as Tokokok, Balanataman, and the coastal strip were fully planted. The leader of Vunabalbal village, a man named Abram ToBobo, went to the newly arrived judge at Kokopo, Dr. Albert Hahl, and pleaded with him to allow the natives to remain (cf. Kleintitschen 1906:126). Dr. Hahl was sympathetic with native claims that they had not enough land to live on, but he was also concerned with the need for economic growth and the fact that little planting seemed to be done outside the plantations. He decided that Queen Emma's claim to have bought the land was justified, but that the natives should have the right to live there so long as they used the land. If in fifty years they had not planted coconuts and still were sparsely scattered over the land in little hamlets, Queen Emma would be allowed to take back the land. Hahl's judgement became the basis for formal policy in 1904 and was essentially reiterated in 1930 by Judge Phillips, who set up what is commonly known as Ralum Native Reserve.[5] I shall use this latter name to refer to the area indicated by Dr. Hahl.

In 1896 or thereabouts, the boundaries of Ralum Reserve were roughly the same as they were in 1961. There were further attempts to encroach on the Reserve, despite the judgement, and shortly after 1901, when Hahl was made Governor, ToBobo com-

---

[5] Mrs. Louisa Miller (1958), a descendant of Queen Emma, gives a similar example from the north coast. She describes how Queen Emma in about 1885 "purchased" about 450 acres at Matakabang for "trade guns and other trade goods," merely sending a Filipino to mark out the area. When, years later, she wanted to plant it, the *luluai* went to Dr. Hahl and said the natives would have no land to plant food. Dr. Hahl "gave them back their land" except for some coastal portions, with the stipulation that "if the natives die out" the land would revert to Queen Emma. This judgement, discovered by Mr. B. Cardew, Director of Native Affairs in 1927, formed the basis for making a native reserve at Matakabang.

Hahl himself (1935:34) describes his official policy to mitigate the injustices of pre-1885 land "purchases" in similar terms, discussing it in connection with sections of the 1904 Land Regulations. The stories of Vunamami informants date Hahl's return of Ralum Reserve as soon after the Tokokok war; 1896 seems the most probable date. The case may well have been the precedent for Hahl's future thinking, and the 1904 Regulations merely the systematizing of ordinances and practices made by Hahl as Judge under the N-G.C. régime.

plained about them. Dr. Hahl and ToBobo surveyed these areas, on the northeast corner of the Reserve, and erected concrete markers which slightly extended the area allotted in 1896. Natives complain that settlers persisted in their efforts at encroachment until Judge Phillips settled matters in 1930, erecting concrete markers and giving a firm responsibility to the Department of Native Affairs to guard native rights against further encroachment.

In so doing, Judge Phillips set a legal precedent for native land tenure in Ralum Reserve in a way that markedly differed from the actual practice and attitudes to land among the people of Vunamami. Freehold title to the land was vested in the Custodian of Expropriated Property (as successors to Queen Emma Forsayth) subject to certain "native rights" allocated to named groups, such as "Vunaibu, Vunabalbal and Kunakunai natives." These rights would be lost "in case of removal from all or portion of the land lasting over six months" and could not be transferred "even if only by way of temporary exercise" without consent of the freehold owner. These rights, of "permanent free and heritable right of dwelling and user," applied to large blocks of land, not to specific smaller village areas. They were vested *en bloc* in the Director of Native Affairs as the trustee for the categories of natives listed. No security of usufructuary rights was given to any individual controller or cultivator in the allocation to village groups. A Vunamami man who believed that another man of Vunamami was trespassing on his land could not legally obtain redress "under native custom," since it was alienated land, nor could he go to a District Officer's court, because rights were allocated to the group of villages. Similarly, Vunamami land could be invaded by men from other villages and clans named as having rights to the central area of Ralum Reserve. Although the rights could not be transferred, there was nothing to forbid the adoption of native outsiders—not European or Chinese—into the status of "Vunamami natives," entitled to all the rights of Vunamami natives. At the same time, any Vunamami man who sold land that he (and his clan) effectively controlled to any other eligible native of the named villages—and many plots did change control between 1896 and 1961—was in fact selling something that he legally did not own and could not transfer.

These legal anomalies were inconsequential until about 1956. At that time the Commissioner of Titles was investigating and re-issuing land titles that had been destroyed during the Japanese occupation. The status of Ralum Reserve came up and he advised that if the Director of Native Affairs purchased the virtually value-less freehold of the land, it would simplify the legal position. No action was taken, however. Concurrently a Native Lands Commission had been set up under a 1952 Ordinance to register titles to land owned "under native custom." In the Kokopo area it was actively at work east of the town; it had issued some clear individual titles for plots that had been sold between 1950 and 1956 and was investigating clans and boundaries in several villages with the obvious intention of issuing some form of title. Titles having acquired distinct value, especially as land sales were increasing (the details of this will be discussed later), Vunamami villagers asked if they could receive titles. The Native Lands Commissioner had to explain fully that "their land" was not theirs and did not come under his jurisdiction.

The matter was raised at the Advisory Council of the New Britain District by Vin ToBaining, president of Vunamami Council, on 10 October 1958. According to the minutes, he made a motion asking

The return of certain native reserves in the Gazelle Peninsula to the native people so that they may be subject to registration by the Native Lands Commissioner. Before people thought that these lands belonged to them and now they know that it is land which we can use only. There is a lot of talk about the land and if we take our complaints to the Native Lands Commissioner at Kokopo he says he cannot do anything about them but refers us to the Native Affairs Officer. When we go to him he tells us that we have the use of the ground only. We would like this ground to be handed back to the native people.

This was seconded by Stanis ToBoramilat, vice-president of Vunadidir Council. As a statement of the legal position it is somewhat inaccurate, but it clearly reflects native feelings on Ralum Reserve and the many other so-called "reserves" in the Tolai area, all of which had somewhat confused legal status.[6] Planters, on the other hand, felt that such a motion questioned the validity of all land purchases before 1900. Discussion in the Advisory Council bogged down, and even the limited motion that certain portions

[6] Some "Reserves," such as most of Portion 165 which even natives thought had some plantation rights remaining in it, turned out to be legally "native land (New Guinea 1956b).

of Ralum Reserve be acquired and handed over to Vunamami Council was not acted upon.

By 1961 there had still been no action, but the issue was far from dead. In that year the Commissioner of Titles was faced with the question of whether he should, in reissuing the preliminary title to Ralum Estate (purchased in the interim by Plantation Holdings, Ltd.), alter it to a permanent title, and he again inquired into native objections. Only then did people realize that they might introduce evidence that had been withheld from Judge Phillips in 1928 through the overbearing actions of native police, and the issuance of title was delayed. Also in 1961 the Administration began efforts to set up a single system of land ownership for all racial groups, guaranteeing native rights but aiming at eventually giving individual freehold titles. It was intended, incidentally, to remove the anomalies and paternalism in the legal status of places like Ralum Reserve. The course of the bill through the Legislature was slow; it had to be redrafted several times, and was cut up into numerous smaller bills, and was not finally passed until May 1963.

(c) Native Practice

It is remarkable that despite the virtual absence of any legally enforceable rights in Vunamami between 1896 and 1961, there were almost no disputes over land among residents. The only disagreements seem to have been not over boundaries but between parties that both had claims under native custom, and these matters were settled through mediation, since intervention by a District Officer was legally ruled out. With this in mind I shall give no further discussion of the *legal* position regarding land rights in Vunamami, but shall treat native practice and attitudes, though unbacked by organized sanctions, as though they were customary law.

In 1875 Vunamami had about 700 acres land for a population of just less than 200. In 1910 Vunamami land, bordered on three sides by plantations and on the fourth by the unchanged boundary with Vunabalbal village, covered roughly 360 acres. The population, as a result of immigration from Tokokok and a faster natural increase after 1896, was 229, according to the German census. There was a steady, natural increase until 1942, when the population was probably about 550. During the war, according to native informants and post-war observers, native populations near

Kokopo decreased by about half. Vunamami, as can be estimated from the age pyramid (Appendix F), probably had about 300 inhabitants in 1946. By 1961, when the annual natural increase was over 5 percent (one of the highest recorded in the world), the population was 533. The village acreage remained fixed at 360. The figures alone are an indication of the land problem in Vunamami. How the people of Vunamami adapted to the problem is the interesting aspect.

When land is scarce, migration is the first possible solution. I shall discuss labour migration in detail in Chapter 4. Here it need only be described in outline. Since the 1890's a few Vunamami men have worked locally in Kokopo and on the plantations, either living at home or visiting home occasionally while being supported by their employer. From a low of about five in German times and a high of perhaps ten in the inter-war period, the number of such wage workers had risen to 36 in 1961. These workers represent a cash income for Vunamami, but they have little bearing on the problem of land pressures. Migration to other parts of New Guinea, including Rabaul, has been common since about 1925, when the population was around 425. Until the 1950's this migration was almost solely of men, though since then government employees and missionaries to the Southern Highlands have been able to take families with them. Some ten to fifteen men were absent in an average year between the wars; after the end of the second war, the number, including dependants, rose, and in 1961 there were 66 away. These absentees mean fewer mouths to be fed from the land of Vunamami, but they do not change the number of claimants to the land, either in the present or in future generations. All are included in the total of 533 cited. I searched in genealogies for names of men who had migrated for work and who subsequently had been lost track of, but found none. I searched in Council records for men who had failed to pay their tax after an absence at work, and again found no cases, although it may be that relatives at home keep up payments on their behalf even though they have effectively severed ties with Vunamami. But Tolai taxi drivers in Port Moresby assured me, after six years of absence, that they would go home some day, and they kept up closely with local gossip.

Migrant labourers, in short, maintain their use rights to land and expect to have a place to live and work when they return. It goes without saying that almost none—four skilled workers out of the 66 Vunamami migrants—are controllers of land. By contrast, 81 of the 205 adults residing in Vunamami in 1961 controlled some land. Residents agree that emigrants have rights. The topic was intensively discussed in 1961 when the Native Lands Commissioner, S. S. Smith, conducted hearings (which I attended) to try to establish what "native customary land law" involved.[7] They cited cases of men who had left home at the age of sixteen and returned after ten years to be given land without question.

Two difficulties with returning migrants were recognized, however. Tolai who return and "do not want to live like us" are suspect. What happens is that they are granted land to live on, but if, after two or three years, they do not live up to their clan obligations, contributing to payments and so on, they are told to clear out. Two such cases (neither in Vunamami) were cited, and a third case (also not in Vunamami) was described of a man who went with his wife and two children to Australia to look after the children of Mr. Mouton, and who was later received back when he "gave up all his European customs, except drinking whisky." Vunamami is almost as willing to accept non-Tolai who wish to settle. There were five immigrant men in the village in 1961— two from the Sepik District, one from Chimbu, and two from New Ireland. Four of them are unmarried and live in the households of affluent Vunamami men, essentially as employees. One from New Ireland came to Kokopo as a driver for the Government in 1921, married a Vunamami woman, and has lived on her clan land since then. There are, however, more absentees from Vunamami than there are immigrant workers.

The other difficult returning migrants are those who have taken foreign wives. As a general principle Tolai say that wives married and children brought up elsewhere have no right to expect land to be made available to them, even while the returning husband/ father is alive. They extend this principle even to Tolai wives, if a husband has chosen at marriage to live uxorilocally. In practice

---

[7] The findings of these hearings have been published as Smith and Salisbury (1961), and they may be compared with the present account. Discrepancies will be found, but these are mainly to be ascribed to different intentions in the two places. Smith and Salisbury try to abstract the general principles in terms of which decisions about land ownership are made. The present chapter attempts to sketch what decisions were actually made under various conditions of, for example, segmenting clans, effectiveness of clan *lualua*, or land shortage.

they are much more liberal. Two Vunamami men were married to women whom they had brought back from work in New Ireland. The children of these marriages were not yet adult but were treated no differently from other children. Their lack of land rights was not yet important, and, if the example of other immigrants is followed, they may well be allowed to use land of their fathers' clans, and be treated as clan members.

What would be important for reducing the number of claimants to land would be an outmigration of women, and a giving up of rights by their children. If some of the wives of skilled workers who have jobs elsewhere did not return this would be effective, as would be the marriage elsewhere of the two migrant single women—a nurse and a schoolteacher. Marriage with men from other parts of New Guinea temporarily working in the Kokopo area, besides those from New Ireland and Manus, simply does not occur because the *wok*, as such labourers are called, are universally despised by Tolai. Marriages with Chinese and half-castes do occur—I have heard of none with Europeans—although the small number of non-natives makes them statistically unimportant. They were more numerous in German times when there were fewer Chinese women. Even so, not all such women are lost to Vunamami. A Chinese, named Patrick Choi, married a local woman of Vunagigi clan and lived for many years in Vunamami village, assisting in Vunagigi clan payments and participating in village enterprises. All but one of his Vunagigi children married locally. After his wife died he remained in Vunamami and took a half-caste wife, but he stopped helping Vunagigi clan; he built a substantial metal house, and his father and relatives came to live with him. He was forced to leave, and his children who were unmarried (including those of his second marriage) have been accepted as Chinese. Although Tolai can cite a few outstanding cases of men with non-native fathers and Tolai mothers who live as Tolai— ToKabiu, the secretary of the New Britain Co-operative Association, is such a man—I should guess that most such people leave native society.

A different form of outmigration of women may well be the most important relief of population pressure in Vunamami. It is provided by the different marriage patterns of Vunamami men and women. Most men marry women of nearby villages, whereas many women marry into distant Tolai villages. The resulting shortage of local wives means that a good many Vunamami men do not marry at all. Unlike children born in nearby villages, children born in distant villages are likely not to return to claim land rights in their mother's village; rather, they obtain rights in the distant village of the father. In this way the population pressure in Vunamami is spread to other Tolai villages, where, presumably, land rights are more obtainable. Of course relief of this kind is possible only so long as land pressures are not so acute elsewhere.

The second series of solutions to the land problem involves the acquisition of land outside the boundaries of Vunamami. There are four such solutions: extending Vunamami boundaries, utilizing rights in other villages, buying land in other villages, and resettling in non-Tolai areas. But before discussing these possibilities, we should examine the pattern of land ownership within Vunamami village.

There were 128 plots of land within Vunamami in 1961. They varied in size from an eighth of an acre for some house sites to about ten acres for some of the largest tree-crop areas. Since I was not able to survey all the plots, the following discussion will be based on numbers of plots rather than on areas of land; a complete listing was obtained by inquiries. Estimates of areas will be discussed later, based on averages of three-quarters of an acre for a house site (usually covered with coconuts) and three and a half acres for a cultivated plot, but the gross numbers will give an indication of the pattern. Of these plots, three had been bought by the Methodist Mission and by the Vunamami Council as sites for the church, for two schools (mission and government), and for the Council chambers and co-operative store. Table 1 shows the ownership of plots by controlling clans. Numbers 1 to 3 are clans with *madapai* in Vunamami territory; they still control 60 of the plots, or almost half the village, even though, in Takaptar, there has been an influx of allied clan segments, members of which now use and control certain plots. The next three clans were certainly present before 1890 and control 36 plots, or over a quarter of Vunamami, although the principal lands of these clans are in other villages. The four clans (nos. 7–10) that immigrated from Tokokok in 1894 control only 10 plots. The remaining 19 plots are distributed among ten clans. Of these ten, three appear to be recently segmented portions of Davara (Palnautur) and Vunabalbal (Bitavuvur and Maudang) but their status is unclear. If they are counted with the larger clans it makes the contrast between the pre-1890 clans and the others even sharper.

Table 1

OWNERSHIP OF LAND IN VUNAMAMI, BY CLANS

Controlling Clan (or group)	Total Number of Plots	Number of Plots as			Number of Resident Clan Members	
		House Sites*	Cultivated Plots	Other	Adults	Children
Council and Mission	3	—	—	Church, School, Council and Co-op	—	—
1) Matupit	17	3	14		19	24
2) Takaptar-Tuluai	25	7	18		20	22
3) Tetegete-Balu	18	2	15	1 *taraiu*	6	2
4) Vunabalbal	11	2	9		21	23
5) Davara-Papakan	12	3	9		18	29
6) Vunaibu	13	3	10		15	25
7) Tomomoi	1	—	1		5	8
8) Vunagigi	7	2	5		11	14
9) Vunakua	2	2	—		5	7
10) Bitagunan-Ineinau	—	—	—		6	7
11) Kulmilat	2	—	2		2	—
12) Tobatobon	1	1	—		7	20
13) Vunaruga	1	1	—		1	5
14) Baluta	1	1	—		1	—
15) Palnautur	3	1	2		1	—
16) Bitavuvur	6	1	5		3	3
17) Maudang	2	2	—		8	4
18) Nomoi	1	—	1		10	9
19) Tolom-Gagalip	1	—	1		6	16
20) Tagatagal	1	1	—		7	17
21) Others	—	—	—		23	39
	128	32	92	4	195	274

* House sites invariably include coconuts; some small-clan houses are built on what is really cultivated land.

The population figures confirm this lack of balance. The three original clans average more than one plot per adult resident; the pre-1890 immigrants average two-thirds of a plot, the 1894 immigrants one-half, and the others one-third. All twelve land sales since 1890 of which I have a record (the list is probably not complete, since the line between gifts to children and purchase by another clan is not always clear) were from the three original clans. Five were acquired by the pre-1890 immigrants, three by immigrants from Tokokok, and only one by other clans. Before 1890 the dominance of the original clans in the control of land was even more marked. On the other hand, the recorded land sales would seem not to reflect pressure of population on land, which was greatest among the "others," but to be part of the steady effort of partly established clans to expand their holdings. They also would seem to show—and I am confident they are sufficiently complete for this purpose—that the existing pattern of dispersed clans, and minority holdings of land within areas predominantly controlled by a few clans, existed before the arrival of Europeans. Vunamami is one of the most extreme cases of population pressure in New Guinea, yet this pressure has made relatively minor changes in the internal distribution of land control as between clans.

As between individuals, considerable change has occurred. Before European contact and up to the year 1890 the *lualua* exercised great control over the land, largely because the land was used for subsistence gardening and individuals had little investment in specific garden plots, provided they were assured the use of new plots when they needed them. The clan head controlled a large number of plots and could allocate them both to ensure soil regeneration and to maintain his political support. Even in 1961 the four plots used as subsistence gardens were ones still controlled directly by clan *lualua*. In 1890 few rights of control were delegated.

By 1961 most land had been planted to tree crops and the clan *lualua*'s obligation to reallocate after fallow periods did not arise. Rights of control were widely delegated. Fifty-four of the 195 adult residents controlled one or more plots, the largest holdings being those of two members of Tetegete who controlled seven plots each. Five residents of nearby villages controlled a total of seven plots. In most cases the controller worked his own land, but fifteen adult "children of the clan" used land controlled by their fathers' clans, and in ten cases land was used by a sister, father, or clan relative of the controller. In all, 78 adults worked land in Vunamami, including seven residents of nearby villages.

Six of them worked land on the basis of two kinds of claim.[8] Now that more or less permanent crops are grown, land users rely on village headmen or councillors to guarantee their visible claims to land, rather than relying on claims of clanship supported by the moral authority of a clan *lualua*.

The more equitable distribution of land that has evolved through the persistence of indigenous attitudes towards land tenure has not been the only trend. There has also been concentration: in twenty households, more than one member has his own land, and only fifty out of eighty-five households have plots to work inside Vunamami. Of the thirty-five landless households, eight are of elderly widows, supported by children who have their own land, and three are households of skilled men earning cash incomes greater than they would obtain from farming. The remaining twenty-four, however, have unskilled heads, and these men, mostly young, provide a pool of labour for plot owners, outside employers, and for fishing (Salisbury n.d.). Without them, wealthy landowners could not exploit relatively large areas, yet these landless men often prefer to work for their wealthier kinsmen in hopes of eventually receiving land from them. The way in which a *lualua*'s power depended on his ability to attract subordinates by the promise of an eventual gift of land is still evident today. It will be further discussed in relation to the supply of labour for agriculture in Chapter 3.

Let us now consider non-Vunamami lands that might be used to satisfy the land hunger. Offhand, it would seem impossible to extend Vunamami directly, because the plantation boundaries have been surveyed and the boundary with Vunabalbal is fixed. In practice, however, since at least the 1930's, certain lands lying within plantation boundaries have been used for subsistence gardens with the owners' tacit agreement. One finds gardens in ravines, or in unplanted areas covered with kunai, or occasionally under coconuts in areas near the boundaries. Palm groves planted at the recommended spacing of thirty feet contain a good deal of land that is usable for gardens. Such double planting slightly reduces

[8] "Working land" does not here mean residing on land. All house plots have some coconuts on them, and they have been classified as "worked" by the cultivator of the palms. Discussion of residence patterns (hamlet composition) will be given in a separate publication, for they are as complex as those described for Truk (Fischer 1958, Goodenough 1956).

the yield of copra, but plantation owners consider a slight loss in yield a small price to pay for good relations with their neighbours, who could rob an unfriendly plantation owner of much of his coconut crop. Most Ravalien palms were destroyed when a Japanese bomb dump exploded after being set afire by a Tolai saboteur, and subsequent owners have lacked the capital to replant them. About ten acres were used by Vunamami for gardens in 1961, including a market garden producing crops like lettuce for sale, and two acres of Malapau were also used.

In 1961 Plantation Holdings, Ltd., decided to sell Ravalien plantation. The only prospective purchasers appeared to be the people of Vunamami and the neighbouring villages. Negotiations were protracted (see Chap. 7), and final terms were undecided in early 1963. Subscriptions were still inadequate, and the Vunamami villagers were thinking of buying only the derelict areas of the plantation. Despite the higher cost of buying land in small parcels, two small purchases were made in 1963. Vunamami Council bought about ten acres to extend the Vunamami village school, and two associations of women bought another ten acres for £700 to be used as subsistence gardens. If the purchase of even the undeveloped land of Ravalien is eventually completed it will add 224 acres to Vunamami.

More important in providing usable land to Vunamami are the rights held by Vunamami men, through their clans, to use land in other villages. Many indeed control land outside Vunamami. Their claims heavily outweigh the claims of outsiders to land inside Vunamami (see p. 90). Thus in 1961 outsiders worked eight of the 128 plots within Vunamami, five controlling their plots while the remainder were daughters of Vunamami, married into neighbouring villages but using land controlled by their brothers. Thirty-four Vunamami villagers actively exercised clan rights outside Vunamami village, 32 worked plots, and two controlled plots worked by residents of other villages. Five workers did not control their plots, three working them by permission of Vunamami controllers—the latter have not been counted as "actively exercising rights"—and two by permission of controllers in other villages. In all, as shown in Table 2, 53 plots were affected by these rights.

As one would expect, the clans that exercise these rights are primarily those with less land in Vunamami, especially those that are segments of an important clan based in nearby villages—

Table 2

OWNERSHIP OF LAND OUTSIDE VUNAMAMI, BY CLANS

Owning Clan (or group)	Plots with Rights by Native Tenure	Plots Leased or Purchased
1) Matupit	2	—
2) Takaptar-Tuluai	4	1
3) Tetegete-Balu	1	—
4) Vunabalbal	13	1
5) Davara-Papakan	5	—
6) Vunaibu	4	3
7) Tomomoi	—	—
8) Vunagigi	4	6
9) Vunakua	2	1
10) Bitagunan-Ineinau	—	1
11) Kulmilat	—	—
12) Tobatobon	9	—
13) Vunaruga	—	—
14) Baluta	—	—
15) Palnautur	—	—
16) Bitavuvur	—	—
17) Maudang	—	—
18) Nomoi	4	—
19) Tolom-Gagalip	1	—
20) Tagatagal	4	1
21) Others	—	1
	53	15

namely, Vunabalbal, Davara-Papakan, and Vunaibu. If these plots
outside Vunamami are included in total landholdings, these three
clans average over one plot per adult resident in Vunamami—
nearly as much as the original clans. For the 1894 immigrants and
the "others," however, landholdings outside Vunamami are few,
and largely the result of special circumstances. Tobatobon, for example, claims nine outside plots because an old man named Peni
spent considerable time in Vunamami as a mission teacher and
now lives there in retirement near his children's relatives. He
owns his house site, and as a minor *lualua* of his clan he also owns
eight plots in his native village of Tingenavudu. It is not certain
whether these lands, when he dies, will be available to distantly
related fellow-clansmen living in Vunamami or will be taken by

more eligible relatives in Tingenavudu; his children, of Vunaibu clan, are well educated and have their own land. The four Nomoi plots are worked by two pairs of brothers. All but one, the youngest, who has no land in Vunamami itself but works for other landowners, claim rights on the land through wife or father, and they are skilled manual workers who have a cash income in addition. They actively sought out claimable land in Vunabalbal as a way of increasing their wealth. Thus, although the average number of plots inside and outside Vunamami per adult for these two categories of clan exceeds one-half, the benefits of the outside holdings are by no means widespread.

When individuals or households are considered, the same picture of individual variability emerges. Ten of the 32 controllers control (and 10 of the 32 workers work) plots inside Vunamami in addition, so that rights outside Vunamami village add only 22 names to the lists of controllers and workers. Five of the workers live in households working land inside Vunamami because of another person's claim; in two households both husband and wife have taken up rights outside Vunamami. In all, thirteen of the thirty-five households with no Vunamami land work plots in other villages, four working two plots each. Most are households of younger men. The remaining 36 plots outside Vunamami are worked by households with Vunamami land as well, 19 of them by four households and 17 by thirteen households.

The voluntary nature of these claims to lands is notable. In only a few cases, like that of Peni, have the lands been inherited by automatic matrilineal principles. More commonly an individual has sought out a relative with land elsewhere, has assisted him in planting land and received in exchange land to work and later to control. In other words, it has been a deliberate acquisition of land by someone reviving social ties that could have been left inactive, and working hard to earn the land. The native Tolai system with its multiple ties gives the politically inclined person much scope for manoeuvre, and the energetic person can reap considerable rewards. Vunamami residents may have been under extreme pressure from having insufficient land near their homes, or alternatively from having too much incentive to stay at home. They may be extreme in their exclusion of non-residents. A more typical Tolai village pattern may be for, say, residents to work one-fifth of their land outside the village boundaries and for non-residents to work one-fifth of the village land, thereby giving a net balance of claims.

Under pressure the system has proved highly flexible, although it is difficult to see how Vunamami could go further in unbalancing the system of claims. Even so, the way in which people perceive that the limit has been reached is not in disputes over claims, but in complaints of the inordinate waste of time needed to travel between the scattered and distant plots that are typical of fragmented holdings.

One indication that the pressure has long been close to the limit has been the purchase of large blocks of land from relatively distant villages, to the east of Kokopo. This began shortly after the end of the Second World War, when Enos Teve, then Paramount Luluai of Vunamami Paramountcy, bought some five acres of kunai land at Kabakaul (irregularities in this and later transactions will be discussed later). Enos is of Vunamerom clan, a segment of Tuluai, but he was born in Vunamami and received some land there from his father, of Vunaibu clan. Although, as a *lualua* of Vunamerom, he controls land to the west in Balanataman and has lived part of his adult life there, he now lives on Takaptar land (Takaptar is also a segment of Tuluai), and works with Takaptar associates. Vunamerom has been included with Takaptar in all tabulations. In the next few years Enos' example was followed by several men of Vunagigi clan (Beniona Tokarai being the principal), of Vunaibu clan (principally ToMakavunga), of Vunabalbal clan (ToLiligau), Vunakua (Jack ToKanit), and Tagatagal (Polos ToPultima). They bought land in the villages of Kabakaul and Taui. Most of these purchases were investigated by the Native Lands Commission and title registered as individually owned plots in 1958 (N.L.C. Kokopo, cases 5, 6, 8, 9, 10). The acreage so registered is 48.20, but there are some additional plots owned in areas that are registered under clan names by the Lands Commission (Popadu and Kabakaul, N.L.C. Kokopo, cases 3 and 4), bringing the total acreage of purchased land up to perhaps 60.

It is not fortuitous that these areas were chosen. Davara clan is a major landowning clan in this area of temporary land surplus. In 1950 two of the *lualua* of Davara clan were living in Vunamami: Oris ToIlam and Tionatan. (Oris died in 1958, and by 1961 Tionatan, then seventy-six, had distributed his land.) Oris' wife was the sister of Beniona, who was himself married to a Papakan woman, unrelated to the Davara segment in the east but their clan sister nonetheless. Jack's wife was also from a segment of Davara. Polos lived next door to Oris. All the principals involved in the purchase of land in Taui were educated men, and a deal was arranged; but the residents of Taui objected. In 1955 Taui men used slings to try and drive out the Vunamami purchasers, but matters were eventually settled when Oris distributed the money he had received among the other members of Davara in accordance with traditional principles (see p. 72). It was this dispute that interested the Native Lands Commissioner in the Taui area, when he arrived in 1956, and thereby led to the issuance of titles.

Despite the registration of individual titles, the attitude to these plots is not one of exclusive personal ownership. In most cases the areas have been planted to tree crops, but while the coconuts have been growing, the land has been available for subsistence gardening by kinsmen, clan dependants, and neighbours and friends of the owners. So, too, in the plans for future disposal of the land, there is a balance between the claims of children and of the clan. Beniona is effectively providing for his children and his clan. He intends all his purchased land to be *pia na vunatarai*—clan land—for his clan. This is logical, since one of his sisters has married into Rainau village, which borders Kabakaul to the east, and her sons are his clan heirs. His own son, of Papakan clan, has one plot in Kabakaul worked by virtue of his clan link with the Davara segment there. This son is temporarily working as a schoolteacher in Madang, and Beniona cultivates his plot for him along with his own. Enos' position is roughly the same as Beniona's. His clan segment in Balanataman is provided for, thanks to his active searching out of plots to claim in inland villages like Malakun and Ngunguna. His lands in Vunamami itself are "his own" to provide for his son (one plot is already transferred). The land to the east he says is "for Vunamami"—a phrase which I interpret in two senses: first, the plots were bought in order to demonstrate to other Vunamami residents, especially to those men of the assorted segments of Vunamerom, Takaptar, and other Tuluai clans who work with (and under) Enos, how to get land and how to use it efficiently; second, they will support the dependants of these men in the future, thus consolidating an amorphous group into a clan segment, springing from Enos the founder.

A final aspect of these land purchases is how they combat fragmentation. The average size of the eleven plots is five and a half acres; they are closely grouped and, as with Beniona's son's plot, some nearby land is also worked by Vunamami men.[9] This has made it practicable for the landowners to build houses in the area; they can spend an entire working week "at Kabakaul," returning to Vunamami for Saturday's market and Sunday's church. Houses are sometimes shared, and enough people are around to combat any sense of loneliness; in 1961, many women and some men were making subsistence and market gardens under the growing coconuts. The accepted solution, if land can be obtained, seems to be a satellite village four miles from the main one, or just beyond daily commuting range on foot but within visiting range of the social services of the main village.

Resettlement at distances of more than four miles has been tried under government sponsorship and pressure, some fifteen miles to the south across the Warangoi River, on land that was covered with virgin forest, which the Administration bought from the Baining people. Under what is known as the Vunamami Council scheme, thirty acres were added to Vunamami land, and under the "Warangoi 15-Acre Block" scheme another fifteen acres were added. The tenure of these forty-five acres, though clear in law, is complex in native terms. Their reconciling of the two types of tenure can be understood only in the light of the history of the schemes and the pattern of land use. To clarify these points, I shall anticipate some of the discussion of land use in Chapter 3.

Three resettlement schemes had been tried in the Tolai area by 1961. The first, the so-called Vudal scheme, was begun in 1952 for residents of Rabaul Council area, and by 1958 was clearly failing, though just why was then unknown.[10] The Administration wished to experiment with a new method when it acquired land beyond the Warangoi. In 1958 it leased 330 acres in an area called Sunam to Vunamami Council, for the latter to sublease to individuals in ten-acre blocks. In this way the Administration hoped

[9] And by Vunabalbal men of Vunaibu, Papaken, and Vunabalbal clans who are close friends and relatives of the Vunamami men.

[10] Early reports blamed the failure on poor native organization and lack of motivation. In 1961 it was found that early investigations of soil conditions had been incorrect. These investigations, made in the dry season, reported a low water table and conditions suitable for cocoa growing. In fact, drainage was in wet weather poor, and the land became swampy and unfit for cocoa. Withdrawal ("lack of enthusiasm") rather than argument is a usual Tolai reaction to European experts (here agriculturalists) who think they know best.

to get the Council to work up enthusiasm, to select needy work-ers, and to enforce effective cultivation practices. The experiment was a qualified success. But officials thought better results would be obtained by settling individual peasant farmers on fifteen-acre blocks, and giving them greater freedom—hence more incentive to good farming—by letting them lease directly from the Admin-istration as Australian settlers did. It therefore set up the Warangoi 15-Acre Block scheme, beginning in 1959 with another thirty-three blocks.

The Vunamami Council Scheme achieved all its aims. Enthu-siasm was intense from the start in 1958. Sixteen ten-acre blocks were allocated, one to each village in the Council, and corvée la-bour was used by each village to build large dormitories, to clear the bush, and, following Agricultural Department advice, to plant sole cocoa, that is, cocoa unmixed with coconuts, bananas, or sub-sistence crops. The work was done in record time, with rows marked out in exemplary fashion thanks to diligent assistance by the Agricultural Extension Officers. But the early enthusiasm meant that several organizational inefficiencies were unrecognized. Trucks could carry out parties of corvée labourers with food for a few days, and enthusiasm would tide them over the discomforts of a short stay in primitive conditions before the truck took them home. No provision was made for growing food at Sunam, or for social amenities. The short periods of hard corvée labour at ir-regular intervals were effective for major tasks like clearing the forest, but for the smaller synchronized and repetitive tasks of starting the cocoa nursery at exactly the right stage of growth of the temporary shade plants, and of planting out the seedlings and thinning the shade, they were ineffective. Several entire blocks were planted with either too little or too much shade.

At this point the Administration asserted its belief that the only form of land tenure and use compatible with a parliamentary democracy and economic development was that in which indi-viduals had clear title to blocks of land which they could farm for themselves. This idea had been part of their original plan for the Vunamami scheme, but it had not been fully understood by the Council, which had stressed the community nature of the en-terprise—a 330-acre plantation, the size of the European ones, but run by Tolais, who had planted the first 160 acres. In practice, each block was "controlled" by the entire village that had worked to clear it, but to fulfill Administration regulations each block was registered in the name of a responsible member of the appropriate village who acted as manager. For Vunamami's block the registered owner was a man named Andreas, who had come from the far western Tolai area to live with a Vunamami wife, and who had been on the working committee that helped the village councillor. Like the other village managers, he was provided with a house on the village block in Sunam.

Presumably the Administration intended villagers to look upon their corvée labour as a contribution to the Council, which would in turn use its cash equivalent, in the form of an annual rent, for the public good. But the villagers did not see it this way. In their view, they had worked hard on the land, and the Council had unfairly given it all to Andreas. Everyone remembered the discomforts they had suffered. The response when further corvée labour was called for to develop the remaining seventeen blocks can be imagined. Nor were Andreas and the other managers happy—isolated in virgin country miles away, with no members of their own villages, no local food supplies, and no means of transportation to obtain food—or even a way of communicating when they needed food sent to them. No villager would accept the lease of the remaining blocks for fear both of the hardships and of accusations of favouritism. The new Vunamami block was finally taken by Vin ToBaining, president of the Council, the Vunabalbal block by Tamai, the village councillor.

Intermittent, and reluctant, corvée by small parties usually supervised by the village councillor continued at more or less weekly intervals, however. The managers of the first blocks began to alternate periods in the village with periods at Sunam. The village officials deputed young, unattached men to take over the supervision of the newer blocks—Tamai's substitute was a seventeen-year-old clan brother living in Vunamami, ToBaining's was a thirty-year-old man from the Sepik District. On the newer blocks some food crops were grown, but the clearing of forest proceeded slowly; the bush often grew up faster than it could be kept down, and little progress was made with cocoa planting. The maintenance of the original plots varied in February 1961 from good in two cases to nothing at all in four (D.A.S.F. Extension, Taliligap, Land Resettlement Report, Feb. 1961). The four lessees who did not maintain their plots forfeited their leases; technically they voluntarily surrendered them to the Council, but it did not take much persuasion to get them to do so. Four new lessees were appointed, and no attempt was made to ensure they were from the villages of the original lessee. Iudas ToWaninara of Vunamami, the driver of the Council Land-Rover, was one of these.

Critics of the Council Scheme attributed its decline to an insistence by the Council on unworkable "communalism." This criticism is unjustified, I believe, and is based on a faulty understanding of the labour and capital demands of plantation development as well as on a stereotyped idea of indigenous practices. A consideration of the third scheme, that of individually owned fifteen-acre blocks, will emphasize my point, although only one plot is Vunamami-owned.

These blocks were allocated in 1960. By early 1961, according to the D.A.S.F. reports, they were a veritable patchwork. About five of the thirty-three still had areas of uncleared virgin bush; eleven were well into the early stages of planting tree crops. Marking out was common, either for cocoa or for coconuts, and there were many shade plantings for cocoa that were barely maintained or kept pace with. On most cleared areas secondary bush had sprung up, and the owners were battling to keep this growth under control with food crops (bananas, manioc, taro, spinach, etc.) and by clearing, while working intermittently at the task of tree planting. On my visits to the area only four or five of the thirty-three houses were occupied by people working there. At least three of the owners worked full time in government offices and spent only vacations working on their plots. They were extreme cases of the general pattern: the plots are additional sources of income to progressive individuals from other areas, who spend their spare time at the Warangoi but who at other times either leave the plots alone or employ casual labourers. In other words, the scheme is not resettling the landless poor.

Naturally, the development of the plots reflects the amount of supervision that owners have given their casual labourers. One Tolai from Wairiki village just across the Warangoi employed a worker from the New Guinea mainland on a full-time basis. He gave him £2 a month plus food, housing, and tools, and treated him very much as a member of his household, working with him frequently at the Warangoi. When the Wairiki man went home to his village the labourer stayed on the fifteen-acre block, but the owner complained that without supervision the worker grew good food crops for his own consumption and was lax in tree planting.

Along with the difficulties of supervision, non-resident owners are hampered by lack of money-capital for hiring labour. In 1951 the owners who were full-time office workers had the best-looking plots, despite their casual supervision, one of them having hired five full-time workers who completely cleared and planted his block in five months. All the owners realized that with money they could hire labour and they made persistent representations to government officials, from the Assistant Administrator on down, for loans from the Native Loan Fund. In January 1961 an offer was made by the Fund administration in Port Moresby of ten loans of £144, an amount considered sufficient for food to tide a resident owner-worker over the first year of clearing. Local Agricultural Extension officers, who were closely watching the scheme and understood that the pattern was one of entrepreneurial development, stressed that development costs to native owners were no different from those on European plantations, or about £40 an acre, plus any costs of management; £800 seemed closer to the needs of a block owner. But in October 1961 the £144 loans were made, after ToBaining finally brought the issue up in the Territorial Legislature.[11]

Several of these fifteen-acre blocks may eventually rival European plantations as efficient cocoa-producing areas and may make some rich Tolai even richer, but the contribution of this scheme to Tolai resettlement and relief of population pressure is negligible. In 1961 it was using as much scarce monetary capital as European development was, and was importing cheap "foreign" labour into the area, and further aggravating population problems, instead of utilizing existing local surpluses of labour. The Council Scheme avoided these pitfalls during the establishment period when ownership by a large corporate body, employing its own members for tasks requiring intensive labour, worked smoothly. The working

[11] In 1963 the Vunamami block owner, Tiriau, was using his £144 loan entirely to pay labourers. For initial clearing he had used local Baining workers at 5s. a day; in 1963 he had two full-time employees from western New Britain on a salary of £3 a month plus keep. He himself alternated between living in Vunamami, where he had plantings and worked as a contract carpenter, and supervising work at the Warangoi. (Letter of Dale ToPin, September 1963.)

members expected to become corporate owners, as was traditionally the case with clan land cleared from virgin forest, and it certainly would have been wise to have issued some receipt for labour
contributed (possibly as a certificate of share capital in the over-all
enterprise) instead of relying on such implicit understandings. The
error lay with the Administration, which did not understand the
basis for corvée labour. The Council's error came later in the
failure to plan for routine maintenance and cropping, although
this oversight grew out of the agriculturalists advising them to
plant sole cocoa instead of first establishing food gardens so that
workers could live there permanently. There should also have
been progressive development of coconut and cocoa mixtures, as
the local people eventually realized. This would have made it
possible for a permanent labour force to live nearby, and the rapid
provision of social services and social ties among the resident
group would have been an inducement to the labourers to stay
there. Individual ownership of the fifteen-acre blocks is no inducement for permanent residence, nor is local patriotism, although
initial development of a "Council village" at Sunam went some
way towards attracting a labour force. But the Administration's
insistence on individual leases effectively halted this trend to the
establishment of social services, and now the blocks, under both
schemes, are largely in the hands of salaried caretakers, visited
occasionally by the absentee owners. The fifteen-acre scheme assumed that owners would make efficient cultivators; a more practical scheme would seem to be to recognize the falseness of the
image of "sturdy pioneer settlers" and to turn efficient cultivators
into owners through some scheme of profit sharing among resident
managers and casual labourers, giving them share capital in a
corporately owned enterprise. The only cash outlay of such a
scheme would be the basic salaries of caretakers, with the returns
to other labour coming when crops were sold. If it became desirable to change the pattern of ownership when the plantations
were bearing, it would be a simple matter for caretakers to buy
larger shares, or to sell their shares at a profit to people who
wished to take over the work of cropping. This would have been
consistent with the trend of indigenous thinking and could have
acquired legal status by being made into a co-operative (see Chap.
6).

An indication that such arrangements could work, even with
no legal incorporation, is provided by a group of plots in the

Vunamami Council area. Owing to various historical accidents, an area of land called Talimut was still unplanted and unclaimed by individuals in 1949,[12] although it was divided into areas owned by the three villages of Vunamami, Vunabalbal, and Ulagunan. In the first enthusiasm for growing cocoa each village cleared the land and planted cocoa, using corvée labour. For some years routine maintenance was also left to corvée labour, a different person being appointed to work it each month. This had not worked for Vunamami village, because appointees had balked at the three miles of travel to Talimut. By 1961 an arrangement had been in effect for about three years whereby a different supervisor was appointed in rotation for each month. If the plantation was kept up, he received ten shillings at the end of his time. He could usually do the work by spending one day a week there, tidying up while collecting beans to be taken to the nearby co-operative fermentery. The salary was clearly only a token one, the major return being the services obtained from the village fund into which proceeds were paid, and which was being created by fairly equal and not onerous labour contributions throughout the village. Ownership by the village with salaried but profit-sharing managers was the solution worked out by the people themselves.

CONCLUSIONS

In 1875 Vunamami had about 700 acres of land for some 200 residents. Something less than one-fifth of an acre of cultivation can feed an individual, and the great fertility of the volcanic soil means that the area lying fallow at any one time needs to be only slightly more than equal to the area under cultivation in order to ensure fertility maintenance. A balance between use-rights vested in individuals to secure their food and a return to their labour, and formal title, vested in various levels of corporate clan grouping, to maintain the balance between fallow and cultivation and to give flexibility as population varied, worked satisfactorily. The people were land rich.

European settlement cut the land available to 360 acres for 220 people—ample for subsistence gardening but progressively less than adequate as cash cropping of coconuts was encouraged. Rapid population growth compounded the problem, and labour emigra-

[12] The history of this plot is discussed more fully in Chapters 3, 7, and 9.

tion acted as a palliative only. Government assistance obtained an additional 45 acres for the Vunamami population between 1958 and 1961, but the major attempts to solve the population problems were locally inspired. Because of the flexibility of indigenous tenure, Vunamami villagers could exercise use rights over some 200 acres in other villages, while restricting use of their own land by outsiders to 25 acres. Perhaps ten acres of plantation land were squatted on. Sixty acres of "native land" had been bought from clans in the east, making a total of 605 acres of native land, and 45 acres of land leased from the government to support the population. Fourteen of these acres were taken up for public purposes, and a village plantation existed at Talimut. Land available still did not meet the demand, although the possible purchase of Ravalien plantation promised to alter this.

The question that this history poses is what form of tenure is best suited to a society that has more and more cash cropping, universal use of money and literacy, and modern political development, but lacks many of the institutions of developed societies, including professional land lawyers, zoning laws by local authorities, capital markets and credit facilities to finance entrepreneurs, and good communications—institutions which can protect the small holder against groups that are politically stronger and can enable him to compete economically with producers who are also capital owners and wholesale marketers. Without these institutions, fee-simple tenure inevitably leads to a concentration of land in the hands of absentee owners and to depressed agricultural wage levels (see Geertz 1963b). Uncodified native land tenure is no more satisfactory, because the small holder must look more and more to a national government for his protection. Even if native tenure were progressively codified it would still be inadequate, for its great virtue of flexibility would be lost in the process. Still, the changes that native tenure has undergone indicate where the small holder needs protection and suggest the form that interim institutions could take.

The formal title still regarded as held by a "controller," a clan *lualua* (or, in some modern examples, a village councillor or council president), as a trustee for a group of people, although nominally the same title as that indigenously held by a clan *lualua*, actually serves different purposes now. It provides wider public support, by the group which the controller represents, to guarantee the rights of the individual land user, and it regulates inheritance problems if no arrangement has been made by the user when alive. It is the legal mechanism of a small-scale society that has no lawyers. In lieu of zoning regulations, it ensures that a range of people are consulted if any major change of land use is proposed, though it gives them few powers to act in opposition to the user. And, as a kind of substitute for a capital and labour market, it designates a labour pool which can be called upon to assist in major tasks, provides some sanctions to encourage the provision of labour, and justifies the collection of capital funds for the development of the land. The possibility of obtaining use rights and eventually converting them into formal title motivates much investment by otherwise landless men. The quasi-religious attitude to land ensures that information about its use and potential are widely circulated, without the existence of land registers or agricultural and legal textbooks. The 1961 compromise of modified native tenure attempted to provide these services, when no land legislation had faced up to the problem of providing them and there were no introduced legal institutions for the purpose.

A better compromise would be to provide the services within a formal legal framework. The history of the Warangoi Council Scheme suggests how such a legal structure might work—with councils assuming "formal title" to all lands in their own area, thereby justifying the exercise of residual zoning powers and the maintenance of land registers. The council would permit individual users (or groups of users) to work land by a contract which would assure to them all the rights they currently held but which could be changed by mutual agreement. Usually, the contract could remain implicit, and would consist of the understandings implied in the local "native tenure." But written contracts could be drawn up specifying the understandings if parties wished. Although there would be no urgent need for a legal profession, the need would inevitably grow as more contracts were written down and the use of a standard legal terminology became necessary. This would entail a translation of indigenous concepts, but once agreed upon, a standard form of translation would apply over fairly large areas. Thus, indigenous social forms would not simply be perpetuated, but would be modified to meet the needs of the developing society.

III

Agriculture

In the 1870's in the Vunamami area land was used almost solely for subsistence gardening. The descriptions of the landscape by contemporary observers make this quite clear. "At this place, Kininigunan, there are large portions of the coast range from which the whole of the bush has been cleared or burnt off, and the ground overgrown with most luxuriant thick coarse grass of the most vivid green, interspersed with clumps of bush in the small ravines and with cocoanut palms on the beach and in clusters also over the land, crowning the low range of hills which bounds the prospect inland" (Brown 1908:146). "The trees near the beach formed a wider band in the East, with the grass belt behind them only reaching the beach in the more westerly areas. Beyond Raluana Point thick forest again covered the coastal slopes, but again, behind the forest, grassy slopes continued inland until the higher ridges were encountered some two or three miles inland" (Parkinson 1887:38).

Raluana Point is really part of the rim of the immense volcanic crater forming Simpson Harbour, where the ocean has broken through. The slopes to the west of it are the vertical interior of the old crater; to the east and south of it the land is a plateau of soft pumice and tuff, sloping down from the crater rim, and from the upthrusted crater of Mount Vunakoko some ten miles inland and directly south of Raluana. The volcanic rocks have weathered to give an extremely fertile soil, though the topsoil is rarely more than nine inches thick. Most Vunamami land is pumice plateau. The plateau meets the coast in a cliff some fifty feet high.

Few rivers drain the plateau. Most water rapidly soaks into the spongy rock and seeps underground to emerge at the foot of the coastal cliffs in springs of fresh water. The heavy downpours of tropical storms have, however, cut deep ravines, with almost vertical walls, into the plateau. They are up to fifty feet deep and rarely more than a hundred feet across, except at the coast, where they join and debouch in wide valleys. The landing place at Ralum is where several such ravines, and the fresh water they bring down, have resulted in a break in the coral reef and a level plain directly behind the beach. The ravines are normally dry, although they may flood during a storm, and large blocks of pumice float down them.[1]

The humus in the dry ravines is several feet thick, and the ground is moist so that plants grow rapidly, but the flash floods render them unsuitable for garden cultivation. Many of them are still "bush" in appearance (what in South America is called "galeria forest"), but the occasional plantings of bananas, cocoa, taro, sugar-cane, and so on in spots where some flood protection is provided show how some gardeners are prepared to risk a total loss in exchange for the high returns from such locations. Even so, the ravines are most important as a source of "wild" products, such as bamboo and rattan, or medicinal herbs. This is less true today than it was in the 1870's, and people complain of how far they must travel for such products, as compared with even thirty years ago. Brown's and Parkinson's descriptions of ravines covered with bush are probably entirely accurate. Some forty acres belonging to Vunamami are in ravines.

The second type of non-plateau land is the area between cliffs and beach. Although the upper part of the cliffs (as near Raluana) may be bush, lower down is an area of water seepage, and here bananas are the main crop. Flat, sandy areas at the foot of the belt of bananas are ideal for coconuts, fringing the beach of black sand in true tropical postcard style. Settlements of fishermen are common. Behind the *motonoi*—the landing areas and places where equipment is stored near a fishing hamlet—there is often an area where the fish are sold to inland villagers. The same people come in the dry season to collect fresh water, since the *motonoi* have fresh-water springs. *Motonoi*, banana land, and cliffs, together with the Ralum plain comprise another twenty acres.[2]

[1] East of Vunamami, where the pumice is thinner, two permanent rivers flow down ravines to drain the land. The appearance resembles the ravines elsewhere, except that the bush is heavier than in the dry ravines.

[2] There has been steady erosion of the main Vunamami *motonoi* since 1870, as indicated by the size of the church built there in 1878 and the current search for a new inland site on which to build. I use the present tense to apply to my estimate of 1870 *motonoi* size.

The plateau land is generally uniform, though irregular areas of subsidence, or incipient gullying, create hollows of rich soil and make it appear irregular. These variations encourage local tree growth, and the custom of naming plots by their distinctive trees reflects this. A tree, a fertile place close by, and the promise of other trees for shade are also the basic needs for settlement. Coconut palms grow so rapidly and provide so many necessities of indigenous life that a clump of them has long been the distinguishing mark of the hamlets, as we realize from Brown's and Parkinson's descriptions.

Within certain limits, it is possible to estimate the number of trees that were needed for subsistence in the 1870's. A mature palm can produce some seventy-five nuts a year. Each hamlet needed trees to provide green nuts (*a kulau*) for liquid for drinking and for entertaining visitors. It needed ripe nuts (*a lama*) for food, mainly for grating and squeezing to give coconut cream. Coconut cream is something of a delicacy (though Europeans to whom it is offered tend to regard it as the only native food), and it is usually eaten only two or three times a week. Each taro corm, a common food, is cooked with the cream of one coconut, making about three nuts a week for cream; counting another three for drinking, one person can be considered to eat around three hundred nuts a year, or the crop of four trees. Thus a hamlet of fifteen individuals would need some sixty trees, covering about an acre of ground. Vunamami's population of about two hundred probably had about fourteen acres of coconuts scattered over its six hundred and forty acres of plateau land.

This estimate is perhaps low, since it is based on minimum needs and on yields from palms grown under plantation conditions. If people in the 1870's ate more nuts than they do now, and if yields were markedly lower, there must have been more trees. The question of yields will be discussed more fully later, but here a major difference between native and plantation practice must be indicated. Coconut palms have shallow roots, and to allow for horizontal spread, modern plantations grow the trees at thirty-foot intervals. The crowns of the palms do not meet but give islands of shade in a wide sunlit area where kunai grass grows freely. This is not true of native plantings, however, which are at about twenty-foot intervals. There the ground is covered with a mat of coconut rootlets, and the crowns meet to form a continuous canopy. The shade prevents the growth of kunai, so that the groves are splendid dwelling sites, especially if there is a breeze to dispel mosquitoes and a dense thatched roof to protect one from falling nuts and "dries," or dead palm fronds. Small clumps of coconuts aggregating twenty-eight acres, yielding only half as much as plantation palms, would have fed and housed the Vunamami population.

In 1875 the Vunamami coconut palm acreage may well have been below the basic requirements, for the people of Lumluvur had recently bested the ward of Kunakunai in battle and had topped their victory by destroying Kunakunai's palms. They still talked scornfully about Kunakunai—"Just kunai"—as a wasted and barely habitable land.

But kunai-covered ground, in this land of high soil fertility, is easily cultivated. An acre of land under long-fallow cultivation can support five or more persons (see Salisbury 1962a: 81), and Vunamami in 1890 would have had to cultivate only forty acres or so at one time. Indeed, it is possible to cultivate the volcanic soil with almost no fallowing at all, as I learned from observation of subsistence gardens in 1961. Such so-called permanent cultivation does, however, involve some grass fallowing of odd patches for short periods. As an outside estimate, fallowing requires as much time as cultivation (the true figure is probably closer to a half as much), so that another forty acres might be needed for fallow. The total land needed for subsistence agriculture would this be less than eighty acres.

The tools required for preparing grassland were strips of bamboo and digging sticks (Danks 1892:618, Parkinson 1887:118, Kleintitschen 1906:60), adzes being used to cut bamboo and wood. Men slashed down the tall kunai with three-foot strips of bamboo and left it to dry for burning; they then turned up large clods in areas to be planted, using six-foot-long sticks, sharpened and hardened by fire. The women broke up the clods and took out the kunai roots by hand. Yams were the first crop, maturing in six months, to be followed by weeding and replanting with taro, which took almost a year to mature; after the taro, bananas and sugarcane were planted (Parkinson 1887:119). Fences are described only for inland wooded districts, but the same need for protection from pigs would presumably have existed also for the fields of villages on the grassy plain. All early accounts emphasize the number of pigs seen, the use of kunai land for pasture, and the diligence with which natives hunted down pigs that ran wild (Kleintitschen 1906:65). By 1961 pig keeping was rare, and pigs were kept closely confined, for sale to Europeans and Chinese and not for home consumption. Killing and butchering were unavailable skills when I imported a live pig for slaughter. And by 1961 there were no fences except those around the pig pens.

Some 165 of Vunamami's 700 acres in 1870 can thus be accounted for. The remainder was predominantly open kunai, but it is likely that the bush in the ravines spread somewhat more widely than it does today. The symbolic opposition between "inhabited places" (*gunan*) and "bush" (*pui*) is a constant theme in Vunamami life, expressed in the abundant mythology about bush creatures (opossums, bats, tree-kangaroos, etc.), the symbolism of the *tubuan* religion, where the spirits are welcomed in the bush by the men in their secret clearings (*a taraiu*) and only later emerge for ceremonies in front of the women in the village. Wild foods are delicacies, timber is a necessity, birds are shot for their feathers, all medicine and esoteric herbs come from the bush. The ravines ensure that some bush is within two hundred yards of any house today, but everything points to a much closer proximity to bush in the 1870's.

It is difficult to explain the 1875 land-use situation in purely ecological terms. The land could have supported a much higher population with ease, yet Tolai informants stress the smallness of families in 1875, and most important, the relatively late age at marriage and the fact that many men were never married at all because they could not afford a bride. It is possible that the Tolai had only recently arrived in the area[3] and were expanding, but the

[3] I find little real evidence to support the conclusion of many *Kulturkreislehre* writers, that the Tolai arrived only around A.D. 1700. There is concrete linguistic, cultural, and traditional evidence linking the Tolai with New Ireland, and especially Lavongai, but attempts to give absolute dates for these links usually rely on the dating of the origin of the *tubuan* ceremonies as "two generations ago." These dates may be accurate for particular varieties of the ceremony (see Chap. 8), but they do not refer to the generic origin of the ceremony. (See the origin myths cited by Meier 1909:110, Kleintitschen 1924: 135–142.) My reconstruction of the economics of shell-money production points to a recent cultural florescence around 1770 (Chap. 8). My own limited survey of *madapai* names over the whole Tolai area shows a concentration inland on the central plateau, near Ratavul; the bush mythology attached to some older *tubuan* (see Parkinson 1907:578) points in the same direction. I would conjecture a long establishment of some Tolai inland in the area, practicing garden agriculture with bush fallow, but a population expansion to about 1870 levels some one hundred and fifty years earlier, possibly when a volcanic eruption cleared large areas of forest and made grass fallowing possible.

large areas cleared of virgin forest suggest a longer occupancy, and the slow increase of population in the nineteenth century argues against a recent expansion. Rather, it appears that the Tolai had developed an equilibrium of low birth rate and low death rate, such as occurs in several Pacific societies (Nag 1962), as a means of stabilizing a relatively high standard of living. Intermittent warfare was endemic, and it predisposed people to a wider dispersal of settlements and a correspondingly lower aggregate population density than would theoretically have been possible.

1875–1896

The arrival of the Europeans brought changes, though not always the ones an outsider might have expected. European steel axes, for example, meant nothing to the coastal natives except as weapons, hafted on long poles.[4] But guns were coveted. For a muzzle loader, or for tobacco, a Tolai would barter his produce or even himself. Tobacco was an improvement on the herb the Tolai had been smoking, a custom called *a yuka* (Kleintitschen 1906:59), and the readiness with which they accepted it was typical of their attitude towards most new plants that the Europeans brought. In early 1884, Parkinson was astounded to see that plants he had introduced a year earlier from Samoa were already being cultivated in Tolai gardens. Cotton, then an important South Sea crop, was one of these (Parkinson 1887:59). To this day there exists an extremely large number of plants that have become indigenously cultivated after being introduced in European gardens or experimental plantings. Only a few have become economic crops, either for consumption or for sale, but they are familiar and have been tested by native plantings. Among them are the various anona fruits—soursops, custard-apples, introduced by Brown in 1875 (Brown 1908: 100), and sweet-sops—teak and ficus rubber trees, garlic and capsicum, kapok trees, dry rice, giant varieties of coconut, tobacco, citrus and guava (both Brown's introductions), and innumerable garden flowers. Those that have been accepted as important in native production are few—peanuts, manioc, pineapples, runner beans, tomatoes, cacao.

[4] This is in marked contrast to areas where fallowing was under bush (see Salisbury 1962), and contrary to my own expectations in 1959 (quoted by T. S. Epstein, 1963:293) "the availability of steel tools . . . made it easier to clear larger areas of bush." A short period of original research was needed to establish the point.

Of importance for agriculture, but to my knowledge unre-
corded in the literature, and possibly also a case of local adaptation, was the replacement of bamboo slashing implements by
lengths of sharpened steel strip. Even today these implements,
called *sarip*, are manufactured locally from imported steel strips,
which are sharpened and given handles. In 1876 hoop iron was one
of the three main commodities left by Dr. Brown with his teachers
for the purchase of food, since he refused to exchange tobacco
or guns. The forty-one pounds left would have made almost one
hundred sarips—more in number than the tomahawks that he also
left. Although only small areas required clearing of kunai in 1876,
it would seem that the Tolai were quick to appreciate the labour-
saving usefulness of the sarip.

The next agricultural innovation that the traders' presence gave
rise to was the sale of food crops. It will be recalled that traders
first sought labour recruits, and shell, yet from the start the villagers were eager to trade food. In 1875 when Brown went to
various villages he listed the objects offered him as "yams and
taro" (Diary, 15 Oct. 1875), "fish, yams, useless shells, fish nets,
spears, bananas" (Diary, 21 Oct.), "eggs, fowls and coconuts"
(Diary, 15 Dec.), and "fowls, eggs and yams" (Diary, 17 Jan.
1876). Yet it would appear that the Duke of York Islands did not
produce enough food to support even the few newcomers very
well. To judge from comments in Brown's diary (not reproduced
in his book) on the foods he managed to buy and the scarcity at
home, and occasional remarks about voyages to the mainland "to
buy food," it would seem that hunger as well as missionary zeal
lay behind his frequent travelling.

It is striking in both Brown's book and his diary that he rarely
mentions coconuts being offered for sale in 1875 and 1876. He
talks a lot about the sale of shell and trepang, though he himself
did not buy these commodities. Only in the diary entry 2 August
1876, when a fire destroyed a trade store in the Duke of Yorks and
"5000 coconuts belonging to Blohm were burned," is there a clear
mention of coconut trading. The year 1875 was probably the first
in which there was copra trading, yet on 1 July 1878 Brown noted
that "copra is king." Powell, who arrived in June 1877, mentions
trading for shell and expeditions to catch turtles, but he talks
more extensively of copra trading.

European writers often give details of early trading practices.
Powell says that prices were "a thimbleful of beads for each pound

of copra, though this alters as time goes on and more traders come to make opposition" (1884:37). Parkinson says that at first a stick of tobacco could be exchanged for twenty-five or thirty coconuts (1887:85), and Danks, in a letter to cousins planning to begin trade in the area (4 Feb. 1881), advises them as follows: "Bring trade tobacco, of which twenty sticks go to make one pound; fantail hatchets; beads, white and red being most desired, but blue only occasionally asked for; knives of different sizes. The people here do not make the copra and then sell it to the trader but *simply bring the nuts* and the latter cut them up for themselves. Competition is keen, five firms now being active, only as many as eight and in some places fifteen coconuts being obtained for one stick of tobacco" (partly quoted in Danks 1933:151). A trader should deduct from £2 10s. to £3 for trade and then freight before realizing the profits cited in Chapter 1.

Accurate figures for the total amounts of copra obtained in these years are lacking but the *Deutsche Kolonialzeitung* of 1886 estimated that the whole Bismarck Archipelago exported 1,000 tons in the year 1879–1880. In 1885, besides the three main depots of Ralum, Matupit, and Mioko, there were fourteen trading posts collecting New Britain copra and nineteen collecting from other islands. An estimate would be that half of the 1,000 tons was Tolai copra. This would represent half of the total Tolai output of coconuts estimated on the same basis as for Vunamami.

We can now consider how this market for coconuts affected Tolai cultivation practices. They do not seem to have drastically increased their plantings (see Weisser 1887:25). If 1875 was the first year of trading for nuts, any palms planted then would not have borne fruit until 1883, and would have steadily increased their yield thereafter. In fact, the only dramatic increase in copra came before 1879–1880, from zero to 1,000 tons (for the Archipelago). From then until 1894, when plantation crops began coming in, the increase was slow but steady. In 1883[5] over 1,350 tons were exported from the Bismarck Archipelago. In 1884 one company

[5] The figures quoted by Epstein (1963:294) are unreliable as they are taken from Blum (1900:157) a secondary compilation of government figures and unreliable for early accounts. The tonnage given here is the total exported by Hernsheim and D.H.P.G., and does not include that of Queen Emma, the third company, which was establishing itself at Ralum in 1883. The 1892 figures were reported on a basis of the eighteen months from January 1892 to June 1893 (*Nachrichten* 1894:20) and should be divided accordingly, as in the present text.

exported less (Parkinson 1887:35), but this may have been due to the expansion of Queen Emma's activities. In 1885 the total exports were 1,550 tons, worth M. 455,000 (*Kolonialzeitung* 1888). In 1892, 1,703 tons were exported, two-thirds by Queen Emma. Then in 1895, the total, enlarged by plantation copra and new plantings on the north coast, shot up to 2,437.2 tons (*Nachrichten* 1896:31).

The reason for the slow increase in native plantings is not mysterious; Dank's letter, cited in Chapter 1, points clearly to it. Existing plantings were adequate to take care of Tolai needs for manufactured goods, and the people found bargaining a better—and quicker—way of increasing the amount they received. In 1879 the local producer was happy to get trade goods worth some six marks for a ton of copra (Blum 1900:169) which would bring 444 marks in Europe; Dank's quoted figure of 50 marks of trade per ton in 1881 seems high, and may include the trade goods paid for food and immigrant labourers. In 1884 fifteen marks' worth of trade goods equalled one ton (Lyng 1919:47), which fetched 320 marks in Europe (*Kolonialzeitung* 1886). By 1898 the Tolai had increased their price to one hundred marks' worth of goods for one ton, and the trader was getting only 218 marks a ton in Singapore, after shipping costs of 20 marks (Blum 1900:169). This would mean, assuming that a constant Tolai population of 20,000 produced half the output of the Bismarck Archipelago, that the value of trade goods received per capita per annum rose from 0.15 marks in 1879, to 0.51 marks in 1883, to 0.62 marks in 1885, to 1.71 marks in 1892 (interpolating a trade goods price of 40 marks per ton) to 6.10 marks in 1895. In Vunamami, one of the chief trading villages, the per capita income in 1895 was no doubt twice as high as the average, and probably four or five times as high in the 1880's. A rapidly rising standard of living was clearly possible without any great increase in production.

The acreage planted can be estimated. Total Tolai production of coconuts, both for subsistence and for cash crops, has been estimated as the equivalent of 1,000 tons of copra in 1879; by 1892 the production had risen (assuming subsistence needs had been met by new planting) to 1,852 tons, the increase being half the total export crop of 1,703 tons. If the Vunamami planting increase was in the same proportion, the acreage of bearing coconuts would have risen from 28 to 48. Since Vunamami undoubtedly had higher demands for trade goods than smaller villages, it may have increased its acreage to as much as 60 acres, 35 for cash cropping and 25 for subsistence. The village planting of about three acres a year would work out at seven coconuts per family head, casually planted in garden areas along with food crops.

On this calculation, 200 of the 700 acres of Vunamami territory were under native cultivation or were unusable in 1892. At the same time, Ralum plantation had planted 450 acres, of which one-quarter was probably Vunamami land, and one-quarter each was from Keravi, Balanataman, and Tokokok villages. Some of the earliest planting had been done by local people "helping" the new settlers in return for regular feasts, but most contemporary European residents interpreted the failure to plant the remaining 387 acres of kunai as simple laziness—"natives plant only enough to get needed amounts of tobacco" (*Nachrichten* 1896:30). This is the background to planter impatience, itching for expansion of plantings, for their provocation of the war of 1893, and for the major expropriation of land thereafter. But Dr. Hahl's establishment of Ralum Reserve in about 1896, leaving Vunamami with 360 acres including 20 of ravines, 10 of *motonoi* and beach, 60 of coconuts, 40 of gardens, and 230 of kunai and bush, was not inequitable in terms of 1896 land use.

1896–1922

The real changes in land use came as a result of Dr. Hahl's ruling that if the land was not settled and planted to coconuts in fifty years it would revert to Queen Emma. If the land was to be settled, there had to be more people. Before 1896, according to informants, marriage was often delayed because of the high bride prices, sometimes more than 100 fathoms of shell money (*tabu*).[6] Kleintitschen (1906:192) confirms that men were usually twenty to twenty-five years old before they married, and many poor men never married at all because they could find no one to finance them. Indeed, few individuals had *tabu* stocks of this size. When ToBobo, the representative of Vunamami and Vunabalbal to Dr. Hahl, decreed that bride prices should be lowered to ten fathoms, the change was dramatic, informants say; all men married before they were twenty, and young children abounded in what had formerly been an "old" community. An annual increase of 3 per-

[6] The 1883 rate was 50 to 100 fathoms (Parkinson 1887:104).

cent would fit the known figures for Vunamami populations. The acreage needed for subsistence production would have risen proportionately.

At the same time ToBobo decreed that all available land should be planted to coconuts. Informants say that his instructions were rapidly carried out. In 1961 I tried to check this statement by inquiring when palms were planted. All trees planted by ToBobo himself had fallen, the last in 1960. All land in Kunakunai ward up to two hundred yards from the Toma Road and not in ravines was planted by 1914; land farther from the road was less planted and some plots were still subsistence gardens in 1961. In Lumluvur it was difficult to get accurate information, since most palms had been destroyed by fires from the Japanese storage depot in Ravalien plantation, but the usual pattern of working out from the track along the ridge seems to have been followed. I estimate that 150 acres were planted in the eighteen years between 1896 and 1914; most of the remaining 80 acres were planted during the wartime occupation, before the Mandate of 1921.

The effects of this planting can be seen in many ways. Table 3 gives estimates for copra exports from Vunamami, including total and per capita income, along with export figures for the Bismarck Archipelago as a whole. The table assumes that palms over six years old produce 4 cwt. of copra, and that five-year-old palms produce 2 cwt., as in 1961 (see Appendix A). It further assumes that the annual rate of planting before 1896 was three acres a year, from 1896 to 1914, eight acres, and from 1914 to 1922, ten acres. Vunamami income figures assume a steady increase of two marks annually in the price per ton of copra from the 100 marks received per ton in 1896, an assumption that corresponds roughly with the fact that in 1909 sixty nuts were bought for one mark, the equivalent of 112 marks per ton (*Monatshefte* 1909:535). Prices were chaotic early in the First World War; I have used the government rates of 1917 and 1918, which remained fixed until 1921—that is, 187 and 172 marks per ton—and have interpolated the 1916 figure. These total income figures have been converted to per capita income figures based on the known Vunamami population of 229 in 1910 and a natural increase of 3 percent per annum thereafter, though a lower rate of increase before then. The calculated population in 1896 was 190 and that of 1920 was 300.

Up to 1912, the Vunamami estimates, based on considerations of local history, follow the trend discernible in the figures for total

Table 3

VUNAMAMI COPRA EXPORTS AND INCOME, 1896–1921

Year	Vunamami*			Bismarck Archipelago*	
	Total Volume (1,000 kg.)	Total Value (Mks.)	Income Per Capita (Mks.)	Total Volume (1,000 kg.)	Total Value (M. 1,000,000)
1896	6.1	610	3.2	2,367	552
1897	6.3	642	3.4	2,425	557
1898	6.5	676	3.5	?	?
1899	6.7	710	3.7	?	?
1900	6.9	745	3.8	?	577
1901	7.1	781	4.0	?	989
1902	7.9	885	4.4	2,867	708
1903	9.5	1,083	5.4	3,293	694
1904	11.1	1,288	6.2	4,225	890
1905	12.7	1,499	7.2	4,465	1,080
1906	14.3	1,716	8.0	4,194	1,376
1907	15.9	1,940	8.8	4,877	1,522
1908	17.5	2,170	9.7	5,587	1,344
1909	19.1	2,407	10.6	7,910	1,952
1910	20.7	2,650	11.5	8,778	2,899
1911	22.3	2,899	12.4	8,571	2,987
1912	23.9	3,155	13.3	8,849	3,622
1913	25.5	3,418	14.0	11,200ca.	?
1914	27.1	3,686	14.6	?	?
1915	28.7	?	?	?	?
1916	30.3	4,545	17.0	?	2,688
1917	31.9	5,965	21.6	?	4,896
1918	33.5	5,762	20.3	16,800ca.	5,968
1919	35.3	6,072	20.7	?	7,072
1920	37.3	6,419	21.4	22,400	12,912

* Vunamami figures are estimates derived from assumptions stated in the text. Figures for the Bismarck Archipelago are derived from official Annual Reports. After 1912 these sources cite only combined figures for the Bismarck Archipelago and the New Guinea mainland. I have calculated the Bismarck Archipelago as providing 90 percent of total production in 1912 and 80 percent for succeeding years.

Bismarck Archipelago output, representing 0.3 percent of total output. Vunamami was one of the first villages to produce cash crops, and it expanded at the same time as plantations did. But after 1912, European plantings inland and in other areas of the Territory expanded rapidly, while Vunamami expansion stayed

constant. My assumptions give rise to the (no doubt spurious)
evenness of Vunamami expansion, but the trend is clear. Even with
the population increase, per capita income increased slowly until
the new plantings began bearing around 1902. Thereafter until
1914 per capita income trebled, despite rapid population growth.
The First World War, after its initial disruptions, raised prices
and incomes another 50 percent, but then controls and the population increases stabilized incomes. Vunamami became almost
completely planted with coconuts at a time of great prosperity; it
must have been hard for Vunamami people to visualize anything
but a continuation of this trend, though in retrospect one can see
the imminent threat of declining incomes.

LABOUR USE, 1870–1922

So far we have discussed the changing appearance of Vunamami
land. The changes in the behaviour of the Vunamami people are
the other side of this picture, and can be most simply described
in terms of the percentage of time spent by the population in
various activities. Table 4 shows these figures not merely for
1896–1922, but up to 1961. The figures for 1870 are hypothetical
and represent a reconstruction based on 1961 time-use budgets
(Appendix B), modified in the light of the historical evidence
available. They accord closely with time-use figures for an aboriginal population given in Salisbury (1962a:108). For purposes of
exposition, however, I shall take the 1870 figures as given and
trace the effects of changes upon them.

In the earliest phase of European contact the major time savings
came from the introduction of the *sarip* and the reduction in inter-
hamlet warfare. Both affected men's time more than women's
(cf. Salisbury 1962a:109). Formerly, agricultural tasks had been
"fairly evenly divided between the men and the women" and
"usually done only early in the morning" (Danks 1892:618), so
that the drop from 25 percent of time spent in agriculture to only
20 percent seems appropriate. Men spent their new extra time
in the male pursuits of trading and ceremonial. There is direct
evidence (see Chapter 6) that trading activities increased markedly,
and indirect evidence of more travelling to collect shells and to sell
to traders. Fishing is today a marginal activity, occupying time
otherwise unusable; as long-distance travelling increased and proved
profitable in the 1870's, I assume that less time was spent in fishing.

Table 4

TIME ALLOCATION IN VUNAMAMI, 1870–1961*

Activity	Percentage of Resident Labour Force Employed at Varying Dates							
	1870	1880	1895	1914	1928	1940	1950	1961
Sickness: inactivity	10	10	10	10	10	7	6	6
Warfare	10	7	—	—	—	—	—	—
Ceremonial (courts, church, corvée work)	8	10	12	10	9	8	10	11
Trading (markets, *tabu* buying, copra selling	15	23	28	13	11	11	12	7
Fishing	30	27	20	13	17	20	15	7
Crafts (incl. housebuilding)	2	3	4	4	2	2	5	5
Agriculture	25	20	20	20	20	20	13	8
Coconut planting	—	—	3	10	—	—	4	4
Copra production	—	2	3	12	14	11	10	9
Cocoa planting	—	—	—	—	—	—	—	5
Cocoa production	—	—	—	—	—	—	—	7
Wage labour	—	—	—	8	16	20	24	31

* The 1961 figures are derived from a census of employment, from figures of attendance at ceremonials and meetings, and from a sample of time budgets of village workers, adjusted for seasonal variations (see Appendix B). Earlier figures are derived as explained in the text, using aggregate yield and acreage figures where relevant. Figures underlined show significant increases in time spent.

As we have seen, Vunamami men did not at first spend time in the novel chore of drying copra, nor did they use additional time for planting coconut trees. Danks says (1892:618) that traditionally, "a provident father [plants] a number of trees when a son is born, and in seven or eight years . . . as soon as the child can do anything, he has a small plantation of his own." Certainly, however, an increasing amount of time must have been spent collecting nuts. By 1896 the selling of copra and attendance at markets had become much more time consuming, although the excitement and profitability of marketing had no doubt waned. The major time expenditure now involved the manual transport of loads of produce to European bulking points and their routine sale rather than local traffic and talk with neighbouring communities. Ceremonial and long-distance voyaging for *tabu* increased at this time, but the abolition of warfare meant a great saving of time, and a further saving resulted from also, no doubt, a decline in fishing.

In 1898 there occurred another minor technological change—the introduction of the shovel. In April, Dr. Hahl ordered the construction of a road connecting Ralum with the top of Mount Vunakoko, passing through all the villages. The road is today called the Toma Road, and it is still the main highway through the Vunamami Council area. Dr. Hahl worked up enthusiasm, describing how easy it would be to travel along the new road to and from the market, and he donated picks and shovels to the road workers and allowed them to keep them when the road was finished. The workers also got small gifts of tobacco (*Kolonialblatt* 1898:796), and on 11 August 1898 a troop of Marines from a cruiser marched triumphantly up the road to erect a monument to Bismarck at the top. Shovels were quickly put to agricultural use, and are used today.

The time spent in planting, using shovels, may be directly estimated. On cleared plantation land the lowest cost of planting and tending an acre of coconuts up to the bearing stage is about two-thirds of the annual cost of a workman (Australia 1953:24, 27).[7] Vunamami costs may be slightly lower but the approximation is probably close. To plant eight acres yearly would require five men working full time, or about 10 percent of a labour force of fifty. The increase in this activity of 1896 was dramatic, but it did not inhibit other activities. In their affluence Vunamami men spent even more time in voyaging for shell, and in ceremonial (see Chapters 8 and 9). There was some cause for complaints of Government and missions that not enough time was spent in plantation work, and for the efforts to force Tolai into wage labour by means of regulations forbidding trading in shell and restricting ceremonials to the month of May. But it was not innate laziness by Tolai that caused the situation, only their reaction to unfamiliar prosperity.

As the new plantings began to bear the issue solved itself, for plantations stopped buying nuts and began buying only dried

[7] This amount of labour is spread over six years. In these and succeeding calculations I have treated this as a cost in only one year—a justified assumption if a standard acreage is planted each year over a long period, since some work is done on all non-bearing plantings at their various stages of growth. This approximates the Vunamami pattern. Throughout New Guinea the average labour used in copra processing was 74.5 man-days per ton. New Britain plantations are efficient and on fertile soil and the average for them, recalculated by myself, was 64.4 man-days per ton.

copra. With their indentured labourers fully employed setting out more plantings and therefore unable to handle the rapidly increasing quantities of locally grown nuts being brought in for sale, the plantations started quoting prices for native-dried copra rather than for nuts (Blum 1900:169). The Law of 18 October 1900, making it illegal to buy nuts because this "encouraged the native's tendencies to do nothing, which is improper," merely recognized an existing situation in Vunamami. From the Vunamami point of view (see Appendix D) the incentive was the emergence of new consumer demands, and copra processing was a way of using time to satisfy demands.

I have no figures for the amount of time it took to process copra in Vunamami by the old method of sun or smoke drying. The preliminary tasks would be much the same as those involved today in the peasant production of hot-air dried copra, that is, collecting the nuts, opening them, and extracting the meat. But whereas the meat can be left virtually unattended in a hot-air drier, it must be constantly spread and turned if it is left in racks over a fire; and sun drying means that it must be tended over several days, brought out of the dew every night, and quickly gathered up in case of rain. I guess that a ton of copra took about 70 man-days of labour processing in 1896—slightly more than was taken on efficient New Britain plantations in 1950 (Australia 1951:49) and almost twice what Vunamami growers now need with hot-air driers.

On this basis, copra processing took 427 man-days of labour in 1896, or about one and a half workers. By 1902 still only one and two-thirds workers were required, but then the labour demands rose rapidly to the equivalent of six workers in 1912, and about nine workers in 1920. As percentages of the adult male labour force, these figures equal 3 percent in 1896, slightly more in 1902, but 11 percent in 1912, and 15 percent in 1920.

At the same time, female workers also found additional employment. Sales of food products to feed plantation labourers from Buka had begun in the 1880's when there were only 150 of them, and in 1888 we know that hundreds of women came to Ralum plantation to sell food (Pitcairn 1891:176); but there were never sufficient supplies and Mrs. Parkinson sent out boats daily along the coast to buy more (Webster 1898:87). To feed the 1,000 labourers near Kokopo would have required that the nearby indigenous population increase its production by only 10 percent.

Shovels, which the women used backwards as hoes, probably increased their productivity by this amount in any case. But between 1900 and 1921 the number of labourers near Kokopo increased to 3,241 (Annual Report 1921:74). This probably increased the amount of women's time spent in growing crops for sale from about 2 percent of their total time (10 percent of 20 percent) to about 10 percent. No additional time was spent by the men, as the land for these gardens was land they had cleared for coconut planting. Subsistence cropping of land under immature palms is still the practice in Vunamami.

Before 1914 a few men did maintain market gardens to supply the Europeans with oranges, Chinese cabbage, beans, cucumbers, radishes, pineapples, mangoes, grenadillas, and so on. In Vunamami an area was devoted to pineapples for local sale and for bulk sale to ships.[8] Keeping chickens for sale, and purchasing them for resale to Europeans at a profit were also male agricultural activities. But these activities were not important ones in Vunamami, which regarded itself as an enterprising "copra village." When I inquired in 1961 why inland villages such as Gunanba supplied most of the European fruits in Kokopo market, I was told that they had not planted coconuts when ToBobo gave the word. As Vunamami grew rich, Gunanba, seeking a quick way of earning money, had turned to market gardening. In German times market gardening and copra were seen as mutually exclusive alternatives, although then, as now, there were of course exceptions, and Vunamami still has a few market gardeners.

The growth of wage labour in Vunamami in the decade 1900–1910 must also be noted, though it will be discussed in Chapter 4. Until 1920 few New Britain men worked as plantation labourers, but in the decade 1900–1910 several Vunamami men obtained élite jobs as domestic servants for government officials (including Dr. Hahl), as police, or as plantation overseers. Genealogies indicate that there were always at least five persons so employed.

Corvée labour, too, increased after the 1898 road building. Subsequent Annual Reports all describe road construction and improvement by villagers, supervised by *luluai*. In 1900 (p. 78) the Tolai were "doing well" but by 1902 the hated roadwork was causing "difficulties and disturbances" (p. 95). The five-mark head tax,

---

[8] Mrs. L. Miller (1958) mentions such a plantation, with horses and carts and metal-roofed houses "near where Mr. Weir lived." It is not clear whether she is describing Vunamami or a similar development elsewhere.

instituted in 1905, was welcomed in Vunamami as freeing them from corvée obligations, though poor inland villages objected. The increase in Vunamami taxes to ten marks in 1910 was also "willingly paid." Anything was preferable to roadwork.

In reviewing the period up to 1922, Table 4 brings out a simple generalization—the increase in the "commitment" involved in time use. This appears as an increase in the time spent in activities lower in the table. The four first categories—sickness, warfare, ceremonial, and trading—are very definitely "optional" activities, in which one indulges by choice, or by accident. The time one spends on them in one year is not the inevitable result of last year's activities, nor does it necessarily commit one's activities for years ahead. Becoming a wage labourer, on the other hand, involves a full-time commitment, and in the same way planting land and harvesting tree crops mean that one is tied to processing them into the indefinite future. One who engages in subsistence agriculture, craftwork, or fishing is far less committed to a future pattern of activity than is one who plants coconut trees.

In Vunamami the increase in "commitment" was not sudden. The changes caused by the presence of Europeans at first allowed a wider choice among traditional "optional" activities, which still continued to occupy roughly half the Tolai's time. The favourite choices were the socially rewarding fields of trading and ceremonials. "Commitment" came after Vunamami was already rich, as the planting era, up to 1928, more and more demanded time to be committed for the future. Even so, Vunamami men spent considerable time in optional activities. For few people was there no choice at all in what they should do. In economic terms, there was still a seller's market for labour.

This explains the democratization of land tenure that accompanied the planting era. The first planters were the heads of the main clans, with pre-eminent claims to land and great involvement in politics, ceremonial, and trading. The land acquisitions by upwardly mobile men of the pre-1890 immigrant clans, like Vunaibu, were also for planting. To secure the labour they required for processing their copra, they allowed their dependants in exchange to use some land for gardening and for planting a few coconuts. With the continuing labour shortage the usufructuary rights gradually became securer tenure, until, by 1961, the delegation of control to the current (or last) user was virtually complete. If there had been a surplus of labour without "optional" avenues of employment, it is likely that the power of clan and lineage heads would have continued to increase after 1896 and a landlord-tenant system might well have developed. Optional non-productive activities are needed during a period of technological change which reduces labour demands, if underemployment is not to rigidify the class structure.

1922–1942: COPRA FOR PLANTATIONS AND FOR PEASANTS

By 1922 Vunamami was a community of peasant copra producers. The land also provided bush in ravines, and subsistence gardens away from settlements and roads. The copra was produced by inefficient sun or smoke-drying techniques. All the copra was sold at a fixed price of thirteen pounds a shilling to the trade store of Ravalien plantation, which marketed it at considerable profit. In effect, Vunamami had become a captive labour force for the plantation.

This was the unintended consequence of the wartime regulations designed to maintain the pre-war status quo and to ensure the smooth flow of copra (see Rowley 1958:Ch. 13). As Vunamami was well within the two-mile limit from the plantation boundaries within which no new trade store could be established, there was no outlet for copra except Ravalien. When price regulations were abolished in 1921, the lack of competition, the swelling Vunamami production, and the immediate post-war slump meant that prices could go nowhere but down.

The rapid sale of Ravalien and Matanatar in 1923, following their expropriation, happily spared Vunamami the uncertainties that threatened other areas. The new owners, first Mackenzie and later the Rowe brothers, were not temporary managers but specific individuals, with special ways of doing things. Their standards and habits became known and could be calculated on, strategies could be worked out to combat them, and a certain *modus vivendi* established, even if this meant blaming the Rowes for every misfortune that struck the area.

To understand the nature of these misfortunes and the importance of organizational changes during the 1930's, one needs to know certain details of the operations of copra production. For convenience, I shall describe those operations as they were performed in 1961 on plantations and by peasant producers, and then consider the changing practices of the 1920's and 1930's.

The average size of the European plantations in Kokopo is about two square miles. In 1961, these plantations were covered in mature (or senescent) palms, and increasingly were being interplanted with cocoa. In the 1920's, however, they were almost exclusively planted to coconuts. Most had a single large centralized plant, located at the edge of the plantation near a public road. The foci of the plant were the dormitories for the indentured labourers (who came mainly from the most recently administered areas of New Guinea, the Sepik in the 1920's, and the Highlands in 1961) and the driers. In 1961 the driers were mostly large hot-air driers burning either kerosene or coconut husks and shells (called "skins"), but plantations also used some driers of the old type, huge sun-drying trays, on rollers so that they could be moved into shelter from the rain. In the 1920's sun driers were the rule and hot-air driers the exception. From the plant radiated a series of plantation roads, along the floor of the ravines or across other land unsuited for geometrical planting. The manager's house was always at a distance from the plant, in a place where there was a view and a cool breeze.

Work on a plantation is so planned to keep the driers operating to capacity round the clock as far as possible. A relatively skilled gang stoke and service the drier; a number of less skilled workers extract meat from nuts, roll sun driers in and out, and bag the dried copra for transportation; other parties are sent out daily to the changing tasks of the plantation—planting, weeding, road clearing, and most importantly nut collecting. The nut-collecting parties are small, and go out armed with sarips. To uncover nuts they slash down the kunai, which grows three feet tall between the widely spaced palms, and carry the nuts to collecting points on the plantation roads. Not only is slashed kunai a good soil mulch, but tall kunai feeds raging grass fires which can easily render palms sterile. Although most nuts are found directly under palms, it increases yields and gives insurance if all kunai is cut every two or three months. Plantations that clear only small circles under the palms are considered to be badly run plantations, and likely to fail. A quarter of an acre cleared and the nuts collected from twelve palm trees is about an average day's work for a single labourer, yielding perhaps 200 nuts and about 70 pounds of copra.

The labour cost of a ton of plantation copra on New Britain was 64.4 man-days (Australia 1953), and roughly half this was incurred in cutting kunai and collecting nuts. In contrast to the transporting of nuts to the central plant to provide fuel, which is done efficiently by tractors and trailers, and in contrast, too, to the maximum use that is made of the cash investment of the drier, plantation labour is used profligately in nut collecting.

Peasant planters, however, in 1961 as in 1921, collected nuts very efficiently. This is partly because of the closeness with which the trees are set out. In the shady groves, weeds and kunai do not grow. A nut collector takes a bush knife to slash creepers, or fallen dries, but he can easily collect the nuts from one or even two acres in a day. Also, peasant women and children, who could not clear kunai, can easily collect nuts at odd moments.

In 1961 Vunamami growers did not carry nuts for long distances. Within the half square mile of Vunamami village there were twelve small copra driers inexpensively constructed out of corrugated iron, forty-four-gallon drums, and thick wire mesh. No planting was more than two hundred yards from a drier, and the nuts could be brought in manually to the nearest drier site. Each planter made his own pile there, measuring it in units of sixty nuts (*a pakaruat*) and leaving the nuts to dry naturally as long as possible short of sprouting—perhaps three or four months. Dry nuts yield their meat most easily.

A *pakaruat* of nuts yields enough meat to fill a wire-mesh "tray" (*a watar*) in most driers, and driers contain from eight to sixteen sliding trays, arranged in banks of four. When a grower has sufficient nuts to fill most of a drier, he organizes a work group to extract the meat. Some participants are his dependants or are paid by him; most are usually other growers with whom he exchanges labour. Two men can fill a small drier in one day, five men may be needed for a large drier. Whatever the arrangement, the "host" provides an evening meal of rice and meat for his workers, costing him some three shillings a head.

The routine of production makes it possible to keep the driers burning continuously once they are fired, using the coconut skins as fuel. As a grower finishes extracting the meat from his coconuts (*ra nibik*), the previous drier load should be dry. The grower and his helpers (who often include the owner of the dry copra) transfer the dry copra to coconut-frond baskets and then load the trays with new wet meat. The drying process takes a little more than a full day—four loads in a six-day week are usually "capacity"—so that there is some staggering of extracting and some overnight storage of wet meat ready for loading the next morning, but the system generally works smoothly. The copra owners help with the loading, and the owner of the drier usually provides nighttime stoking as part of his hire charge (*a totokom*) of two shillings per tray used. This works out at about £8 for drying one ton of copra.

It is only when the copra is fully dry that it is carried for long distances—in Vunamami exclusively to the two purchasing stations of the Bitatali Co-operative Society, which are on the two main roads through Vunamami Territory. At the Co-op, the copra is bulked, shipped by truck, and sold (through the New Britain Co-operative Association) to the national Copra Marketing Board.

The economics of modern small-scale copra growing in Vunamami can now be appreciated. On a five-acre plot a grower spends up to five man-days every three months collecting nuts. He spends another four days extracting the meat (or repaying the assistance of other growers) and some fifteen shillings entertaining workers, again every three months. Transporting the finished copra—six or seven full baskets each time—to the purchasing station takes only a few hours. In one year he can produce a ton of copra for between 36 and 45 man-days of labour, plus £11 of cash costs. This is in addition to the capital costs of plantations, their establishment, and their mechanical plant, which are discussed in Appendix E, along with other figures of returns to capital investment. But these overhead costs to the peasant producer are minute compared with those of large plantations, where equipment worth £700 turns out 51 tons of copra.

A Vunamami producer who sells through the Co-operative receives an immediate "first payment," fixed for long periods at below the anticipated world price. Later on he receives a second payment, called a P.C.B. payment, after the wartime Production Control Board which preceded the current Copra Marketing Board, based on the amount by which realized market prices for all New Guinea copra during the year exceeded the amount advanced by the Marketing Board to the Co-operative. He may also receive a third payment as a Co-operative Society refund if the Co-operative itself makes a profit. If he grosses sixpence a pound for his copra, his ton gives him £56, less £11 cash costs, or £45

for about 40 man-days of work or a rate of 22*s*. 6*d*. per day's work.
On a plantation at a weekly wage of £3, he would have to work
for fifteen weeks to earn this amount, during which time he would
have produced about two tons of copra. His employer would receive £112 to pay the £45 labour costs plus £67 for interest,
depreciation, and management. Such high management costs can
be supported only by paying substandard wages for unskilled
labour. This would be economically justified if there were an over-
all land shortage, as a means of providing employment on small
areas of land, and to yield much greater crops per acre than do
the extensive cultivation techniques of Vunamami (see Appendix
A). It is unjustified given the land and labour situation in 1961
in New Guinea.

The situation in 1922 with smoke drying was different. A peasant grower had to dry small quantities at a time, and had to remain near his fire (or mats) in order to turn the meat and bring
it in in case of rain. He usually did his drying near his house, and
either built his house in his coconut grove or transported whole
nuts to his house. He either collected too frequently over all his
plantings, or else collected too seldom from small areas, in order
to have a single *pakaruat* for drying. He then had to transport the
poorly dried copra all the way to Ravalien, where the price he
received had to yield a profit to the plantation after paying marketing costs and possibly the costs of redrying by plantation labourers. Under these circumstances, the risks and organization needed
for marketing justified the large payments to the plantation "for
management."

After 1922 copra growing became less profitable for Vunamami
growers. No one was interested in acquiring new land for planting. Continually increasing quantities of nuts, as new plantings
came into bearing, absorbed larger amounts of labour in processing. But at the same time the population explosion begun in 1897
increased the work force available. Underemployment set in,
keeping people working at copra processing despite the low return, and making employment on plantations, including Ravalien
and Matanatar, a feasible alternative. Informants date this cessation of planting and beginning of plantation labour to 1924. By
1928 regular workers from Vunamami were being paid as much
as seven shillings a week as supervisors on Matanatar, where experimental plots of cocoa were being grown. Fishing became rela-

tively profitable also, and there was no incentive to increase the efficiency of copra processing.

The later 1920's and early 1930's, then, saw a growth of other occupations. Some of the most important men, already wealthy from early copra growing, turned to seine nets to increase their wealth. Levi ToLingling, the father of Enos Teve, was one of these, and his metal-roofed house of the 1920's remained as evidence of his prosperity, until the Japanese commandeered the metal during the Second World War.

Other men turned to the growing of market-garden vegetables. In the four years between 1921 and 1925 the Rabaul market expanded from a place on the edge of Chinatown where a few women squatted "under a big tree with baskets of pawpaws, green oranges, bananas, grenadillas, pineapples, and coconuts (Overell 1923:9)" to a varied and larger market, in which tomatoes and cucumbers were grown by commercial gardeners in and around Kokopo (Annual Reports 1925). Vunamami was also prominent in this trade, although land for market gardens was scarce because of the extensive and tightly planted coconut groves. Gradually, market gardeners began encroaching on the plantations of Ravalien and Malapau, planting between the widely spaced palms. This was probably the occasion of the several disputes reported during the mid-1920's over plantation boundaries, notably one involving Enos Teve and Pero, the head of the Matupit clan, just before 1928 when Judge Phillips' investigations began. Tolerating limited encroachment would appear to have been part of the *modus vivendi* with the Rowe brothers, by which, as indentured labourers became scarce, the plantation could obtain relatively skilled but cheap casual labour from Vunamami, in return for winking at illegalities. This scarcity of plantation labour also led to a cessation of plantation tapping of twenty acres of ficus rubber planted between Ravalien and Matanatar. Local people were allowed to tap the trees, and the plantation then bought back the latex sheet from tappers for one shilling per basket. Surprisingly, Vunamami people remember this period of low copra returns but diversification of labour as a "good time"—*a bona bung*.

The Depression climaxed Vunamami's declining interest in copra. Copra prices, which had slowly declined to £13 10s. a ton by 1929, dropped sharply to £4 11s. a ton in 1933, and local prices paid were 40 pounds a shilling (New Guinea 1933). It was fortunate for Vunamami that Ravalien plantation did not stop buying altogether; Malapau did, and it allowed independent Chinese traders to set up purchasing points within its borders. When Vunamami growers sold their copra to the Chinese, Mr. Rowe retaliated by barring to Vunamami the road across his plantation, leading to the beach *motonoi* of Bitadivulo. Though this contravened Judge Phillips' (and Dr. Hahl's) decision that Vunamami had permanent access rights to *motonoi*, the District Officer accepted Mr. Rowe's argument that he had barred the road because cattle pasturing under the palms were let out by natives crossing his land. Peace was restored only when Vunamami men retaliated by blocking a road across Reserve land which led to an outlying part of Ravalien. Tempers could run high when Vunamami was little interested in copra, and copra buyers had to scrape to earn every penny they could.

Vunamami's lack of interest meant that they did not rapidly adopt the design for hot-air copra driers, using scrap metal and oil drums, worked out at Malaguna Technical School, though it had been quickly accepted near Rabaul. In part, also, the non-acceptance of driers was due to the fact that few Vunamami boys studied at Malaguna Tech, and the few who did rarely returned to agriculture. But in 1935, Enos Teve, newly appointed *luluai* of the village, organized a *kivung* or "association" to collect funds and to build a drier in the village. It was a large drier with extensive concrete foundations and cost £75, or about £300 in present-day terms.

But for all that it was an innovation, the new drier (finished in 1936) did not transform the pattern of copra processing in Vunamami, very largely because as a single central facility it involved high transportation costs. It was built near the main Toma Road, central to Vunamami ward and accessible to Vunabalbal village or even Bitarebarebe along the road, but inconvenient to Lumluvur ward. No road connected the wards across the ravine, so that it was easier for Lumluvur men to take wet meat a short distance along the ridge and sell it for drying to Ravalien plantation, at one-third the price of dry copra, than to make a double journey to Vunamami ward and back. Even in Vunamami, there was no distinct advantage for growers living at some distance, since the labour saved in drying was offset by the labour of transportation. Everyone had contributed to the central drier fund, so no one could build a competitive drier, even though several smaller driers, more conveniently located, would have been better. Vunabalbal followed the same pattern and built one large central drier.

The greatest importance of the drier was that it revived interest in copra; by drying copra more efficiently and increasing its quality, it raised the price received for it. The smell of smoke-dried copra, and its dark colour, can permeate an entire load, and if sun-dried copra is bulked in with smoked copra, the whole load is paid for at the lowest prices. And since the hire charge for the drier was nominal, producers could receive maximum prices. Indeed, though the drier operated almost at capacity, it was in effect a public utility, operating at very little profit. With copra prices rising, Vunamami people had a sense of raising their income by their own effort, and as never since the 1920's, new plantings were started. Trees planted by ToBobo to mark the boundaries of the Reserve were replaced when they fell. Areas of contested ownership on the Ravalien side of Lumluvur were planted. The area of Talimut, originally Tokokok village land but adjudicated as part of the Reserve by Judge Phillips, was divided up among the villages of Vunamami, Vunabalbal, and Ulagunan, and planted with coconuts as a village plantation. The volcanic eruption of 1937 did not interrupt the increase of prosperity as copra prices rose. By 1939 a Vunamami man received three shillings for a forty-pound basket of dry copra, or one shilling for a basket of wet meat. Copra production, and its transport to the docks, continued right up to the day of the Japanese landings.[9]

1942–1951: THE WARTIME INTERLUDE

The Japanese occupation caused violent, if temporary, changes in Vunamami land use. The Japanese did not immediately appropriate Vunamami land but segregated their military establishments, locating them on the plantations and forbidding any intercourse between the troops and the local population. They did, however, use large areas of the plantations for a new food crop—rice, cultivated on a large scale by imported Indian prisoners of war. As always, there were some Vunamami people who adopted the new crop, and with Japanese help in husking it, its cultivation grew.

[9] Mrs. L. Miller (1964) describes the bombing of a Norwegian copra vessel in Rabaul Harbour on the day of the landings and the chaos next day when she tried to recover the copra she had sent to the docks for loading.

More dramatic was the immediate conscription of every male, able-bodied or not, to build airstrips. Until they were completed —in record time—Vunamami men worked day in and day out, spurred on by an occasional public beheading of a fugitive or a malingerer. Malnutrition was common, because food had to be brought by women from the distant villages and food levies were made to support the occupation troops. The women were kept working continuously by the speedily recruited native police, the *kempe tai:* "All they said was 'dig, dig'."

At first, traditional foods were grown, and reasonable levies were made. But when food supplies from overseas were cut off in 1943, the Japanese became more demanding. They ordered every possible area to be used for gardens—all kunai ground between widely spaced palms, all waste areas. Non-bearing palms, such as those at Talimut, were cut down to make way for gardens. The half-acre of hard waste ground at Bitatali, where now the Council House stands, had to be cultivated, though it meant a week spent bringing in baskets of topsoil. Vunamami amusement at Japanese ignorance of soil conditions turned to astonishment when the sweet potatoes produced were larger than any seen before. The *kempe tai* enforced these rules, and the Vunamami people, exhausted and underfed, could only submit or be executed.

But complete segregation of the military was not possible. The plantations are like fingers of land stretching inland; the Reserves are the intermediate strips between them, and communication between plantations in those days was largely along the coast road. As Allied bombers made this road unusable and forced the dispersal of camps and vehicles away from the coast, a network of roads had to be constructed inland. These cut across the Reserves in an east-west direction, going down into the ravines and up the other side. The ravines, in plantations and in reserves, had chambers cut in their soft pumice walls to shelter men and vehicles. Slit trenches were dug everywhere, by villagers and troops alike.

These Japanese roads were built with an appreciation of the problems of erosion and swamping that beset the main roads built by both Germans and Australians. The result, in 1961, was that although some of these roads had received little or no maintenance after 1945, they were still negotiable by two-wheel drive vehicles provided that overhanging vegetation was cut away. Few of them appeared on official maps, yet they provided easy communication criss-crossing the Reserve, unknown to most government officials.

I myself, after some hesitation, found it safer and easier on my car to use these narrow, overgrown lanes than to follow the washboard main roads.

When V-J Day came, Vunamami could not immediately recommence its normal pattern of land use. The population was housed in a camp at the original Vunamami *motonoi* to facilitate the supply of rations and medication, while the camps and hospitals in the Kokopo area, set up for liberated prisoners of war and internees and for captured Japanese personnel, were being evacuated. Food growing, including extended cropping of the area of dry rice, and fishing were the main activities. One of the main problems discussed by village leaders at this time was how to husk the dry rice and make it edible, using hand methods.

Copra processing began again, though slowly. All the drying equipment had been lost in Allied bombings. There were no trade stores to buy the copra and market it, nor were there trade goods to get in exchange. But the coconuts were there to be collected. The wartime Production Control Board set up a buying station at Kabakaul, though it was limited by the scarcity and irregularity of commercial shipping and of copra sacks. For a time it had to sell trade goods in order to satisfy the demand.

With no trade stores to buy small amounts of copra and bulk them for export, Vunamami growers were obliged to find a new outlet. Some individuals with large acreages made contact with the P.C.B. directly and were able to open accounts.[10] The difficulties they encountered and the development of Tolai copra marketing will be discussed in Chapter 7. For the rest, there was for the first time the possibility of direct bulk sales to overseas shippers. Growers were free from their dependency on plantations, and it was possible to work out a reorganization of peasant production, in which bulk purchasing points were conveniently located for the producers.

A reorganization of the drying process was also possible, now that the Vunamami central drier had been destroyed, and the materials themselves lay everywhere in the wake of the occupation.

[10] To have an account implied that the seller's sales were recorded, and a second payment was made to him based on the price eventually realized by the P.C.B. on the world market. Accounting problems meant that the P.C.B. (and the later C.M.B.) demanded a minimum size of shipment. The minimum has increased steadily, and in 1964 the Kabakaul depot was closed to facilitate greater centralization in Rabaul. Both actions have put the smaller producer at a disadvantage.

Forty-four-gallon drums littered the countryside. (One drum uncovered in 1949 contained methyl alcohol, and the ensuing party
in Vunamami resulted in the death of nine of the most socially
active men born between 1915 and 1920.) Thick wire mesh had
been used and discarded in constructing parking areas, beach landing places, and fences. And there was a plentiful supply of small,
rusty pieces of corrugated iron. Although new materials were not
available the scrap materials were usable.

Four men built small driers in Vunamami in 1948, and others
followed suit. In 1950 Enos Teve tried to reintroduce the centralized processing pattern and used the funds of a *kivung* (described more fully in Chapter 7) to build an even larger drier on
the site of the old one. This move was resented by individuals
who had built makeshift but functioning driers, some of whom
were also members of the *kivung* and had not been consulted
over the use of their funds. The large drier was quietly but effectively boycotted, and even more small driers were built. By
1953 there were about sixteen driers in the half square mile of
Vunamami—more than the total number in 1961 when twelve
were in use. The change in numbers was not simply a matter of
some having collapsed or rusted away, for three of the 1961 driers
were new and efficient. Rather, the first wave of drier building
led to an oversaturation of the area, but as driers were gradually
rebuilt or dismantled for their usable metal, only efficient, properly
located driers were retained and a new organizational system
evolved. The present pattern of dispersed small driers, each servic-
ing twenty-five acres, with a minimum of transportation needed,
was virtually established by 1950. Though the appropriate technology had been learned by 1935, it was the disruption of plantation control between 1945 and 1949 that made it possible for the
new organization to develop.

Interest in planting revived then as a consequence. Within
Vunamami there was accidental planting, as undiscovered nuts
sprouted and rooted in the maze of slit trenches and bomb craters.
Most of these were allowed to grow, as a way of replacing senescent, blasted, or sterilized trees. Haphazard planting and extreme
closeness mark such areas. In a few areas where most palms had
been destroyed, as in Lumluvur during the fire at Ravalien bomb
dump, widely spaced regular planting was begun. People began
looking for new land to plant east of Kokopo. Again in 1950,
copra was king, but now in indigenous style.

1950–1960: THE COCOA ERA

As early as 1949, cocoa was being urged by Agricultural Extension Officers as a peasant cash crop. Here we must consider the Vunamami reaction to this proselytization.

Three men from the Vunamami area, but only one from Vunamami village, attended Mr. Ryan's initial meeting in late 1949 at Kerevat. From Vunamami went Enos Teve, and from Ngatur, just southeast of Malapau plantation, went Elison and NaPitalai. All three were enthusiastic and began planting cocoa immediately on return. Enos planted an area in Balanataman village near Ngatur which was part of his own clan land, and also land in Vunamami village belonging to his wife's clan. These early plantings, unsupervised by Agricultural Officers, were badly shaded and not properly lined, but Enos was inspired with the missionary fervour of the Agricultural Officers, and within a year nine Vunamami men had followed his example; there were also seven new planters from Vunabalbal village, eleven from Bitarebarebe, and two from Tingenavudu. In addition, Enos, as Paramount Luluai and Council president, persuaded the three villages of Vunamami, Vunabalbal, and Ulagunan to use Talimut, standing idle since its palms were cut down, as a "village cocoa plantation" or demonstration plot for the Vunamami area. As an example it had less effect than did the three active individual planters near Ngatur. Within a year there were 302 growers in the six villages near Ngatur. In the various villages near Ngatur Enos had persuaded his clansmen to plant seven areas of cocoa that were bearing in 1961; in Vunamami and Vunabalbal he had only three smaller plots bearing cocoa; by 1961 his larger plots to the east of Kokopo were not yet bearing.

The records of Talimut fermentery permit the history of cocoa planting to be traced in detail. As the plantings began to yield beans, growers registered at the fermentery, and thus the approximate date of first planting can be obtained for each grower by allowing four years as the interval between planting and plentiful bearing. Table 5 summarizes these records. Following the first plantings by Enos and others, there was a steady increase up to 1952, then a lapse of three years, and again a steady increase more or less to the present time. The early growers were for the most part landed and progressive older men; others were drawn in only after 1953–1954, when the early planters began reaping large re-

Table 5

COCOA GROWERS IN FIVE VILLAGES NEAR VUNAMAMI

Date*	Vunamami (pop. 502)	Vunabalbal (pop. 408)	Bitarebarebe (pop. 480)	Tingenavudu (pop. 195)	Ulagunan (pop. 265)
July 1950	10	7	11	2	0
September 1950	16	12	19	22	15
December 1950	19	17	28	24	22
June 1951	22	34	33	32	33
September 1952	30	47	52	35	42
September 1954	32	48	55	35	43
April 1955	37	57	77	41	47
September 1955	42	65	79	43	53
April 1956	49	70	84	44	55
September 1956	49	74	87	50	57
June 1957	53	75	95	55	63
(Copra growers in August 1961)	101	91	67	32	43

* Dates at which growers began planting are calculated as four years before the registration of growers at Talimut fermentery. Records of Bitatali Co-operative Store provide the numbers of copra sellers in 1961. Plantings by local residents in locations closer to other fermenteries are omitted in these figures, and constitute a small source of error. Populations are taken from the 1961 village census sheets.

turns from cash sales. These second planters tend to have been smaller landowners, younger men newly acquiring land, or women tending small numbers of trees.

The land and labour demands of cocoa growing largely explain this pattern. At first it was thought that sole cocoa—cocoa planted alone with leguminous trees to shade it—was the only way to plant; thus only those landowners with unused garden land or plots in ravines could plant. As has been described, such generally available land tended to have remained in the control of clan *lualua*. These men could also obtain the needed labour from their clan dependants. Even so, some of the earliest plots, planted without supervision by Agricultural Extension Officers, proved worthless after a few years. The most productive plots were those planted later in regular rows, under supervision, on the flat lands near Lumluvur, where many palms had been destroyed. Standing coconuts were left for shade, as were those newly planted before 1950. By 1956 it was apparent that cocoa grew well, and with the least amount of care, under the high canopy of established close-planted palms. Small coconut growers realized that they could interplant with cacao and so the number of growers increased.

This effect can be seen in the figures for all villages. Land-short Vunamami reached a saturation level, when growing was restricted to owners of clear land, with growers numbering only 6 percent of the population. In other villages, where land was more available, the number of growers gradually increased until it reached between 12 and 20 percent of the population.[11] All experienced a pause in new plantings in 1953 and 1954. After 1955 all villages recruited new planters at a similar absolute rate of about nine a year. It is my impression, from a knowledge of the non-bearing areas in Vunamami in 1961, that the Vunamami increase continued well beyond the 10.5 percent level of 1957, whereas other villages had reached a saturation level before 1961, with between 18 and 28 percent of the populations as growers.

But as with coconuts, the availability of land is only one aspect of land use; availability of labour is the other. To establish sole cocoa, planting with artificial shade under plantation conditions takes about 115 man-days of labour for each acre of 222 trees; the same number of trees planted under established coconut palms and needing no additional shade take only 87 man-days (Australia 1958:30–34). In a situation of labour surplus and land shortage, cocoa can therefore be a more practical crop than coconut palms, which require more land and less labour.[12] The labour of establishing cocoa is also spread more evenly over several years. The initial plantings in Vunamami took only about 1.7 man-years of work in 1950, less than 10 percent of the time of the nineteen planters. As new acreages were planted and earlier plantings needed tending, labour needs increased to six man-years in 1954, or 20 percent of the time of thirty planters. By then, harvesting began to require labour too, so that expansion of plantings was only possible as newcomers became interested in cocoa. More recently, the spreading out of the labour of establishing cocoa has been de-

[11] These figures also reflect the greater number of Vunamami men in wage employment and explain the higher incomes of inland villages. These differences will be considered in later chapters.

[12] This has been an important consideration for plantations with limited land. For plantations, too, interplanted cacao trees cut down the growth of kunai under palms, reducing the cost of collecting coconuts, while barely affecting yields. This has helped many plantations that had been losing money when producing only copra.

liberately exploited, both in the newer areas east of Kokopo and on
the Warangoi. Coconuts have been deliberately planted first, and
subsistence crops have been interplanted, both by the owner and
by any related person. The subsistence crops help to keep kunai
growth under control. When the slow, part-time planting covers
the entire area, the first coconuts are well established and can
provide shade for new cacao plants. Cacao planting can continue
gradually as other coconuts develop and as the subsistence gardens
move across the area. Using spare-time cultivation, the cocoa
grower can maintain himself and create a valuable capital asset
at one and the same time.

But, as we have seen, for the peasant producer the return on
labour spent in harvesting and processing the crop is the vital consideration. All Vunamami growers, for reasons considered below,
have their beans, wet and freshly extracted from their pods,
processed at a centralized fermentery. The fermentery normally
accepts wet beans only on a Tuesday. Cocoa is a fairly seasonal
crop, however, with most pods ripening in Vunamami during the
"main flush" of April, May, and June, and smaller quantities in
all other months except October when there is a "secondary flush."
At flush times the fermentery may start a second processing cycle
on Fridays as well. During the flush season, then, the grower,
his wife, and one helper (say a teen-age son) can pick the ripe
pods on an eight-acre plot on Monday. On Tuesday morning the
three of them can open the pods and extract about one hundred
pounds of wet beans, which one person carries to the fermentery
in the afternoon. He waits on one of the back roads for a truck,
contracted by the village to pick up growers and beans, and pays
an average of three shillings for transport to the fermentery. For
the remaining forty weeks of the year the grower works alone,
collecting and opening half as many pods, and spending two days
at his work. According to the average-yield figures for Vunamami
(see Appendix A), this acreage yields almost one ton of dry
cocoa, or about two and a half tons of wet beans. To harvest it
takes five man-days a week for twelve weeks, and two man-days
for forty weeks, or 140 man-days in all.

In cash terms, at 1960 prices of around 8d. a pound for wet
beans, the grower received almost £187, less transport costs of
£15. The apparent return for his labour was about £1 3s. 10d.
per day. At 1954 prices of 1s. 3d. per pound, the return was al-

most twice as much.[13] The rush to plant in 1955 can be easily understood. In 1961, work on peasant cocoa returned roughly as much as work on copra, in 1954 cocoa was much more rewarding.

The labour cost of Vunamami cocoa seems higher than that of plantation cocoa, though plantation costs can be estimated only indirectly. In 1957 a ton of *dry* plantation cocoa cost £116.57, including a component of £36.73 (equal to 134 man-days) for native labor (Australia 1958:6–15). From this must be subtracted labour employed in fermenting. Fermenting, comparatively mechanized, cost Tolai ferementeries £28.90 per ton of dry beans, or 40 percent of the total cash costs of plantations. At most, fermenting amounts to 40 percent of the plantation labour, or 53 man-days; a more likely figure is around 30 man-days per ton. The labour costs of producing two and a half tons of *wet* beans on a plantation is thus between 81 and 100 man-days.

The inefficiency of Vunamami in cocoa, like the 1920 inefficiency in copra production, would seem to be due to defects in organization. Most obvious is the amount of time wasted in transporting cocoa to the fermentery—26 out of 140 days in my calculations. Much of this time is spent waiting for trucks or waiting at the fermentery for the clerk to weigh the baskets. Some saving is made, over the figure used, because a truckload of cocoa from some thirty growers is accompanied by only about ten of them, each one with the identification tags of several growers. (Against this, for areas smaller than the eight acres used in the example, the same amount of transportation time is needed for smaller quantities of beans.) Also, the grower waiting for a truck is not necessarily idle, for he may be weeding or otherwise tending his trees.

The organization of the cocoa industry draws largely on European initiative, and is still in a phase of adaptation to Tolai conditions. The present scheme, the cooperative Tolai Cocoa Project, will be considered in Chapter 7, but the situation in Vunamami developed before this project and these early arrangements will be described here.

[13] A grower price of £187 a ton represents a London price of about £300, after adding £30 for fermenting costs and £80 for marketing and transportation. Since these costs are more or less fixed, a London price drop to £170 as in 1961, cuts the grower price to about 2½*d.* per pound of wet beans.

Agricultural Extension Officers taught the value of centralized processing when they introduced the crop, and from the start advocated that the fermenteries accept beans only on one day each week so as to ensure large-volume ferments. In 1952 the group of growers in Vunamami Council decided to build a fermentery in the area where most cocoa was then growing, Ngatur. The growers were also active politically in the Vunamami Council, and obtained a loan from the Council, and the council clerk supervised the bookkeeping of what was called the Vunamami Cacao Marketing Account. The small fermentery began operations in October 1952. Extensions by July 1954 cost £259 6s. 6d. but the account had a favourable balance of £4,000. This was enough to cover £2,000 for a hot-air drier and £2,000 for a second payment to growers of ninepence per pound wet beans. Yet Agricultural Department officers realized that extensions financed so precariously could not meet the enormous increase in output in the next few years. The Tolai Cocoa Project was the direct outcome, taking over the Ngatur fermentery and extending it into a large and efficient unit.

From the start, growers in villages on the Toma Road had been allocated different account numbers from those at Ngatur, and they had brought their beans to the Talimut village plantation, where a clerk came to weigh them and issue payment. The volume of local beans reached practicable levels in the main flush of 1954 and a small fermentery was built at Talimut, though it required expansion, financed by a government loan of £1,000 in August 1955. The village plantation and the availability of land from the nearby, almost derelict plantation of Giregire determined the site. Large loans for expanding the fermentery later on had to be secured by the tax revenue of the Vunamami Council, so that participation in the Co-operative Cocoa Project was restricted to Council residents.

Vunamami village by 1961 was outside the ideal radius for using Talimut fermentery, but it did not have a sufficient volume of cocoa to justify a fermentery of its own; 40,000 trees is standard. Nor were there other Council residents near the coast that could join together for a coastal fermentery: the nearest Raluana village along the road had not entered a council, and plantations border Vunamami on the east and west. Use of plantation facilities was ruled out by the pattern of operation that the Vunamami growers had become used to. The Cocoa Project did not "buy" beans from growers. Beans remained the growers' property until final sale, with the Project acting as both processing and marketing agent. The Project (like the Copra Marketing Board) gave a first payment (often only as a first credit) when the wet beans were brought in. After selling the dry beans it made a final payment based on the volume of wet beans delivered, and the price realized for dry beans from that particular fermentery. Since 1961 these final payments have been made at six-month intervals to coincide with the non-flush periods of low income. Selling wet beans to plantations would mean returning to the dependent conditions of the 1920's and giving up the control over marketing which Vunamami people felt had contributed to much of their post-war prosperity.[14] The problem of a more convenient fermentery site had yet to be solved.

In other ways the labour for cocoa harvesting had become well organized. The weekly routine of pod collecting (*a ginigit*) on Monday and the opening of pods (*di puar ra kakau*) and selling of the beans on Tuesday was closely adhered to, and other tasks were also arranged on a weekly basis. The additional labour demands of the flush season could largely be met by the assistance of wives or other dependants. The possibility that seasonal demands might conflict with the less insistent and more regular demands for assistance in processing copra were met in an interesting way.

Aboriginally, there existed a right by the first-settling clan which owned the sacred men's (ancestral) places in the bush (*a taraiu*) to forbid (*watabu*) certain activities by erecting a sign (*a bagil*) composed of *tankets* and other shrubs.[15] This was commonly used, as in many other Pacific areas, to forbid the processing or picking of coconuts so that a large supply would be available when a ceremony was anticipated in three months' time. Until the 1950's *bagil* were used also to encourage efficient copra production, discouraging the wasteful expenditure of time and ef-

[14] This feeling was not shared by all Tolai villages in 1961, as I point out in Chapter 8. In Vunamami, however, there was an almost religious fervour over support for the Project. The raw figures for Table 6 shows no individual decline in sales to the Project that would suggest diversion of crops to plantation buyers in 1961. The decline in sales by early planters is the continuation of a trend of declining yields for them, masked in earlier years by additional acreages starting to bear.

[15] Other forms of taboo signs, like thrusting a dry coconut leaf into the ground (*a turaul*), are used to proclaim property rights, to bar roads, and so on.

fort on tiny quantities of nuts, preventing stealing by letting no one claim that he "was only borrowing a drinking-nut from a relative" when entering someone else's planting, and enabling driers to be used to capacity once they were fired. It also ensured that large amounts of cash became available on the expiry of the *bagil*, and this might be synchronized with tax collection, the organization of ceremonies, or the annual church fund-raising drive. In 1961 such a *bagil* was the first choice for raising money to buy Ravalien plantation, though in June 1955 Vunamami Council had agreed that it was time to discontinue *bagil*, since growers were now able to look after their own crops. In April 1961 all the villages near Vunamami erected *bagil*. The Vunamami *bagil* bore a sign reading "*A Watabu ure ra lama/Vunamami/April 14–June 26/1961* [A taboo on Vunamami coconuts]." The Vunabalbal sign was more elaborate: "*A bagil/Vunabalbal/April 21 1961 tuk tara July 30 1961/a warkurai dania ka iat/ure ra lama/Onaitariing @1/-.* [Vunabalbal's *bagil* from April 21st until July 30th 1961, by order of the village itself, applying to coconuts. Infractions 1/- fine.]" On the expiration of the Vunamami *bagil* those villagers present contributed eight inches of shell money each (*a pidik*) to a man of Tetegete-Balu clan, as thanks that the coconuts were "given back" to them by the founding ancestors of that clan. More practically, the *bagil* ensured that no one spent time on copra processing during the cocoa flush.[16]

Yet another way of assuring the labour of dependants and at the same time allowing the value of cocoa plantings to pass to the sons of the planters is the practice of using land belonging to the planter's wife and then registering the name of the planter's son as the cocoa grower at the fermentery. Of the first eighteen Vunamami names registered in 1954, four were then youths, the sons of important fathers. Even so, three of these four youths in 1961 were working away from Vunamami as skilled carpenters or drivers, and their fathers were employing casual labour on the bearing plantings, grossing over £200. One name on the list was that of a small child. Another "grower" at registration already had a large fully bearing acreage, planted for him by an uncle who was one of the earliest major growers at Ngatur. As soon as cocoa processing became sufficient to use his full-time labour, he

[16] It also meant that large incomes were available in August 1961 for ceremonials and for the church fund raising in September (see Chapter 7). This is now an established yearly cycle.

resigned his job as a government clerk and returned to his village to manage a portion of his uncle's acreage.

The practice was not confined to the rich early planters. Nine of the thirty-three growers registered between 1958 and 1961 were youths or small children. Two were women—one a widow with young children and one the elderly mother of a child "grower." Of twenty more growers I was told of, not yet registered because their cocoa was not yet bearing, six were women and three were absentee workers. One of the latter cases has already been described for its tenure complexities. The registered grower's father planted land east of Kokopo which belonged to his wife's clan, aided by his son who then became a migrant worker. The father later divorced his wife, and in 1961 she contested his right to harvest the incipient crop in the name of their son. The return of the son would solve the question, and this is likely to occur when the trees begin to bear. Migrant labour is a useful fill-in for a young man during the four years between the intensive work of first planting and full production.

Table 6, showing the crops harvested by the various categories of growers in each year, is translated in Table 7 to show the increasing time expenditures involved in cocoa harvesting and the patterns of income change involved. It will be seen that between 1953 and 1957 the thirty harvesters increased their time spent in

Table 6

COCOA CROPS OF VUNAMAMI GROWERS

Growers	1961 Effective Acreage (total)	Yields of Wet Beans in Pounds, by Years (00's omitted)							
		53–54	54–55	55–56	56–57	57–58	58–59	59–60	60–61
Ten earliest	48.17	42	62	97	179	181	237	230	207
Nine next	24.83	32	64	15	29	45	66	82	98
Eleven next	54.83	0	34	57	83	117	180	191	167
Seven later	19.33	—	—	—	—	2	13	19	24
Twelve next	39.67	—	—	—	—	—	3	26	56
Four latest	5.67	—	—	—	—	—	—	—	2
Total		74	160	169	291	345	499	548	554

Source: Talimut fermentery records. Crops grown in the area of Ngatur fermentery are omitted, as are the quantities credited to Talimut village plantation and to the Vunamami church account. Categories of growers are those used in Table 5.

harvesting from six days each per year to twenty-four days each. Even by 1961 they were spending only some forty days each, on an average of four effective acres of cocoa (or six acres interplanted). The other twenty-three growers were spending only

Table 7

VUNAMAMI INCOME AND LABOUR FOR COCOA HARVESTING

	53–54	54–55	55–56	56–57	57–58	58–59	59–60	60–61
Gross price for wet beans in pence per lb.	12	15	8	7	9	10	8	6
Aggregate income in £	371	1,001	564	842	1,289	2,078	1,822	1,384
Average income per grower in £	12	33	19	28	35	42	38	26
Harvesting labour in man-years	0.6	1.3	1.4	2.4	2.8	4.2	4.6	4.6
Return per man-day in shillings	40	50	27	23	31	33	27	21

SOURCE: Talimut fermentery records.

small amounts of time harvesting their smaller plots, but could expect their work to increase perhaps six times in the next few years.

After the phenomenal prices of 1954 and the relatively enormous returns to the earliest growers, there was a period of almost stable incomes as increases in the numbers of growers and the output of beans were matched by decreases in prices. Since 1960 world cocoa prices have been low, and the trend towards declining returns for labour input has probably continued.

During the cocoa era, one other crop was for a brief time a competitor for Vunamami interest: rice. Until 1950 shipping services were irregular, and considerable quantities of rice were still being grown, usually on a casual basis in garden areas principally devoted to green vegetables (*a ibika*). Husking the grain was a major chore, however. One of the first productive ventures of the Vunamami Council in 1950 was to invest in a hand-operated rice-husking machine, but even with this machine the volume of rice husked steadily declined. When the Council obtained a diesel generator in 1954 the rice-husker became power operated, but the decline continued. Nor was interest revived by teaching the techniques of rice-growing at the local Central School, which used the council machine for hulling the rice it grew. In the year 1957 the machine was hired only once, and from then to 1961, though it was oiled and maintained, it was not used at all. Rice can easily be grown in New Guinea and it is the main store-bought foodstuff, but its returns are too low to be competitive with cheap imported rice, which has been readily available since 1950.

LAND USE IN 1961

The patterns of land use and labour expenditure in 1961 are summed up in Appendix A and Appendix B. Here, I should like to put the detailed findings into the historical background and to show how the pattern will necessarily have to change as time goes on.

In 1961 subsistence gardening was still an important activity in Vunamami. These gardens contained a large variety of crops, including as the main staples *tigapu* or Chinese taro, and sweet manioc. A few bananas were grown, especially in the areas of seepage, in hollows or ravines. European vegetables such as beans, tomatoes, and cucumbers were grown where bonfires of roots had fertilized the soil. But the main crop was *ibika*, a shrubby plant growing up to four feet high, from which the shoots and dark green palmate leaves can be picked for cooking as a vegetable relish. It tastes like a bitter spinach and is the invariable accompaniment of Vunamami meals.[17] The few food gardens close to Vunamami—four plots still not planted to trees—and occasional unshaded areas near houses were all *ibika* gardens. A housewife feels she must have fresh *ibika* near her kitchen, and it was to meet the encroachment by male cash crops on this female preserve that the women's associations in 1963 purchased (at a high price) ten acres of Ravalien plantation.

The other main garden area for Vunamami was the new land at Kabakaul to the east of Kokopo. Housewives would walk out to Kabakaul and spend two or three days there, always returning with a load of *ibika*. These gardens did, however, have quite a

[17] An even more bitter leaf, *karakap*, is occasionally substituted as a delicacy. It is a low-growing herb, akin to a nettle. Both *ibika* and *karakap* can be cooked to European taste in coconut cream, which absorbs the bitterness.

few root crops and European vegetables growing in them, mostly for sale to plantation owners or to the European population of Kokopo. A common routine was for a woman to walk to Kabakaul on Thursday morning and to return early on Saturday with a load of fifty pounds of *tigapu* and thirty pounds of *ibika*. The *tigapu* would be sold in the market on the way home, and half of the cash used to buy taro from inland villagers. The *ibika* would be distributed to other women who would reciprocate the next week-end.

Ibika itself also provided some cash returns, about twelve bundles worth twelve shillings being bought each week by plantation labourers in Kokopo. And Vunamami women were the major suppliers of *ibika* stems for planting (termed *a inoa*) in Rabaul market, although this meant only that one Vunamami woman took in a load of fifteen one-shilling bundles every three weeks. It is noteworthy that *every* Vunamami woman sold produce in Kokopo market at least once during 1961, even those with husbands whose cash incomes were large enough to make market sales unnecessary. For women, selling in the market place is not essentially a means of obtaining cash income, but is rather a demonstration of gardening skill, in which specialty crops grown in Vunamami are exchanged (using shell money as a means of delaying the exchange) against specialty crops grown elsewhere. Vunamami, thanks to its women, still is (or could be if biscuits were not a prestige breakfast, and rice and corned beef a prestige evening meal) virtually self-sufficient in food crops, at a cost of only fifteen and a half acres of land and 11 percent of the labour of its farmers.

A few men also did some market gardening of vegetables for sale to Europeans in Kokopo. William ToKavivi and his brother were the most prominent, although they were not mainly dependent on market gardening for their livelihood. They lived right on the boundary of Ravalien plantation, and cultivated about ten acres of plantation land on a commercial scale. Unfortunately, in 1961 their production was not staggered sufficiently for the small market they served. Their lettuce, for example, glutted the market for three weeks and was largely unsold, whereas at other times lettuce was often unobtainable.

The remaining agricultural labour of Vunamami, and the remaining acreage, were about equally divided between copra and cocoa, between planting and cropping. These over-all figures in fact conceal great variations. The wealthier, landed men aged forty and over owned large plots of mature coconuts in Vunamami village, and included those early planters of cocoa who used the valleys and flat lands near Lumluvur ward. These are the "stable" areas of the village, and the time budgets of their owners also show stable work patterns. Two days a week were devoted to cocoa production, and four days a month to copra. They regularly attended meetings, ceremonials, markets, and so on.

The less wealthy men tended to have smaller acreages, often dispersed in other villages. Some had interplanted with cacao under the standing palms not long before 1961; others were still interplanting. In any case, their plantings were too small to occupy them on a regular basis—perhaps half a day being spent every other Monday collecting pods, and half of the following Tuesday taking beans to the fermentery. Monday morning would be taken up with corvée work for the Council, weeding local roads, and Tuesday afternoon would go in odd jobs near home. An occasional few days helping process someone else's copra, or fishing, or working for the church on Wednesday and marketing on Saturday—each a small block of time, inefficiently involving them in unnecessary travel—such was their pattern of work. They were not unemployed, but they were underemployed. Yet when an urgent task arose, like the clearing of virgin forest at the Warangoi in 1958, theirs was the labour that permitted it to be done. Without them the new land at Kabakaul could not have been quickly cleared and planted. But in the next five years their time will become more and more absorbed in cocoa harvesting.

The third main category of agriculturalists, and the third main category of land, was involved in the new plantings at Kabakaul and on the Warangoi. The eleven men with such land were mainly youngish men, between twenty-five and forty, with considerable education (category 2 in the time budgets) and often a paid white-collar position. Two of them were self-employed craftsmen (category 5) and had small acreages fairly near Vunamami which occupied them on Mondays and Tuesdays. When necessary tasks arose—a contract to build a dormitory on a plantation, for example—they worked at that job until it was finished, but every spare moment went on tending the new plantings, whole blocks of time being involved. In ten years they would be rich land-owners, fully occupied harvesting their copra and cocoa, and in fact in the same position as the old élite of 1961.

CONCLUSIONS

At a casual glance, Vunamami agriculture in 1961 would appear to conform to the classic type of peasant agriculture: land short and capital short, and involving considerable underemployment. The expensive capital equipment of plantations is lacking and human labour is used instead. Productivity per acre is low, and fragmentation and subdivision of holdings are common.

It is a form of agriculture that is roundly condemned by plantation owners and agriculturalists. Plantation owners believe that this is a waste of land in low per acre productivity, in a country where highly productive plantations cannot obtain more land because of discriminatory regulations against land alienation. With reason, they complain of the failure of Vunamami farmers to use sprays, fertilizers, and pruning equipment for their cacao trees. Black-pod and other cocoa diseases were spreading in 1961, and despite teachings by agricultural extension officers little was being done to combat disease within the area of Vunamami. Europeans see the underemployment as laziness by choice and say, "Why don't they come and work on plantations?"

There is some foundation for their criticism. Vunamami cocoa production is inefficient even in terms of productivity per man-day, and it is very vulnerable to diseases and decreasing yields. Both techniques and organization are still rudimentary and agricultural research could help a great deal. Greater capital investment (e.g., in fertilizers) would probably increase yields and might increase the efficiency of labour on small plots. Copra production, though efficient in terms of labour input, needs attention to the long-term problems of replacing senescent palms. Additional work is needed at times for the underemployed.

Yet Vunamami agriculture has, over the years, shown itself to be highly flexible, and its 1961 condition must be looked at from that point of view. Investment is being made, and in a highly rational way. Cash is the scarcest resource, with labour and land being relatively available. Vunamami farmers invest by planting new land with cash crops, spending 10.2 percent of their time in such investment (Appendix E). They have increased the area under cash crops by 105 acres over the period of roughly 1955 to 1961, constituting an increase of around 3 percent per annum in the total acreage under cultivation. A net investment of 10.2 percent of gross annual income (involving a 30 percent investment by the most forward-looking group of youngish but wealthy farmers) would put Vunamami farmers on a par with countries like Chile, Mexico, Argentina, or Canada in 1920, in Rostow's (1960:44) tabulation of ratios between net investment and G.N.P. In its agriculture this is a growth economy, though of a sort that differs from plantation growth.

It may be suggested that Vunamami growth is uneven, since it depends basically on eleven enterprising farmers. This is not necessarily bad. Recently the net investment in land improvement by even the less wealthy has approached the average figure of 10.2 percent, being now about 9 percent. The people who pull the average figure down are the older wealthy farmers, but their low investment in land improvement (2 percent) is easy to explain, since they made their land investment five years earlier and are now fully involved in harvesting the proceeds. As later chapters will show, they seek avenues for investment of their high cash incomes. Their time-expenditure figures indicate that they are so far mainly interested in trading or business activities, but to a limited extent they are making cash investments in their land. The two men who bought sprayers for disease control in 1961 and the men who hire "foreign" labourers to care for their plantations belong to this group. On their larger acreages plantation techniques are most likely to be effective. They, then, are beginning to invest along lines that are more familiar to agricultural economists.

The uneven pattern of growth seen in Vunamami at one moment of time is but a reflection of how any changing economy must appear in cross-section. Any such economy has a dynamic part and a less dynamic part, with the less dynamic part imitating the dynamic part after a time lag—in a cocoa-growing economy a lag of five years. There must also be a group of young men, destined to be dynamic leaders but currently unsuccessful, who are ready to adopt new dynamic innovations in the future. It is, in fact, a good sign that not everyone is uniformly spraying and fertilizing his cocoa, for it gives added confidence to the prediction that, as the mass of less wealthy new planters become more fully involved in cocoa harvesting over the next decade, they too will begin to adopt practices now used experimentally by the few. By then, the prediction would be, the dynamic few will have progressed to something new.

The growth and flexibility of Vunamami contrasts markedly with what Geertz (1963*b*) has called "agricultural involution," or the state where labour-intensive cultivation practices are used, resulting in steadily decreasing returns per unit of labour input, but where there develops such a degree of involvement in the techniques used that they cannot be changed. Labour-intensive practices tend to make agriculture the stagnant, low-wage sector of a national economy. It implies underemployment of the rural population.

In Vunamami underemployment is present, but it is restricted to a few categories of workers. Even they can earn during two days of work on their plantings almost as much as they would earn working for five and a half days on a plantation. The avenues of spare-time employment open to them, such as fishing or casual labour for fellow-villagers, even though offering very low returns, make them better off than full-time plantation labourers. There is little incentive for them, the followers, to experiment with labour-intensive techniques of cash cropping. Wage rates remain high in Vunamami.

This availability of alternative occupations, as has been shown, has always made it hard for wealthy men to obtain hired labour. No one consents to call anyone else "master," much as Adam Smith observed in explaining the rapid growth of American wealth before the Revolution. The unsuccessful farmer cannot cease farming and become an absentee landlord, so he works on the land himself and continues experimenting with ways to save his own, highly valued time. He may then diversify his enterprise into other fields, but agriculture remains, as in Vunamami, an active growth sector of the economy. An abundance of land, as was discussed in the Introduction and as Adam Smith showed, is basic to this pattern. What I believe the Vunamami case shows is that the availability of alternative occupations is also a necessary condition if the general wage rate is to remain high and the labour-intensive road to stagnation is to be avoided.[18]

[18] Eighteenth-century North America also had this diversity of alternative occupations, thanks to the complex technology of craft production that had been brought from Europe and to the diversified consumption patterns involved. It was in this area, I think, that the demonstration effect of earlier advances in Europe was most important in facilitating American economic dynamism. The lack of alternative occupations in countries having no immigration from technologically advanced areas may well explain the difficulty encountered in starting economic growth.

IV

Wage Labour

In Vunamami there may at first appear to be no indigenous concept of wage labour. What Kleintitschen (1906:237) says about indigenous feelings is clearly accurate, even today: no Tolai willingly submits to any other person, to become his servant or his employee. Wage labour as Europeans define it did not exist in 1875.

EMPLOYMENT CONCEPTS

Yet as we have seen in the discussion of how big men obtained "help" (*marawut*) in planting new areas of land, it was possible to get additional labour for large-scale tasks, supplementing household labour which sufficed for regular jobs. The principle underlying both casual help and household work was one of reciprocity: you help me today in building my house, and I would do the same for you in a month's time; as a member of the household you did your job while everyone else did theirs, and everyone benefited equally. The initiator of a task and his helpers were equals, freely and reciprocally assisting one another. An initiator would acknowledge his indebtedness by feeding those who were helping him, and perhaps giving them gifts when the work was finished; he would treat his workers as members of the family or as guests, and would *wapuak* (support) them as he would his children. In practice, the principle of reciprocal help covered, as it still does today, a more asymmetrical relationship in which one person did all the helping, without reciprocity, and the other did all the supporting. In modern Tolai the word *wapuak* is commonly used of a salary, and in such cases it pays for wage labour, though the principle is still one of reciprocity and equality.

Fishing provides some of the clearest examples of how the market for casual labour worked indigenously. The technology of fishing has already been well described (Parkinson 1907:95–106, Bley 1900:107–112, etc.), and since I have discussed elsewhere the economics of the fishing industry along the Kokopo Sub-district coast (Salisbury n.d.), I shall merely summarize here. The main techniques are the use of fish traps (*a wup*) and large nets (*a ubene*) that are pulled onto the beach after encircling schools of fish. Four-man canoes are used to inspect the anchored traps and to tow the nets; larger canoes are used to carry out the traps along with their floats and their anchors to a distance from shore. All the canoes and traps are individually owned, as are some of the nets, although big ones valued at up to £100 are usually owned by a group or association (*a kivung*).

The major recurrent task in trap fishing is inspecting the traps and extracting any fish that have been caught. Two men can do this, but usually three go along—one to hold onto the float, one to raise the trap, and one to take out the fish, mostly mackerel weighing between seven and ten pounds. Owners do not have to visit their traps personally in their own canoes; it is customary for any crew of men at the fishing beach or *motonoi* to inspect all the anchored traps in any available canoe. A fixed portion of the catch then goes to the owners of the traps and of the canoes—half the total catch to the trap owner, and one fish to the canoe owner —and the rest goes to the crew. The first claim, however, is that one fish goes to the crew to be eaten on the beach.

The owning of canoes and traps can thus be seen as a business investment, on which a return is received. It will be discussed in Chapter 7. Crewing is essentially unskilled labour for the benefit of the canoe and trap owners. The returns for crewing can be estimated from the records of thirty-seven occasions when I was present when traps were visited. On the average, crews received 0.46 fishes per head per morning's work as pay in kind, plus one-ninth of a fish to eat on the beach. Fish can all be sold at a standard rate of one per fathom of *tabu* (shell money), making the return for about five hours of crewing equal to half a fathom, plus food.

Reciprocity is involved to some extent. A small number of men are regular fishermen, who go to the beach perhaps every other day. They mostly own canoes and have fish traps at anchor, so that when birds are seen flying over the traps and the call goes out that fish are in them, they make up the crew and use one or other regular fisherman's canoe. Among them there is reciprocity, for today crew member A may go out in individual B's canoe, and find fish only in individual C's trap; tomorrow he may go out in his own canoe and find fish in B's traps; on the next day individual C may go out and find fish in A's traps. But there are also casual visitors at the beach, or young men not yet owning a canoe and still learning how to weave fish traps, who are only too willing to work for a morning with the near certainty of a meal, and the expectation of half a fathom of *tabu* as well. Reciprocity is unlikely for such young men, who form a labour pool.

For net fishing there is also a need for regular labour. About nine men are needed, four ready to paddle the canoe should a school be sighted, paying out one end of the net, while another four hold firmly to the other end on the beach. When the school is encircled both parties haul in the net, while other men plunge into the water behind the net to keep fish from leaping out. All nine work together to clean the net and hang it up to dry. The nucleus of a work group is usually the owners of the net, but others on the beach will assist. The large fish all go to the owners of the net, and are sold by them as a business; the smaller ones are divided among the workers nominally as food for them to eat on the beach, although there are usually some left over to take home to their families. Although the return to net owners is high, the return for unskilled labour is merely food, though often in quite large quantities. It is also noteworthy that there is virtually no chance of non-owners having their work reciprocated, since there is rarely more than one large net at any *motonoi*. Some major partners in net-owning groups also provide only capital and rarely work on the beach; they are employers only.

A further instance of non-reciprocal labour in the fishing industry is provided by the manufacture of fish traps. Although almost everyone nominally makes his own, putting in about ten days' work, what often happens is that a skilled man makes only the most difficult part of his trap—the springy central core through which fish enter, but through which they cannot escape. He then gets a less skilled person, often one of the youths mentioned above, to do the tedious job of tying hundreds of cane strips to the spacing rings to make the basket. Food is provided while a youth is so working, and usually a final present equivalent to about half a fathom of *tabu* for a day's work. Reciprocity is again possible, for the skilled man may eventually make a core for the youth, but it does not necessarily occur.

But the anchoring of fish traps is the occasion of reciprocity

par excellence. This job requires a group of at least ten men to
paddle three large canoes and to dive for the coral to weight the
"anchor" basket. The trap owner announces a launching widely,
and well in advance so that all owners whom he has previously
helped, or who wish his help in the future, are able to attend.
Such a group receives only a meal on return to the beach, though
tabu must be given to the owners of the canoes used. Each launching involves most of the trap owners at a *motonoi,* and the names
of people present are remembered.

Before 1875, housebuilding and clearing bush for planting gardens were the main tasks requiring large labour forces. Bush
clearing on a large scale is now rare in Vunamami, and modern
housebuilding is usually a job for a skilled carpenter rather than
for a large crew of unskilled workers. But occasionally, even
in 1961, tasks of the old sort served to illustrate the general principles of labour payment.

I have already described how entire villages willingly spent
days at the Warangoi clearing virgin forest "for the Council,"
essentially without any return except that it was "their" Council,
which reciprocated by "helping the people." The Council on such
occasions provided transport, housing at the Warangoi in large
sheds, and a limited amount of food, mostly from members of the
village who did not come to work. On a smaller scale in the clearing of newly acquired land at Kabakaul, Beniona and others recruited large labour forces to cut the kunai and bush in return for
one big feast and some foodstuffs at other times. The major incentive for such work would seem to be to obtain permission to
use cleared areas as garden sites while the owner's coconuts are
immature. In this way the exchange could be seen as work for
food, though on a delayed basis.

A similar reputedly traditional practice which I witnessed in
connection with the weeding of a vegetable garden was called *di
kul ra bung*—"they buy the day." The principle of "buying days"
is that the individual needing a work team advertises when he wants
it. Everyone who turns up on that day receives his food, and in
addition some large gift or entertainment is given to the group as
a whole. On the occasion I witnessed, the workers were members
of a corporate Women's Group[1] (*kivung kai ra waden*) and the

---

[1] This *kivung* or association was based primarily in Vunabalbal village,
and was independent of (though overlapping in membership with) the two
associations described in Chapter 7.

payment went into group funds. Potential reciprocity was evidenced by the fact that the wife of the man whose garden was weeded was herself a member of the group, and would presumably work for other members who later "bought a day."

Housebuilding on the same village basis as for the clearing of bush at the Warangoi occurred periodically. Every Sunday after church the jobs for the coming week on the village schools, the church, or the missionary's house, would be read out. Frequently these involved house construction—a new schoolteacher's house or an additional classroom of native materials, repairs to the church, or a new house for the minister. Monday was the day for any government work, such as school or road repairs, and Wednesday was the day for mission work. Turnout for such work was good, at least among those not employed in wage labour elsewhere; major projects were considered almost as a holiday, and a meal was usually available afterwards, especially if the work was done for an individual like the schoolteacher or the minister.

A more sophisticated version of the same practice occurred at Balanataman during my stay. Three villages of Balanataman, Keravi, and Nanuk had tendered £70 for a large government timber-frame building, due for demolition in Rabaul (see Salisbury 1967) and when their tender was successful had taken it to pieces and shipped each section to the village at a cost of £48 10s. Three Raluana carpenters, on contract, had built concrete footings, and had assembled each side of the building separately on the ground. Word was sent to nearby villages that there would be a "school raising" on the thirtieth of August. I went with the Rev. Elias ToVutnalom and a small group from Vunamami, and in all about fifty men and forty women appeared. After a short service and a sermon on Jesus' schooling, the whole group joined in raising the fifty-foot-long frames into position while the carpenters nailed braces at the corners, and the first nails were blessed. When the frame was in position the trenches around the footings were filled in and some fifteen hundred cubic feet of earth was brought in baskets and two wheelbarrows to raise the inside level. In three hours the frame was ready for roofing. By one-thirty all the workers were eating taro cooked in coconut and fish, and when they left they each received a basket of food. My own weighed about four pounds, and contained sweet potato in coconut cream with a little fresh fish and an unopened seven-and-a-half-ounce tin of mackerel.

Elements of a festival, of publicizing the school buildings and of entertaining distinguished guests all enter into the situation, as they do with most large projects. It can hardly be argued that a communal work bee was the cheapest way of raising the frame; a day's crane rental would have cost £6. Yet without the use of cash or sophisticated equipment such jobs can be done, and large labour forces recruited, provided reciprocity is envisaged; the food keeps workers happy, and the work becomes almost a sport.

The second way of obtaining the assistance of outside workers in a way that need not necessarily entail reciprocity is the technique of "adopting" a worker into the household. Bürger (1913: 21) describes this practice as *warmamel*, though I did not hear this term used, only the more general one of *wapuak*. Several Vunamami men in 1961 had adopted outsiders into the household and were feeding them and housing them and giving them periodic presents. The outsiders performed whatever tasks were delegated to them but were otherwise free to do as they wished.

One of the individuals concerned, Bonomi, an expert fisherman from the Sepik District, first settled in Vunamami village on this basis in about 1910, though he left shortly before the Second World War and returned only about 1950. The custom is clearly an old one, extended in its present form to non-Tolai; before 1875 it undoubtedly existed in the form of big men "adopting" distant affinal or classificatory kin. A resident work force, usually of single males without land of their own, could provide the means not only for extending the household head's landholdings but for giving him political power. Household heads now commonly refer to an adopted employee as "my boy" (*kaugu bul*), though this may be a translation of pidgin usage.

Adoptive employees are indeed still often distant kinsmen. Two men in Vunamami had classificatory fathers living with them, whom they "looked after" with food and such. In return the "fathers" washed clothes, cleaned the house, gathered food, and washed dishes. When I was looking for a household servant I was persuaded by a friend to take the brother of one of the "classificatory fathers" into my house. It was phrased as though I were doing my friend a favour, "looking after" his "father" for him, rather than that I was employing a servant. In three other cases, distant young relatives were living at Sunam, working the blocks of older men in return for food, housing, and a monthly salary.

In five other cases the adoptive employees were non-Tolai. One, Bonomi the fisherman, did not live in the same house as his sponsor, but in his boathouse. He looked after the sponsor's canoe and worked on his fish traps, but had much time free. He owned his own canoe, crewed very frequently, and did skilled repairs (in return for presents) for any member of the village. His sponsor, in providing him with food, was really performing a public service in retaining a handyman and permanent caretaker of the *motonoi*. Three other employees were from New Ireland, Talasea, and the Highlands and were specifically looking after their sponsors' cocoa within the village areas. All had come to the Kokopo area to work on plantations and after their time was up had sought work in the area instead of returning to their villages. The fifth individual was a youth from Kainantu. A Tolai policeman from another village befriended him while serving in Kainantu, and in order that he could get the advantages of schooling in the Gazelle area, he had been adopted by a female relative of the policeman. In return for his board he did odd jobs around the house, like a member of the family of the same age.

The last group of "adopted employees" were adopted in only the most tenuous sense. They were plantation labourers who, on their week-ends off, came to work for Vunamami landowners. They received a cash wage for this, but what appeared more influential in getting them to work was the prospect of a week-end out of the plantation barracks and in a village, eating fresh food instead of rice and tinned meat. Though Tolai have no respect for plantation workers—the term used for them is *"a wok"*—they seemed to be sorry for them and to offer them many of the "comforts of home." As can be seen, there is a wide range of situations that can be covered under the principle that a person working for a household is doing so in exchange for his keep.

Both reciprocal casual work and "adoptive employment" fall clearly in indigenous thought in the domain of subsistence activities: both are for food (*a nian*). There is a third area which Europeans would categorize as wage employment, but which is outside the indigenous ideas of subsistence: the hiring out of specialist skills. The general term for paying such a specialist is that *di tokom ia*—"one hires, or rents him." The payment is a *totokom*. The same word is used for the rental of a material object such as a canoe, or a motor vehicle, and also for the payment of taxes. These latter usages will be discussed in Chapters 7 and 8; here I shall discuss only the hiring of traditional specialists.

An indigenous profession that is still active is that of composing songs and dances, and this will serve to illustrate the pattern of specialist employment. To become a composer, or at least to become a composer whom people will hire, requires that one obtain an "authentic" source of inspiration. There are a small number of such expert sources, and they are particularly common in the Duke of Yorks and in northern New Ireland and Lavongai. The aspirant pays the expert for his teaching, and receives some special betel nuts (*a buai na pepe*, or *a buai na kodakodo*) from a palm near the expert's own source of inspiration (*a kaia*). He returns home to grow his own palm from the nuts, as his personal source of inspiration. The inspiration is felt to be like a dream in which a spirit (*a tabaran*) shows a vision (*wartetenia*); a composer's personal spirit is sometimes referred to as a *turangan* (guardian spirit), or sometimes as *ra buai kai ToAn* (the betel of Mr. So-and-so). A typical invocational song opening is "*Pilak ra buai kai ToMelem*" (Choose the betel of Mr. Expert . . .).

As his outlay for admission to the profession or for "raising (*watut*) the *tabaran*" an aspirant pays his master some fifty fathoms of shell money. He himself can then charge a fee of twenty to thirty fathoms for each song he composes. For every *matamatam* (clan ancestral ceremony) about twelve dances and songs are needed, each performed by a different village, under the sponsorship of an important leader there. The *matamatam* frequency of once every three years in each village means that a dance team from a particular village performs somewhere about four times a year. It gives a sponsor prestige to stage a new dance (although he does not always do so), so that there is a possible average of commissions for composers of two or three a year for every village. In practice, of course, the number of commissions any composer receives depends on his reputation.

In 1961 there were two active composers in Vunamami village; one had only one commission and the other had three. A composer from Balanataman, whom I met at every *matamatam* I went to, must have been employed almost full time. Each commission involves the composer in about two weeks of seclusion in the bush while he composes and teaches the song and the steps to two assistants. While in seclusion he and the dance leaders are fully fed and housed by the sponsor. When the dance is ready the three emerge from seclusion and show what they have done. The composer plays the drums while the leaders dance and are joined by villagers who wish to be in the eventual team. After a ceremonial meal, skeins of *tabu* are handed over to the composer and his assistants; during the next few weeks the composer attends most rehearsals, and, of course, the eventual performance. Twenty to thirty fathoms can be seen as the wage for two or three weeks of composing; at ten shillings per fathom this would mean an annual wage to full-time composers of £260 plus full board and lodging.

Canoe building is another important profession, although the master carvers employed in Vunamami all come from the Duke of York Islands. Enos Teve in 1957 commissioned a ten-man canoe, said to be the first on the coast, and for the month's work involved he paid the master carver 200 fathoms. Four Vunamami men worked with the carver, doing the routine chipping of parts marked out. All the carving party was fed and lodged, and the assistants received ten fathoms of *tabu* as a gift at the end of the month. It will be noted that the rate for assistance is in the neighbourhood of half to one-third of a fathom daily, as it is for crewing. The annual rate for a full-time master carver would be £1,200.

Other skills in varying demand are those of carvers of dance sticks (*a bair*) and slit-gongs (*a garamut*), and the making of cores for fish traps. The two skilled *bair* carvers in Vunamami did not receive any commission in 1961, but they normally charge five fathoms for a stick that may take two days to carve. I heard of no cases of anyone's being paid to make a fish-trap core in 1961—there were enough skilled men for demand to be met by their making cores on a reciprocal labour basis—but on a *tokom* basis the rate is two fathoms for about a single day's work. An expert *garamut* carver receives fifty fathoms for a commission of about two months (Laufer 1961:467).

Before 1875 the number of skills payable in this way must have been much greater. The production of stone adzes and of the wide range of clubs described by early writers has completely ceased. Early writers talk of the large fees charged by sorcerers,[2] for using love magic (*a malira*), for causing harm or death through the *ingiet*, or for working divinations. People may still pay for the working of love magic, as I was secretly shown many techniques,

[2] The amount charged by the inventor of the bullet-repelling ointment in 1894 is reported as 1,000 fathoms, but this was undoubtedly exceptional.

but no one admitted either to doing so or to accepting a fee. *Ingiet* practices were openly described, because they were something that people no longer did.

Although it is dangerous to generalize from 1961 to pre-1875 (for I have been unable to find any mention of early rates of pay for specialist services), the idea of high and graduated payment for different degrees of skill would seem to be an aboriginal one. There is indeed a full vocabulary for referring to such skills. There is the general word for a master craftsman, *a melem*, who is an expert in (*ila tana*) his special skill; an ordinary skilled person is a *tena* in the special skill, and it will be remembered that when the *melem* shows him skills he *wartetenia*, or makes him a *tena*. The word *tena* can be used extremely widely: a baby can be *a tena tinangi* (who always cries), and a habitual liar is *a tena vaongo*. In addition to the generic term *a totokom*, there are also specific terms for each specific payment.

One other sort of skill that is not paid for by individual employers but on a community basis is that of many ritual specialists who benefit the entire community. In payment for witnessing a performance, all individuals contribute, and the collection goes to the performer. Such contributions are called a *nidok* and usually amount to about eight inches of *tabu* per person; contributors *dok* the performer, and an audience of one hundred for a *tubuan* ceremony would result in a ten-fathom *nidok* taken by the sponsor. The way in which *nidok* can be used almost as a profit-making business will be discussed in Chapter 8, but a non-profit example will suffice to illustrate the "skilled employment" aspect— that of the tabooing of coconuts described in Chapter 3. The men who ritually imposed the taboo, and later removed it, Alwas ToMatinur and Polos ToPultima, were individuals of appropriate clans who had acquired the skills needed for the ceremony. They would have been able to collect a shilling from each person who broke the taboo, in return for averting the supernatural consequences from him; when they removed the taboo, each person present—and this included most of the village—paid a *nidok* of one shilling. In practice, Polos acted as the treasurer of the church fund, and the entire proceeds of about £5 went into the fund.

THE HISTORY OF WAGE LABOUR

Let us now look at the arrival of Europeans and the way in which it affected the indigenous labour market. Parkinson (1887:78–79) tells of the first day on which, with a group of fifteen Bukas, he set out to clear kunai for planting coconuts. It was a market day, and numbers of Tolai, many of whom must have been from Vunamami, passed by. First a few stayed to watch, and then more, until the work team was surrounded by armed men. Parkinson kept his hand on his revolver, but heard everyone talking of *papalum*. Shortly after, first one, and then many men joined in, until everyone was helping. At the end of the day he realized that *papalum* meant work. He gave everyone tobacco, and people were pleased, saying "A lot of work, a lot of tobacco; little work, little tobacco."

Tinai, a man of almost ninety in 1961, put this story in perspective. As has been said, the payments given by Parkinson and Queen Emma were regarded as payments for adoption into the local communities, and thus for the right to live there, to make gardens, and to gather nuts. Clearing bush for gardens (another meaning of the term *papalum*) is a task where reciprocal work is normal; they helped Parkinson, and in return he gave them the only "food" that Europeans brought with them—tobacco. Considerable planting of palms was done on the same basis; Parkinson was a member of the community. He further reinforced this picture of his position by accepting the many gifts of food and produce that local people brought—payment was refused by the local people, for one does not sell food to fellow-villagers. On the other hand, return gifts of tobacco were made rather freely, and periodically Parkinson did what other big men do—he gave a feast and a dance (*matamatam*), and in that way reciprocated the small food gifts. His Buka labourers were part of his household, and he took care of them as any Tolai household head would do, providing them with housing, food, tools, and periodic gifts in return for their help.

The missions, too, fitted into the pattern. Dr. Brown brought with him his assistants, teachers from Fiji and Samoa, and looked after them, feeding them and providing for their wants. We have already (Chapter 1) seen the list of goods that each one received for the period when Brown was away. Local people who were accepted into the church were also looked after, if not quite so well. Clothing was particularly important as the return gift from the mission to its faithful servants. We have also seen the success of the Roman Catholic policy of giving lengths of cloth to each parishioner who attended church for seventeen consecutive weeks. This was not just bribery. For the people it was the mark that the wearer had been accepted into the (very extended) "house-hold" of the mission. The extreme version of this adoption was the Roman Catholic buying of orphans and slaves to form a board-ing school and settlement at Vunapope. They were completely "of the mission."

The Methodists also insisted that a village "adopt" its teacher; that it give him land, build him a house, and provide him with food. The teacher in return provided skills and teaching, and oc-casional presents of tobacco, cloth, hoop iron, and the like. Vil-lages, as has been described, vied with one another for the privilege of having their resident teacher. The missionaries became, not out-siders in a foreign country but, from the villagers' point of view, "our missionary" or "our teacher."

Kleintitschen (1906:58) thought this phrasing silly, commenting that people "are proud that *their* missionary [my emphasis] or European has a boat, as they like to pass themselves off as co-owners." Because of this they were always willing in 1900 to pad-dle canoes for missionaries, with the missionary providing food and a small payment. My interpretation would be that, although by 1900 readiness to work for European employers was at a low ebb, a job like paddling a canoe gave a sense of being a partner with the employer in an exchange of services, rather than of being a hired hand. Kleintitschen comes closer to this explanation when he says that people were also ready to carry messages, "as it made them feel important." The importance was that of being the part-ner of the message sender. All the sender needed was to give the message carrier sufficient tobacco to smoke on the journey.

But while missionaries and the Parkinsons could preserve the sense of reciprocity in their relationships with villagers, most Euro-peans gave no opportunity for any such feeling. They shouted at local people, hit them, and would not listen to what they had to say. Even Dr. Brown's pleased noting of a native remark that *"Missionary he no savvy fight him me fellow"*—an anglicised version of pidgin "Missionaries do not hit us"—gains additional importance as a recognition as early as 1878 of the asymmetrical relationship demanded by most Europeans other than missionaries. The virtual refusal by Tolai to sign on for employment with re-cruiters of plantation labour, while New Irelanders flocked aboard, as remarked on by both Parkinson and Danks, further illustrates this early aversion to European-style wage labour. For the few without land, *tabu*, or family, however, even work for Europeans on such a basis might be preferable to "adoption" into the household of an overbearing Tolai; tobacco, rice, and meat might be preferable to an insufficiency of native foods: there were exceptions to the general rule.

Around 1895 a new pattern began, as sympathetic administrators like Dr. Hahl also began treating local people as human beings, learning their language and listening to what they said. To become adopted into the household of such employers was to retain a sense of equality, and Vunamami people began working as house servants. I have already mentioned how Dr. Hahl's cook of fifty years before pressed me for news of how his "little girl" Berta now was. Much the same sort of "family relationship" prevailed in the police force—as it still did in the 1950's (see McCarthy 1963)—with the police as the protectors of the European patrol officer on expeditions into the bush, and the officer "looking after" his men's food, their work, and even their personal problems. Two Vunamami residents still living in 1961 had been policemen under the Germans.

By 1900, as Kleintitschen and others noted, the readiness of Tolai to enter into (casual) wage labour had declined markedly. Kleintitschen attributes this cynically to constitutional laziness and to the availability of money from the new Tolai coconut plantings. As has been shown in Chapter 3, at this time any landless youth or orphan could be "adopted" by a Vunamami landowner wishing to extend his plantings; why should such a youth wish to engage in non-reciprocal labour? The availability of money is also not the right explanation, because those who supplied casual labour were not those who obtained money from copra. Kleintitschen was right, however, in so far as the wages paid by Europeans were seen as worth less (taking into account the conditions of work) than the returns from Tolai employers. In one case, however, Kleintitschen notes (1906:57) that there was a readiness to work for Europeans on a paid basis—as carpenters. Again he interprets this cynically, as being due to the opportunities for pilfering nails and materials, for there was a sudden surge of demand for plank-built houses. I should interpret the same interest in carpenters' work as a desire to learn skills for future employment in villages, and as due to the father-son type of relationship between a carpenter and his assistant. I do not know the rates of pay for assistant carpenters in 1904, and so cannot say whether this work was also more attractive financially.

The pattern of Vunamami employment thus became set for the next twenty years: personal service with (not *for*) Europeans (including the police force), an aversion to unskilled plantation labour, and an interest in skilled trades. As we have already seen, in the 1920's this pattern was altered by a decline in Vunamami incomes, an increase in population, and a decrease in the amount of work for village employers, when Vunamami lands were fully planted to coconuts. A few more skilled occupations opened up. Three Vunamami men were accepted as ministers in the Methodist Mission. One Vunamami man had been a driver for a plantation near Kokopo in the 1920's. In the later 1920's the District Officer, Edward Taylor, hired the first Tolai as a clerk in the government offices, Alwas ToMatinur. But the number of such jobs remained small. Young men without land began to engage for work on nearby plantations as the returns from village employment dropped and work became intermittent. Fishing, by all accounts, became much more popular. The 1926 gold strike at Edie Creek and the subsequent large-scale mining at Bulolo and Wau provided some new employment opportunities. But still Vunamami men opted for personal service occupations: of the men in Salamaua or Wau at the Japanese invasion only one of those over twenty-five (though a larger number of the youths) was doing mining work.

As far as it is possible to reconstruct the pattern of the later 1930's from the work histories of men still alive in 1961, some 37 percent of those employed by Europeans were in white-collar occupations, and all but two of these were working for the Methodist Mission, one as a minister, two as missionaries, one as a typesetter, and one as a teacher trainee; one man was a government clerk and another was a government teacher trainee. All except the trainees and one missionary were over twenty-five. Two men, or 11 percent of the employed, were in semi-skilled blue-collar work —an older man as a carpenter, and a younger man as a driver. The remaining 52 percent of the employees were relatively unskilled. One older man worked as a labourer locally, and one was in the police force; the other eight, or 42 percent of the wage employees, were in mainland New Guinea, five at least of them as house servants.

Twelve of the thirty-one whose histories were obtained were working on their own land in Vunamami or were fishing, but this probably underrepresents the number of farmers, since the histories of many obvious homebodies were not collected. No man born before 1914 seems to have gone to mainland New Guinea, whereas nearly 60 percent of the males under twenty-five years of age in the sample were working there when the Japanese invasion came. Thirteen Vunamami men in all were cut off from the village by the war.

A sample work history of this generation—one that was badly depleted in 1949 when the nine men died after drinking Japanese methyl alcohol—is that of Punion. Born in 1917, he had only a village mission school education when he went to work at Kinabot plantation at the age of fourteen. He spent about three years there, and then helped his father in the village for awhile before signing on again as a cook in Kokopo for a Mr. Brazier. Two years there were followed by marriage and more time in the village, and then a period as personal servant to a patrol officer, based in Salamaua, but spending much time patrolling the bush. When his employer was transferred after eighteen months to the Sepik, Punion was left in Salamaua as servant to the manager of the Salamaua Club. His employer went on leave soon after, and Punion returned to Vunamami for three months. On returning to Salamaua to complete his time he learned that his employer had died; his contract was taken over by the Salamaua Hotel, where he was working when the Japanese arrived. They took him to Lae to build airstrips, but when the Allies landed he "went bush" to the Wain country. He later returned and was employed by the Allies, again building airstrips, spending time at Moresby, Lae, Goodenough Bay, Bilibili, Finschhafen, Gasmata, and Jacquinot Bay, where he was on V-J Day. He had risen to the job of foreman and had learned considerable skills as a mechanic and carpenter.

On his return to the village he was appointed *luluai*. He built the first post-war copra drier with scrap metal, and was a member of the "Komiti" of villages near Vunamami which preceded the Council. In 1961, his copra and cocoa plantings were about average, but he operated one of the busiest and most profitable copra driers in the village. He was the person turned to whenever a village automobile needed repairs. He was trusted and much respected as a solid citizen, who, although he was not an outspoken or an aggressive leader, was heeded when he spoke. In his quiet, comfortable way he had been the chief male helper of the women's association in the village. Despite his gay and adventurous youth (and as a participant in the methyl alcohol party he was saved only by forcing himself to vomit when the first man dropped dead), he

was a warm, rotund family man. His two sons, born in 1937 and
1939, had received a good education. The older one was a sergeant
in the Pacific Islands Regiment (Service Corps section); the
younger, after Malaguna Technical, and training as a medical
orderly, lost his job for drinking and helped his father. His post-
war family were all still at school, and formed a closely knit
group.

Punion was, of course, above average in his abilities, and was one
of the senior members of the group that was in New Guinea during the war. This group was one of old comrades, uniting people
from many villages. When they got together their conversations
sounded the same as those of their European counterparts, the
"Old Territory Hands" (*man blong bipo*), with reminiscences of
Tiger Lil of Salamaua, of Coastwatcher *kiaps* and wartime airstrips. The dean of them all was Nason ToKiala, president of Vunadidir Council, whose employment history went back to early
gold-rush days, as the personal servant of an important official.
They had all acquired European skills and abilities to deal with
Europeans on an equal footing, respecting those who were com-
petent, but undisguisedly scornful of the many who were preju-
diced or incompetent. They got on well with the returning Administration officials, most of whom had had similar wartime experiences.

In the years following the war, the blue-collar workers of this
generation returned to the village and became the backbone of it,
restoring the plantings, taking over the jobs of village administration and Komiti, and working as drivers, mechanics, medical
assistants, and carpenters in the Kokopo area. By 1961 only four
of this group were still employed in wage labour, two as drivers,
one as barman at the Kokopo Club, and the other as a servant;
the rest were all farmers, some doing carpentry on a contract basis
as well.

The pre-war white-collar workers mostly returned to their employment after the war, although their period of village work re-
integrated them into their village and made them less committed to
the mission or the government bureaucratic system. For all of
them farming became as important as wage employment.

For the generation that was born in the 1920's, a new pattern of
employment developed after the war. Seven men from Vunamami
—the first to do so—formed part of the class entering Standard 6
at Malaguna Tech in 1939; five more followed them in 1940, and

another group in 1941. When the Japanese invaded, all returned to Vunamami, but they had acquired skills in English and in technical subjects. When the war was over they and their counterparts from Vunairima were the only local people with education. The Vunairima graduates, not surprisingly, became teachers and missionaries, or alternatively worked as self-employed carpenters. The Malaguna group became the clerks and technical workers for the government; three became clerks for government offices or stores, two became medical orderlies, two drivers, two (with some older men) enlisted in the police or the army, and two of the youngest went back to school. A group of four Vunamami men, two from Vunabalbal, nine from Nodup, four other Tolais, and two men from the mainland formed a major part of the New Guinea Police Band for three years immediately after the war; over half had been in the same class at Malaguna.

Yet by 1958 most of these men were back in Vunamami utilizing their skills in village employment, while also investing heavily in planting cocoa and acquiring new land. Within Vunamami the Councillor, ToDaula, the two storemen at Bitatali and Bitaulagumgum Co-operative Stores, a medical orderly at Butuwin hospital, Polos ToPultima (a furniture manufacturer and church treasurer), one carpenter, and one Land-Rover driver came from this group.

A sample work history of this group is that of David ToLungata, born in 1927, son of Peni ToKarel, a missionary. He had had only one year at Malaguna when the Japanese came, although he had already acquired some skill at plumbing. At the war's end, he enlisted in the army and (perhaps as some joke by the recruiting officer) went into the pipe band. He left the army in 1951 and returned home to marry, to plant cocoa, and to do occasional plumbing and carpentry. His elder brother, who completed his training at Vunairima, is one of the most successful carpentry contractors and can call on David when he has too much work on hand. David's history is straightforward and typical of the generation, except for the level of his education.

Of the generation that finished school after the war, only ten of the sixty-three have not at some time been in regular employment. Those who finished soon after the war tended to follow their seniors and go into the police, navy, or army. Most of them have now returned to the village. The majority of those still in wage employment are men with technical skills who have settled in distant places like Moresby, or those with white-collar positions elsewhere in the Tolai area. Among the group aged between seventeen and twenty-one, seven are still undergoing training at teachers' colleges or at the medical college, four are outside the area in skilled or white-collar occupations, three are living at home but working in skilled or clerical occupations, one has taken up unskilled work elsewhere, and three others are working at home.

EMPLOYMENT IN 1961

Table 8 lists the 1961 occupations of men born in Vunamami since 1925. It indicates an over-all trend to returning home both to

Table 8

OCCUPATIONS OF MEN BORN IN VUNAMAMI, 1925–1944*

	Year Born			
	1925–29	1930–34	1935–39	1940–44
Residents				
White-collar work	5	1	2	1
Skilled wage work	1	1	1	2
Self-employed	2	2	1	—
Farming	8	11	4	2
Unskilled wage work	3	2	2	1
Total resident	19	17	10	6
Absentees				
White-collar work	2	4	4	2
Skilled wage work	1	3	3	2
Unskilled	1	3	—	1
Schooling	—	—	—	7
Total absentee	4	10	7	12

* Occupations are those of October 1961. This table differs from Table 9 in omitting immigrants to Vunamami and older men. It groups police, army, etc., with skilled wage work. Most residents in the village were farmers as well as wage workers; only those without wage work have been classified as farmers. No older men were absentee workers in 1961.

farming and to skilled occupations, but among the three older groups there seems to be no significant change in the proportions entering different types of employment; for the group aged seventeen to twenty-one, it was too early to tell whether their higher education would lead to even more white-collar employment. Age thirty appears to be the stage in careers when Vunamami men wish to return home, to educate their children locally and to establish a farm for the future. In 1961 this had been possible for those over thirty, largely because of the great local increase since 1951 in opportunities for white-collar work and the skilled trades. Whether this expansion would continue, giving opportunities for the men reaching thirty, was a crucial question. If Vunamami were indeed in a state of self-sustained growth this would be the case; the degree to which a full range of occupations is available within a community could then be considered an index of a society in take-off. To see the likelihood of this being the case, let us review the occupational opportunities in Vunamami of 1961.

Table 9 lists the wage employment of men residing in Vuna-

Table 9

MALE WAGE EARNERS RESIDENT OR DOMICILED IN VUNAMAMI*

Occupation	Residing in Vunamami	Domiciled in Vunamami, Resident in	
		Rabaul District	Elsewhere
Council/government officials	4	—	1
Schoolteachers	4	1	3
Missionaries	2	2	—
Medical assistants	2	4	1
Clerks, storemen	2	—	1
Total white-collar	14	7	6
Craftsmen, self-employed	7	—	—
Craftsmen, employed	1	—	3
Drivers	2	1	3
Police, army, navy	—	—	4
Total skilled manual	10	1	10
Unskilled	12	7	5
Grand total	36	15	21

* Figures do not include non-Vunamami residents working in Vunamami, or "adoptive employees" residing in a Vunamami household, or casual labour within Vunamami, as explained in the text.

mami, and those of men born in Vunamami and/or paying Vunamami Council tax but not currently residing in the village. Two women were also in wage employment, one a nurse in Rabaul District and one a teacher in Moresby.

Of the thirty-six wage workers residing in the village, three of the teachers and one of the missionaries came from other Tolai villages and lived in accommodations forming part of the school and church. It will be noted, however, that Vunamami supplied seven white-collar workers for other Tolai villages so that the village can be considered potentially self-sufficient for these occupations. The figure of seven self-employed craftsmen includes all those who obtained income from this source in 1961, though all worked varying amounts less than full time.[3] I should estimate that there was sufficient work altogether for at least three full-time workers. Three village residents who looked after Warangoi plantation blocks for distant relatives but received a cash income as well as board, and returned to their village homes periodically, are included as resident unskilled wage earners. Not included are unpaid "adoptive employees"—the five non-Vunamami men, one skilled and four unskilled, living in the village as members of households, and distant relatives living with but working for a household head.

Some of the positions occupied were outside Vunamami. Two government clerks commuted to work, one to Kokopo and one to Rabaul; one medical assistant commuted to Butuwin hospital; one storekeeper worked for Bitaulagumgum Co-operative. Over half of the work of the self-employed craftsmen was for Europeans outside the village. The one skilled employee was a garage mechanic, and eight of the unskilled workers worked in Kokopo, mainly for the Government Works Department, but also for the Sports Club. Yet it would also be fair to say that these men were performing work related to the running of their home village, in administration, in caring for the sick, in constructing roads, and so on. In 1961 it was clear that the indigenous community would soon have its own sports club, and would need its own barmen.

Perhaps most striking is the way in which social services within the village had become specialized and paid, especially since the advent of the Vunamami Council in 1951, but to some extent also through the activities of the mission. For many years, as has been shown, the local missionary and mission schoolteachers were paid in kind, essentially by the congregation. By 1961 five local men were employees of the Council, all of the revenue for which came from the local community—the Council president, the local coun-

---

[3] Three others who called themselves carpenters but who received no income from this source in 1961 have not been included.

cillor, a driver, a medical aid post attendant, and the caretaker of
the council chambers. The government schoolteachers were paid
from taxes, but local unpaid work provided housing and school-
rooms. Another driver was paid locally, as was almost half of the
craftsmen's work, and the two storekeepers. Four other workers
who entered Vunamami daily to work for native employers—an
assistant storekeeper, another council driver, the council clerk, and
the council policeman—are not listed in Table 9.

Vunamami attitudes towards further monetization of work done
for fellow-villagers were ambivalent. On innumerable occasions
since 1951 the Council had had major projects of school or well
building, preparing market stalls, providing food for celebrations,
or making artifacts for display or gifts. In almost all cases the first
suggestion had been that these tasks be done on an unpaid basis
by village work. Councillors readily accepted the tasks for their
villages; the European adviser in most instances then said, "Why
don't you pay people to do the work?" The compromise was
usually that the Council provided food for such work parties.
But there was no reluctance shown to paying carpenters or other
skilled workers, and the latter vied to bid on Council projects.

Although the employment of non-locals for casual labour was
readily accepted, cash was not usually paid between relatives, except in the case of the managers of the distant Warangoi plantations. An exception was the case of "buying days" (*di kul ra bung*),
especially where the work was to collect funds for a corporate
body. In February 1956 there was a Council discussion of this
"long-standing practice," as the president described it. People wishing to "buy a day" paid the fee (*totokom*) to the village. In 1956
the councillors wanted the custom to continue and were unhappy
that some people did not turn up for work. The payment of from
five shillings to one pound for a day's work by a team was then
formally recognized in a Council Rule which imposed penalties
on those who did not turn up for work.

The 1961 work by a women's *kivung* has already been mentioned. Nineteen women turned up at about 9:45 A.M. to weed
a garden of about two-thirds of an acre, which was already planted
with bananas, *ibika*, sugar-cane, and beans. Rarely were there more
than seven working at any moment, as children demanded care
and there was much joking and horseplay, but they finished by
about one o'clock. Although the payment of one pound to the
kivung was said to be at twice the usual rate, and the equivalent

of about ten shillings' worth of taro was supplied as food to the
group, the garden owner still got a bargain. The fact that his wife
was a member of the group and would reciprocate later for other
"buyers" was undoubtedly important.

By contrast, also in 1961 when the village was collecting funds
to buy Ravalien plantation, Enos Teve suggested that a village
work team of sixteen, eight men and eight women, might be
"bought" on Mondays and Wednesdays, the days when government and mission work is done on an unpaid basis. The proceeds
at the rate of forty-eight shillings a day would go into the village
fund. He suggested this at two meetings, but got no support, and
the issue lapsed. My interpretation of the lack of support would
be that his suggestion made reciprocity unlikely; regular users of
labour would not be neighbours, helping one another out, but men
with large plantations, who would profit from cheap labour more
than the village fund would.

The volume of intra-village work on an "adoptive employee"
basis can be judged from the fact that nine unmarried men who
had left school and who ranged up to age thirty-nine were living
in other men's households and were not in wage employment.
Four of the commuters from Vunamami were also not heads of
households, and presumably contributed cash to household fi-
nances.

WAGE INCOMES

To estimate the total income for the village obtained from wage
work I shall take the conservative course of omitting unpaid exchanges of services—undoubtedly in Vunamami terms they are
part of the category "subsistence" (*a nian*). I shall also omit payments to casual labourers, and consider only Vunamami residents.[4]
Contributions to Vunamami by emigrant workers were nominal,
except for tax and contributions to major savings projects. They
are ignored.

Wage rates varied. The official minimum wage paid by most
European employers to unskilled casual workers was £3 a week,

[4] It would be too difficult to consider how much money the white-collar
worker domiciled in Vunamami, but resident elsewhere in Rabaul District,
spent in Vunamami, and how much those resident in Vunamami but domiciled elsewhere spent in their home villages. I shall assume that the two
figures balance.

but Vunamami employers paid £5 a month plus food as the *wapuak* for non-Tolai adoptive employees. For casual plantation workers the standard rate was five shillings a day plus food. Drivers received £3 a week when new to the work, but could expect to go up to £4 after a little time; unskilled foremen with Public Works received £5 a week. The salaries of teachers and medical assistants were fixed by the Public Service scale to take account of their receiving housing and food and were exceptionally low. Thus the Council medical assistant received only £7 a month, although he actually lived at home and did not use any facilities. Teachers' salaries started at the same level but increased more rapidly with training and experience. Carpenters expected a flat £7 a week if they were employed on a time basis by a plantation to repair buildings. Working on a contract basis they could earn £16 or £18 a week, but such work was not available full time except to the most skilled, who had established reputations with the Kokopo Chinese and with plantation managers. The less skilled often worked for £7 a week, helping friends out on contracts. The full-time Council clerk received £25 a month, the supposedly half-time president £16, and the supposedly quarter-time councillors £3 10s. to £4 10s., depending on length of service. The president also received a major income as a member of the Legislative Council.

The total estimated income from wage work for the year 1960–1961 is thus £5,790. This figure may be compared with the £3,217 earned from sixty-six and a half tons of copra, and the £1,778 earned from cocoa. Despite its rural appearance, Vunamami is very much a wage-earning village.

The pattern of a wage-earning rural community has been rarely described in the literature. The two commonly described patterns are those of the cash-cropping village and of the dormitory peri-urban community. A cash-cropping village gets its money by exporting both the cash crop and its young men, who find little to keep them at home, especially if they have skills, literacy, and a knowledge of the "sophisticated" enjoyments that towns offer, ranging from consumer goods and cinemas to better educational facilities for their children (see Van der Veur and Richardson 1966). The result is a village without the trained people who could provide it with skilled services. It thus becomes even more of a backwater, a partial society dependent on, yet kept backward by the towns. The peri-urban dormitory community has been well described for New Guinea by Belshaw (1957) and A. L. Epstein (1963). It may well cling to symbolic vestiges of traditional culture, but as the expatriate town expands, the local community loses its basis for independent existence and becomes a dormitory for the employees of foreigners. It becomes an appendage of the town, housing town workers who cannot afford to move to better accommodation, and gradually changing from an independent community with its own standards to a substandard if "quaint" part of a foreign town.

The prosperous rural village, where employment opportunities exist within the local society or nearby, is a third possibility. It must develop a lively cash-cropping economy to finance the services that the population needs, and neither lose its active population to the towns nor become swamped by an expatriate urbanism. The comparative stability of Vunamami's occupational distribution between white-collar, skilled manual, unskilled, and farm occupations suggests that it is such a village. Young men can go out to gain experience and to take important positions throughout the wider national unit, but the village does not suffer. In the past the young men have always returned home. Whether they will in the future depends on several things, but mainly on whether the expansion of opportunities at home that attracted the educated men back in the 1950's will continue, providing jobs for their younger brothers, and on whether there will be farms and land for them and their unskilled cousins, either in Vunamami itself or in resettlement areas. In 1961 the prospects of plantation purchase, of increased school building, of co-operative wholesaling, and of diversification of Council projects gave every indication that these conditions would be realized.

V

Market Place Trade

The market place in Rabaul is a show-place for European visitors to the Tolai, who are impressed by the availability of European-style produce, by the approximately 7,000 individuals who pass through on an average Saturday, and by the approximately £2,000 worth of produce that changes hands. As we have seen, a simplistic interpretation would consider this market an alien introduction either by Chinese during the First World War or by later governmental encouragement, but in either case a major infusion of commercial patterns of thought into the economy. A slightly deeper interpretation would see the market as having been facilitated by the pre-1875 existence of marketing but essentially a notable introduction of modern Western concepts of trade to replace indigenous patterns. The present interpretation differs from these and sees it as a gradual development of a primarily inter-Tolai regional marketing system.[1] The relations between this system and the presence of Europeans and Chinese are complex, but before they can be discussed the pre-1875 marketing system must be reviewed, together with the concepts involved in it.

[1] It is based on a six-month survey, not only of Rabaul market but of several of the smaller markets that dot the Tolai area. Dr. T. S. Epstein collaborated in the early phases of the Rabaul market study, and has published a report on her material, focusing on the sellers (T. S. Epstein 1961). My own material concentrated on buyers in Rabaul market in June and on qualitative interviews with sellers. Epstein's excellent numerical data agree closely with those obtained from buyer surveys, but my fuller study contradicts many of her qualitative conclusions regarding the role of barter, attitudes to marketing, and the role of men. The reason seems to be Epstein's inadequate qualitative study of the market place before sampling and questionnaire administering, which biased the selection of samples and determined the omission of questions that would have elicited the pertinent information.

MARKETS BEFORE 1875

In 1875 market places were common in the Kokopo area, and many of the old market sites are still used for their original purpose. Along the coast there was a row of market places one behind each of the larger fishing beaches or *motonoi* of Mioko, Vunamami, Keravi, Vunakabi, Bitakua, and Davaun at roughly one-mile intervals. These served as the meeting places where each coastal village exchanged fish for products brought by its neighbours inland. A second row of markets, spaced a little wider than at the beach, was located some two or three miles inland, at the southern boundary of the second village inland. In the Vunamami area there was a market at a site called Bitalama between Vunabalbal and Bitarebarebe villages, and one inland of Balanataman and Ngatur villages at a site called Kulmilat. Near Vunamami the Tolai population extends only five or six miles inland so that the farthest inland groups could come to the second row of markets. Farther west a third row of markets existed (Danks 1887:315), and published sources mention a market at Toma where the Catholic Mission of Paparatava was established. Schmiele (*Monatshefte* 1896:263), travelling from east to west along a row of markets in 1888, before the western area was pacified, reports five markets in about thirteen miles, confirming this distributional pattern.

In the Vunamami area, at least, there was little trade along the rows, but coastal and inland markets were paired. To a coastal market would come members of one or two coastal villages, and their inland neighbours, but no one from groups farther inland. The coastal people would bring mainly lime obtained from burning coral, cooking bananas, and fish; the inland people would bring mainly taro and betel nuts. At an inland market there would be the same pattern of only neighbouring villages meeting at their common boundary, with the downhill group bringing goods obtained at coastal markets to exchange for those grown by the uplanders. The middle group apparently acted mainly as middlemen and produced only limited quantities of goods themselves.

Villages using a pair of markets constituted a district and were often traditional enemies of the next district; Parkinson (1887:79) distinguished "Vunamami District" from "Raluana District" in this way. But friendships between coastal and inland villages were only between immediate neighbours; beyond this range there was permanent hostility, and no possibility of private travel. Even between neighbouring and trading villages there was the risk of fighting. Parkinson (1887:78) and Danks (1887) both describe how men came fully armed to markets though not overtly to trade; their wives brought the produce and did most of the exchanging while the men stood in the background, presumably to protect their wives against men of the opposing village, although, in Danks's words (1887:316), if the opportunity for a sharp trade appeared they would leap into the affair.

What the men seem mostly to have been looking for were the less obvious commodities that were also brought to market from time to time. Ochre (*taar*), megapod eggs (both primarily from volcanic areas at Matupit), and live cockatoos are articles of this sort still seen in markets; feather headdresses and stone clubs, originally obtained from the Bainings, are mentioned in early reports (e.g., Powell 1884:169). By analogy with other areas in New Guinea, it would be expected that a wide variety of now seldom used implements or items of decoration, such as shells, feathers, spears, and musical instruments, would have entered into this occasional trade, which was primarily the concern of men rather than of women.

But though Danks talks of men bargaining, the manner of trade among women was then and is now a silent one. Each woman sits demurely near her produce, which is divided into separate units —heaps, bundles, packages, or strings. When a trade is to be made the other party puts down a standard unit of similar value and picks up the exposed goods. There are standard terms[2] for most units of goods: a bundle (*pulpulu*) of cooked food, a packet (*vaum*) of lime, a bunch (*kure*) of six taro corms, a stalk (*kor*) of bananas, a string (*warvivi*) of four coconuts, a knot (*vinvin*) of peanuts on the stem, a standard fish (*en*) (which may be two undersized mackerel strung together or even a dozen smaller fishes). The units are related to one another numerically, most of them on a one-to-one ratio,[3] but some in different ratios—a stalk of

---

[2] Many sources (e.g., Kleintitschen 1906:182) list these and other terms as special vocabularies for counting different categories of goods on the lines of other Oceanic-language grammars. It is an interesting speculation whether, in these languages too, the terms referred to units in fixed-equivalence barter systems as among the Tolai.

[3] Polanyi (1966: Ch. 10) in his study of the Dahomean fixed-equivalence trade in slaves attempts very complex analyses of the meaning of "one-to-one" trading, concluding that it meant "trading even, or fairly." The present analysis sees the term as a straightforward statement that standard units

bananas and a bundle of food being worth two units, a *kure* of taro worth six, and a standard fish worth twelve. Equal also to a single unit in 1961 was a six-inch length of shell money (*a pidik*), with a half-fathom (*a peapar*) equalling a *kure* of taro, and a fathom equalling a fish. For 1881 Danks (1887:307, 315) quotes a *tabu*-fish exchange rate of half a fathom (or six *pidik*) to one fish, a *tabu*-banana rate of one fathom (or 12 *pidik*) for four stalks, and a banana-betel rate of one stalk for one stalk. Danks gives a taro-*tabu* rate of ten *kure* of taro (*a pakaruat*) for a fathom: Parkinson (1887:104) says eighty taro for a fathom. Unlike the dramatic decline in the purchasing power of the dollar and the pound, the fathom of *tabu* has roughly halved in value in eighty-five years. The barter rates of other commodities have remained fixed, and in the short run of five to ten years, at any rate, *tabu* rates seem almost unvarying.

The key concept in women's marketing is *kul*. This term is often simply translated as "to buy," but it also means to sell. Bürger (1913:22), in a full analysis of its usage,[4] concludes that it refers more generally to exchanges in which there is immediate reciprocity (*Zug um Zug*), including the special case where goods are given for cash (*Ware gegen Bare*). This is borne out by the repetitive form of the verb *di kukul*, "they are buying and selling," the abstract term *kunukul* which means "marketing," and the collective term a *warkukul*," a reciprocal buying and selling" or "a market."

The Tolai term *bung* which has entered pidgin with the meaning "a market," a word which Tolai understand but do not use among themselves, has an interesting derivation. Markets occurred before 1875 on fixed days—Danks suggests every third day—or by special appointment. *Ra bung* (the day) thus meant the special day, and when one talked of *kubu ra bung* (appointing the day) one meant, unless otherwise specified, appointing a special market

---

of two different kinds of goods were exchanged "one to one" rather than "six to one" as was the case with taro-lime package exchanges in Vunamami. Differences between the standards in different areas are not ruled out.

[4] Danks (1887:307) gives a different analysis: *kul*, refers he says, to purchase, *buapa* to exchange, the two terms being distinct. The term *buapa* was not familiar to my informants, although it is listed in Mainwaring's Tolai dictionary. It most probably referred to formal ceremonial exchanges at delayed intervals between big men, and as such was distinct from the immediate reciprocity of *kul*. I see no inconsistency between Bürger and Danks: they are talking about different things.

day. Schmiele's evidence of passing five markets in thirteen miles on such a day shows that markets were synchronized over a wide area in 1886, though Danks (1887:315) indicates they were staggered in 1881.

Another term that is often translated as "to sell" is the word *ivure*, from which is derived the abstract term *a nivura*. Its sense is actually more restricted. To call a woman *a tena nivura* (an expert at *nivura*) is to insult her; to call her *a tena kunukul* is complimentary, for it indicates that she regularly fulfils a woman's expected duty of market buying and selling. When I asked women in my market survey how much they had *ivure* they were indignant, but if I asked how many items they had *kukul* they answered readily. The connotations of the two terms were vividly brought out by a discussion in the Vunamami Council in June 1955. The councillors were unhappy about rising prices for produce (mainly for sale to Europeans) and insisted that they should remain stationary. They said, according to the pidgin minutes, that women go to the market "*long peim na selim ologeda samting bilong ol*" and not "*long bisnis*." Men present at the debate translated this for me into Tolai as *ure ra kunukul, wakir ure ra nivura*; the English translation would be, "for exchanging goods reciprocally, not for selling at a profit in trade." What is shameful for a woman in *nivura* is that she is "selling for profit"; for a man it is not only permitted but it is prestigious to do so.

The clarification of this difference also sheds light on a phenomenon reported by Kleintitschen (1906:203), that husbands control how many fruits a woman may take to market, and in the evening demand from her the *tabu* she has received. Only if the woman has cleared her own garden may she keep the proceeds. My own experience is that this is only partly true. Most Vunamami women in 1961 attended Kokopo market regularly each Saturday, deciding how much food to take to market themselves. When they returned home their husbands did not demand their *tabu*—in fact, much of the *tabu* from food sales was usually spent buying other foodstuffs for family consumption. A few Vunamami women earned *tabu* in Kokopo and Rabaul markets selling quantities of lime which they themselves had manufactured, and this they claimed as their "business" (*nivura*). For such activities Kleintitschen's generalization is incorrect. On the other hand, in support of Kleintitschen's generalization, in Rabaul market many women sit at stalls selling large amounts of European

vegetables such as Chinese cabbage, and receiving cash for them.
But in the early afternoon each woman's husband can usually be
seen arriving and demanding from her the day's proceeds.[5] The
production of vegetables for purposes of profit-making is normally
a male affair, and in this case he *does* control the quantities marketed and the proceeds. For a woman to "profit" from what she
herself has made is permissible but unusual. She may assist her
husband in his business and may perhaps use his profits to barter
for food (perhaps making use of shell money or cash as a means
of exchange for effecting the barter), but it is more likely that
she will barter home-grown food for exotic foodstuffs at fixed
rates of equivalence.

It may be appropriate to sum up some of the main features of
this trade in fixed equivalences. There are relatively few ethnographic accounts of such trade in operation, but mainly speculative
reconstructions of earlier practices (e.g., Polanyi *et al.* 1957,
Polanyi 1966). The present account may clarify some issues raised
there.

In the first place it should be noted that although the equivalences are standard, the quantities involved are variable within
limits.[6] When taro is scarce the size of corms in a bunch decreases,
though the number remains at six. Naturally in a scarce market
the largest bunches are sold first but there is no sense of bargaining over price. The small size of the taro bunch is determined by
the season or the weather, not by the seller's decision. She divides
her crop into bunches of approximately equal size, balancing large
corms with small ones. The trading is not phrased as a competition
between sellers and buyers, each trying to get the better of the
other, but as each side providing whatever is available, and exchanging "fairly" with the other side.

This attitude towards "fair exchanges" is not unknown even in
the United States. Every child knows that a chocolate bar equals
a package of gum equals a package of raisins equals five cents.
Barter is common if one child has a spare package of raisins in his

[5] Epstein (1961) failed to observe this practice and incorrectly inferred
that the women present at the stalls controlled the major business trading
in European vegetables. The effect of a Sepik riot in Rabaul confirms the
present interpretation.

[6] For a similar analysis of trading in standard but variable size units of
merchandise see Mintz (1961). There is also a range of variation in the
size of the units of *tabu*. This will be discussed further in Chapter 8.

lunchbox and someone else has a package of gum. But if units began to have different cash values the system would be upset. An increase in the world price of cocoa in the 1950's could not mean a change in the price of a chocolate bar. The manufacturers realized that the solution was to reduce the size of chocolate bars; sellers accepted this as "fair" and the barter system continued.

This should not be taken as implying that Tolai marketing is today, or indeed ever was, entirely a matter of direct barter of goods. Direct barter does occur in all markets but only rarely. In Rabaul market it occurs when sellers have just arrived and have not yet sold any of their stock. They may then take some items of that stock to other sellers to exchange for what they want to buy. I have seen Vunamami women in Rabaul use packets of lime in this way, but the people to whom they gave packets were always women whom they knew. A seller sitting down and approached by one bringing an article of merchandise would accept it without question, as a gift, and would then bring out a return gift from her personal basket rather than from her displayed stock. It is my impression of other barters observed in Rabual market[7] that they too were with known acquaintances, and involved choice or special items.

Much the same attitude was displayed in some of the infrequent sales of food for sticks of tobacco in Rabaul market. Thus nuns from the Sacred Heart Convent used only tobacco for purchasing, yet when their van arrived in the parking area, many women would run up to it bringing bundles of food. Far from being undersized or poor-quality items, these were usually of the best. The women who ran up all seemed to be personally known to the nuns. Only for items not contributed in this way did the nuns have to tour the market; even then their payment in tobacco was accepted without question. This was in marked contrast to attempts to pay with tobacco observed in Kokopo market. Some European women there would march imperiously round the market, especially when the rush was over and many vendors were away from their merchandise, and would sweep up piles of food into their baskets and leave sticks of tobacco in their place. Threatening gestures and unfavourable comments often followed their re-

---

[7] Including barters on 3 June, a day which Epstein surveyed and for which she asserted that barter did not occur. She surveyed only goods that sellers displayed as stock, however, whereas barter is often of items kept in personal receptacles.

treating backs, as vendors returned in haste to collect their pay.

This was not simply a difference in local custom: in my own food transactions within Vunamami village, people expressed a preference for being given tobacco in exchange. They would come to my door and "give me freely" (*tabar*) some choice vegetables or eggs; to offer money in exchange would have been an insult, making this a market transaction between strangers, but for me to express my gratitude by giving an equally free gift of a stick of tobacco was not only acceptable but expected. It confirmed that we were friends, as long as the rate of barter was a fair one. Bartering in this type of "preferred customer" relationship appeared more obviously in Kokopo, though it still probably accounted for much less than 5 percent of sales. I am not sure whether this apparently greater frequency was real or merely due to better observation, though the two are to some extent linked. Kokopo market serves a smaller area, and sellers tend to know one another and to be more regular; I also knew more sellers personally and was more regular in attending. A seller can reserve choice food items for other sellers only if there is a strong likelihood that they will attend and can reciprocate. In a large impersonal market with irregular attendance it is usually safer to rely on negotiable means of exchange.

In fact, the vast majority of transactions in all markets are made with either *tabu* or cash as the means of exchange. Overtly the transactions appear as simple sales. But the *attitude* to most transactions by women is that they are part of a barter system, in which the "fixed equivalences" enable the barter to be "delayed" and not immediate. Obtaining the maximum cash return from goods is not a socially approved goal for this form of women's trade.

For such a trade to exist in reality and not just as a social fiction presupposes that there is an approximate over-all balance between what is produced of the various goods entering into the exchange, as stated by the standard equivalence rate; it presupposes that there are ecological factors making different areas suitable for different products. The extent to which the traditional complementarity of ecological areas persists to this day will be reviewed later in this chapter; the extent to which there is a balance in the quantities produced will be considered in Chapter 8 as part of a review of the balance-of-payments flow of *tabu* between villages. For the moment these approximate balances will be assumed to exist, and I shall focus on how a fixed-equivalence or delayed-barter system, such as they permit, can be logically integrated.

It must also be recognized that there has also always existed in Tolai, alongside the barter system, a pattern of trading for profit (*a nivura*) in special commodities that seldom appeared on the market. This was traditionally an important male sphere of activity, but some women participated in it with some commodities. The mechanisms used in this trade will mainly be considered in Chapter 7 under the heading "Businesses." Perforce, prices in this business trade bore some relationship to (or could be expressed in terms of) the means of exchange in delayed barter, yet prices were not standard. Each transaction was an independent one, and the possibilities of middlemen buying and selling were open.

Let us return to the techniques and attitudes of delayed, fixed-equivalence barter. As we have seen, competition between sellers to reduce prices and increase sales is ruled out by the rigidity of standards. Yet there can be intense competition between sellers to demonstrate their abilities as producers. A housewife can use the market place both as the arena where she can display her prowess as a producer and as the testing ground for her abilities to select good merchandise to replace what she has sold. To "push" one's own merchandise is to establish a spurious reputation, and is not "good form," so sellers sit quietly beside their produce, waiting for customers to approach. When someone stops to inspect the merchandise, often very closely, a discussion is likely to ensue. In sales to other Tolai, where the competition as gardeners, and judges, is relevant, interest by a buyer in, say, a particular bunch of taro may result in the vendor's pointing out borer marks that the buyer did not see, or saying where better taro can be bought. It is as if the demonstration of her discrimination were more important for the seller than actually selling her produce. To tour the market with a Tolai seeking a special product, such as peanuts for planting, is like touring an agricultural show with one of the judges. Lime for betel chewing, for example, can vary tremendously in quality. If the producer did not leave the salty coral in a pile long enough for rain to wash out all the salt, the taste will be evident. Insufficient heat in the drier used for calcining can leave the lime chalky; the degree of slaking can vary. Both sellers and chewers at Kokopo knew the reputations of almost every lime manufacturer; buyers prided themselves on using select packets of lime, high-quality and smaller in size than the usual, and sales by a reputedly inferior producer aroused fairly acrimonious comments among sellers out of earshot, about her abilities and the buyers' ignorance (especially if they were immigrant New Guineans). In Rabaul market most people are strangers, but Vunamami women generally have a high reputation as lime producers, and the one or two sellers sitting in the "Vunamami site" dispose of all the one hundred or one hundred and fifty packets each one brings while women from other villages rarely sell out stocks of fifty packets.

Yet this competition over quality is not always free of a commercial tinge. It is not only the seller herself who may point out the defects in merchandise and the advantages of someone else's product; a neighbour may also do so. I have on several occasions been taken on a tour of instruction in the finer points of, say, choosing taro, by the neighbour of a seller whose goods I had examined. When I indicated that I was interested in size rather than in taste, or in a bunch that could be bought for money rather than for *tabu*, my guide would then sell me an appropriate bunch. Having clearly demonstrated her superior knowledge, she could condescend to commerce. Vendors overtly disclaim an interest in making sales, by affecting not to look at the *tabu* or money that is thrown down for their goods. They wait until the purchaser has moved on before picking up the payment. But however nonchalant, a vendor can always say exactly how many sales she has made.

This lack of competition among sellers is sometimes an active collusion against buyers, especially if these are of a different ethnic group. Thus at Kokopo at the start of field work I was struck by an apparent dearth of eggs. Those displayed were small and grouped in twos as the equivalent of one shilling. In large stores where most Europeans bought eggs the price was five shillings a dozen, although supplies were unpredictable because of shipping difficulties. The Chinese were the main buyers of market eggs, and many of them, speaking Tolai, would automatically ask the price of eggs as they passed vendors. On being told "two" they would say "three" and move on. Once, the local store unexpectedly being out of eggs, I bought two of the four eggs on display by a vendor for one shilling. I immediately heard talking all around—"He bought at two"—and within minutes I was offered dozens of eggs, previously hidden in baskets and all larger than the two I had already bought. I could hardly resist buying

larger eggs when I had already bought small eggs at two for a
shilling. From then on, I never again had occasion to buy market
or store eggs, for my neighbours kept me well supplied. As I have
said, neighbours refused to accept cash, but an exchange rate of
two eggs for a stick of trade tobacco (worth ninepence) proved
a mutually acceptable "fixed equivalence." For me, buying tobacco
wholesale, I got fresh eggs at less than store prices; local people
got a better price than the three for a shilling expected from Chinese buyers.

The last aspect of fixed-equivalence barter that must be borne
in mind is that the goods involved are ones that the seller can
use herself, or can store for future sales if they remain unsold.
Items like lime packets will fetch the same price at next week's
market, and there is no loss from not selling on any one day. If
the goods are usable by the seller, the incentive for making sales
is provided by the enhanced pleasure to be obtained from eating,
say, taro instead of cooking bananas. Only if the exchange stands
a chance of being completed is it worthwhile letting go of the
goods one already has; cutting prices would ensure that the exchange would not be completed and so would make the seller
worse off than he would be if he retained his own goods. As will
be seen, these conditions do not apply to an increasing range of
goods sold in the market. The change to commercially oriented
marketing is a story of steadily developing specialization.

CHANGES AFTER 1875

When the Europeans came, their pattern of trading at first closely
followed the indigenous ones. The major exchanges were of food
against tobacco, as has already been described by Brown, and by
Parkinson when he set up his plantation and was "adopted" into
the indigenous barter system. By contrast, the activities of the
traders were fitted much more into the pattern of business trading
for profit, with shells being bought at first, and subsequently the
growth of sales of coconuts. Men were the sellers in this and
bargaining with the European traders was common. Traders who
underpaid were often driven out, as happened to Cook at Matupit.
Chapter 3 has already shown how the increase in the number of
traders and the bargaining abilities of the Tolai steadily drove up
coconut prices, bringing large increases in Tolai income without
additional work of planting. The political effects of the coastal

attempt to prevent direct trade between Europeans and inland, and a break in their monopoly position, culminating in the war of 1878, have also been described. European traders contributed directly to the development of a broker role for the male Tolai by their practice of leaving a supply of trade goods with a trusted man in each village, and calling back periodically to pick up the coconuts he had bought. Persistent European complaints of short weight suggest that Tolai traders did better out of this scheme than was anticipated. Clearly male trade was greatly increased by the advent of Europeans and relatively large profits were available for the coastal entrepreneurs.

The advent of mission peace and the establishment of plantations around 1880–1882 combined to produce considerable economic changes. The missionaries were very proud that peace meant that people living inland could come down to the coast unharmed as they had never done before. Parkinson saw the same changes and thought of them as showing *his* control over the area. It would seem that there were also economic advantages in the change to all native parties. For the farthest inland peoples the trip to the coast was clearly advantageous in both the food-barter trade and the men's trade in coconuts. The inlanders cut out the middlemen of the central villages and had access to a wider choice of European goods. Walking down to the coast with goods, especially coconuts, was a small cost, especially when there were such additional benefits as getting a free supply of salt water (see Pitcairn 1891:176). For the coastal people, too, once they had grown used to the loss of their monopoly position in European trade, there were advantages in cutting out the middlemen—in having taro brought right to them, for example, and in selling fish and lime directly to those who lived far inland.

Only for the central people was the change of dubious value. They lost the advantages of middlemen's profits, or choice of prime products from coast and inland, but they gained in direct access to European buyers. It would also seem likely that the advent of plantations and their labourers provided for the first time a market for foodstuffs that were grown everywhere and thus rarely entered into indigenous barter—sweet potatoes, spinach (*a ibika*), yams, and so on. The central people could market these crops to Europeans instead of pursuing their former work of carrying fish inland or taro to the coast. For all parties, in short, the advent of peace and plantations meant a large expansion of marketing activities. It must also, however, have reduced the importance of inland market sites, since only local exchanges would have been made there while goods destined for further exchanging would have bypassed them. Some inland sites presumably became inactive early.

The setting up of specific food-buying sites at plantations, and the custom of buying only at specific times on appointed days, was also an extension of the indigenous custom of markets being held at the no man's land between villages, and of appointing days for markets. To a European, the method of buying may have seemed like the accepting of a tribute—the women sitting quietly with their produce in little piles in front of them, until Mrs. Parkinson came out with her servant, who went down the line, giving an equivalent in tobacco for each pile as Mrs. Parkinson nodded, and shovelling the food into bags. In fact, however, it was but an extension of the usual Tolai procedure. The plantation bought whatever was offered at fixed equivalences. Even this did not fulfil plantation needs, and boats went out from Ralum to obtain extra supplies up and down the coast.

Although there was a decline in the opportunities for middlemen's profits in the male business trade for coconuts, the volume of trade nonetheless increased. Europeans recognized the indigenous distinction between it and barter-exchanging by selling large trade-goods items—axes and cloth, for example—only for coconuts, never for food. Only for coconuts was shell money (and after 1902, cash) paid, although sticks of trade tobacco were universal media of payment.

Yet the possibilities for making money out of trading still remained. The Raluana *tultul* mentioned in Chapter 1 sold four chickens for a shilling and "still had four sticks of tobacco in hand" (A. S. Booth, Letter to Gen. Sec. M.O.M., 13 Dec. 1910), though the rate of exchange was eight to ten sticks of tobacco for a shilling. He must have been buying chickens at from four to six sticks for four chickens in order to make his profit, amounting to 67–100 percent on his outlay! The same letter in which this incident is related also bemoans the way in which prices to Europeans were going up; how some stations were still able to buy chickens at three for a shilling (presumably at three sticks of tobacco each), but how the policy advocated in Australia of eschewing tobacco and using only coins would double the costs of food buying.

The refrain of a constant inflation of prices for Europeans had begun, in fact, in 1878, and it continues to this day (see Danks, Letter to B. Chapman, 6 Sept. 1880). As long as Tolai men could demand *tabu* for their special products from Europeans, and as long as Europeans were dependent for their *tabu* on selling manufactured goods to the local men, the control of prices for such goods obviously lay mostly with the Tolai. We have already seen how this led up to the German regulations of 1901 and 1902 officially prohibiting the use of *tabu* by Europeans. It is noteworthy to compare the rapid increase in prices to Europeans—chickens, for example, fetched five shillings in 1961, a twentyfold increase in just over forty years—with the virtual stability of barter-exchange prices as expressed in *tabu*.

Opportunities for trade were quickly seized. The planting of areas of pineapples for sale to visiting ships has already been mentioned as occurring in the 1900's. And we recall Overell's description (1923:159) of how Jonah, the new *luluai* of Raluana, tried to inflate the price of eggs by not allowing women to sell eggs to plantations or to the mission at the price of two for one stick of tobacco. He told the women to hold out for one stick each and tried to corner supplies offered at the lower price. The response to the availability of new crops, including peanuts, around 1930 should also be interpreted in this light. There have always been Tolai men ready to seize an opportunity for trading gains.

The same readiness to trade is evident in the way in which new market places have arisen wherever customers exist. When Chinese workers, freed from indenture and no longer fed by their employers, wanted to buy fresh foods, Tolais would come to sell to them, and so in the First World War there developed the market at Vunamai on the edge of Rabaul Chinatown. The pre-1939 market in Kokopo was also on the edge of Chinatown, under a large tree, and another market appeared near the mental hospital at Bitalovo, closer to Vunamami. The military hospital set up when the Allies landed in 1945 occasioned a market near the old Chinatown site, and this market was moved to a larger site when the Vunamami Council was inaugurated in 1950. Shortly after Nonga hospital was built near Rabaul in 1957, a market appeared across the road. At the Vunapope hospital a large market is held daily, mainly for women in the maternity wards, who are encouraged to enter hospital early for pre-natal care, to escape the burdens of village life. The nearby market at Mioko is adjacent to Bitaula-gumgum Co-operative store, to which come numbers of trucks with copra. It is also at the road junction where all roads from the east converge before entering Kokopo and must be passed by all plantation labourers walking to town. It does a lively trade in betel nut and pepper. Kulmilat, an old inland market site, is at the crossing of two well-used roads; it is adjacent to Ngatur fermentery, and for that reason has recently become active after a long period of decline. All the traditional market sites behind the *motonoi* between Kokopo and Davaun, halfway to Rabaul, were active in 1961, advertising when fish was on sale by hanging one from a stick by the side of the Kokopo–Rabaul road. When Sepik labourers and police rioted in August 1961 and wrecked Rabaul market, stalls immediately appeared alongside every road outside Rabaul. In 1961 any public event—a choir competition, school sports day, or District Show—brought forth its sellers. Not many on such occasions offered traditional market goods, except for cooked food and betel-chewing needs, but the sellers of cigarettes, buns, soft drinks, and sweets did a thriving business.[8]

So far as I can discover, there was no attempt to regulate or improve markets (except for plantations managing the buying of food supplies) until Local Government Councils came upon the scene, in 1951. Woven bamboo mats on wooden legs (termed *bet*) had often been made by regular sellers to display their produce (especially European produce like tomatoes, beans, cucumbers, lettuce, and fruits), but the councils made the provision of *bets* an obligation for villages in the area of each major market. Penalties were imposed for putting foodstuffs on bare ground, though it was permissible to pile coconuts or root crops on the ground in areas where trucks had easy access. Rabaul market was recognized as the responsibility of not just Rabaul Council but of all four councils combined, and all contributed cash towards the construction of two roofed sheds and toilet facilities, and towards cleaning and maintenance. It was not until October 1961 when Administration officials convinced the Councils that more covered space

---

[8] Some discussion of this casual retailing of European goods on festive occasions will be given in Chapter 7.

and permanent stands were desirable, that a charge of one shilling was levied on each seller in the market to help defray these expenses.

MARKETING IN 1961

Throughout the Gazelle Peninsula, Saturday was the big marketing day in 1961, and on that day about eight thousand people passed through one or another market, mainly Rabaul and Kokopo. Some small markets ceased operations on Saturday because their potential customers preferred to drive on to the greater variety and hustle and bustle of the bigger centres. On week-days all other markets handled a much smaller volume, and were of a different nature. On Saturdays the largest volume in Rabaul market was of inter-Tolai food exchanging, but on week-days the sale of foodstuffs to resident Europeans, Chinese, and Papuan office workers was more important. Kokopo market on a Saturday was split between inter-Tolai food exchanges and sales to European plantations; on week-days it became almost exclusively a market selling to the immigrant New Guinean population of Kokopo town. The smaller markets were either regular sellers of foodstuffs to a "captive" population, as at the hospitals, or mainly sellers of betel-chewing materials for immigrant workers and transients. It was the latter type of market that closed on Saturday.

(a) Kokopo Market

As a way of analysing some of the mechanisms operating on a large and complex scale in Rabaul, let us look first at the smaller Kokopo market, essentially the same as the Rabaul market but lacking certain special features determined by Rabaul's large size. In 1961 Kokopo market was on a site halfway between the Government Offices and the Kokopo Sports Club, where some trees shaded the edge of the playing field. Between it and the access road was an open area where cars and trucks parked, and on the edge of which bulky foodstuffs—mainly sweet potatoes and *tigapu* (*Xanthosoma* taro)—were displayed in piles. Most of these were bought by European plantation owners to feed their workers. Under the trees and covering an area about forty by one hundred feet were six uneven rows of uncovered *bet* (stands) of sticks and woven bamboo. On these were displayed most of the foods in which Europeans were interested—tomatoes, eating bananas (*mau*), oranges, whisk brooms, pineapples, pawpaws, eggplant, pumpkin, custard-apples, cucumbers, star-apples, sour-sops, mango, squash, *galip* and *pau* nuts, lettuce, Chinese cabbage, peanuts, melons, beans, sweet corn, lemons, and eggs—along with many of native interest—betel nuts, bundles of cooked foods such as roasted cassava or fish or taro in coconut cream, lime in packets, green vegetables of several varieties (*a ibika, karakap,* etc.), *pitpit,* cooking bananas, pepper catkins, and so on. On the edge of the playing field, but keeping to the shade as far as possible, were piles of bulky Tolai foods such as taro, cooking bananas, and hands of betel nut.

On Saturday mornings sellers began arriving about seven-thirty, with the main flow coming between eight-thirty and nine. The number of sellers varied between 130 on a small market day and 275 on a large market day. The European buyers, plantation families and white-collar workers, arrived in their cars in a sudden rush between eight-thirty and nine, and then there was a steady dribble of new buyers until almost eleven. For these European buyers, a visit to the market was one step in a Saturday morning of collecting mail at the post office, shopping at the two large European stores nearby, and dropping in for a social drink at the Sports Club before returning home for lunch. Most of the sellers in the market were women; perhaps one in fifteen was a man, and none of the men had "native" foods for sale. But other men drifted in to the market area, or sat by the entrance near the road during the morning, so that by noon there might be a hundred Tolai men there. Around noon, the Tolai women began drifting back to their villages, although there were usually about forty still there at four in the afternoon. After noon an influx of plantation and office workers began, building up as football matches started on the playing field.

Most of the sellers walked to the market, coming from places as far as five miles away. Fifty or so came by truck from villages farther to the east. These trucks arrived at the market with a few men, several women, and large quantities of vegetables on board. Most women and produce were unloaded in Kokopo, and numbers of men boarded the trucks for the trip on into Rabaul. A few came by truck from Raluana to the west, and from inland villages.

In addition to the indigenous pattern of inland villages having taro and betel and coastal villages having lime and cooking bananas, one noticed many other specializations. Most of the sweet potatoes and *tigapu* came from areas to the east where these crops were grown on land under immature coconuts; women from Vunamami and Vunabalbal with gardens at Kabakaul were among this group of sellers. Villages behind Balanataman and Ngatur which had not been planted early to coconuts had large quantities of oranges, lemons, pineapples, beans, and Chinese cabbage. Among the men many specialties were noticeable. One man occasionally appeared with numbers of live crabs; several inland men brought five cockatoos every week; one man did a good trade selling shelled peanuts in paper bags for two shillings a bag. Most men brought large supplies of a single European product—usually pineapples, Chinese cabbage, beans, or oranges. Most of the Vunamami women brought goods of several kinds; a typical load would include fifty pounds of *tigapu*, left in seven piles near the parking lot, and a *bet* display of one pawpaw, three cucumbers, twelve small tomatoes, and a bunch of *karakap*. Inland villages tended to bring larger loads of a single crop, and less variety of produce, but the over-all pattern was clear. The women grow a main staple on which they depend either for sale or for home consumption, and at the time that they are preparing for market they collect for sale whatever else is ripe in their gardens.

The average amount brought in by each seller was just over eleven shillings' worth. The average amount of food purchased by each market seller to take home at the end of the market was about three shillings' worth, in addition to whatever was left of her own produce—an amount that varied greatly. The average amount bought at the market by each European car (and this included not only families buying for themselves but also purchases for servants and plantation workers) was just over twelve shillings' worth. I was not able to obtain reliable figures for the purchases of betel, cooked food, peanuts, and so on, by transient men or office workers, but I should estimate from a small sample that 150 men each purchased an average of about one shilling's worth of some food.

Although the number of sellers varied widely, there seemed to be no correlation between the number of sellers present and the amount that each one brought. Europeans said that more sellers came in wet weather than in dry weather (presumably because crops grow faster in the wet). From my observation, however, there seemed to be no steady decline from April to December, the comparatively dry months of the year. On the contrary, the amount of goods on display varied widely and unpredictably.

The number of European buyers was remarkably constant, varying only between 75 and 85, and the amount bought by each increased only slightly on good market days. The amount purchased by each market woman also appeared constant, although the total volume changing hands obviously varied according to the number present. The number of plantation labourers coming into Kokopo also varied extremely widely, depending on whether or not there were football matches, but since such small amounts of goods were bought by these labourers, the sales were of minor significance in the market picture.

On 13 May, a fairly slow day, I counted 160 sellers. By listing all the goods left in the market at nine-thirty, after most of the European buyers had left, and by allowing for purchases made by the market women themselves, I calculate that the sellers brought in 1,972 shillings' worth of produce—a little more than the average of eleven shillings' worth per person. Of this produce, 1,239*s.* worth was "native" and 733*s.* was European, although Europeans had also bought *tigapu*, cooking bananas, and sweet potatoes, as mentioned. Of the European foodstuffs, 163*s.* worth was unsold at nine-thirty, and I estimate that only another 30*s.* worth was sold later. Of the native foodstuffs, 707*s.* worth was still unsold at nine-thirty. I estimate that Europeans later bought about 50*s.* worth of this, market women another 150*s.* worth, and men in the afternoon another 150*s.* The resultant flow of goods brought in and taken out is tabulated below:

	Brought in	*Took out*
Market sellers	1,972*s.* of produce	490 *s.* produce unsold
		480 *s.* produce bought
		1,002*s.* cash and *tabu*
Europeans	852*s.* cash	852*s.* produce
Plantation labourers	150*s.* cash and *tabu*	150*s.* produce

The unsold European articles at nine-thirty on this day were 58*s.* worth of oranges and 20*s.* of lemons, 30*s.* worth of pawpaws, and 30*s.* worth of pumpkins. All the lemons belonged to one seller; two sellers had brought 36*s.* worth of oranges, three had brought 25*s.* worth of pawpaws, and two had brought 17*s.* worth of pumpkins. The native vegetables unsold included (unusually, for taro usually sold out) 180s. worth of taro, 180s. worth of *tigapu* and sweet potatoes, 136s. worth of betel, and 79s. worth of lime. Except for the taro, probably only small quantities of each native foodstuffs were left by the end of the day, or when market women left for home.

At eleven o'clock on the morning of 5 August, a slightly busier market day, there were 47s. worth of tomatoes left to twelve sellers, 76s. worth of lettuce again to twelve sellers, 19s. worth of pineapples, 26s. worth of cucumbers, and 35s. worth of beans. The total European goods unsold were worth 331s. Three weeks later, also a busy day, there was no lettuce left in the market, but there was still a surplus of cucumbers and tomatoes, and also a large number of watermelons. On both these days in August, the volume of *native* produce left unsold was low—169s. worth on the 5th and about 200s. worth on the 26th.

The striking feature in comparing market days is thus the changing volume of European goods *unsold:* it increases dramatically as the number of sellers increases, whereas the amount of native produce unsold remains more or less steady, or even decreases as the proportion of the total goods in a larger market. The reason for this, obviously, is the fixed size of the European buying group, which means that anyone trying to go into larger-scale production of European foods is very likely to flood the market and be left with most of his goods on his hands. The woman who brings in a few cucumbers because they happen to be ripe can always take them home again and eat them herself, but a man with 20s. worth of lemons is left with a surplus that is far more than he can consume. It is much safer to concentrate on native foods, especially the root vegetables. If they do not sell, they will at least keep for a few days and can be eaten by the family; and if they do sell, more can be dug up for the family, which will in the meantime enjoy the variety of foods obtained in exchange for what was sold.

The degree to which marketing is an exchange can be illustrated by the list of sales and purchases by nine Vunamami women on 5 August. They sold 75s. worth of goods, including 20s. of *galip* nuts by one woman, 16s. of cooked *karakap* by two women, and 6s. of spring onions by another. Other articles sold included eggs, lime, cooking bananas, fresh *ibika*, and sweet potatoes. On their return home they had bought 14s. worth of *tigapu* and 2s. taro (as it happened, there was hardly any taro in the market that day),

7*s.* worth of betel, 3*s.* of watermelons, 2*s.* of sweet potatoes, and one shilling's worth of tomatoes. They had also spent 15*s.* on goods in trade stores: 4*s.* on bread, 7*s.* on cake, and 4*s.* on tinned fish. Of the 32*s.* remaining, only 6*s.* was in the form of coins, and the rest in the form of *tabu.* Two women, in fact, had spent cash out of their own pockets in stores, in order to save the *tabu* they got in the market. The only women who had not sold all their goods were one with *ibika* who brought home two bundles, one with twenty-four packets of lime remaining, and one with eight eggs left. The lime could be sold the following week, and the remainder could easily be consumed at home. Part of the reason for the rather large amount of *tabu* retained was the unavailability of taro, which can usually be bought only for *tabu:* but under any circumstances women like to end up with *tabu* if possible. European money can be obtained in many ways, but *tabu* can be obtained only through indigenous channels, and most indigenous foodstuffs can be bought only with *tabu.*

Items of Vunamami produce traditionally entering into the coastal-inland trade were lime and cooking bananas. They still are important, but they constitute only 13 percent of the goods sold by this group. The proceeds of this sale were more than spent in buying traditional inland commodities (allowing for the substitutions of *tigapu* for taro). Goods sold to Europeans and Chinese constituted the same portion of sales, and again more money than was received was spent on food purchases from Chinese stores. But the majority of Vunamami sales were of indigenous foodstuffs that in earlier days did not enter into trade—*galip* nuts, cooked *karakap, ibika,* and sweet potatoes. Vunamami women sold these to other Tolai, and to immigrant New Guineans, but they bought only a much smaller quantity of foods of a similar type—melons and sweet potatoes. Here the exchanges are unbalanced, and it is in this area that the possibilities of profit-making are emerging. It is also noteworthy that sweet potatoes appear as both bought and sold by Vunamami women; a growing portion of the market trade is indirectly between individuals of the same village. Of course, no Vunamami woman would pay another Vunamami woman money for sweet potatoes, but many would prefer to buy from outsiders in the market place rather than try to obtain them from local friends by non-market means.

The obverse of the Vunamami exchanging pattern can be inferred. A larger proportion of what inland villagers bring down is of traditional crops for sale to the coastals, but a larger proportion of what they take back are the indigenous crops in which the coastals have recently begun to specialize. To a considerable extent, but somewhat less than the coastals, their sales to Europeans and Chinese give them money with which to buy foods in trade stores, while their sales to immigrant New Guineans give them a cash profit.

Kokopo market is thus still about 20 percent of a traditional nature, involving the traditional exchange commodities utilizing *tabu* as the means of exchange; about 10 percent is an indirect exchange between Tolai and Europeans and Chinese of entirely new foodstuffs, using money as the means of exchange. Most of the market involves the sale or exchange of non-traditional commodities between groups that traditionally did not trade at all. The wider implications of these novel trade channels will be considered in the discussion of Rabaul market, where they are even more evident.

The nature of price fluctuations, both on a single day and over the long term, can be understood in the light of the foregoing discussion. The most dramatic swings were, naturally, in the prices of European foods, notably tomatoes, which varied from ten or twelve good-sized ones down to three or four, comparably sized, for a shilling. Cucumbers varied from seven to two for a shilling. The average price corresponded generally with the periods of glut and scarcity, but within the same market there were sometimes marked discrepancies in price. The reason for this can be best understood by considering the pricing strategy of the small-scale producer of these variable price commodities. As a woman looks around her garden for what to take in to market, she sees she has a few tomatoes and collects them. She remembers roughly whether tomatoes were plentiful last week or not, but for today's market she has to judge the state of the supply from her own garden and those nearby. If she estimates that about six tomatoes is the price and she has seven ripe, she will pick all the ripe ones, and sell them for a shilling; with nine tomatoes ripe she will pick three underripe ones and reckon on making up two piles or basketsful in the market. In other words, she has tentatively fixed the price in her own mind in her own garden; with such small quantities, and the "lumpiness" caused by the custom of selling everything in one-shilling units, she has little room to manoeuvre in the market place.

What happens there must be considered in the light of the arrival times for buyers and sellers—almost simultaneous, with sellers still coming in when the first buyers are leaving. An early seller who has priced her goods—tomatoes, shall we say—fairly low is likely to have them bought immediately; they disappear from the scene and late-arriving sellers do not see them. Higher-priced tomatoes will tend to be left, although at the same time no early seller knows how large the tomato market will be; it is quite likely that after a little while there will be only high-priced tomatoes in the market, and they will be taken by some European desperate for tomatoes. On the other hand, a late-arriving seller sees only the piles of those who have been unable to sell because their prices are too high. She could in theory alter her pre-calculated prices slightly while setting out her goods. She could raise prices and reduce the number of tomatoes from six for a shilling to five for a shilling, or she could lower prices and put six ripe ones together for one shilling pile, and expect not to sell the six small ones. But if she has only twelve tomatoes she gains little either way. Raising prices slightly will leave a few tomatoes over but will not equal another shilling's worth; lowering prices will perhaps sell one shilling's worth, but at the cost of certainly *not* selling the remainder. The pressures are towards maintaining the pre-calculated price, hoping that when later buyers arrive, the low-priced sellers will have disposed of all their stock. What one tends to find, then, on looking at the market as a whole is a variety of prices, tending generally to rise during the trading period, but with bargains available as long as new sellers are arriving. But as soon as sellers stop coming the low-priced goods disappear from the market. Only when there is an obvious glut on the market is there likely to be any cutting of prices by individual sellers, and even then only when the flow of buyers has almost stopped. Given the small volume of any one seller, and the lumpiness of prices which can only change by ordinal steps (5 for a shilling to 4 a shilling, etc.), changes in prices made during any one session of the market are rare.

Paradoxically, most of the price changes I observed—perhaps half a dozen in nine months of weekly visits to markets—were of native foodstuffs like sweet potatoes and *tigapu*. One case of reshuffling tomato piles and one of oranges were all that I noted in the way of price changes in European produce. The changes in native food piles did not involve altering the numbers per pile, but grouping bigger tubers together. For native foods, of course, the market lasts longer, since there is always the chance of plantation labourers' buying in the afternoon. And each seller usually has a larger stock of native produce, so that slight changes in price do not mean losing much in total sales. A lower price for a seller with fifty-four *tigapu* may mean the difference between selling only five shillings' worth and taking home twenty-four fair-sized tubers, or selling seven shillings' worth and taking home twelve small tubers that would not be salable. Since what is taken home is not wasted, many women may choose the second alternative. In general terms, then, it is in a market where buyers and sellers are matched in numbers and power, where there is a reasonable possibility of additional marginal buyers and where there is the largest volume of sales, that the finest adjustments of prices occur, even though these prices are nominally fixed equivalences. Where nominally there is the most price freedom and lack of fixed equivalences, there is actually little short-term sensitivity to changes in supply and demand but large, somewhat random, variability of price in the one market; the longer-term trends in price are the result of people's estimates at home, outside the market, of whether there will be glut or scarcity, and thus show only a general and not very exact relationship to actual supply and demand conditions. In such markets suppliers lower their risks by dealing in small quantities and by not specializing; by so doing they in fact make it even less possible to respond precisely to finer changes in supply and demand, or to make precise judgements about the future state of the market. It is not surprising that neither the marketing nor the production of European vegetables becomes what a European would think of as "rationalized."

(b) Small Markets

Besides the Kokopo and Rabaul markets, two types of smaller markets may be briefly mentioned: first, "traditional" markets arranged on special occasions, and, second, regular markets such as Kokopo on a weekday, Mioko, and Vunakabi (apart from its fish sales).

The "traditional" arranged market that I observed occurred as part of a celebration in honour of the ancestors of Vunabalbal clan (*a matamatam*) which was organized by John ToMarangrang of Vunabalbal village (see Chapter 8). To enable villagers of Vunamami and Vunabalbal villages to obtain taro, should they wish to contribute to the feast, he sent word to Wairiki village, a main taro supplier to Kokopo market, to "appoint a day" (*kubu ra bung*) when they would come to the piece of ground called Bitatali on the border of Vunabalbal and Vunamami to sell their taro. They came on 9 August, two days before the dance on the 11th; this, rather than seasonal factors, explains the absence of taro from Kokopo market on 5 August mentioned above. At eleven o'clock seventeen women and a man arrived on a truck hired for them by John, bringing 115 bunches of taro with leaves, 39 bunches without leaves, 14 piles of *tigapu*, two bundles of betel and pepper, and one banana stalk. They insisted that they would only accept *tabu* at the full half-fathom rate for each bunch; John argued that *tabu* was in short supply and that they should take money, but they were adamant. Bystanding Vunamami men were amused: "They're insisting on *tabu* now, but when we sell them fish, all the *tabu* will come back."

Sales went slowly, and for the first hour more sales were made with lime packets (one for each taro corm, or six for a bunch) than with *tabu;* some of the *tigapu* were sold for cash. By two o'clock 57 leafy bunches, 18 leafless ones, one pile of *tigapu*, and the stalk of bananas still remained. The Wairiki women were annoyed that they had been assured a good market yet so little had been sold; John was annoyed that they were so stubborn in demanding *tabu;* the truck driver was annoyed that no one was ready to go home. Finally, John himself paid *tabu* for the taro that was left, and the Wairiki women departed in an atmosphere of mutual recriminations.

In some ways the arranged market admirably illustrates the formal rules of pre-1875 trading—the nature of the products, the border position of the market, the insistence on standard equivalences, the high incidence of direct barter. One can equally well consider it as an illustration of the tempering of traditional principles of reciprocity by commercialism. Wairiki women obviously chose this market instead of Kokopo for the greater chance of making *tabu* sales. John and the other Vunamami people clearly thought that by inviting the Wairiki women and virtually guaranteeing sales, they were entitled to expect to be treated as special customers and given some preferential advantages over conditions in a regular market. But the Wairiki women were equally aware of their strong monopoly position. The eventual adherence to formal rules was in effect a safe compromise for both sides, neither getting the "illegitimate" advantages it had hoped for. Viewed in this light, the apparently smooth adherence to "traditional equivalences" in the distant past may well also have been the compromise result of similar efforts by both sides to increase their advantage. The possibilities of change may always have been implicit, if opportunities opened up for one side to seize the advantage from the other side.

The smaller markets in the Kokopo area include that at Kokopo on a week-day, those at Mioko and Vunakabi (ignoring fish sales there), and the one at Vunapope hospital.

At Kokopo the number of women sellers present varied between two and five, and their total stock in trade was almost exclusively betel, pepper, and lime—about 20s. worth of betel and pepper and five or six lime packets; a few bunches of bananas, a pawpaw, or a pineapple might be brought in addition. Total sales averaged about five shillings' worth, but there was occasionally a sell-out. Vunamami women did not market in this way; the women here were from villages to the east, or were wives of workers in Kokopo. At Mioko, the number of sellers varied between eight and seventeen and averaged eleven, with an average total stock in trade of 30s. of betel and pepper, 30s. worth of lime, and about 20s. worth of various fruits and European commodities. A relatively small group of women from nearby villages, attending on a fairly regular basis, did all the selling. They sold about half of their produce on a typi- cal day. Vunakabi was a more occasional market, with no sellers on many days and on others only about as many as at Kokopo; yet on days when there was much activity at the fishing beach, a dozen or more local women might turn up to sell betel or cooking bananas to labourers from Malapau plantation or to passers-by on the Rabaul road. The market at Vunapope hospital was bigger, sometimes with as many as twenty or thirty women sellers, many of them maternity patients awaiting or recovering from delivery. Hus- bands would bring a load of food for their wives, and the wives would use some for immediate consumption, and some for sale, saving the money received for later purchases. Husbands with large amounts of produce available could thus take advantage of their wife's hospitalization for her to earn money by marketing.

All these market places depend on the existence of a special buy- ing population: in Kokopo, on urban workers or the families of government employees; at Mioko, on plantation workers, passing trucks and Tolai coming to sell copra, or Europeans returning to plantations; at Vunakabi, on the workers on Malapau plantation and passers-by on the road; and at Vunapope, on other hospital patients. Because of the special character of the buying groups, only sellers of the one or two major commodities attend and they are willing to take only a few risks with additional commodities which might attract new types of customers. And though the sellers may be at the market place fairly regularly, the income they derive from selling is nominal. They are women who otherwise would not be profitably employed—pregnant women, wives of town workers, or women with numbers of young children. They are happy to convert the family's surplus food production into cash, but they do not try to increase production for the market, nor do they make entrepreneurial experiments.

(c) Rabaul Market

Rabaul market on Saturdays in 1961 was very much a larger version of Kokopo market. At the northeast edge of the town of Rabaul is an area of native land called Vunamai. It fronts on the major east-west road in Rabaul, Malaguna Road, and the Chinatown area of trade stores, businesses, small restaurants, and dwellings is opposite to it. The market precinct is enclosed by two roads that turn off Malaguna Road about sixty yards apart and are connected at the north end, about one hundred yards in. The actual market was located at the northern end of the precinct, away from Malaguna Road, and consisted of two permanent, covered sheds. The one facing the westward entrance road was of wood with a low-hanging thatched roof; the one on the eastern side was of metal and concrete construction. Outside the precinct to the north straggled a few small stalls of bamboo and thatch, and on the open grassy space between the sheds and the road there were a few wooden stands on which lime packets were displayed. Everything was open, and trucks could drive right to the market sheds. The sheds provided the only immediate shade, though there was a grove of trees west of the market near the Rabaul Council and Tolai Cocoa Project offices.

Goods were arranged much as in Kokopo. European foods were displayed in the better shed, the eastern one, with bulky root vegetables for sale to Europeans on display on the roadward side of the European shed. Bulky native foods like taro and stalks of bananas were mainly displayed on the grassy area, where many native trucks pulled in to unload; betel-chewing necessities, lime, peanuts, cooked foods, some fish, and native green vegetables were grouped in and around the thatched shed. There was, however, more duplication in the kinds of foods displayed in different areas than at Kokopo, and the newer stalls at the northern end contained an overflow of sellers of all goods.

Sellers began arriving early on a Saturday, about six-thirty, with the main flow between eight and nine. According to Dr. T. S. Epstein, the number of sellers on the Saturdays in June 1961 averaged 1,920, and in July my own counts indicated a continuation of this pattern. On 29 July, however, a Sepik worker molested a Tolai woman and was assaulted by her aggrieved husband; this set off a riot of numbers of Sepik workers and off-duty policemen, in which market stalls were destroyed and Tolai market women were beaten. On the following day Sepik policemen, "guarding" against unarmed protesting Tolai, ignored their officers' orders and shot down several Tolai. For the rest of that year the number of sellers was only about 1,250. The imposition on 7 October of a vendor's charge of one shilling for a place in the sheds and sixpence for a place in the sun may have discouraged attendance also, but this was not at all clear, since the numbers attending were at that point slowly beginning to rise for the first time since the riot. One other major effect of the riot was to alter the balance of male and female sellers of European foodstuffs. Instead of the pre-riot pattern of thirty to forty male sellers among about three hundred women in and around the European shed, with a flow of men coming at about two-thirty in the afternoon to collect the proceeds from the sales, after the riot there were about eighty male vendors, nearly half the total number inside the shed.

Unlike the Kokopo market, the Rabaul market had a series of peaks in the flow of buyers, the greatest number of whom came by truck, car, or taxi. Between seven and eight the buyers were mainly Chinese, along with some Tolai from the villages near Rabaul which were importers of basic foodstuffs. The trucks bringing in the female sellers and their loads also brought in numbers of male buyers in an increasing wave which reached a peak around nine o'clock and then fell off. Europeans from all over town began arriving about eight-thirty, and the flow continued for an hour or an hour and a half. Throughout the morning there was a steady stream of non-Tolai workers, coming mainly on foot from jobs around town and including many house servants buying for their employers. Their numbers were vastly augmented at noon, when office workers (mainly Papuan) arrived in taxis. At eleven or so, an exodus began of trucks taking back food supplies to nearby

Tolai villages, and these trucks returned again and again for additional loads after noon. Trucks from outlying areas began loading for their return journeys at about two. After that the market closed down rapidly, and by three-thirty it was almost empty except for the enormous piles of market leavings—coconut-frond baskets, discarded banana leaves which had been used as wrappings, betel husks, and banana skins.

Nearly all the sellers came by truck, and there were standard rates for particular distances. From Vunamami to Rabaul the round-trip fare was 6s. for a woman with a load, 4s. for a man; from Wairiki, farther out, it was 10s. for a woman, 6s. for a man; from Raluana a woman was charged 4s. Wairiki sellers could go to Kokopo market for 7s. and Raluana sellers could do so for 2s. Most eastern villages had one or two trucks within the village that collected and returned all the sellers from that village, but these trucks would also pick up other passengers en route if they had room. There were recognized points along the Kokopo–Rabaul road where pick-ups were made and passengers waited.

Eastern villagers had a choice of markets, and only those who had large quantities of compact merchandise, or who had additional reasons for going to Rabaul, would spend the money for the truck fare to Rabaul. From Vunamami a few vendors—usually one or two each week—took in lime, almost exclusively, and they sold one hundred to one hundred and fifty packets each. On one particular Saturday, for example, they were accompanied by the wife of the Methodist minister, who had to attend a meeting in Rabaul. She brought in 28s. worth of planting material for *ibika* (*a inoa*), and since she happened to be the only seller of this in the market, she quickly sold out. For villagers along the north coast or to the west, Rabaul was the only major market.

Table 10 summarizes the results of a survey of vehicles leaving the market precinct. A total of about 300 trucks, 200 utilities or pick-up trucks, and 50 panel vans, 130 Land-Rovers passed through the market every Saturday, roughly half of these being empty vehicles leaving after unloading. Europeans and Chinese drove about half of the utilities and Land-Rovers counted, and most of the panel vans which attended the market each week. Practically all the 350 private cars belonged to Europeans or Chinese, but most of the 260 taxis leaving the market with loads were hired by Papuans or other New Guineans.

A sample of about 6 percent of all loaded vehicles leaving the

Table 10

VEHICLES AT RABAUL MARKET AND THEIR
PURCHASES, JUNE AND NOVEMBER, 1961*

Type of Vehicle	Average Number	Average Amount of Purchases per Vehicle	Average Number of Passengers per Vehicle
Full truck, Tolai†	155	184/–	12.5‡
Full truck, European	6	50/2	3.2
Utilities, Tolai	60	42/9	4.3
Utilities, other	81	41/5	1.9
Land-Rovers	128	49/3	2.0
Panel vans	49	53/2	3.1
Full taxis, Tolai	64	19/–	2.2‡
Full taxis, other New Guinean, etc.	198	22/7	2.2‡
Cars, European	230	21/8	1.9
Cars, Chinese	135	26/1	2.3

* Based on a total count of departures, classified by vehicle type; a one-sixth time sample of departures, classified by type and number of passengers; a roughly 6 percent sample of vehicles was interviewed while loading.

† Full truck, Tolai, figures are for June only. For November the figures were 127 vehicles, buying 246/9 produce, with 14.0 passengers each.

‡ Indicates that the driver was not counted as a passenger.

market was checked as each vehicle was loaded, and details of numbers of passengers, their purchases of market produce, place of origin, unsold produce, travel costs, and so on were recorded.[9] The figures for volume of purchase and numbers of passengers for three Saturdays in June (3, 10, 24) and one in November (17) have been averaged in the table.

On 24 June the average value of produce brought in by sellers and taken back unsold was 30s. per Tolai truck, in addition to the amount purchased. In November the amount was only 17s. per truck.

A count was also made of pedestrian buyers leaving the market, but owing to the number of possible exits from the market, and the reluctance of interviewers to approach certain categories of

[9] For the June survey the assistance of six agricultural trainees was kindly provided by the Agricultural Extension Officer, Taliligap. Dale ToPin and Orim of Vunamami assisted in June and November.

buyers, the count was discontinued after one Saturday. The figures obtained are thus only a guide to orders of magnitude. A total of 1,538 people were counted leaving the market at the major exit at the southwest corner on 10 June. Spot checks by myself at two time periods indicated that these figures were only 60 percent complete for this exit, and that about one-fifth as many pedestrians left by other exits, giving a grand total of around 3,000 pedestrians leaving the market. Of these, 113 were Chinese, and 95 were Europeans—figures that have high reliability.

New Guinean pedestrians were classified in terms of the dress worn: shorts or *laplap* (waistcloth), shirt, singlet or no shirt, dress or blouse and *laplap*. From this count and my corrections, I estimate that about 150 New Guineans wore shirts and trousers or shorts—mainly Papuan or New Guinean white-collar workers—and 90 women (mainly their wives) wore dresses. About 1,000 men wore waistcloths and shirts (mainly Tolai and house servants); about 750 men wore singlets with waistcloths or shorts, or shorts alone (mainly plantation labourers); about 600 men wore waistcloths alone (both Tolai men and labourers). About 500 women (mainly Tolai) wore waistcloths and blouses. These figures undoubtedly include some double counting. There was an outflow of women between nine and ten-thirty, some with many purchases destined for resale to Europeans in town, but the large majority without purchases, leaving to buy goods at stores using money obtained from market sales. They returned later to leave on the trucks after noon. Tolai men, arriving on later trucks and having met friends and purchased betel, peanuts, and so on, left to make the round of town stores in midmorning, and did not usually return to the market place unless they had further purchases to make. They were picked up by trucks at collecting points along the main road. Plantation labourers drifted in and out of the market place, from about eleven o'clock on.

One hundred and thirty pedestrians were interviewed about their purchases. They seem to have been selected for approachability, and because they were carrying purchases, rather than randomly, but gave the following average volumes of purchases.[10]

[10] The categories of dress proved sufficiently discriminating to permit the total count of pedestrians to be divided into subgroups. The figures of average purchases by dress category did not, however, prove reliable. The averages for ethnic subgroups shown in Table 14 were calculated on the basis of questionnaire responses, not dress.

```
 3 Europeans  ................   5/4
 1 Chinese  ...................   3/–
14 men in shorts and shirts  ....   3/5
 2 men in shorts and singlets  ....   1/–
24 men in waistcloths and shirts .   3/8
35 men in waistcloths only  ......   4/1
 6 men in waistcloths and singlets   1/–
26 women in blouses  ...........   2/–
19 women in dresses  ...........   3/8
```

My spot checks indicated that people who had not bought anything were not interviewed, and that these included large numbers of Tolai men, Tolai market women, and plantation workers. The survey averages for these groups should be reduced to less than half in projecting to estimate total purchases.

Combining these figures, ignoring double counting as it is probably matched by failure to count other people, and making allowances for the number of house servants accompanying Europeans in their cars, an estimate of the total traffic in Rabaul market on four Saturdays can be compiled, as is shown in Table 11.

June 10th in these estimates appears as a larger market than the others. It was a holiday week-end, when some out-of-town Europeans were in Rabaul, and there was some stocking of foods for the Monday holiday. The drop in Tolai attendance after the riots appears clearly in the number of vehicle passengers, and I may have overestimated in my guess of November pedestrians. Yet the volume of sales shows much less change. This virtual stability of sales despite variations in the number of sellers becomes even more striking when one takes into account the amounts taken back unsold—£222 on 24 June and £108 on 17 November. Large market days made for disproportionately large gluts.

These gluts were of the same kind as at Kokopo—that is, European vegetables or fruits—and they occurred especially for producers who had begun to specialize in a single commodity. Thus on 14 June (a week-day) when total sales in the market were about £127, unsold produce worth £30 remained at 2:00 P.M. One-fifth of this was green beans, and half of the beans were provided by three sellers, each left with an average of twenty shillings' worth. The other seventeen sellers of beans had less than four shillings' worth each. Another £12 worth was of other European vegetables, particularly Chinese cabbage, lettuce, and cucumbers, with two volume sellers providing the bulk of each com-

Table 11

ESTIMATED ATTENDANCE AND PURCHASES AT RABAUL MARKET, 1961*

	Europeans		Chinese		Tolai		Non-Tolai	
	Number	Amount Bought	Number	Amount Bought	Number	Amount Bought	Number	Amount Bought
3 June								
left in vehicles	360	£421	352	£303	2,668	£1,601	480	£160
left on foot	95	25	113	17	1,505	77	891	83
Total	455	£446	465	£320	4,173	£1,678	1,371	£243
10 June								
left in vehicles	527	£631	469	£402	2,846	£1,688	627	£219
left on foot	95	25	113	17	1,505	77	891	83
Total	622	£656	582	£419	4,351	£1,765	1,518	£302
24 June								
left in vehicles	441	£505	424	£364	2,549	£1,554	545	£174
left on foot	95	25	113	17	1,505	77	891	83
Total	536	£530	537	£381	4,054	£1,631	1,436	£257
17 November								
left in vehicles	479	£339	400	£301	2,079	£1,527	627	£219
left on foot	95	25	113	17	1,000	52	891	83
Total	574	£364	513	£318	3,079	£1,579	1,518	£302

	Total Attendance	Total Purchases
3 June	6,464	£2,687
10 June	7,073	£3,142
24 June	6,563	£2,799
17 November	5,684	£2,563

* Pedestrians counted on 10 June only, with a guessed drop in Tolai pedestrians for 17 November. Vehicular attenders estimated as explained in text for 10 and 24 June, and 17 November. For 3 June, all estimates are based on a half-hour vehicle count which ran 10 percent below comparable figures for 10 June, extrapolated using averages based on 10 and 24 June. They are cited only to permit comparison with estimates based on a sample of sellers on the same day, cited in T. S. Epstein (1961).

modity. The three native commodities of which there was a surplus were coconuts, betel, and lime—all storable items and all handled by many sellers who had sold the majority of their stock. The same generalization is thus applicable in Rabaul as in Kokopo: it does not pay to specialize in goods for the minority European purchasers, because a surplus and lack of sales can occur too easily.

Data on the composition of the demand in Rabaul market were obtained by interviewing a sample of buyers, both pedestrians and vehicular passengers as they were leaving the market. Tables 12, 13, 14, and 15 summarize these data. The interviewers were

Table 12

PURCHASES BY VEHICLE PASSENGERS IN RABAUL MARKET
IN JUNE AND NOVEMBER, 1961*

	Tolai	New Guinean	European	Chinese
Number of vehicles checked	57	47	30	40
Number of passengers	842	191	101	98
Travel costs	1,989/-	ca. 305/-	?	?
Volume purchased	10,567/-	1,975/-	1,286/-	1,778/-
Goods purchased (in percentages)				
Betel and lime	4.8	10.3	1.9	2.9
Drinking coconuts and refreshments	1.7	8.2	5.9	4.9
Cooking bananas	24.4	9.0	2.8	1.5
Taro	10.8	6.8	4.0	2.1
Sweet potatoes	7.5	10.4	9.0	7.0
Tigapu and other roots	15.4	15.7	4.0	3.7
Native greens	3.5	2.8	1.1	1.5
European greens	.6	5.5	26.5	16.3
Salad vegetables	.3	2.3	13.0	5.5
Eating bananas	1.9	3.3	5.0	3.8
Fruits	1.1	.6	8.8	2.2
Eggs	—	.4	5.7	22.0
Chickens	0	1.3	3.9	22.8
Fish (fresh and cooked)	1.2	4.3	1.6	.5
Coconuts	24.4	17.6	5.8	2.1
Miscellaneous (brooms, etc.)	2.2	1.5	1.1	1.2

* Half-castes are included with Chinese; European and Chinese purchases include some made for feeding New Guinean employees. The total sample interviewed constitutes about 12 percent of the number of European and Chinese vehicles, and 24 percent of the New Guinean vehicles visiting any one Saturday market. In this and subsequent tables "Drinking coconuts and refreshments" include peanuts, *galip* nuts, sugar-cane, cooked food, and watermelon. "Other roots" include yams, *mami*, manioc. "Native greens" include *ibika, karakap*, pumpkin greens, watercress. "European greens" include Chinese cabbage, green beans, pumpkin, egg-plant, chocoes, corn, etc. "Salad vegetables" include lettuce, cucumbers, tomatoes, parsley, spring onions. "Fish" includes fresh and cooked fish, and shellfish. "Fruits" include pine-apples, pawpaws, mangoes, grenadillas, oranges, lemons, limes, five-corners, etc.

Table 13

PURCHASES BY TOLAI VILLAGE GROUPS DEPARTING BY TRUCK FROM
RABAUL MARKET IN JUNE AND NOVEMBER, 1961*

	Village Group					
	Matupit	*Malaguna*	*Near*	*Plateau*	*West*	*East*
Number of vehicles checked	8	7	16	8	10	8
Number of passengers	175	117	181	154	116	96
Travel costs	186/–	154/–	216/–	474/–	462/–	497/–
Volume purchased	3,326/–	1,827/–	1,632/–	962/–	1,829/–	992/–
Goods purchased (in percentages)						
Betel and lime	3.4	4.7	2.1	8.5	1.2	6.1
Drinking coconuts and refreshments	1.2	.9	3.6	2.3	1.3	1.8
Cooking bananas	31.6	25.7	40.0	16.8	5.9	10.6
Taro	9.7	15.2	18.0	14.6	13.6	13.1
Sweet potatoes	8.7	10.2	9.6	4.3	4.5	2.4
Tigapu and other roots	21.5	17.7	12.0	33.5	3.0	6.1
Native greens	4.9	3.9	3.8	3.5	1.4	1.6
European greens	.1	1.0	1.5	.1	.6	.9
Salad vegetables	.1	0	0	2.3	.4	.4
Eating bananas	2.3	1.1	1.4	4.1	1.6	.8
Fruits	.6	.4	1.2	.8	—	6.2
Eggs	—	—	—	—	.1	—
Chickens	—	—	—	—	—	—
Fish (fresh and cooked)	.1	.4	.6	.4	2.2	6.2
Coconuts	13.8	17.0	2.4	.8	62.4	39.9
Planting materials, brooms, flowers, etc.	1.9	1.8	3.0	5.2	1.3	1.6

* "Near" villages are Iawakaka, Nodup, Pilapila, Rapidik, Ratavul, Ratung, Talakua, Toleap, Talwat; "Plateau" villages include Nangananga, Navuneram, Rabarua, Ratavul, Tavuilui, Vunairoto; "Western" include Kabakada, Kuraip, Napapar, Rapitok, Reber; "Eastern" include Gunanba, Kokopo, Malakuna, Ngunguna, Ramale, and Toma. The sample is approximately 31.5 percent of the number of Tolai tricks and utilities attending one Saturday market. Categories of goods are described in Table 12. The first three columns are peri-urban food importers; the next two are the major suppliers of food-stuffs; the last column are suppliers of small specialist products like lime.

Table 14

PURCHASES BY PEDESTRIAN BUYERS IN
RABAUL MARKET IN JUNE 1961*

	Tolai Women	Tolai Men	Purchased on Behalf of	
			New Guineans	Europeans and Chinese
Number of buyers questioned	32	22	42	34
Volume purchased	65/–	44/–	127/–	120/–
Goods purchased (in percentages)				
Betel and lime	26.1	25.0	35.4	—
Drinking coconuts and refreshments	20.0	13.7	6.3	.8
Cooking bananas	18.1	—	4.7	—
Taro	3.1	—	—	—
Sweet potatoes	—	—	11.0	3.3
Tigapu and other roots	9.2	18.2	7.9	—
Native greens	3.1	—	4.7	—
European greens	4.6	—	5.5	20.8
Salad vegetables	—	—	1.6	36.7
Eating bananas	6.2	—	4.7	8.3
Fruits	—	—	.8	16.7
Eggs	4.6	—	.8	5.0
Chickens	—	40.9	15.8	8.3
Fish (fresh and cooked)	4.6	2.3	.8	—

* Purchases for Europeans and Chinese in column 4 were made in twenty-six instances by house servants, in four instances by Tolai women buying for resale, and in four instances by Europeans and Chinese. Categories of goods are described in Table 12 p. 208.

instructed to approach vehicles as they were loading (or pedestrians as they were leaving) and to record for each what was bought, as well as the answers to questions about destination, ethnic group of passengers, fares paid, whether the goods were for their own consumption or for resale, and so on. When one interview was completed, interviewers moved to the nearest vehicle or pedestrian. Because of the haphazard nature of the interviewing, one could not expect any constant bias within various sample subgroups. The different time taken to observe, say, a taxi and a truck loading and obvious preferences by interviewers meant that different classes of vehicles were differently represented in the samples and would have to be multiplied by different factors to esti-

Table 15

PERCENTAGES OF MARKET SALES TO DIFFERENT
ETHNIC GROUPS, BY PRODUCTS*

	Tolai	New Guinea	European	Chinese	Total
Betel and lime	2.4	2.4	.3	.6	5.7
Drinking coconuts and refreshments	1.2	1.1	.9	1.0	4.2
Cooking bananas	11.6	1.2	.4	.3	13.5
Taro	5.1	.8	.6	.4	6.9
Sweet potatoes	3.5	1.6	1.2	1.5	7.8
Other roots	7.7	2.0	.6	.8	11.1
Native greens	1.7	.5	.2	.3	2.7
European greens	.3	.8	4.1	3.5	8.7
Salad vegetables	.2	.3	2.1	1.2	3.8
Eating bananas	.9	.5	.8	.8	3.0
Fruits	.5	.1	1.4	.5	2.5
Eggs	.1	.1	.9	4.7†	5.9†
Chickens	.4	.7	.6	4.8†	6.5†
Fish (fresh and cooked)	.6	.5	.2	.1	1.4
Coconuts	11.3†	2.0	.9	.4	14.6†
Miscellaneous	1.0	.2	.2	.2	1.6
Totals	48.5	14.9	15.4	21.2	100.0‡

* Percentages underlined indicate that a disproportionate part of the demand for that product is provided by one ethnic group—over two-thirds of the total demand being by Tolais, or over one-third of the total demand by one of the other groups. Total demand estimated by multiplying sample demand figures in Tables 13, 14, and 15 by factors listed in the text.

† These are subject to considerable sample error because they depend on interviews with a small number of bulk buyers.

‡ Totals may be discrepant because of rounding.

mate the total volume of purchases made by different ethnic groups. These factors were given by comparing the size of sample subgroups with the total figures obtained from the vehicle and pedestrian counts.

For Tolai trucks and utilities the sample represents 31.5 percent of the total for one Saturday; it represents 12 percent of the total for both European and Chinese vehicles, and 24 percent of the New Guinean–Papuan vehicle passengers. The factors for converting the sample figures for pedestrians into aggregates were 12 for Tolai women, 17 for Tolai men, 20 for New Guinean and Papuan workers and their wives, and 3.3 for Europeans and Chinese. In view of the large proportion of purchases made on behalf of employers (or for resale to Europeans) by New Guinea males and Tolai women, it seemed more meaningful to classify these in terms of the subgroup of ultimate consumers rather than in terms of the buyers. I have been inconsistent in this matter, since many European and Chinese vehicle purchases included produce for New Guinean household servants or plantation employees; but the amounts so included were always relatively small, and were usually conditioned by European tastes, as well as by those of the ultimate consumers. This is shown, for example, by the preference for *tigapu* and cooking bananas among New Guineans buying for themselves, whereas Europeans and Chinese rarely buy anything but sweet potatoes for their employees.

Interviews for a single subgroup conducted on different Saturdays have been grouped to increase sample size, as have pedestrian interviews conducted on week-days as well. Variation *within* subgroups is rather large, so that differences between Saturdays are not significant for any single subgroup. On the other hand, differences *between* subgroups are consistent over a long period. For three items—Tolai coconut purchases, and Chinese purchases of eggs and chickens—a large proportion of the total surveyed derived from a very small number of bulk purchases, rendering projections based on them subject to considerable sample error.

With these reservations, let us look at the figures. They confirm many of the qualitative descriptions already given. The way in which Tolai and New Guinean pedestrians largely came to buy betel requisites or refreshments before leaving for town is shown by comparing the left-hand columns of Tables 12 and 14; the virtual monopoly of purchases of "European greens" by Chinese and Europeans, of salads and other fruits by Europeans, and of eggs and chickens by Chinese, appears in Table 12 and Table 14. The separation between "native foods" and "European foods" seen in the physical separation of the areas in which they were sold is reflected in the distinctive patterns of demand for these commodities.

But other distinctions are brought out. In the first place, the volume of sales between Tolai (Table 15, col. 1) constituted 48.5 percent of all sales. Over 95 percent of these sales were of "indigenous" foodstuffs—root crops, coconuts, betel requisites, "native greens," fish, and drinking coconuts. Europeans and Chinese only accounted for about one-third of all purchases, and these were of varied commodities, only about half of them being of the "specialized categories" of European greens, salads, other fruits, eggs and chickens. If the average Saturday turnover was £3,000, over £1,400 was contributed by inter-Tolai sales of indigenous produce, only £350 by sales to Europeans and Chinese of "European" vegetables and fruits, and another £300 by sales of chickens and eggs to them. With immigrant New Guinean demand further supplementing inter-Tolai sales, and with sales to Europeans and Chinese almost unchanging from week to week, the greater incentive to specialize in indigenous foods is evident.

This may not always be true in future, for the immigrant New Guinean workers, or at least those urban workers who left the market by taxis, had a pattern of demand that fell somewhere between that of the Tolais and that of the Europeans. They ate more sweet potatoes and less taro, more salad and European greens and fewer native greens, and more *mau* (eating) bananas. As their numbers increase, so will the market for what were in 1961 "European" foods.

A comparison between the demand patterns of immigrant workers and Tolais also indicates some interesting similarities and differences. Betel requisites were the principal item sold to New Guineans, although the purchases by Tolai pedestrians indicate that the sales to Tolai in general were comparatively low only because most groups grew their own supplies at home. Consumption was probably about equal in the two groups. Although the aggregate sales of starchy foods to Tolai were about five times as great as those to New Guineans, there was not so much qualitative difference in their demands as the Tolai description of themselves as eaters of taro and cooking bananas would suggest. Though other New Guineans prefer *tigapu* and sweet potatoes, they bought some taro and cooking bananas; Tolai, on the other hand, bought large quantities of sweet potatoes and *tigapu*. Their relative cheapness, perhaps a reflection of their status as "poor substitutes" in Tolai eyes, made them of considerable importance in Tolai areas like Matupit and Malaguna which imported a large proportion of their foodstuffs. If Tolai prosperity continues to grow at the 1961 rate, it is likely to involve further increases in the demand for the prestige crops of bananas and taro. Cash prices for these are likely to rise even if the *tabu* prices do not (i.e., *tabu* will appreciate relative to cash). This rise will be held in check only by the possibility of substituting other root crops for the prestige foods. On the other hand, if incomes remain stable or decline, the substitution of sweet potatoes and *tigapu* for taro and bananas would seem likely to increase.

Table 13, while bringing out the great importance of the demand from the two villages closest to Rabaul—Malaguna and Matupit—in determining the nature of Rabaul market, does not show at all clearly the traditional interdependence of the inland taro and betel producers from the west and the east, and the coastal producers of bananas, lime, and fish from Matupit, Malaguna, and the "near" north coast villages. In part this is because the sample includes some coastal villages in the east and west, but the demands by all groups were much more similar than would be expected on this basis alone. Even the western villages, traditionally the "bread-basket" of the Tolai area, bought an amount of carbohydrates worth one-quarter of their total market purchases. The eastern village purchases also included one-third starches, although those of all the villages near Rabaul included about 70 percent starches. The western and eastern village figures were somewhat depressed by the large amounts of coconuts bought by individual businessmen from those areas for processing into copra.

In summary, then, the figures indicate that the Rabaul market had gradually undergone a transformation. The earlier interdependence of different ecological areas which was clearly apparent still in Kokopo market had gradually been replaced by a different form of interdependence. One major interdependence was between the land-short villages near Rabaul, which could no longer produce their own food and had therefore tended to specialize in urban labour for cash, and the rural villages which produced food crops for them. On the other hand, the so-called rural villagers were not simply peasants producing for sophisticated urbanites. Each "rural" village had its individuals who specialized in producing different bulk crops for the market, and who themselves purchased from other producers the vegetables that they needed for subsistence. The villagers of Matupit and Malaguna may have become what Finney (1965) has called "rural proletarians," whereas the people of Vunamami and other "outer" areas have become "commercial farmers." Most of their trade is still conducted through the mechanisms of delayed barter exchanges, using *tabu* and standard fixed equivalences. Profit is, supposedly, not the driving force for barter exchanges, and as long as the exchanges are more or less even, there is no reason why this should not continue to be so. If the system is thrown out of balance, it will not be because of direct European influences or demand for vegetables, but rather because of an inability of Tolai food production to keep pace with the rising demand in all areas, produced by population increase and by the declining food production of areas that are becoming fully planted to cocoa and coconuts. This natural increase is the dynamic factor in the picture of Tolai marketing, and it represents part of a steady change within the Tolai economy itself, facilitated by the constant presence of a male interest in profiting.

VI

Co-operatives

Not all marketing in which Vunamami is involved is conducted in the market place. Virtually all the copra produced in Vunamami is now sold through the local co-operative society, named Bitatali. This co-operative also runs a general store, which sells most staple foods, and luxuries like cigarettes, operates a petrol pump and sells oil and kerosene, stocks limited quantities of tools, utensils, and clothing, and buys some large items at discounts for Co-operative members. After the nearby society of Bitaulagumgum, it was in 1961 the most successful of the eleven co-operative societies in the Tolai area. It had 762 signed-up members, mainly from the villages of Vunamami, Vunabalbal, Bitarebarebe, and Tingenavudu. For 1960, it had copra sales of £11,422 and retail store sales of £10,591, for a net profit of £2,360. I estimate that over 90 percent of all local purchases of the kinds of items stocked in the Co-operative store were in 1961 bought there, though many special items, such as cameras and drip-dry shirts, were bought exclusively from large European or Chinese stores. Items bought during visits to Rabaul or Kokopo, from the two small trade stores stocking small amounts of staples and operated part time by Vunamami residents in Lumluvur ward, account for the rest of the purchases.

As will appear, the entirely non-traditional organization of the co-operative could equally well be considered as a rather special type of "business." But because of its equally strong trading aspect, it merits treatment immediately. As a straightforward description of an introduced institution, it will prepare the reader for the way in which such an organization can include many indigenous forms in its operation, and in that way it will serve as an introduction to the discussion of businesses in general in Chapter 7.

GENERAL

The official organization of co-operatives in the Tolai area consists in having all co-operative societies meeting certain standards register with the Government Registry of Co-operatives in Port Moresby. This obligates them to keep standardized accounts and lists of membership, and to maintain an approved balance between reserve funds and the distribution of dividends or patronage refunds (rebates). In return, societies receive advice and supervision from Co-operative Officers, who are paid from government funds and not from local revenues. Local societies meet all other charges, and all other employees are local people. In practice a Co-op Officer's advice and supervision may extend to minute details of day-to-day operation in a new co-operative with inexperienced members and staff; an active co-operative may run virtually independently, making its own decisions about retail mark-ups or profit distribution, provided that these do not conflict with what "Moresby"—the Government Registry—and the ordinances demand.

The Co-op Officers have their base (and their chief means of controlling society policies) in the New Britain Co-operative Association, located in Rabaul. The "members" of the Association are the local societies, not only in the Tolai area but throughout New Britain and New Ireland. Each society subscribes for shares in the Association to the value of three-fifths of its own subscribed capital. The Association is primarily the wholesale agency for the societies, selling them merchandise and buying their copra for bulking and resale to the Copra Marketing Board. It does a smaller amount of business wholesaling to private storekeepers or unregistered co-operatives, redrying copra rejected by the C.M.B., and buying large items at trade discounts for individual members. It trains store clerks both on the spot, and by selecting candidates for the training school in Moresby. Its board of directors includes some twenty of the most influential Tolai of the region, and meets approximately once a month. Meetings of delegates from the societies occur less frequently but draw over a hundred individuals, and are occasions of lively debate and politicking. The chairman (usually one of the directors) is elected annually; the secretary is a Tolai. Most official business is conducted in pidgin for the benefit of the Co-op Officer, but most business from the floor is discussed in Tolai.

The Association's history, like that of co-operatives in the Territory as a whole, is a checkered one. Between 1948 and 1953 many small societies began operating unofficially, some with advice and some without, but most were short-lived or plagued with difficulties. In 1953 Co-op Officers arrived in Rabaul to organize and assist this movement. They were not specially trained, but were usually dedicated ex-administrators imbued with the idea that "co-operation" was a simple panacea for the slowness of indigenous development. Enrolling members, creating enthusiasm, and presenting members with goods to buy and an opportunity to sell copra directly instead of through European or Chinese middlemen would, they thought, automatically lead to success. Their proselytizing soon created nineteen societies with a membership of 13,315, each member subscribing £5. Societies were encouraged to build impressive permanent buildings with concrete floors and metal roofs, and to stock a wide variety of goods, including high-priced tools and clothing. The Association hired a large staff, bought vehicles, and was negotiating for a motor launch.

But the ambitious dream was economically unsound and within a year many societies were bankrupt. Some failures were due to poor bookkeeping, illegal extension of credit, thefts, or the absconding of storekeepers. But more were due to the economic impracticality of the visionary Co-op Officers. Prices charged were usually higher than in Chinese stores; merchandise was stocked because it was thought natives *should* buy it rather than because they *would* buy it; the grandiose predictions were not realized, enthusiasm waned, and with it the volume of sales. If societies did not fail, their sales volume rarely justified the scale of capital and overhead expenses incurred. The turnover of Co-op Officers was high, as each one tried to cope with one or more of the problems of training staff, controlling Society buying and pricing, and organizing the management and capital structure of the Association. Successes in one area were negated by failures in others, and by 1957 only twelve societies remained. Three more were in bad straits and either withdrew or were expelled in 1959.

The surviving societies were ones in which initial enthusiasm had been high and literate personnel had been available, located where copra marketing was a major business. Throughout, they had been running at a small profit but had appeared to be in difficulties because their profits were needed as a reserve and as working capital, to complement the subscription capital that had been mostly spent on fixed assets. In 1957 an officer trained in economics succeeded in writing off losses and depreciating the big initial capital expenses, bringing order out of chaotic balance sheets. The Association became a more modest business, balancing overhead against volume, carrying goods that were in demand, and rarely trying to educate consumer tastes. In that year Bitaulagumgum's reserves became sufficient, according to Moresby, to allow payment of a patronage refund. Bitatali followed with "rebates" in 1958, and other societies did so later.

From this base steady improvement was shown. Association turnover rose from £64,000 in 1957, to £125,000 in 1959, and £161,000 in 1960. In 1961 the number of registered Tolai societies was back to eleven, and new unregistered societies throughout New Britain depended on the largely Tolai association, particularly for trained personnel. As will appear, Co-op Officers were still trying to solve the problems of insufficient working capital to support the increased turnover, but at the same time they were considering profitable avenues for expansion within the managerial and financial limitations of societies—a bakery to supply the growing Tolai demand for bread and scones, a restaurant and department store in Rabaul, purchase of a plantation, and a new warehouse for the Kokopo area.

THE VUNAMAMI SCENE

The history of the area points up the importance of trained and active Co-op Officers in the success of societies. It might also seem to imply that, without close supervision, co-operatives are doomed to failure by a shortage of trained accountants and by temptations to bookkeepers who handle large sums—and the demands of extended kinsmen on these bookkeepers. To show that this is not necessarily the case, and to emphasize the local contribution, let us once again look at an example from the inside viewpoint: namely, the Bitatali Society, its history and its 1961 operations.

(a) Bitatali History

Before 1953 Vunamami was involved in three co-operatives. One had a majority of Raluana participants and was a restaurant, set up near Kokopo market and the nearby hospital (later replaced by Butuwin). It was called *Unaruk* (The Come Inn). It was capitalized largely by the unofficial "tax" of £4, collected in

Raluana village, and at first was financially very successful, using local resources and having a highly educated managing group. Unfortunately the bitterness between the ardent Council enthusiasts of Vunamami and the anti-Council group of Raluana in 1953 resulted in Raluana's being expelled from the Council-controlled market, and the restaurant closed down. I could not discover what happened to its funds, but it is remembered as a shining example of what co-operation can achieve if it is not bedevilled by factionalism.

Largely with it as an example, two "co-operative" stores had been started in Vunamami village by 1952, both of them on the piece of land called Bitatali, though on the opposite side of the Toma Road to where the present store stands. The working nucleus for both stores was the group of young men born between about 1925 and 1930, who, before the war, had become friendly with their Raluana contemporaries at Malaguna Tech. Leadership was provided largely by three men: Enos, the Paramount Luluai, Alwas, the retired clerk of the Kokopo District Office, and Beniona ToKarai, who had taught in the Methodist post-primary schools in Vunairima and Raluana before the war. Enos had organized the group to build a school on his own land, next door to Bitatali, so that they could complete their education under Alwas and Beniona, as soon as Vunamami returned from the beach camp in 1947.[1] Soon after, Enos, again assisted by Beniona and Alwas, and helped by the unavailability of consumer goods generally, began advocating a store "for the people." A subscription levy was taken throughout Vunamami and Vunabalbal villages, and a store was built on the plot of land at the boundary—Bitatali. The school provided a pool of reasonably well-trained clerical staff.

I could obtain no figures about the capitalization of the store, the contributors, or the mode of operation, because its records were destroyed when Bitatali Society was formally organized. It operated for several years, but some informants suggested a history of frequent changes of storekeeper (all of them from the group of educated Vunamami and Vunabalbal men), and of recurrent shortages of funds when accounts were made. In April 1952 the Council passed a motion that all co-operative businesses had to be registered with the Council, presumably to control just

[1] This voluntary school was the nucleus out of which Vunamami Council developed Nganalaka School in 1951.

such irregularities. Everyone agreed with pride, however, that "we had a store for the people before the Co-operative was founded."

The second store on Bitatali was started by the young men themselves. Eight of them, headed by Sailas ToBitaoko, were angry at the way in which Chinese traders who grew no coconuts themselves could get rich from copra trading. The eight had money and decided to pool their funds, buy copra, and sell it to the P.C.B. One man argued that everyone should put in £100: Jack Kanit, who took over as council clerk at about this time, urged a more realistic approach of bringing in more participants and seeing how much could be obtained. The number of participants was raised to twenty by inviting other youths and some of the more educated older men, including Vin ToBaining, and altogether £230 10s. was subscribed. The group was composed of members of a number of unrelated clans, and could not adopt the usual practice of giving itself the name of a clan. It named itself ToVurmatana (Mr. Mix-up) to indicate this, but I shall call it the Group of Twenty. Jack Kanit and Osea ToKankan were put in charge of the bookkeeping, including purchase of dockets and other clerical supplies.

The first efforts were unsuccessful. The first forty-eight bags of copra bought were rejected at the P.C.B. Depot at Kabakaul as too wet, and had to be dried again in Enos' copra drier. But the group learned fast, and their next four shipments were all accepted. The biggest surprise came when a cheque was received for the proceeds. It was so large that the members were "frightened." They had to have a bank account to be able to cash cheques of this size. ToBaining asked "What shall we do with the profit?" All agreed with Jack's suggestion that they should keep the money intact, reinvesting profits until the sum reached five to ten thousand pounds. Most members were young men without land or families and would have no other means of obtaining houses when they would need them. Such a sum would buy twenty houses, they vaguely thought. Or they might decide to buy a truck for copra transport, so as not to be dependent on the Council truck which they had been hiring. But they all felt that they needed advice, and fortunately for them a Co-operative Officer was just then appointed to New Britain.

The arrival of the Co-op Officer in 1953 thus dates the turning point in Vunamami; unfortunately, the early minutes of the Group of Twenty (on which the previous account is based), though

meticulously kept by Jack, were undated. In January 1953 the
new officer was introduced to Vunamami Council, and in August
there were heated Council discussions of who should go from the
area to the training school for storekeepers. By November Vunamami village, together with Vunabalbal, Bitarebarebe, and Tingenavudu villages and numerous individuals from further up the
Toma Road, had formed and officially registered the Bitatali Co-
operative Society. A total of 732 individuals subscribed £3,660
as capital. The earlier retail store was incorporated as part of the
society and ceased operations as soon as the new store was built.
Beniona was the carpenter for both Bitatali and Bitaulagumgum
stores. Bitaulagumgum Society immediately began active copra
trading but Bitatali at first concentrated on retailing to Vunamami
and buying copra from other villages, leaving Vunamami copra
marketing largely to the Group of Twenty, all of whom were
strong supporters of the new society.

I did not have a 1953 census list of the Vunamami area, but I
should think that the 732 members included an adult from every
household in the three first-named villages at that time. Between
1953 and 1961 new co-operatives were formed further up the
road and distant members withdrew from Bitatali; deaths and
migrations caused other accounts to become inactive, but in 1961
458 of the original 732 accounts were still active. Thirty new accounts had been opened, mainly by villagers who had been away
from the area in 1953. The 125 active accounts of Vunamami
residents included all households in the village. Beniona became
the society president, attending meetings of the Association as the
chief Bitatali delegate and actively promoting interest in the Co-op
among the Vunamami villagers. Osea and Sailas soon went away
to attend training courses and on their return took up duties as
clerks at Bitatali and Bitaulagumgum, respectively. Sailas could
still live in Vunamami, however, bicycling the two miles to work
each day.

From this point Bitatali's story is more or less typical of those
of other societies. It had spent all its original capital of £3,660,
three-fifths of it, or £2,196, having been subscribed as capital
shares of the Association; £1,036 went for a store with a tin roof
and concrete floor, and with good shelving and other fixtures,
and for a small shed for storing copra. Though working capital
was low, credit from the Association made it possible to buy
a fairly lavish stock—valued in August 1954 at £1,330, with copra

worth £485 also in storage. During the preceding six months also, wages for the storekeeper had come to an additional £85. Yet the tremendous local enthusiasm for the new venture meant that the accounts showed a paper surplus of £537 for the period. The grandiose level of capital expenditure and stocking was encouraged by the Co-operative Officer, who saw it as a good way of advertising that Co-ops were "real businesses," not hole-in-the-corner operations.

Indeed, the volume of copra sold to the C.M.B. and its high price— £3,477—carried the society through its first six months when consumer purchases amounted to only £437. In the following year another Group of Twenty member was hired (ToDaula). Expenditures for wages more than doubled, but retail sales increased even more, to about £2,500. At the same time, however, copra sales dropped substantially, to only £4,001 for the year. Several loads of copra were rejected because they got wet in the open shed. At the end of the year the books showed a net loss of £364, but the society still had enough funds and local support to survive, at a time when many other Tolai societies were being liquidated as bankrupt.

The Group of Twenty continued to function as a sort of loose associate rather than as a competitor to Bitatali, by buying the rejected copra and redrying it. It had increased its capital sufficiently to buy a diesel truck for £600, but as Bitatali weathered its storm and gradually began increasing its copra purchases, the Group of Twenty began to encounter trouble. Too little copra was available to make it economically justifiable to buy a truck for transporting Group copra only. Maintenance costs for the truck were unexpectedly high. Instead of the capital tripling or quadrupling as it had done at first, funds remained almost stationary. Recriminations began as to whether the principals in the Group were not misusing the truck, or misappropriating funds. Early in 1959 Eliap, who by then was the most successful carpenter in Vunabalbal, informed the group that he did not want his money remaining unprofitably in the business. Though others objected that he was needlessly breaking up something that was only temporarily in the doldrums, he got his way, and over £500 was distributed among the twenty. It was much less than they had hoped for, but a respectable yield on capital over ten years, during which the group had provided a service to the village and training for the Co-op.

The revival of the Bitatali Society involved allowing stocks of goods to run down and writing off some of the unsalable items that had been acquired in the first enthusiasm. ToDaula became a clerk in the District Office and the wage bill returned to £12 a month. By April 1957, although retail sales and copra purchases for the year were virtually unchanged, at £2,653 and £3,864, respectively, there was a profit of £236. Shell Oil had promised to install a tank and petrol pump, and at the annual meeting a rebate of threepence in the pound was voted. The meeting also raised the copra buying price to fivepence a pound to meet competition for Chinese traders.

This decision was unfortunate, because copra prices promptly fell, leaving the store with copra on hand worth £1,273; a rebate had to be foregone in 1958. Figures for 1959 showed the first effects of the demise, late in the year, of the Group of Twenty, with copra purchases up to £4,600 and retail sales up to £2,867. Profits soared to £1,247 and a very conservative rebate of sevenpence in the pound was voted. The advent of the petrol pump, increasing sales and making it worthwhile for copra to be brought by truck from distant villages, plus the full year of Vunamami copra buying, made 1960 a banner year. Copra purchases rose 110 percent, to £9,823, and retail sales rose 160 percent, to £7,533. The rise continued in 1961 to the figures of £11,422 and £10,591, respectively. Profits for the two years were £1,766 and £2,360, respectively, permitting rebates of one shilling and eightpence, and one shilling and sixpence in the pound. Turnover declined somewhat in the first six months of the fiscal year 1961–1962, but this could be entirely attributed to the decline in copra and cocoa prices. There seemed no waning of Vunamami enthusiasm for the Co-op.

(b) Bitatali Operations

The Bitatali store was run by one full-time clerk, Osea To-Kankan, with a helper to work in the copra store and to pump kerosene and petrol. For part of the year a trainee clerk also helped, before returning to operate a co-operative in his own area. It will be appreciated that the copra represented by £11,422 is approximately 200 tons, or about 1,500 pounds brought in every working day. Growers would bring it in loads averaging 60 pounds—the content of one coconut-frond bag, and the yield from one bet of a drier. These had to be weighed, a docket issued for each with the grower's Co-op number on it, and cash paid out. The price per pound was sixpence at the beginning of the year; it dropped to fourpence for several months and increased to fivepence again in November. The bags were emptied into a large bin, and when time was available the copra was rebagged into standard-weight sacks. About once a week, a truck, hired on contract by the Association from a Rabaul cartage firm, called to pick up the copra at the store. The storeman would do the loading, helped by any bystanders.

The store itself almost always had two or three people in it, in addition to Osea, who was there from soon after seven in the morning till after six at night. The advent of transistor radios, the first of which were allocated by the Association during 1961, one to a society, to familiarize people with the idea of radio listening, was part of the attraction. When Radio Rabaul started broadcasting in 1961 enthusiasm was intense, especially for the record request programmes, and the store was often jammed.[2] Daily store turnover can be seen to be in the region of £35, or about 230 sales of 3s., and for each sale a receipt ("docket") had to be issued, again with the purchaser's number on it. Slow service, especially when a customer was buying cloth, say, and wanted to see each colour and quality, and while dockets were written out, was accepted as normal, everyone present joining in the gossip in the traditional pattern of general stores. In fact, for one to state one's desires before making some sort of conversation with people present would have been considered very impolite. Only the occasional European plantation truck driver, quickly dropping in because he was unexpectedly out of cigarettes, behaved so rudely. But with the carbons of all the dockets needing to be tallied to yield each customer's patronage total, orders for new stock to be made out, and returns to be sent to the Association, it will be realized that the storekeeper was kept busy, if not exactly harried.

The pattern of buying by Vunamami was a little different from that of other villages. In Vunamami in 1960 purchases, at £2,782, exceeded copra sales of £2,749 by one percent, whereas other villages sold 11 percent more copra than they spent. At breakfast time in Vunamami one could see numbers of children on their way to the store to buy biscuits or scones, and sugar or tea for those families where there was a full-time worker. And again before

[2] By the end of 1961 only two Vunamami residents had bought their own sets.

the evening meal children would go to the store, this time to buy
rice and tinned meat or mackerel pike, kerosene for the family
lamps, and cigarettes for after dinner. During the day casual shop-
pers passing the store on their way to or from work, up or down
the Toma Road, would come in for everyday necessities such as
soap, matches, cigarettes, and flashlight batteries. Men or women
bringing in copra for sale would usually buy some larger item—
powder, cloth, or a lamp—with whatever loose change they got
in return (paper money they saved). Passengers from passing
trucks would come in to have a cold soft drink from the store
refrigerator while the truck filled up with petrol. More distant villages with fewer wage workers did not have the same demand
for "corner store" purchases.

The net effect can be seen in Table 16, which lists the replacement stock ordered by Bitatali Co-operative in August 1961. The
total stock of the Co-operative was valued at this time at just
over £1,000, and the £970 worth of goods ordered must represent fairly closely the retail purchases. It will be noted that no
major consumer durables are listed—no pots and pans, bicycles,
cameras, shovels, or lamps. A few of these items (but not bicycles
or cameras) were stocked at Bitatali, but they were mostly collecting dust. For these items, and for quality clothing such as
drip-dry shirts or tailored waistcloths (*sulu*), Vunamami residents
preferred to shop at stores in Rabaul where there was more choice,
more confidence in quality, or substantially lower prices (as, for
example, for Chinese aluminium pots and pans in Chinese trade
stores). For everyday needs, however, Bitatali supplied probably
90 percent of the Vunamami demand—the major exceptions being that most visitors to Rabaul, for whatever purpose, would
bring back a loaf of fresh bread, and that people working in
Kokopo would buy their meat, fish, and major-brand cigarettes
in the Chinese stores there, where prices were threepence lower
than at Bitatali.[3] Some of the sales of Bitatali were also conducted
from Osea's own house in Lumluvur, where he kept some stock
in a shed for residents of that area; he bought copra there in the
morning and at night. Prices were the same as at Bitatali proper,
and dockets were issued for many items, although others—in-

---

[3] This pattern would seem to have been established by 1958, although
at that time Bitatali was still trying to compete in the market for tools and
pots and pans, and food and tobacco tastes were somewhat less sophisticated than they are now.

Table 16

REPLACEMENT STOCKS ORDERED FOR BITATALI
STORE, AUGUST 1961 AND MARCH 1958*

| | | Retail Value | | March |
	Quantity	£	s.	1958
Food				
Rice	65 × 56 lb. bags	154 —		44 16
Biscuits	16 cartons	62 13		56 —
Tinned fish	744 × 15 oz. tins	74 8		19 4
Tinned meat	144 × 12 oz. tins	28 16		—
Scones	72 dozen	8 14		9 8
Sugar	7 × 70 lb. bags	24 10		9 6
Salt (1961, butter (1958)	2 × 56 lb. bags	7 —		6 15
Tea, coffee, dried milk	various	4 4		1 4
Soft drinks	20 dozen bottles	12 —		7 4
		£376 5s.		£153 17s.
Tobacco				
Major brands†	129 cartons	90 4		5 5
Local brands	20 cartons	20 —		—
Twist tobacco	63 lbs.	94 10		64 1
Pipe tobacco	6 lbs.	13 16		18 1
Matches, cigarette papers, etc.		4 1		4 18
		£222 11s.		£92 5s.
Toilet Goods				
Soap	3 3/4 cartons	14 14		15 6
Hairdye, peroxide, powder	4 dozen	4 4		4 10
Mirrors, scissors, sticking plaster		2 11		2 2
Razor blades (1961), toothbrushes (1958)	4 cartons	9 12		1 16
		£31 1s.		£23 14s.

Table 16 continued on p. 228

Table 16—Continued

	Quantity	Retail Value		March 1958
		£	s.	
Clothing				
Cloth, various grades	330 yards	70	11	3 9
Coloured shirts (1961), various (1958)	1 dozen	4	16	3 12
		£75	7s.	£7 1s.
Miscellaneous				
Gasoline	1,043 gallons	195	11	—
Kerosene, oil	144 gallons	35	2	22 —
Flashlight batteries	9 dozen	5	8	1 4
Corrugated iron (1961), cement (1958)	12 sheets	13	10	10 10
Chewing gum, stationery, files		4	1	4 15
Bicycle tubes (1961), pots, pans, tools (1958)	1/2 dozen	1	10	13 18
		£255	2s.	£52 7s.
Total purchased		£960	6s.	£329 4s.

* Figures were compiled from stock order forms seen in Bitatali store, by courtesy of Osea ToKankan. They correspond closely to the pattern of retail sales, with total stock just over £1,000. March 1958 figures are given for comparison.

† Major brands were Rothman's and Craven A; the local brand was Three Cats.

cluding beer, at that time illegal for native consumption—were private sales by Osea himself. Everyone referred to this copra collecting point and storage shed as "Osea's store," but it was not marked as such and I shall consider it merely as a branch of Bitatali, for Lumlulvur residents.

(c) Meetings

The Co-operative was not merely a supply agency and social gathering place but a political centre as well. Three full meetings of the society were held between April and November 1961, at each of which some 320 of the total active membership of 488 were present, together with their young children. Informal meetings of senior members of the society were held after the two general meetings of the New Britain Association, and in August when there was a possibility that the Co-op might be involved in the purchase of Ravalien plantation. Not only did representatives of Bitatali attend the general Association meetings, but two Vunamami men, Enos and ToVin, were on the board of directors of the Association. They met more regularly and reported on important issues at informal village meetings.

An analysis of these meetings throws considerable light on the decisions that a co-operative has to make, the management problems that face them, and the way in which the local society fits into the broader structure. I shall therefore discuss them in some detail.

Essentially, each of the three meetings of the local society had a special purpose: the first, to consider the accounts of the 1960 fiscal year; the second, to distribute the second payment on copra delivered in 1959; and the third, to distribute the rebate on 1960 business and to present a report of the first six months of the fiscal year 1961.

Fiscal years run from 1 April to 31 March, so the annual meeting of 14 April 1961 was held promptly to consider the accounts just closed. It needed only a totalling of the turnover for the last six months, copra and store business being taken separately, and a totalling of the receipts from the C.M.B. and the invoices from the Association to arrive at the gross profit of £1,342 for the six months. Store expenses (mainly copra sacks and salaries) were £272, leaving £1,070 to be added to the profit of the previous six months of £1,529. Of the net profit, £239 went to the statutory reserves which co-operatives must maintain, and as a donation to the training school run by the co-operative movement, leaving an available profit of £2,360. Osea presented these figures in Tolai to the meeting. The Co-operative Officer then spoke in pidgin, asking why the turnover and profit had dropped in the last six months. Was it because people were trying to help Chinese stores rather than their own store? He explained the overhead costs and the need for reserves, and pointed out that in addition to the £2,360 profit, there was also a second payment of £1,784 due from the C.M.B. What did people wish to do with the £4,000

total? This was an important issue; why had so few people come
to decide it? (I think the only people absent were those in wage
employment.) He then said that the Association needed money;
it had started with only a small amount of share capital to finance
a small amount of business. Now the business had grown to an
annual turnover of £161,000, but it was still financed by the
original £37,000 share capital. The Association as a whole had
£25,000 to share out, and if half of this were reinvested as share
capital, the business would be healthy. It would be the same as if
everyone invested another £2.

Discussion was heated, but at this time my Tolai was so limited
that I caught only the points made in pidgin. These were: (1) that
those people who did not help by patronizing the Co-op should
be the ones to pay up; (2) that those who had sold copra should
receive the second payment; and (3) that everything should be
shared out. Beniona proposed a motion that everything should
be shared out, and the meeting closed.

In retrospect I feel that although the Co-op Officer made a very
good attempt to explain the technical points and to instruct the
members about share capital, he succeeded only in arousing suspicion. Scolding them for patronizing trade stores might be seen
as confirming that there was something wrong, since trade stores
charged less for some items; immediately asking for the profits to
be returned could suggest that the money was not there, or that
the little men would never see their money, for it would only go
into the hands of the big men of the Association. The officer
either did not realize, or chose to ignore, the tensions that existed
among certain elements of the membership, and by looking at
things from the point of view of the central Association, he lost
the interest of the local members. He should have let the discussion of what to do with the profits and rebates proceed to its
inevitable conclusion—that it should be shared out—before discussing the need of the local store to have more share capital to
pay for the stock it held.[4] It would have meant describing in detail,
as he did for me later, the history of how £25,000 of the original
£37,000 invested had been spent on fixed assets, how the original
stocks had been obtained largely on credit, and how much of the
money used to pay for current stock purchases and for copra in

[4] He used this technique successfully at the subsequent meeting of Bitaulagumgum.

transit was the undistributed profits of the previous year or C.M.B. second payments for two years back. Delay in distributing was a surreptitious means of preserving working capital. In many ways people had justifications for their suspicious attitude to requests for more contributions.

By the time the C.M.B. money was finally distributed, on 16 October, a change in attitude had taken place. Everyone was happy that the money would be distributed. The figure of £2 had become accepted as the standard new subscription, with those receiving less than £2 subscribing it all, save for loose change, and those receiving more than £4 subscribing one-half. The two Co-op clerks and the Co-op Officer sat behind a table. As the first one called out the name and number of each member, and the amount he was entitled to, the second handed over the appropriate sum and whispered how much should be reinvested, while the third accepted the money and noted the amount in the share register. Two members who received over £10 invested all of it plus money out of their own pockets, and six other men with payments of around £6 invested everything except the small change. In all, £950 was reinvested from the £1,784 distributed; Vunamami villagers subscribed £243.

At the third meeting on 21 November to distribute the rebates on 1960 business, the same procedure was followed—distribution of rebates followed by reinvestment of £2 or half of the sum received. A novelty was the decision by the directors to pay out a dividend of one shilling per one-pound share. Although this meant that every member received the same sum of five shillings in 1961, the Co-op Officer was looking ahead to 1962 in suggesting this, for then members would own different amounts of share capital and would appreciate that they were receiving different returns on their different investments.

But at the same time people were much more ready to question what the share capital was needed for, and how it should be collected. They also brought up other disturbing issues regarding the Co-op. Three members from Malakun village asked why a flat levy on all members could not be made, and there were the usual demands that all money should be distributed to those who were entitled to it. The most perturbed questioning came when the Association secretary ToKabiu of Malaguna asked quite simply whether the Association's profits of £1,680 could remain there as additional share capital, instead of being distributed to member societies. ToUraliu, the hard-headed manager of Malakun fermentery, asked why Bitatali and other well-run societies should pay to keep poorly run societies going, especially as no attempt had been made to recoup losses incurred because of the bad advice of the early Co-op officers. ToDaula of Vunamami pointed out that Bitatali had a great interest in the purchase of a block of land in Kokopo and wanted to apply any funds available for this purpose. Yet the Association, under orders from Moresby to permit no expansion until capital was increased, had vetoed this. In addition, societies could not plan their affairs because the date for distributing Association rebates was not fixed. TaVul of Vunabalbal summed up by saying that people were worried, on account of rumours they heard and could not verify: (1) that the price of copra was about to change, (2) that the rebate share-out might not take place, and (3) that the Europeans were going to deceive people once again.

The copra price rumour was true. The disastrous fall in copra prices from £72 to £52 per ton, which had caused a drop from sixpence to fourpence a pound in the price at the store, had slowed somewhat. The Association meeting the week before had discussed a raise to fivepence per pound; people who had already sold at fourpence felt cheated, and copra sales stopped completely until the announcement of the price increase was made.

Other factors remained in the background. The March–September turnover figures had fallen sharply, and profit was down to £410 against £1,070 for the previous six months, almost exclusively from store sales. Comments were made on the need to stop pilfering losses by keeping idlers out of the store, and on the possibility of conflict of interest, since the storekeeper also ran a private store. At this point Koniel of Malakun, a former vice-president of Vunamami Council, brought a halt to the acrimonious discussion by saying that too much time was being spent in complaining; it would be better to take local issues of this sort to the Board of Directors, and to get on in the present meeting with the distribution of rebates. Nonetheless, it was past eight o'clock by the time the £1,750 of rebates and £170 of share dividends had been distributed, and another £950 of share capital subscribed. Of these amounts, £478 had gone to Vunamami village and £242 had been reinvested, making a total increase of £485 in village savings invested in the Co-op during the year.

The local picture, of enthusiastic good will when issues are explained but otherwise of suspicion (based on rumours, imperfect knowledge, fears that others are reaping benefits, and that the people at the top are getting rich), needs to be complemented by a consideration of the Association meetings. These are the occasions where the directors of the member societies come together to discuss policy, where knowledge is most available, and where conflicting interests could theoretically be brought into the open.

The same issues came up in the April Association meeting as in the society meeting. Share capital had been discussed at the November 1960 Association meeting, and the suggestion had then been to obtain a voluntary levy of £2 per member, but few co-operatives had acted on this suggestion. Profits of the entire association were announced as £4,198, and the question was raised of whether to divide this out to societies, retain it in the Association treasury as working capital, or (the Co-op Officer's suggestion) give a "party." Nason ToKiala quietly said he could see the point of distribution, but what was the point of a party? The Co-op Officer explained the propaganda value for attracting new members and the educational value of demonstrating the success of the Co-op movement. Beniona replied that a cash distribution would get more members than a party and the issue was settled. At the same time the Association members were enthusiastic about setting up an education committee to "teach the people" about the need for patronizing the Co-op and for increasing share capital. Names were immediately suggested—Nason and Napitalai, and Beniona and ToDaula from Vunamami—but as Nason said, "We would be happy to do this work, but it is no good if the same men are always exhorting the people to do better; others must help too."

The Association showed similar common sense over executive issues, discussing the merits of truck brands or of tenders for the copra cartage contract. When the question was raised of why people sold copra elsewhere than at the Co-op, the prices at trade stores were all known, as were the transport costs from villages to the stores, and the usual amounts of the C.M.B. second payments. Despite the Co-op Officer's attempts to show that trade stores actually paid less for copra than the Co-ops did, the questioning made it clear that really they were paying more than the C.M.B.

first payment justified and were gambling on the size of the second payment.

Yet on topics where there was a lack of knowledge, Association members were eager to learn. It was in April that the Co-op Officer first mentioned the possibility of share dividend payments as well as patronage refunds, and the idea was discussed at length. When a member of the Planters' Association (a former Co-op Officer) came to ask for support in opposing the abolition of the national Copra Stabilization Fund Levy, everyone questioned him about the fund. The issue he raised was that the Stabilization Fund had been built up during a period of rising prices after 1950 by contributions from the long-established growers. They had received no share-outs, since prices had never fallen to support levels. The fund had reached £6,000,000, a satisfactory level, and the government proposed to stop making the levy. But now newly established growers outnumbered those who had contributed the £6,000,000, and it was the newly established growers who would benefit from the fund. He proposed continuing the levy, though at a lower rate, and progressively refunding the early contributions out of current receipts. Some members could not see the problem, but the senior men (as established growers) supported his stand, and a motion was passed *nem. con.*

But on another level the same problems of suspicion of people at the top, and of doubt about European sincerity, were present as in the local meetings. The secretary of the Association, ToKabiu of Malaguna, was absent in Kavieng, so when the Co-op Officer said that he had heard murmurings about ToKabiu, whom he supported, and that he would like them to be expressed openly, accusations flooded out. Some said that ToKabiu was paid too much for too little work; others accused him of using the Co-op car for his own purposes and of having refused to give people lifts when the car was empty, of having shouted at Tolai as Europeans do, and of having bragged about his visit to Australia. The Co-op Officer pointed out that ToKabiu used the car on business late at night and was his own driver for evening meetings, and that he worked an irregular seven-day week of invaluable work rather than a simple nine-to-five routine. When discussion started on how to replace him it became clear that no one else could do the job as well, and that training a replacement would take time. If the question of misuse of the car could be solved by paying a driver overtime when necessary, and if ToKabiu could be taken down a peg by censure, the rank and file would be happy for him to continue as secretary.

Distrust of Europeans came out when one member asked from the floor whether it would be possible to buy Mr. Black's trade store in Rabaul, which was going out of business, although it was on a busy corner close to the market and truck stop. The Co-op Officer quickly answered that it would cost £25,000 and there was not enough money available. Someone asked whether the £4,000 that was ready for distribution could not be used, and the Co-op Officer had to go into detail about the financial position of the Association and the societies, listing the £37,000 originally paid in, and spent as £13,000 for society assets, £12,000 for Association assets, and £12,000 for working capital, and the current position of having £17,000 at the bank but being due to distribute £25,000 to the members. He confided to me that there was another £10,000 due from the C.M.B., but for an hour he had to defend his stance that there were insufficient funds to buy the store. Feeling ran high, and many members were still unconvinced at the end, and resolved that the next time such an opportunity arose they would start fund-raising in good time.

In August an opportunity did arise of buying a large block of land, zoned for industrial use, within the proposed extension of Kokopo town. The decision to buy was quickly made in a meeting of delegates from the four societies affected, Bitatali, Bitaulagum-gum, Kulaun, and Tingenalom, and a drive for share capital was begun. Storemen were empowered to accept subscriptions, and the move to get £2 per head share capital at the next distribution was reaffirmed, with the results already described.

At the November Association meeting the Co-op Officer had little to do except explain how reluctant Moresby had been to *permit* any distribution of C.M.B. second payments, and how they had done so only in order to see how much would be reinvested from it. They had been satisfied with the response and had author-ized payments of rebates and dividends to all four Kokopo soci-eties. Without prompting, all speakers then advocated *not* distrib-uting the Association profits to societies but retaining them as working capital within the Association, provided the capital was put to work and was not used for parties. Then followed an in-terminable analysis of why profits had fallen so sharply, and why people did not bring their copra to the Co-operatives. An aggressive pricing policy was decided upon, to take the fight into the trade stores' camp.

By the end of 1961 the co-operatives, in Kokopo Sub-district at least, were in a very healthy state. The Co-op Officer had encouraged this most by being available with specialist advice when needed, but by learning when to withdraw at other times. Issues raised at Association meetings were discussed by societies and meaningful decisions made. And despite their occasional suspicions, the members were always glad to accept what was pointed out to them as the "right" thing to do. Often there was real moral fervour: people (*ra tarai*) should stand together (*tur warurung*) in the face of threats from Chinese trade stores or from Europeans, and should work to make Bitatali/Bitaulagumgum/New Britain grow. Scorn was poured on "the others" (*diat*) who did not stand together, who sought only immediate personal gain, or were too stupid to understand. Thus the leaders exhorted, as they "worked to teach" their people. And the people responded, to the tune of £485 in Vunamami alone. If anything, the European advisers were overcautious, while the Tolai pushed for expansion.

VII
Businesses

In preceding chapters we have already examined certain enterprises that a European would include under the term "businesses." Land purchases and their development as cocoa plantations, market gardening, the acquisition of specialist skills of either a traditional or a modern kind which are then available on a contract basis, middleman transactions, termed *a nivura*, in marketing either to Tolai or to Europeans, the trucking businesses that carry both vendors and buyers to market, co-operatives themselves and the group copra-buying organization which preceded co-operatives in Vunamami: all are examples of what may loosely be called "businesses," of highly varying types.

In present-day Tolai the pidgin term *bisnis* is also applied to all these activities, grouping them under a common rubric, although certain aspects of each activity are differentiated as not-*bisnis*. Thus land purchase and cultivation for subsistence is not-*bisnis*—that is, it is "food." The distinction would seem to be that "food" activities produce goods to be exchanged for other subsistence commodities, housing, and so on; yet as we have seen, in the claims of sons to cash incomes from copra planted on their father's clan land, regular cash incomes are also becoming classified as "food." A distinction is also made between *bisnis* and work (*papalum*), in that work is something that one is obligated to do. This may refer to the traditional role obligations of a male or female, or of a father, mother's brother, or elder sister, or to the modern obligations of a hired labourer or a contracting carpenter to his employer. A person's *bisnis* by contrast is something that he does voluntarily, or by his own decision. Yet a man who operates a *bisnis* may often say that his "work" is running a fleet of trucks, or buying copra for resale. He thereby implies that he is so involved in his *bisnis* that it is now an avocation for him; he is no longer merely trying to earn a selfish profit, but is performing a service for others.

Another aspect of this same distinction between *bisnis* and "work" is that the latter is concerned almost exclusively with labour; the word derives from *palum*, "to cultivate," and it is what one does to a garden (*a uma*), regardless of who may own the actual land, whereas *a bisnis* always involves the ownership of some capital asset. This may be non-material, like the copyright on a dance, or material, like a copra drier or canoes. It may be land. In fact the term *bisnis* is used by many Tolai as the translation of the terms *vunatarai* or *niuruna*, for which I have used the gloss of "clan." As I have elsewhere shown (Salisbury 1962c) the Tolai clan has few of the political, affective, or socialization functions of the monolithic solidary clans described in some classic African studies; it is a specialized corporation concerned with the owning of material assets, like land, and non-material assets like certain ceremonials. It seems to cause no confusion for the same term to be used for such a traditional corporation and for the profit-making, capital-owning organization that an individual has voluntarily established. There is for Tolai a clear conceptual unity.

TRADITIONAL BUSINESSES

Even if the ownership and use implied in indigenous agriculture are not considered as "business," there would still seem to have been many indigenous activities that would nowadays be classed as *bisnis*. Apart from the term *nivura*, however, there seems to have been no single word to describe them.

Just as fishing provides some of the best examples of traditional wage-labour practices, so it provides some of the best examples of capital-using businesses. The returns obtained by fish-trap manufacturers have been indicated, incidentally to the description of returns to labour. Since the manufacturer receives half of the catch in his trap whenever a crew goes out to visit it, regardless of whether or not he himself is a member of the crew, this can be regarded as profits from his investment in the trap itself and from organizing the group of three canoes and about twelve men that spent an entire morning anchoring his trap. The investment is a risky one, for a storm may destroy the trap the day after anchoring, but the *average* yields in 1961 were high. On the average, traps lasted four months, and each owner received one fish every eight

days, or fifteen while the trap lasted. His investment could be calculated as either two and a half weeks of work, plus two fathoms
of *tabu* for canoe hire, or thirteen fathoms of *tabu* in all, from
which fifteen fathoms could be expected as a return in four months.
With continuous reinvestment of returns, a person buying traps for
tabu would get roughly an 80 percent return on his capital per annum (Salisbury n.d.).

Net fishing (*a ubene*), as described earlier, is more clearly a
business in the European sense, since more than mere investment
is needed if a good yield is to be returned. Not only must a substantial labour force be organized but the net must be dried and
repaired after each use. The nets represent a large capital investment—I have no figures of the labour cost of indigenous net manufacture, but modern store-bought nets may cost £100—but the
yields are high. Only large fish are considered as earnings by the
group owning the net, which sells them for *tabu* and cash; the
small fish are distributed among the net team as "food." Nevertheless the accounted-for returns from fish sold each year for one net
group in recent years have been between three and four times the
value of the nets themselves.

The owners of nets (and specific examples will be described
later) are either very rich individuals or associations (*kivung*) of
members of one or more closely related clans who call themselves
by a clan name. They "pay" themselves "food" from the small
fish, but the *kivung* organizer retains the profits (*a tinavua*) in the
name of the *kivung* at least until the end of the year, when there
may be a small distribution.[1] The bulk of the profits is usually re-

---

[1] A. L. Epstein (1963) gives interesting comparable figures from Matupit.
In Matupit it appears that all fishing is organized on a collective basis for
each individual fishing beach (*a motonoi*), whether by nets or traps. Annual
distributions are then made of all *motonoi* proceeds. In Vunamami individuals are the units for trap fishing, taking their own portions of the catch
each day, and only net fishing is collectively organized; the collective units
are clan *kivung* rather than entire *motonoi*. These patterns seen markedly
different superficially, but there is an underlying identity. A few of the
small *motonoi* near Vunamami are owned by a single clan, and if any
owned a net they would distribute among all *motonoi* users, just as in
Matupit. On the other hand, in Matupit fishing is a major industry at which
many people work regularly; collaborative work is more common and
rewarding and periodic distributions more feasible among the many participants. In Vunamami fishing is very much a part-time activity, and there
are few regular fishermen; any system of reward division among a large
group and not reflecting the different degrees of participation would be

tained, supposedly for future investment by the *kivung*. I assume
that this was also the indigenous pattern, when the richest men (*a
uviana*) were also the leaders of local clan segments, and the guard-
ians of all the *tabu* of the clan members. The other members deposited their shell money in the *uviana's* storehouse; the *uviana*,
though free to use the deposit for his own enterprises, was obligated to provide the payments needed by clan members. In such
a case the *kivung* organizer and the guardian of the clan *tabu*
would be the same person, and there would be no point in his distributing any *tabu*, since his store would pay any debts incurred
by clan members. At the same time the yields from net fishing may
have been quite different before 1875 in view of the immense
amount of labour presumably involved in indigenous net manufacture (and the consequent organizing ability required of the leader),
the shorter life of nets, and the presumably lower efficiency of
fish catching. The principles were presumably the same, however.

The role of the rich man and the guardian of clan stocks of
shell money was noted by many early observers (e.g., Parkinson
1907:56), most of whom regarded the *uviana* as tyrants, only concerned to lay their hands on every morsel of shell money that
their subordinates acquired, and delaying and begrudging making
payments on their behalf. George Brown (1898:785), in the
generalized life history of a person he calls TePang, gives an interesting picture of the sorts of investment such a person might make.
TePang invested *tabu* in acquiring skills as a sorcerer and as a member of the *ingiet* society, and while making people sick by the use
of one skill, he profited by charging them for cures made by using
his other skill. He lent the shell money he earned at rates of at
least 10 percent for relatively short periods, and in this way became
a "man of power." With such a reputation he did not even have to
make straightforward loans and wait for them to mature; he could
make twice as much, far more quickly, by acting as a professional
loan collector. A man who had made a loan of, say, ten fathoms,
would come to TePang and pay him one fathom; TePang would
give the lender his principal of ten fathoms, and immediately go to
the debtor and demand eleven fathoms—the original loan plus the
interest. Brown claimed that there were Tolai words for getting on

doomed to failure. Danks (1887:310) talks of partnerships to buy fish
traps, with the profits from the partnership divided either daily or at the
end of the season. He does not indicate how the choice of method was
determined.

credit, borrowing, lending, pledging, redeeming, and interest, though he did not list them.

Parkinson (1907:83–84) tells of other Tolai financiers with original schemes of multiplying capital. One man, at a time when people did not know where shell money came from, purchased unworked shells, hung them in a tree, and convinced people that he had the original "money tree." He then sold people the rights to gather what fell from the tree and made considerable profits, presumably by secretly placing "ripe" *tabu*, obtained from his fees, under the tree in sufficient amounts to convince people that fortunes might be made, and to carry on paying him more fees. A similar scheme of "stock promotion" by paying "dividends" out of later contributions was that of a woman who spread a rumour that she knew how to make *tabu* rolls increase in size. She repaid early depositors with *tabu* that she received later, and induced an ever increasing flow of deposits. The bubble eventually burst, however, and she was punished by the German government for fraud. Despite the obvious post-1885 date of this incident, I daresay it was indeed an original scheme, since education about stock markets had still barely begun in New Guinea in 1961.

These examples, and similar case histories such as that of the magician who sold bullet-proof ointment before the war of 1893, are quoted by early writers usually to illustrate either the gullibility of those who believed in what the writers considered to be ludicrous schemes, or alternatively the deceitfulness of people who invented the schemes. Everyday examples of profitable businesses are not cited. But Danks (1887:316) puts such activities in a context of "the commercial acumen" of people. According to him, the coming of peace stopped enforced idleness and "gave place to industry and to comparative comfort and wealth. The innate industry of the people shone forth the moment property and life became safe. I have known a man make fifty fathoms of tambu during the fishing season and ten or twelve from his plantations." Danks mentions (p. 310) partnerships to buy fish traps, with the division of profits either daily or at season's end, and similar joint enterprises in planting crops. The major profits were to be made from *tabu* finance, then from fishing, and then from planting. He cites lending at 10 percent interest (called *wawaturu* on the Duke of Yorks), presents given on the return of a loan (*kubika*), borrowing small sums to avoid breaking into a coil of several hundred fathoms (*a vuvuring*), failure to repay loans (*watukum*), and the mutual advantages to both depositors and big men of the deposit system, as all depositors rally round to guard their money, and the more depositors the safer the money is. Even so, he indicates that many big men refused to repay on demand, especially if they were the mother's brother of the lender, as would usually have been the case.

I interpret Danks's description as meaning that all these customs existed commonly before 1875, and that the arrival of Europeans and inter-district peace encouraged their development. On the other hand, except for the trade in coconuts, few businesses involved matters of concern to Europeans; most were traditional in nature. Financial manipulations using shell money were both the most lucrative area for businesses, and the most commonly engaged in. They are still lucrative, as we shall see in the next chapter, and still the concern of the "big men."

MODERN BUSINESSES

It was not until about 1900 that Tolai began conducting European-style ventures. In 1899 Ah Tam began selling planked rowing boats for two or three hundred fathoms of *tabu*. Bley (*Monatshefte* 1900:104) mentions this as the beginning of large-scale and frequent voyaging to Nakanai to collect shell money. He was not unaware of the nature of earlier voyages to Nakanai, for his Tolai grammar of 1897 included (p. 129) the text of a narrative of an eight-week trip by Volavolo men to Nakanai, so that his indication that 1900 marked a major change is probably more reliable than later reports by writers who thought that the post-1899 pattern had always existed.

During the next decade appear the first mentions of businesses directed at Europeans: the planting of pineapples for sale to visiting ships (Chap. 3), and the development of middlemen traders buying chickens for resale to Europeans (Chap. 5). In Vunamami around 1910 rich men began buying horses and buggies for use on the extensive network of roads radiating from Kokopo. Mackenzie (1938:249) describes such a purchase by a coastal *luluai* who brought "an array of tins" full of shillings and marks to pay for one in 1916. ToDik the missionary had one, as did Levi ToLingling, ToInia, and Amos ToKauba, later the Paramount Luluai. To some extent this would seem to have been a matter of prestigious buying of consumer durables, for as the other indication of how wealthy these men were, informants mentioned that most of them also built houses with metal roofs. On the other hand, these men were all shrewd in their traditional business dealings and it would be surprising if they did not use their horses and carts for the commercial carriage of goods and passengers. Their houses with metal roofs are another indication of an emerging Tolai business, that of carpentry. Kleintitschen mentioned this beginning about 1901 when Tolai chose to assist carpenters to learn the trade and to acquire tools, although they refused other work for Europeans. Housebuilding within the villages and the building of large metal-roofed churches at both Vunamami and Raluana during the First World War suggest that many Tolai had invested in tool kits and were in business on their own account.

Between 1921 and 1935 this proliferation of European-style businesses in Vunamami seems to have come to a virtual halt. No one seems to have owned horses and buggies during this period, and no more metal-roofed houses were built. The main activity of the rich men (besides making copra) was fishing. Levi ToLingling in particular is described during this period as making large sums of money and *tabu* from fishing with nets. His principal assistant was his son, Enos Teve, who later became Paramount Luluai, but, as has been described, net fishing requires a large work group, and participants in it are usually co-owners of the nets. It would seem probable that Levi's fishing group included mostly members of his own clan, Vunaibu, of which ToInia was also a member. Levi and Enos used parts of their profits to buy land within Vunamami, and on Levi's death around 1928 disputes arose over whether the *tabu* that Enos had contributed for the purchase was his own or his father's. If the latter, then his father's heirs of Vunaibu clan (who had also presumably been co-members of the fishing *kivung*) were the rightful owners of the land and the *tabu*. Similar acrimony over the division of a *kivung*'s assets, should a business have to liquidate, is a recurrent theme to this day, as will appear.

Enos' business activities while Paramount Luluai of inducing people to contribute to the construction of his copra drier in 1936 have been mentioned (p. 130). To understand why this copra drier should have aroused so much excitement one needs to consider the attitude which existed among Europeans at this time, and which New Guineans felt was virtually a law—namely, that business enterprises by New Guineans were forbidden. J. K. McCarthy (1963: 78–81) has described these attitudes clearly. New Ireland natives

were astounded in 1932 when he told them that there was no *law*
that they could not dry copra but only a tacit agreement among
traders not to buy dried copra. After he encouraged the natives to
begin drying copra, he was quickly demoted to Patrol Officer
from Assistant District Officer and transferred away from New Ireland. For Enos to set up a copra-drying business, with local contributions, and with a hot-air drier comparable with those on
plantations, was revolutionary in the repressive social climate of
the early 1930's.

At the same time fishing by nets was, for Vunamami, still by
far the most profitable business. Enos, his two half-brothers William ToKavivi and ToNiuta, Kamel ToDik, and a number of
other men in either Vunaibu or the allied clans of Takaptar-Tuluai
were joint members in the most successful *kivung*, which made
good profits even during the Depression.

An innovation in 1937 was that Enos expanded the range of
grouping that could be called on to contribute to an enterprise.
Whereas fishing-net *kivungs* were essentially all members of one
clan, together with close relatives or members of allied clans, he
began to invoke loyalty to the Paramountcy group, to get subscriptions for constructing schools, hospitals, meeting houses, and
so on. He went to Salamaua to collect five shillings each from migrant workers from Vunamami, and built a meetinghouse with the
proceeds; other projects were pending when the war intervened.
He also encouraged corporate village ownership of the unclaimed
land at Talimut (see Chaps. 2 and 3), and its operation first as a
coconut plantation and later under cocoa.

When the Second World War came to an end and Vunamami
was residing at the *motonoi*, fishing again became an important
business activity. Early in 1947 Enos formed a new Takaptar-
Tuluai *kivung* of nine members, though the others were now much
younger than he was—the sons or sisters' sons of the former
kivung. Several of them, including Punion, had been absent in
New Guinea all during the war and had ample cash. Each member
subscribed £10 and for £90 they bought a large net. In the first
season of operation they earned £300 plus 200 fathoms of *tabu*.

At this time, too, War Damage payments flowed in and war surplus materials such as trucks, Jeeps, tools, and corrugated iron became available. Punion bought iron and some forty-four-gallon
drums and for about £10 built a small hot-air copra drier. Two
other nearby residents of Kunakunai ward, Demas and ToPupuak,

followed suit, and copra driers became *the* avenue of investment. Before the next fishing season opened, £200 of the capital of the Takaptar *kivung* was invested in building a large and handsome copra drier near Enos' house, and not far from the two smaller driers erected earlier by Punion and ToPupuak, both of whom were members of the *kivung*. Both the latter felt that a wrong use had been made of *kivung* funds, and they received the sympathy of others in the *kivung*. No more fishing was done; the nets remained idle; the partners went their individual ways, and the cash and *tabu* assets of the *kivung* were lost track of. Notwithstanding this contretemps, the construction of small-scale driers progressed steadily throughout both wards of Vunamami, until by 1961 a network covered the whole area. Vunamami men were by then financing driers located in other villages. The standard of construction had steadily improved, and several owners were already on their second or third construction. The economics of this construction will be considered later.

Trucks and Jeeps were another popular avenue of investment between 1948 and 1952; army surplus vehicles were easily available, and many of the wartime workers knew how to drive. At one time there were as many as ten vehicles owned within the village, though almost half were usually not in running order. The need for repairs, and the lack of mechanical skills which made repairs unusually frequent, together with the difficulty of obtaining spare parts, made owning a vehicle a far more expensive proposition than most investors had imagined. Most owners charged fees for hire that yielded a fair profit if only running costs were considered, plus the nominal cost of such vehicles. But when a major bill for repairs arrived they could not pay it, and few of them had the foresight to realize that they would need a new vehicle in only one or two years, and that the charges should be calculated with such a purchase in mind. Hundreds of pounds were spent on vehicles, and even in 1961 many men proudly said they were vehicle owners, although their trucks were rusting heaps near their houses, unmoved for seven or eight years. As with horses and buggies forty years earlier, there was undoubtedly an element of prestige buying associated with "having a truck," but most men thought of trucks as profit-making ventures.

The Council too, soon after its formation, entered the trucking business with high hopes of making good profits from hire charges, in addition to getting Council work done. By August 1952, however, these expectations were starting to fade. Too many people were begging rides on the three-ton truck when it was engaged on other business—even exceeding the maximum of twenty-nine for which insurance was carried—and it was decided that no riders were to be allowed when the truck was on Council business. The rates of hire, unrealistically low, were raised to five shillings per passenger for a trip to Rabaul; all requests for hire were to come through a councillor, and there were to be special charges for such services (or "favours") as bringing back parcels from Rabaul on return trips. The Council budget for expenditures on the truck was exhausted, and money from hires was essential if it was to be kept running. Vunamami village itself presented a petition requesting the Council to fire the driver because he was not a mechanic and was ruining the truck.

In 1954, after several high repair bills and a court judgment of £450 damages against the Council following an accident, there was strong pressure on the Council to dispose of the truck, and the next year it was sold to Enos Teve for £600. The Council then bought a Land-Rover, leaving intermittent large shipments or mass transportation of large groups to be arranged by hiring trucks from local contractors.

The history of private truck ownership in Vunamami village followed much the same pattern. As people saw hundreds of pounds invested with a view to profit-making, only to be lost because of poor pricing, misuse of vehicles, failure to make or provide for repairs, and the high rate of depreciation, the attractiveness of truck hiring as an enterprise vanished. No new trucks were bought by Vunamami residents and by 1961 not a single one was owned within the village. The village needs for mass transportation were taken care of very efficiently by hiring one of the two trucks owned by a man of Bitarebarebe, who had managed to keep his business profitable.

On the other hand, there were within Vunamami four Land-Rovers and Jeeps, three of them operational. Two of the operational ones were owned by rich individuals (one of them Enos) with large and scattered plantation interests, and the third was owned by a group of women but looked after by Punion (see Chap. 4). Transportation in Vunamami was thus effectively rationalized. The major transport need, that of taking copra to the C.M.B. depot or to the Co-operative Association in Rabaul, was met on a regular basis by a European firm which contracted for regular pick-ups at Bitalali. Even the two richest landowners making enough copra on their outlying plantations to merit having their own accounts with the C.M.B. did not produce enough to require a three-ton truck. For their personal transportation to meetings and to their various planting areas, Land-Rovers were an excellent compromise, and they were willing to hire out their vehicles to others when they were free.[2] The other people with special needs for personal transport—particularly ToBaining as Council president and Legislative Council representative—travelled officially in the Council Land-Rover or in government vehicles. For emergencies and for private hire as virtually a taxi the Land-Rover owned by the Women's Group was available.

Stores and retailing, a major avenue for investment by petty entrepreneurs in other less well-developed Tolai areas, were of minor importance in Vunamami. The single large co-operative store was a convenient source of the most regularly used consumer goods throughout Vunamami. Two small stores in Lumluvur ward were useful for occasional emergency supplies of staples for nearby households provided the owners or their wives were home. The owners of both these small stores had full-time regular incomes, and their stores were merely a small sideline, with less than £50 investments in stock. The one item to which this generalization would not apply—the illegal sale of beer, on which the rate of profit was presumably high—was the one on which information was naturally hardest to obtain. It would be my impression that aggregate profits were small, not because of any lack of demand for beer, but because of the need to sell only to discreet and known customers, and also because the supply of "sly grog" was limited.

More profitable, but equally illegal, was the organization of a *pati*, a public entertainment rather like an impromptu night club, for which admission was charged. Food and alcohol were available (both imported and locally manufactured banana liquor), and there were one or more guitar players to provide music. Such events, especially if the organizer proclaimed that his *pati* was to finance a particular project, usually turned into all-night drunken brawls which enlivened many, if not most, weekends.

[2] A similar decline in the proportion of large trucks in use at Rabaul market occurred between June and November 1961. Most new trucks that appeared in November were cheaper Japanese utility vehicles, and this trend, along with a general trend towards the purchase of more cars for personal transport, has continued to spread beyond Vunamami since then.

By far the most lucrative full-time private business ventures in Vunamami were those of the contracting carpenters, which were briefly discussed in Chapter 4. These were undoubtedly businesses, despite their general reluctance to undertake the purchase of building materials and to finance entire construction projects, and their preference for quoting construction costs using the owner's own materials. The average cost of tools owned by Vunamami carpenters—their capital investment—was over £80, and the contractors frequently employed assistants on projects.

There were also a number of minor businesses, including pig raising. This was no longer a subsistence vocation but was solely a business, all the pigs being sold, mainly to Chinese. All pigs were kept in large pens of steel mesh. Poultry raising was also largely for the purpose of sale, although some chickens were eaten locally on special occasions. Most households had one or two that lived off scraps, but all larger flocks were specially fed, mainly from grated coconut. There was also one man, Polos ToPultima, who made furniture to order. He learned his carpentry skills at Malaguna Tech and began manufacturing furniture in about 1955, employing one youth from Vunabalbal and buying timber from the Council. The business had lasted a year only, but Polos still kept his tools and made odd items occasionally on request; his major activities in 1961 were in cocoa planting.

The major business of Vunamami in 1961 was co-operative, not private: the Tolai Cocoa Project Fermentery at Talimut. Over the period 1953–1960, Vunamami growers had built up an equity in the fermentery of about £1,200 through the deductions from the payments for their beans to repay the bank loan to the councils. In 1960–1961 they invested another £245 of new capital in this way.

BUSINESS OPERATIONS

The way in which the small businesses of Vunamami operated can best be understood by considering a few specific examples of each type, and then analysing the general principles of ownership, profitability, and prospects. First, let us look at copra driers: a private drier, owned by Punion, and a drier owned by a group of men from Vunaibu clan.

Punion's drier was his second one. The drier it had replaced, the first drier in Vunamami after the war, had cost him little money but considerable work. He had salvaged the materials: scrap iron for the galvanized roof and metal sides, wire mesh for trays, and forty-four-gallon drums for the furnace. The structure was made of uncut poles. Cash had been required only for nails, sawn timber for the trays, and the chimney stack. Its total cost had been less than £10, and it lasted five years.

The main improvement in the second drier was the use of cut timber for the structure and for the tray supports. Punion re-used the iron, which was of much better quality than the early post-war material. Thus for about another £10 he built a very solid structure with effective tight-fitting joints and trays. There were eight trays, each of which could hold 150 pounds of wet meat (about 70 pounds dried). Punion charged two shillings per tray. During September 1961 the drier completed sixteen fillings, or four each six-day week—all work stops on the Sabbath in Vunamami—and yielded him £12 16s. rental. This pattern was typical of about eight months of the year, with three or more usually being covered by a taboo on coconuts. His annual gross income from the drier was about £100.

To achieve this level of income a degree of efficient management was required. In the first place, there was careful attention to keep the drier's heat in by leakproof joints. In order to dry each load fully by the time the next load of wet copra was ready, the fires had to be stoked regularly. Less efficient driers, which took more than a day per load, seldom turned out four loads a week: that was the maximum, not the average. On only three occasions in the month did Punion miss a filling because the previous load was not dry. On one occasion only no one wished to use the drier. On three Saturdays and one Monday, although coconuts were awaiting drying, no one arrived to extract the meat. On other days Punion was usually ready to assist part-time with cutting the copra, thereby ensuring that the next load would be ready in time. He also attended to much of the night-time stoking.

His drier had been in operation almost five years, and showed no signs of having to be replaced. Further depreciation of the cash investment of £20 was almost nil, although much of the initial investment was of Punion's own work, and his careful work on repairs kept the cash needs for replacements at a minimum. Punion owned the drier outright and had already put sufficient money into the bank for a replacement. From the income from the drier he was comfortably supporting his family and was building a house of solid European construction, with a metal roof and a water tank. Furthermore, less than one-quarter of his time was spent on his drying business; he also had cocoa plantings, did mechanical repairs, raised pigs and chickens commercially, and spent a fair proportion of his time in public service activities without remuneration. The clearing in front of his house served as the meeting place for the ward of Kunakunai. His businesses were operating smoothly and profitably, and he was ready and able to take up any new venture that presented itself. On the other hand, he was happy to be able to live comfortably, gradually building up the material assets of his household, rather than driving himself to grow rich.

The second drier to be considered is one built in 1960 by a Vunaibu clan *kivung* of four Vunamami and Vunabalbal men.[3] They had each subscribed £15 and had collaborated (they were all carpenters) to build a twelve-tray drier of solid cement, metal, and sawn timber on a plot of Vunaibu land in Keravi village. They had no coconuts of their own in the area, so this was a purely business venture.

They charged two shillings per tray, and during the sample month of November dried eighteen full loads, for an income of £22 8s., or an estimated yearly income of £175. Only one day was lost by poor drying, and the remainder by there being no copra cut on particular days (Saturdays, meeting days, etc.). To achieve this good record they had hired a teen-aged clansman who lived in Keravi village to supervise operations and receive money for the *kivung*. The youth was not paid wages but was permitted to "take his food" from the receipts, which remained "inside the group" (*tara balana kivung*). One shareholder was treasurer, collecting the receipts periodically and looking after them. No distribution of profits was envisaged, because the drier was said to be "of Vunaibu clan" and all profits were to remain for reinvestment in other businesses.

Unfortunately in July 1961 the group discovered that there had been no profits since the last collection. The youth had been steadily increasing the amount of his "food" to the detriment of the returns "to the group." The group brought him before the Council, which reprimanded him and told him to work properly. The treasurer was told to collect payments himself, and to give the youth a regular amount for food. I inquired of group mem-

[3] One owner's life history has been sketched in Salisbury (1967).

bers whether the court had said anything about the youth repaying the missing money. They were indignant at this, saying that he was of Vunaibu clan and was entitled to food from the clan; he could not "steal" it. The Council court had no jurisdiction over a clan issue.

After this episode the "manager's" food payment was fixed at £2 a week, leaving about £70 yearly gross profit to the group. Depreciation and repair charges could be liberally estimated at £12, yielding about 100 percent per annum on the original investment.

The only truck-owning business within Vunamami was the women's group called IaMinat (Mrs. Death) which operated a Land-Rover. They had bought this in 1960 for £500, and kept it at Punion's house. He kept the books for the business. The group paid a fixed fee of £2 10s. a month, plus the annual renewal of his licence, to ToPalangat, the husband of a group member and a neighbour of Punion, to act as driver when needed. For normal uses of the Land-Rover fixed rates were charged which did not vary whether the hirer was a member of the group or not. A day's trip to Rabaul cost £4; a trip to Kabakaul, either to deliver copra or to take people to work in the gardens there, cost £1 10s. For Balanataman, the fee was £2 10s., for Raluana school, £1 10s., and for Kokopo 6s., or one shilling per passenger.

Partly because of careful management, the profits were considerable, though the Land-Rover was used only part of the time. The group bought oil in large quantities at £25 a drum, saving £7 over the retail price, and Punion did the oil changing. According to my estimate, Palangat spent less than two days a week driving, mostly trips in spare moments to Kokopo, and I was always able to hire the car at short notice when my own was out of action. Yet a gross profit of £250 had been made in ten months of operation by October 1961, after paying all running and repair costs. Depreciation of £100 should be deducted from this figure, yet little more than quarter-time operation produced a net return of 30 percent of capital.

Again, there had been no plan to distribute profits, though there was a steady increase of assets by IaMinat over ten years.[4] The contributions of a member who had died were retained, and her name was still on the membership list. The return to individual

[4] This continued at least until 1967, when the same Land-Rover was still in use.

members (apart from car bookings by members taking priority over those of non-members) was that the Land-Rover and its driver are available without charge as a village ambulance. The purchase was originally decided on to save pregnant women from having to walk to hospital when in labour, and this was still the most common "emergency" use. The security of having an ambulance at hand, plus the satisfaction to women of talking to men about "our car," were the only advantages they had over other villagers as a result of the Land-Rover purchase.

To understand the ownership of the Land-Rover the history of the IaMinat group must be considered. In about 1951, thirty-four women living mainly in Kunakunai ward decided to get together and collect funds, apparently with no specific aim in mind beyond helping themselves. They built a fence and each contributed a chicken, with the idea of going into business by selling eggs and adult birds. Who fed the chickens is not clear, but I suspect it was Punion, who even at this stage was the bookkeeper and treasurer. Unfortunately, hawks and rats preyed on the chickens, and the venture did not prosper. In 1953 the remaining fowl were sold for £9.

At the same time the women also raised funds by each contributing twelve shells of *tabu* (equal to about threepence) every month. The small amounts were threaded together by Punion, until they totalled twenty fathoms (about £10). The *tabu* was used to buy wet copra, largely from group members, at the rate of one fathom for each five *pakaruats* of coconut meat (i.e., the meat from 5 × 60 nuts). This was dried in Punion's drier. The women obtained an account number with the P.C.B. for £6, and with the rest of their cash they hired a truck to take the dried copra to Kabakaul depot.

They went into the copra-buying business using their monetary capital, while continuing to collect contributions of shell money. By early 1954 they had £140 to their credit, and after two more years this had multiplied to £410. They had still not decided what the money was for, although the need for an ambulance was spoken of. For most members it was enough that it was a successful *kivung* with a large bank account. At this point interest flagged (it will be remembered that the men's group ToVurmatana and the Bitatali Co-operative also had problems over copra marketing and prices at this time) and no more work was done by the group until 1960.

Early in 1960 they learned that a local European wished to sell a second-hand Land-Rover for £550. They felt this was too much and did nothing until Punion persuaded a friend in the government workshops to look at the vehicle. He valued it at £500, and the owner agreed to this price, and to giving a loan of £100 which could be repaid out of profits. A collection among the group realized £14 5*s.*; Punion unobtrusively added £40; and presumably the bank account had earned about £40 interest. The car was bought, licensed, and insured and initial costs were paid for. By October 1961 the loan had been paid off and the group had a credit balance of £150.

The group's next move, in 1963, was to buy an area of land from Ravalien plantation, using £350 of the profits. This purchase is not exactly business in the European sense, except perhaps as a speculative investment, for it was not bought primarily with an idea of making a profit, but for use as a subsistence garden. I have already discussed the Vunamami housewives' insistence on fresh green *ibika* each evening, and the difficulty of obtaining it from distant gardens at Kabakaul. Buying land near the village was to provide this convenience for the women. IaMinat and another group called IaPidik owned the plot as a unitary whole,[5] but all active members were allocated an area within it to cultivate as they wished.

The composition of IaMinat departed from the more usual principle of common clan membership. There were thirty-four names in the membership book in 1961, although not all were active and one had died. All except four lived in Kunakunai ward or in the adjoining part of Vunabalbal, along the Toma Road. But not all the residents of this area were members. I was told privately by some members that certain women had been excluded because they were too ambitious, pushy, or domineering, but I noted at the same time that almost all the excluded women had been born outside Vunamami-Vunabalbal, whereas only six group members had not been born there. To me, it seemed essentially a locally born group which had got together on the basis of neighbourhood, rational-

---

[5] No record of the purchase had been made in the Land Titles Registry by 1967, so that the question of how a group such as IaMinat establishes its legal identity cannot be answered. A group of Raluana men who purchased Kuradui plantation in 1964 registered themselves as Kuradui Plantation Society, Ltd., and obtained a loan from the Native Loans Board under that title.

izing a distrust of outsiders, but pulling in three women not currently resident in Kunakunai ward because they were natives
of the area. The one member who did not meet either criterion
was the wife of Osea, the clerk of Bitatali store located in the
middle of the group's territory. She spent much time in the store
and contributed handsomely to group projects. The group was
also unified by age, twenty-two of the women being between
forty and fifty, with four older and seven younger. The names
of two men, Punion and Demas, a preacher at Vunamami Church,
also appeared as contributors to the group.

The other group, IaPidik, was based on Vunabalbal village and
started in 1961 with the same intentions. This was the group that
hired itself out to raise funds, as described in Chapter 4, and it
collected the other £350 for the land purchase.

The businesses of pig raising, chicken raising, market gardening,
carpentry, and even the inactive furniture manufacturing of Polos
ToPultima were all individually owned. An indication of their
operation can be gauged from Punion's pig-raising business. The
main capital expense was for the heavy-gauge wire mesh used
for the pig pen, which would normally cost about £30 to enclose
a circular pen twenty-five feet in diameter, large enough for one
or two pigs. Punion's pen, which had been built mainly of scrap
metal and cost only £10, held two pigs for most of my stay. These
were purchased as piglets from other men in Vunamami at a cost
of ten shillings each. The one sale I witnessed was of a seventy-
nine-and-a-half-pound pig for £7 17s. to a group of Chinese from
Kokopo, but Punion said that he expected to sell three pigs of
that size in the course of the year, averaging about nine months
for fattening them. For his investment of £11, he received £22.

There were fifteen people who kept pigs in Vunamami village,
but only a few of them bred intensively; many of the piglets
bought for fattening came from plantations that kept prize stock.
In view of the hazardous nature of the breeding business, one can
understand its relative unpopularity. One household, in its first
venture, raised six piglets almost to weaning age. The Agricultural
Officer on a visit saw the piglets and persuaded the owner that they
needed inoculations. The supposedly protective serum killed the
entire farrow. On a total village investment in piglets and fattening
pens (assuming all pens were of new wire) of £465 a return of
£330 per annum could be expected with relatively little risk. If
only half the owners *bred* piglets (as the sales would indicate)

they would receive £22 10*s*. profit from an investment of over £200. The emphasis on fattening is economically sound, in terms of profit rate and of the lower risks.

Perhaps the highest profit rate, however, was to be earned by entertaining. At one *pati* the organizer spent £36 in preparing foods and drinks, plus some three days' work erecting a fence and preparing shelters in case of rain. From one night's operation, in which he did not charge admission but a flat fee of two shillings for each package of food or drink, he grossed £70. This compares favourably with the amounts earnable by small retailers who attend public occasions. Thus at the Vunairima choir festival on 15 August, in addition to the three official stores selling soft drinks, bread and buns, and bowls of rice and meat, there were fifteen individuals with goods to sell at retail—cigarettes, scones, dry biscuits, lemonade, lollipops, tinned meat and fish, pipe tobacco, twist tobacco, cigarette papers, and chewing gum. The largest stock had cost £10 10*s*. at wholesale prices from the Co-operative Association, but the average was about £8. If all goods had sold, the yield would have been £16 10*s*. (or £6 profit) for the biggest stocker, and £12 (or £4 profit) on the average. One seller whose stock I checked before and after, however, had just over £4-worth of merchandise unsold, almost half of it expensive pipe tobacco in which he had unwisely specialized. But this could later be sold in the trade store which he operated nearby, as could also the lemonade, tinned meat, chewing gum, and dry biscuits that remained. Or one could say that this particular seller had made his profit in merchandise, which he could consume himself. In either case, the mark of success in trading of this sort is to sell at least enough to replace the cash used to buy the stock. Beyond that it does not matter whether one takes one's profits by consuming the items that remain, or by selling more goods. The original stock can be replaced, and one is receiving an income as well. The rate of profit on investment is very high, though it is not easy to separate profits from labour costs.

The last two major businesses in which Vunamami was involved in 1961 were the operation of the cocoa fermentery at Talimut, and the prospective operation of Ravalien plantation. Both were matters of intense village concern and many meetings, yet in both Vunamami was associated more or less closely with the neighbouring villages of Vunabalbal, Bitarebarebe and Tingenavudu, which belonged to Bitatali Co-operative.

TALIMUT FERMENTERY OPERATION

Talimut fermentery, it will be remembered, was an outgrowth of the coconut plantation planted in 1938 at the instigation of Enos Teve, the Paramount Luluai, by village corvée labour. It had been replanted in the same way to cocoa in 1950, and the Council had set up the fermentery on the same plot of land, ostensibly to service the village plantation but incidentally to provide for the active individual politicians and entrepreneurs who were privately growing cocoa. The initial loan by the Council to set up the Ngatur fermentery was repaid from the profits of the Vunamami Cacao Marketing Account (i.e., from the amounts of money not paid to growers), so that the original fermenteries at Ngatur and Talimut were paid for entirely by internally generated funds for two years. The government loan of £1000 in 1955 to finance expansion of both Talimut and Malakun fermenteries was made to the Vunamami Council, but this did not detract from the feeling of intense local involvement in "their" fermentery, built with local funds on local initiative.

The eventual securing of a large loan from the Bank of New South Wales to finance all immediately foreseeable fermentery expansion in the Tolai area necessitated formal legal conditions which nominally altered this local involvement but in practice did not do so. The bank could not take over the land or assets of the fermenteries in case of default because they were on Native Land (or Reserves), and therefore a mortgage on individual fermenteries was out of the question. The only security the bank could accept were the tax revenues of the councils, and it insisted on what it felt were satisfactory guarantees of efficient operation and of loan repayment: the setting up of a government-supervised accounting and marketing agency employing a European manager, and steady repayment fixed in terms of the volume of cocoa processed (£35 per ton of dry beans) and not in terms of the profit made. This meant establishing the Tolai Cocoa Project as virtually an agency of the combined Local Government Councils.

Owing to the intelligence and skill of the manager of the Project, K. R. Gorringe, the sense of local identification was maintianed, as it had to be if growers were to be convinced that they should bring their beans to the fermentery, though it meant a lower first payment for them than they might get at nearby plantations or trade stores. The growers were of course acquiring equity in the Project by paying £35 a ton to amortise the loan, and they would also receive a variable second payment depending on the price realized for dry beans. But to accept less money in hand for speculative money in the bush required a confidence in the Project that had to be maintained. By keeping separate accounts for each fermentery and marking each fermentery's cocoa with distinctive marks, the participants were encouraged to build up individual reputations.[6] In addition, fermenteries selling a superior product or operating economically were able to pass on their profits directly to the growers concerned. The manager also stressed the legal distinction that the Project was not *buying* beans from the growers but was merely acting as their agent until the final sale, processing and marketing the growers' property and giving only an advance against payment.

Councils were explicitly involved in the Project as guarantors of the loan, as appointers of local cocoa inspectors, and as members of the board. Each council individually was responsible for the portion of the loan allocated to the fermenteries within its jurisdiction, so that of the £227,020 advanced by the Bank of New South Wales by April 1961, Vunamami Council, with five fermenteries out of the total of sixteen, was responsible for £69,620. It had not yet drawn £10,531 of this, and had £37,725 still outstanding. Vunamami Council growers had paid off £21,363 by means of the levy on tonnage sold.

The management of individual fermenteries was left very much to local initiative, although decisions involving major investments were always discussed at central Project meetings. On these occasions, too, there would be discussion of technical information on the merits of particular kinds of driers, on crop projections based on Agriculture Department planting records, or on marketing or transportation problems common to all fermenteries, and fermentery managers had an opportunity to voice their opinions on Project costs. Especially they could comment on the overhead charges of the Project administration—whether, for example, the expenditure of the £1,000 for a new Project Land-Rover in 1961 was justified, and whether its cost should be divided equally among all the fermenteries.

---

[6] In 1961 a rum bottle found in a cocoa sack was readily traced to a particular fermentery, which was named at the ensuing Project meeting. Cadbury's letter, however, merely expressed regret that the bottle was empty.

The manager of Talimut fermentery was an active young man of twenty-five named ToUraliu. He was originally from Vunabalbal village but had close ties in Malakun. Somewhat of a rough diamond, he had left Vunairima school under a cloud when a girl became pregnant, and he had signed on as ship's crew. He had spent considerable time in Australia between voyages, and had developed language, mechanical, and organizational skills. On his return to his village he had attracted the attention of older men by his organizing of young men's groups, especially if dancing was involved, and by his business use of the capital he had earned. He had first been appointed an assistant at Talimut to the former councillor of Bitarebarebe, and had then been promoted to manager when the older man resigned in January 1958 to look after his own cocoa. He had matured into an effective political speaker and a ruthlessly efficient manager who did not mince words. But he had maintained his popularity and public image of being a man of the people by his skill at dancing and by his hard work and participation in *tubuan* ceremonials. His fees for initiation into the *tubuan* had been paid by a very distantly related big man, who was clearly grooming him as his successor.

Originally the fermentery had been looked on as a major user of local labour, but in practice it had proved more economical to employ only a few full-time workers for the routine unskilled jobs of turning the ferment, rolling out sun driers, and bagging the product. In 1961 five immigrant New Guinean workers were so employed at £5 per month. The fermentery manager received £10 a month, and local women from Bitarebarebe were employed part time during the flush seasons and also on Tuesdays, when beans were bought and more workers were needed. Vunamami villagers felt that one of the advantages of having another fermentery near at hand would be the part-time work available to their womenfolk, but they recognized that the location of the Talimut fermentery restricted such work there to Bitarebarebe women.

In the six months October 1958–March 1959 Talimut sales of 23.6 tons of cocoa fetched £6,278. Of this, £650 went for processing, overhead, and interest costs, £556 for loan redemption charges (the rate per ton had been lowered by then by agreement with the Bank of New South Wales, to £25 per ton), and £5,072 for payments to growers. The processing cost of under £30 per ton compared favourably with the 1956–1957 averages for all fermenteries of over £48 per ton. (But neither cost took account of such central Project expenses as salaries, contributed by the Administration, which amounted to some £15 per ton.) It also compared favourably with Talimut costs per ton in the 1957 period of £64.34 (Australia 1958:52). It would undoubtedly have reduced still further by 1960–1961 when, for the same period, 43.5 tons were sold but labour costs had increased only 20 percent.

Fermentery affairs were much to the forefront of Vunamami interest in 1961. The Talimut plantation was corporately owned and the returns went into a village account. By 1961 the work of cocoa collection and maintenance originally done in turn by all men had devolved on five only, who took turns doing the work for one month at a fee of ten shillings. There was discussion of what to do with defaulters. One man, Darius, had consistently done more turns than he needed to, and at the year's end he agreed to do the work regularly for a fee of one pound a month. On this basis the plantation was working smoothly and grossed £31 (£6 for labour costs) for the village between October 1960 and June 1961.

In January 1961, as cocoa prices fell, a rumour got about that some growers were not selling their wet beans to Project fermenteries but were instead selling them privately to plantations or trading fermenteries.[7] For Talimut the figures for yields over eight years (Table 6) clearly indicate the falseness of the rumour. The truth was that all growers were continuing to patronize the fermentery, but yields from nine-year-old plantations had begun to decline. The decline had so far been hidden by increases in total yield as newer areas came into bearing, but by 1961 the two trends had reached a balance, and total production was almost stationary. For some areas with less efficient fermenteries the rumour may have been true. A planter from an outlying area showed me how, when the Project could pay only threepence a pound for wet beans, he could make a profit while paying five and a half pence. He had just installed a new drier, which lost heat and did

[7] The rumour would seem to have been started, possibly by D.A.S.F. officials, when sales to the Project fell below forecasts made on the basis of numbers of trees planted and estimates of yields. It proved to be a convenient political weapon and was widely accepted even up to 1967, despite the factual evidence against it. Accepting it was easier than changing the yield estimates, though the too facile acceptance of it as the cause of declining sales to the Project delayed the recognition of the seriousness of dieback and black-pod diseases.

not dry evenly; if he could buy enough native-grown beans to keep it operating at a time when his own beans were not in flush, he could have it put into good working order and get his workers trained in time for his flush season. He would charge enough to cover the direct costs of fuel and so on but would ignore depreciation and overhead charges. A Project fermentery was just beginning operations some miles from his plantation, but he had no difficulty getting nearby growers to sell to him rather than to the Project.

The Vunamami Council fermentery managers, Napitalai of Ngatur and ToUraliu of Talimut, were among the most vehement in demanding that something be done about what they regarded as sabotage of the Project. At every Project meeting they asked that a law be enacted, and at every large meeting of villagers, for ceremonies, censusing, or Co-ops, they and the village councillors harangued people about the immorality of destroying something that was "of the people themselves" (*kai ra tarai iat*). When the Agricultural Officer also talked about the (more serious) sabotage by growers who did not clean up their plantations and let black-pod infection spread, Napitalai demanded to know why District Officers never listened to charges against such growers brought by Council cocoa inspectors or imposed the £50 fine decreed in the official ordinance.

In the mid-June session of the 1961 Legislative Council, Vin ToBaining made a dramatic speech in which he demanded Territory-wide legislation; if this was not forthcoming, the councils would make strong rules, and if these were not supported in the courts they would be appealed right to the highest courts in Canberra. On 21 June the Administrator made a special visit to attend a meeting of the combined councils and learn the strength of Tolai feeling on the issue. Every speech stressed how the fermenteries were agencies of the councils, and therefore of the people; if the government let fermenteries go, they might as well let councils go; people who took beans to *kampani* and not to the Project were people who stole other growers' beans by night, or were generally "*groa nogut tasol.*" The Administrator was obviously impressed by the warmth of feeling and by the lack of any negative sentiment, even when the chairman, Nason ToKiala, went out of his way to ask for contrary opinions, and he promised that the Administration would seek ways of helping. During the next three months there were many village meetings in Vunamami,

primarily to discuss the purchase of Ravalien plantation, the forthcoming Council elections, the *matamatam* in Vunabalbal village,
or Bitatali Co-operative, but they all included a half-hour or so of
enthusiastic rhetoric about the need to support Talimut.

At the Cocoa Project meeting on 28 June ToUraliu posed the
managerial issues. The original owners, who had been paying off
the bank loan at the rate of £25 per ton, felt that the fermenteries
were largely theirs, and they seemed to think that the fermenteries
were being taken away from them. Now, with falling prices, the
actual price paid for beans was becoming more important; how
did the Project fix its buying prices and how could traders and
plantations afford to pay more? The Project manager, Mr. Gorringe, explained that the then current loan repayment rate of £25
per ton was equivalent to growers receiving 1.2d. per pound of
wet beans extra as equity in the fermenteries; he had, he said,
succeeded in lowering the rate to £15 per ton, or about ¾d. per
pound. He also pointed out how the amount given as an advance
payment had to be fixed conservatively as *less* than any likely
eventual payment for processed beans. A private trader could risk
speculation on a rise in price; the Project could not.[8] The Agricultural Officer said the Administration was studying the question
of how to determine the equity in the Project of individual growers, and the form of asset ownership when the loan was repaid.[9]

He further indicated that the pessimistic talk about the Project
failing was really unfounded. Production for May 1961 had
reached an all-time high of 190 tons, and the £4,750 repaid on
the loan almost exactly equalled the amount withdrawn for construction and working capital. The Project was in a position to
finance future development out of earnings and was expanding at

[8] On the other hand, the Project was also sensitive to political pressures
by the Administration. When prices fell disastrously in November and
December, 1960, the Project had been forced to maintain its buying price
rather than cut immediately, so that local incomes would be maintained
before the Legislative Assembly elections. By doing so it incurred severe
losses.

[9] The Administration was still "considering the question" in 1967, six
years later. Local fears of a takeover of assets from the growers by an
impersonal company had been increased by the replacement, at Administration urging, of large Project meetings by meetings of a small, exclusive
board. The bank loan was almost paid off, yet growers felt more and more
alienated from the Project. The solution of operating in accordance with
the wishes of the growers rather than for administrative convenience did
not seem to have occurred to the Australian advisers.

a rapid rate. At the July 12th meeting it was agreed that advance payments could go back to fourpence per pound. Yet there were still some fears—uncertainty over who owned the Project, and whether prices were incorrectly fixed—a hangover from the false rumours of imminent failure. For the observer, the episode had been revealing as bringing up, in the stress of the moment, all the normally hidden fears of the growers, and as illustrating the grasp that the local managers had of the crucial issues of financial management even though they lacked the sophisticated European vocabulary to express it, and their European advisers, underestimating their understanding, felt they were not ready for full and clear explanations using that sophisticated vocabulary.

RAVALIEN PLANTATION

The question of the purchase of Ravalien plantation, discussed but not carried through in 1961, illustrates many of the same issues of managerial know-how and capital accumulation. The possibility of buying small plots of land from Ravalien had first become known some years earlier, when Plantation Holdings, Ltd., published its intentions of subdividing for commercial and residential purposes the portion of the plantation nearest Kokopo. The Methodist Mission had investigated possible sites for a new church, and the Administration had inquired about land for a teachers' college, and about ten acres for extensions to Kalamanagunan school. The question of raising money for these purposes had been discussed. But not until 19 June 1961, when Vin ToBaining returned from the Legislative council session in Port Moresby, had the idea of buying plantation land for cash cropping occurred to Vunamami. Although ToBaining did not then know the price, the response of villagers at an evening meeting was almost rapturous. This was "our" land (*kadat*), "we" would buy it back. ToBaining's cautious questions of whether it would be better to let the Administration buy it and subdivide it into twenty-two-acre blocks, or to make the purchase as a village unit, were lost in the general comments that all money in the village would be pooled, and that although people complained of being hard up, there was really an ample supply of money.

For the next village meeting on 27 June considerable preparation had been done on alternative schemes for raising the purchase price (still unknown). ToDaula the councillor had investigated the possibility of obtaining loans from the Native Loans Board, and had learned of the need for providing security for such loans. (The fact that the land was freehold land and excellent security in itself had not been told to him at the District Office, because he had inquired in a context of the loans to settlers on ten-acre blocks in the Warangoi scheme.) Suggestions were made that Savings Bank books could be used as security, or that one-quarter of all copra receipts at Bitatali store could be put into a special fund. ToBaining suggested that, whatever was done about collecting money or obtaining loans, it was most important to continue operating the plantation fermentery as a central facility and to use all its profits to pay off the loan. Clearly, the Cocoa Project operations provided a model of organizational finance. The ensuing discussion accepted this principle and extended it to the relationship between fermenteries and growers; each grower sending to the fermentery should work his own small plot of land, and should consider that plot of land as *pia na bartamana* (private family land), not as *pia na vunatarai* (clan land).

On 3 July the A.D.O. and I were invited to a formal meeting at Vunamami *motonoi*, where the community decision was announced and our support was asked for their efforts. Polos To-Pultima, Lote Turvung and his brother Beniona ToKarai, and Vin ToBaining spoke. They stressed the desire of the people to buy the land for themselves, but said they could not do it without government help. This could come in two ways. The whole area could be bought by the government, which would subdivide it and sell small plots to individual Vunamami residents, who would gradually repay the money advanced. Or perhaps the government could advance a single large sum for the purchase of the whole unit of land, and work out some form of management supervision such as that provided for the Cocoa Project, with the loan repayment to come from profits. Either way, the question of how to subdivide could be postponed until the land was fully paid for. The A.D.O could make the formal request to the government, and my contribution could be to document the village need for land, its financial resources, and its potential for working the area. The villagers filed past in a ceremonial *wartabar*, donating small items until there was a pile of food for each of us. The A.D.O. promised he would write to Port Moresby, as requested, but he cautioned the people that the Administration was not favourable towards the lending of money because of what it considered was happening to the Tolai Cocoa Project, and that any action would have to await an appraisal of the plantation's value. I redoubled my efforts at collecting economic statistics.

At a meeting on 11 July, prior to the Council elections, there was renewed emphasis on the interest of both the Co-operative Association and the Methodist Mission in purchasing parts of the plantation and in contributing funds to the purchase. Another Vunamami village meeting on 14 July discussed the possible operation of the plantation. ToDaula pointed out that in many ways the entire village could be considered a single plantation (though he had to look to me for a figure of how many acres it contained) and that running Ravalien could be done on the same lines. If the village were thinking of repaying a loan out of operating profits on Ravalien, it could equally well do so out of the operating profits of the village itself. Everyone agreed that a fund should be set up to include all village operating profits and that a *watabu* should be imposed on coconuts for a period of three months.

There was intense discussion of who should control the village plantation. It was agreed that there were great difficulties in applying any control (*warkurai*) to Vunamami residents working, or owning land, outside the village limits, although Beniona volunteered to try and collect contributions from emigrant workers. When some of the big men agreed to submit to any controls that were decided upon, everyone agreed that a single management was needed. At the same time there was a need for keeping accounts of who had contributed what to the village fund; this would not be a matter of donations (*wartabar*) but of loans (*di tultaria*), which later could either be repaid or could be used as a basis for subdividing the land.

At the regular Vunamami Council meeting of 27 July the councillors of other villages, confronted by the issue for the first time, were timid and showed little of the business sense that had developed during the month in Vunamami village. They agreed with the District Officer's suggestions that insufficient money was available locally for the purchase and that the government should buy the plantation and subdivide it into blocks.

A month went by awaiting word from Port Moresby, during which I completed a report on "Land Shortage in Vunamami" and sent it to the Director of District Services in support of their request. The managing director of Plantation Holdings arrived for discussions on 5 September, and for the first time firm figures of costs could be discussed by Vunamami. His asking figure was approximately 40 percent higher than my own valuation of the largely derelict land, but it enabled the problems of collecting £10–15,000 for a 420-acre purchase to be faced realistically, and a full inspection of the land and its equipment was arranged. Observers from several other villages that were interested in purchasing other land from Plantation Holdings participated in the discussions and later went to view the properties. Of particular concern to Vunamami was the realization that to purchase the land after it had been subdivided into small blocks would raise the price by something like one-third. This clinched the case for buying the plantation land as a whole unit. It seemed to be agreed that the final form of the purchase and operation should involve a *kivung na Vunamami* collecting subscriptions, and obtaining loans, and so buying an operating plantation including the drier and fermentery. The names of subscribers would be recorded as lending money to the *kivung* in the same way that share capital was lent to the Co-operative. The fermentery would be offered to the Cocoa Project for £3,000, which not only would help with any down payment required but also would ensure the continuity of managerial skills that the Project had built up. Areas within the plantation would be allocated to individuals who thought they could work them—some would require planting up and others only the collection of crops—in return for rental (*totokom*) payments to the *kivung*. It was recognized that while the *kivung* had outstanding mortgages on the property it could not subdivide; subdivision would have to await the repayment of loans, but eventually the claims of cultivators, and of contributors, would be recognized. On the other hand, some people saw advantages in maintaining a single village control (*warkurai*) further into the future, to ensure that good cultivation practices were maintained, to guarantee that produce was sold through the Project and the Co-operative, and to enable reallocation of plots (as was done with Council blocks at the Warangoi) should a tenant not tend his plot well. Using both indigenous terms and concepts and their experiences in co-operatives and the Cocoa Project, the people had in fact worked out the complex structure of a holding company, which would sell operating rights over the machinery to another business and lease land to its own shareholders.

The events that followed appeared as an anticlimax to the promising beginnings. The Administration, though sympathetic to the Vunamami appeal, did not feel able to assist with loan funds, or to provide the degree of supervision it thought would be necessary for the successful operation of a plantation. It offered the help of a valuer to assist in negotiations, and it suggested that Vunamami could lend the village the £5,000 held as a statutory reserve. I was optimistic that with Council guarantees a bank loan could be arranged. It indicated its preference for subdivision of the plantation into large blocks, despite ToBaining and ToPultima's representations to the District Commissioner on 13 September that the urgent need was to assist *many* people in Vunamami, in view of the great population pressure, rather than the extremely limited wealthy few who were already being helped by Government Resettlement schemes on ten- and twenty-acre blocks. It encouraged the collection of funds immediately.

Beniona, William ToKavivi, and ToDaula kept the accounts for the fund, and at first money flowed in. The sum of £90 was received the first day, with contributions from thirty people ranging from one to ten pounds. The *watabu* on coconuts for three months was signed by Beniona, William, Punion, ToDaula, Alwas, Enos, Polos, and for the women Makaret, IaLavol, IaNuk (wife of ToBaining), IaRodi, IaLoi, and IaPapata. The Council on 27 September approved the use of its Reserve Fund, with all councillors seizing on the idea that as Vunamami repaid its borrowings with interest, other villages might then borrow for their land purchases. In that way the money would not "sleep" but would "work," and the Council would be like a bank "for the people."

But by November there was still no news of the valuation; money continued to trickle in to the village fund at a rate of five pounds a day. The fund stood at £264 12s. 6d., but it was from current income rather than from accumulated savings. The largest single contribution was £29, given, surprisingly, not by one of the rich men but by a rather poor, middle-aged fisherman. Most households had contributed something, usually five to ten pounds, but many women and old men had contributed only a pound or so. People were holding off, and although firm in their expressions of a desire to buy Ravalien, were becoming sceptical whether anything would happen. Negotiations between the Administration and Plantation Holdings, Ltd., over the selling price still hung fire in September 1962, although the Administration speedily concluded a purchase for itself of forty-five acres for a teachers' college, and the two ten-acre blocks which this subdivision isolated were sold in 1963 to the Women's Groups, and for the extension of Kala-managunan school.

ANALYSIS

Three general elements emerge from these descriptions of the various types of business in Vunamami: the distinction made between "food" and what is "of the business," the nature of capital-owning groups, and the way in which businesses tend to pyramid capital and reinvest profits.

The distinction between "food" and "business" underlies many activities in Vunamami, as has been shown, for example, in the earlier discussion of the claims of sons to their fathers' lands, which are claims to "food" not to outright title, or in the distinction made between women's marketing and that of men. In those contexts, the distinction could be interpreted as that between subsistence activities and profit-making or luxury activities. In the context of businesses, however, the distinction is one that parallels the economist's distinction between an income flow and a capital stock. The "income flow" in Vunamami may often not be of food or of anything translatable into a cash equivalent: the provision of ambulance services or priority in the use of a copra drier or car, or the ease of availability of green vegetables are this kind of income. But income is recognized by Vunamami people as a main purpose of business investment. European bookkeeping should not judge the success of such businesses merely in terms of the level of capital stock at the end of the year, as compared with the level at the beginning of the year—that is, by an entity that they call "profits." The real return on the initial investment is the flow of income of all kinds (or services) that accrues throughout the life of the investment. Belshaw (1965:71, 74) has shown how this same principal pervades indigenous businesses in the Fiji Islands, even those of a large-scale business like the Vunamoli manganese mining company, where "profits" may be overshadowed by the public services that are provided.

Problems also exist in separating "income" from "capital," especially where the asset has a long life but will need eventual replacement. Accounting procedures solve the problem by not taking all revenue as income, but considering some as replacing of the capital stock, that is, as depreciation. Where the asset was land in the proto-typical Vunamami business, depreciation (or replacement) was not a problem, because fertility was rarely lost; successive generations who cleared virgin bush or planted trees increased the value of the capital assets that they handed on to the next generation, while being satisfied themselves with the income flow of food that they received from the land. With land, the difficulty now is to find ways of ensuring that the increased value of land created by planting it—unplanted land may be worth only £10 an acre, but bearing cocoa land may be worth £100 an acre —does not accrue to the landowning clan entirely as a capital gain but yields a flow of income to the planter (and his children) during his lifetime. A sale of the trees by the planter to the clan, or an agreement by the clan that the planter can dispose of the produce of the trees for a definite period (e.g., by deeding them to his son), would be solutions to this difficulty.

In the modern situation failure to realize the need for replacing assets such as trucks has often been due to lack of experience, but this pattern would seem to be changing. Katakatai ward of Vunabalbal village, for example, owned a truck as a result of a community association venture, very similar to the Women's Group in Vunamami. After the maintenance costs were met out of revenue, the net profit was put in the bank until the full cost of replacement was accumulated; only after this would Katakatai consider spending any residual funds as part of the purchase of Matanatar plantation. Depreciation, in short, was not being spread over the entire life of the asset but was being accounted for as an immediate charge on revenue. This made costs seem high at first, but it encouraged long-term business expansion, and would appear to be typical of Vunamami thinking about businesses.

Alternatively, one could see this practice as an extension of the Vunamami pattern of businesses in which the life of assets is comparatively short—as with nets or fish traps. Each accounting period—or fishing season—included the replacement of most of the assets, so that profits were assessed only after the nets or traps had been replaced. Once the material assets of the business had returned to the level they were at the beginning, all future earnings were profit.

The other main difficulty in separating income from assets occurs where there is only one owner, or where, as with the Vunaibu clan drier, the labour costs of the operator are not fixed. In many cases of owner-operated businesses, such as Punion's drier or pig-raising activities, there is no point in separating the two components, so long as the material assets themselves are not consumed —pigs eaten for household food, copra-drier timbers used for firewood, or carpenters' tools sold to buy clothing. In the operation of a small store, as long as the value of the stock is maintained at at least its initial level (though not artificially by accumulating unsalable items) it may not matter if the owner eats his own stock; he can continue in business. Attempts to deplete the primary stock in such businesses are likely to originate with the family of the businessman, but equally they are most likely to listen to a claim that these assets are "business" not "food." Only if the owner himself faces a major crisis—having to kill a pig for a ceremony, for example—is he likely to destroy his own basic assets, but in such instances we might ask whether it is preferable to maintain the business or to succumb to the crisis.

For businesses owned by more than one person, one key to success is in fixing labour costs—what is "food" and not "business"— even if the people contributing labour are also owners. The actual level of costs is perhaps less important than that they should be predictable. Thus the amount of food a net-fishing group receives during a season's operation may vary widely, but it is known that it will not include any of the large mackerel, but only small fish; owner-operators may use a drier for their own copra as often as they like, so long as all cash returns (or all returns, less fixed costs) are part of the business. One of the most crucial elements in the success of the IaMinat group is that they have secured the services of a treasurer and a driver at a fixed rate. It helps that both are receiving less for their services than they could expect if they were working for an unrelated employer, but the saving is not substantial in relation to the profits of the group. Of more importance for smooth running is the universal confidence in the honesty and fairness of the treasurer, and the knowledge that they can call on the driver at any time of the day or night. The Vunaibu copra drier became profitable when the "food" of the operator became a predictable charge rather than an optional one.

The nature of capital-owning groups is of great importance in this connection, for specifying the returns of income to individual workers defines the residue as accruing to the owners. In Vunamami, if more than one individual is involved in asset ownership, care is always taken to give the owning group a corporate identity, distinct from the individuals who make it up. People may be quite clear that Enos inspired the fishing-net group and directed most of its operations, but he and the other members scrupulously emphasized that it was the Takaptar-Tuluai group; the Group of Twenty called itself "Mr. Mix-up"; the four-man copra drier was designated the Vunaibu drier; the Land-Rover was designated as being either "of the women" or with wry Tolai humour as "Mrs. Death";[10] the Katakatai truck was referred to simply as that. Each business had a treasurer-bookkeeper, and usually a bank account, although the bank account often appeared in official records under the name of the treasurer. When people talk about the use of Bitatali Co-operative account number 66 as the number for donations to the local church (though in the Society books it is listed under the name of Polos ToPultima), they phrase it as Polos "donating" (*tabar*) his number to the church. He subscribed the £5 for the share account. No attention is paid to the situation as it would be considered in a court of government law, that the sums credited to that account belong to Polos.

But corporate identity is only possible if members of the owning group can feel a part of it, and if they can trust the treasurer to act as a disinterested group representative and not as a self-motivated individual. The use of clan names is a simple way of mobilizing a sense of participation by contributors, and of guaranteeing that the group will (in theory) exist in perpetuity apart from the individuals who currently are members. It does not imply that every clan member has subscribed, but it does imply that the clan can be looked upon to sanction breaches of faith within the group. So too with locally based *kivung* like IaMinat, IaPidik, or Katakatai, although all individuals are not necessarily members, the doings of the *kivung* are discussed at public meetings. I heard one of the most incisive discussions of Talimut fermentery operations in the speeches following one stage in the *tubuan* initiation, and discussion of the Ravalien plantation purchase often followed announcements of the weeks' activities in church on Sunday. Such public discussions take time, and group interest may hamper rapid executive action, but the feeling of confidence that is engendered by using clan or group names has, I think, been vital for the success of businesses in Vunamami. The Administration's encouragement of businesses in New Guinea has usually been described as

---

[10] The use of personal names to characterize corporate businesses was probably more common before large-scale village or area projects emerged. It would seem to be an independent invention of an "incorporation" mechanism to enable them to be treated as single legal personalities.

an attempt "to free individual entrepreneurs from the shackles of their kin groups." From the local point of view, this has usually meant encouraging a ruthless few to renege on obligations. And this in turn has caused the break-up of large organizations and the proliferation of small, uneconomic units. What would seem to be more needed is support for the rights of shareholders in large businesses, to enable them to appeal to, say, Council courts if a lack of confidence in *kivung* operations develops. *Kivung*s need the support of some form of Companies Act, to supplement their present informal support by public opinion.

Most cases of lack of confidence in *kivung* operations also turn out to be lack of confidence in specific powerful individuals belonging to the *kivung*, and the feeling that those individuals are getting an undeserved personal income out of the *kivung* instead of acting as trustees for the corporate body. We have considered Enos' use of the Takaptar-Tuluai *kivung* funds to build a drier, the alleged use of the Co-operative Association's Land-Rover for personal purposes by the Co-op secretary and the dissatisfaction over the purchase of a truck by the executive of the copra-buying Group of Twenty. There is indeed a habitual distrust of all business executives—a feeling that if a "big man" pushes a collaborative project, he is doing it because in the long run he will benefit from it personally, at the expense of the small men who helped him earlier. Yet the small man is optimistic. His small contribution will do nothing on its own; if it is joined by the energetic big man into a large *kivung* it may earn something, at least during the early stages of a business, and there is always the chance that this will be the exceptional *kivung* that will last. You stay poor if you stay alone; if you join with a big man you won't be any poorer and you may be much richer. It is often worth the gamble, especially if there are safeguards.

The safeguards are important, as was shown in the Ravalien plantation subscriptions affair. My own estimate of the available cash savings in Vunamami in 1961 was £5,000, yet the amount that was produced by November 1961 as subscriptions for the village purchase of the plantation was only £264. When asked about reasons for holding back at this stage, Vunamami people said in private that it was because of the government's insistence on subdividing into twenty blocks. They saw this as meaning that only twenty big men would profit; the big men, even if they saw their personal advantages from the purchase and spoke out strongly

in favour of subscriptions, presumably also knew that if they subscribed large sums this would be interpreted as the first steps in
taking over. Safeguards were looked for, such as those of incorporation as a company, or of the purchase being by a corporate
unit like the Council or the Village. With the fermentery the
Council had guaranteed that each investor's contribution was safe
against any predation by big men; something similar was needed
if villagers were to subscribe for the purchase of a plantation.

Again this view of the main reason for the failure of businesses
(apart from technical incompetence) differs somewhat from the
view voiced by many expatriates in New Guinea. The latter often
say that it is the demands of minor shareholders for division of
the proceeds of a business which hampers go-ahead entrepreneurs
and causes business failures. The present analysis sees the demand
for division of the assets of a business as coming only when the
executives of a business have lost the confidence of the minor
shareholders. A loss of confidence may be unreasonable from an
outsider's point of view, but it is likely to be based on a personal
assessment of motives or on small signs of incipient mismanage-
ment that are not apparent to outsiders. It may be objectively
well founded, as was the case with the Group of Twenty, though
this did not prevent executives from complaining that it was lack
of support that caused a prospering business to dissolve. The underlying reason for the business failure is to be found in the
behaviour of the entrepreneur-manager, either in his business decisions or in his public relations; the demand for a division of
assets is a symptom of incipient failure, not its cause.

The division of profits is, indeed, the exception in Vunamami
businesses, not the rule. The normal situation, as already indicated,
is for the income return to shareholders to be provided in the
course of business operations in the form of services or "food."
All the remaining receipts are "of the business," from which
maintenance, overhead, and employee labour costs are met; the
balance, which Western accounting would consider a "profit"
to be distributed as dividends, is regarded by Vunamami people
as part of the business assets. A distribution of those assets is demanded only if there is a likelihood of the business collapsing.
When expatriate business advisers insist on the payment of dividends to investors they bring up the spectre of imminent bankruptcy. The Vunamami investor wants to feel that his investment
is safe, and that it is growing. He will not invest if he sees no like-

lihood of services coming from his investment, but having once invested he measures the security of his investment by the assets that the business owns. It is important that these be publicly visible—an aspect that was correctly understood by the first Co-operative Officer—though it can lead (as in 1953) to making uneconomic investments. Trucks may be bought, or driers built, because they are visible and therefore "safe" assets, which will provide a constant flow of services for the owner. No thought may be given to obtaining the cash for repairs and eventual replacement, nor to the possibility of getting the same services for less money by renting or hiring equipment.

A bank account may also be felt to be a safe asset; it is there when needed, and this in itself is a form of insurance. From this point of view, the recurrent pattern of businesses going inactive, often with quite large sums in the hands of the treasurer in his bank account, which the shareholders do not then demand back, appears less irrational. The business corporation remains in existence, and each shareholder can continue to talk about the assets that "he" owns (in part); the assets are (presumably) still there, and could begin growing again should the reasons for the *kivung*'s inactivity be removed, or a new investment avenue appear. If the assets were divided and a final accounting made, the corporation would be seen to "die," rather than merely to "fall down" (*i bura*); the services that the *kivung* was set up to provide would certainly not be provided; the sum of money received by each shareholder would likely be too small to allow him to use it effectively except for purposes of immediate consumption; the man who insisted on the return of his investment would be revealed as someone who wished to destroy the *kivung*, and who preferred to dissipate his assets in consumption.

To put this another way, most Vunamami people when they have once invested in a business treat the amount of their investment as something "lost" or no longer available for consumption. They see investing in worthy projects as a duty, and treat collections for clan copra driers in the same way as collections for the church's mission activities, Council tax, or for sending the village school choir to a competition. The contribution is lost and not to be demanded back; the return for the contribution is the service provided by the drier, the church, the Council, or the school, plus the pride and vicarious sense of participation of "owning a drier," being part of an onward-marching church, having the most progressive council in New Guinea, or winning the choir competition.

The non-distribution of profits and their continuous reinvestment should, if Western business experience can be taken as a guide, lead to extremely rapid business growth. That this can occur appears from the history of IaMinat, where a total of £19 contributed capital in 1953 had increased to £140 by 1954 and to £410 in two more years, which then remained stationary until with new activity it reached £600 in another year, and was still growing in 1963. The Takaptar-Tuluai *kivung* and the Group of Twenty showed the same pattern of growth and reinvestment for considerable periods. The growth of the Tolai Cocoa Project to a £250,000 business, or of the Co-operative Association to a business with a £500,000 annual turnover was essentially a matter of minimizing distribution of profits and using the available cash flow to pay off the bank loan at an extremely fast rate or to provide the working capital for the business increase. In both cases the European advisers avoided explaining the issues to shareholders, thinking that the principles involved were beyond their comprehension. In both cases the advisers were actually following established native business practice, and were risking loss of shareholder confidence.

Yet it is equally true that no businesses achieve the astronomical rates of growth that might be expected with the continual reinvestment of profits that are in the range of 25–50 percent of invested capital per annum. Technical incompetence in either mechanical operations or in such business operations as pricing goods for sale or in bookkeeping and allowing for depreciation, takes a considerable toll of businesses, although the Vunamami material provides few of the gross examples of running trucks without oil, or selling goods at a loss to increase turnover that have become the stereotyped myth of indigenous business practices for many expatriates. Dishonesty, or at least conflict between business and personal interests, also plays a role in preventing growth. "Demands by extended kin groups" do not appear in the present material as detrimental to business growth.

Quite the contrary. One of the major factors in hindering growth would seem to be the difficulty in establishing corporations larger than of about twenty people, and owning capital assets worth more than about £1,000. Larger assets provide services of use to wider groups than the typical *kivung*, yet wider groups are often reluctant to make use of those services if they feel they "be-long" to a "foreign" group. Equally, the wider groups feel re-luctant to enter into co-operative ownership arrangements with people with whom they have no pre-existent common membership in a corporate unit. It is the absence of recognition of wider ties that hinders business growth into larger fields, and it is the ac-ceptance of common understandings among fellow-clansmen (even if these understandings include the idea that one must always be suspicious of a relative) that permit business expansions to get as far as they do. Dewey (1962) has vividly shown how it is the spread of these understandings and informal sanctioning powers on a wider basis than just the clan that has facilitated Chinese business growth in Indonesia.

Yet many of the cases described for Vunamami are of businesses with wider bases of support than just a few members of a single clan—neighbourhood groups, whole villages, alliances of nearby villages, the Vunamami Council, and to some extent the combined councils of the Tolai area. It has been the spread of loyalties and identification with wider-range groupings that has been vital for the growth of businesses, and a precondition for it. The political aspects of this consolidation of groupings and how it has come about will be a major topic in Chapter 10.

The other main deterrent to business growth in Vunamami has been a lack of avenues for productive investment. The limited range of business opportunities available in a village of five hun-dred people is clear, and it was well known to Vunamami people. The progression of an entrepreneur from petty marketing, to copra drying, to truck ownership was one that was readily achiev-able—so much so that an oversupply of trucks had already oc-curred, and an oversupply of driers seemed imminent. One result of such an oversupply is that those operating less efficiently should fall by the wayside, and market forces should result in a closer equilibrium between the supply of, say, trucks and the demand for transportation. As we have seen, this did indeed occur in Vu-namami. But the other result of market forces—that the lowering of the yield to capital in established fields should encourage entre-preneurs to branch out into new areas of investment—had not occurred. Savings remained tied up in inactive bank accounts (and exported by the banks to finance Australian businesses) or were employed in duplicating facilities used only by the local com-munity. There were ample funds available for bigger investments in Vunamami, and as Appendix E shows, well over 10 percent of annual income was saved and available for future investment. It needed to be channelled into businesses catering to wider markets than the village, with shareholding scattered over the area of their market, and employing capital of the order of £10,000 rather than only £1,000. Such businesses will emerge as public confidence in groupings of this size develops, to the extent that wider groupings can feel a sense of participation in such enterprises, and to the extent that government regulation can give shareholders security of investment equal to that which they currently obtain by their informal powers of sanctioning managers.

VIII

Shell Money Finance

Shell money, or *tabu*, has been mentioned frequently in earlier descriptions of land purchases, market-place trade, businesses, and finance. Transactions using cash have been discussed simultaneously, and the reader has been left to assume that cash and shell money are functionally identical, and have been interchangeable (albeit at varying exchange rates). This chapter will pull together the scattered information about shell-money usage, and will give these assumptions closer scrutiny.[1]

A detailed treatment of shell money has been kept until last because it is the economic phenomenon least open to non-Tolai. Most Europeans see it as a quaint survival that will shortly disappear. The present chapter shows how it is the mainspring, not only of inter-Tolai trade and business enterprise, but of a critical area of entrepreneurship in Tolai society. The entrepreneur working with *tabu* can easily realize profits of a larger order than are thought to be reasonable in a cash economy; *tabu* entrepreneurs are "big businessmen." They are also politicians, and their skills are those of organizing people and finance to realize large collective projects, mainly ceremonials. Here, where Europeans interfere least, the Tolai are most free to organize politically and economically, limited only by the financial constraints and regulation imposed by the *tabu* system itself. In this chapter the emphasis is on the operation of the system of shell-money exchange, and not on the implications of Tolai autonomy in a major area of political activity. That will be the topic of Part Three, though the present chapter is a bridge to that part.

It should not be thought that the survival of shell-money usage

[1] The material contained in this chapter has been summarized as Salisbury (1966).

without notable diminution owes anything to European support. Since the 1880's the Roman Catholic Mission has inveighed against the practice as being harmful to "habits of frugality and saving" which would lead to "improvements in family life." The German government prohibited the use of shell money in trade by Europeans. Modern administrators try to discourage it by tolerant laughter. And some anthropologists continue to use nineteenth-century concepts of "primitive money" in relation to *tabu*, and predict its demise, as other writers have done for sixty years.

The Tolai themselves avoid European scorn by concealing most *tabu* transactions. They recognize that the use of *tabu* is a keystone (*a vuna*) to preserving a distinct Tolai identity. They encourage people to acquire cash to buy material comforts, but they all recognize that only *tabu* can maintain the fabric of social relationships. Only *tabu* can give people power. Tabu is a "strong thing"—*a dekdek na magit*—and when Tolai officials and students in Port Moresby combined in 1967 to create a "tribal" Improvement Society they called themselves The Pal na Tabu Society.

TABU STOCKS

There are, at my estimate, some 1,730,000 fathoms of shell money, each containing some three hundred shells, currently in circulation in the Rabaul area. I base this estimate on the stocks of shells of a sample of Vunamami villagers, a few other figures of *tabu* owned by rich individuals in other villages, and on the numbers of rolls of *tabu* displayed at ceremonies in villages from Tingenalom and Wairiki to Rainau. Some figures on *tabu* ownership in Rapitok (T. S. Epstein n.d.) would confirm these estimates.

Tabu stocks can be divided into three components, each of which has distinct characteristics. First, there is what is called *palumtabu*, consisting of rolls (*a gogo*) of continuous lengths of cane on which the shells are strung, tightly coiled and wrapped in leaves, resembling new automobile tires wrapped in brown paper. A very big roll may measure four feet across with coils a foot thick, and may contain between 1,000 and 1,200 fathoms. Most rolls are about two feet six inches in diameter, with coils six inches thick, and contain between two and three hundred fathoms. Rolls with thinner coils are sometimes seen.

Palumtabu is wealth that is publicly displayed and proclaimed as not for everyday use at the time of coiling.[2] It may belong to individuals or to corporate bodies. Rolls of *tabu* given to the ancestral *tubuan* religious groups (*a tabu na tubuan*) are too sacred for women to handle and are stored in secret storehouses of the *tubuan*. These were the oldest rolls I saw. I saw private rolls that had been coiled at dates from 1935 on. Rolls are never transferred intact but are always "carved" (*poka*) and distributed in small quantities to persons present at the carving. These recipients are not obligated to make return gifts for the *tabu*, as they would for *tabu* received otherwise. Coiling thus implies a promise that the coiler will eventually freely donate his *tabu* to all and sundry; there are religious implications also, but the public secular promise is all-important.

The main carvings for which an individual accumulates rolls are for those at his own funeral, and at ceremonies in honour of recent clan dead called *matamatam*. The amount that can be distributed at a funeral is limited to 3,000 fathoms at the outside, since no recipient is supposed to receive more than one or two fathoms, and since only relatives and residents of the nearest two or three villages are supposed to attend the rites. People who come simply to obtain free *tabu* are treated as gate-crashers. The amount distributed for a fairly important man, at a funeral attended by three or four villages, is usually around 1,500 fathoms. Judging from Parkinson's figures (1887:103), there has been no change in these amounts since 1880.

At a *matamatam* a roll is carved by one of the sponsoring hosts for each dance, performed by thirty to one hundred dancers, and *matamatam* are evaluated in terms of the number of dances performed. Thirteen comprise a full afternoon's programme, and though the rolls used are usually small, about 2,500–3,000 fathoms are needed for a ceremony. The sponsoring hosts also display, for the ancestors' gratification, the rolls of *tabu* intended for their own funerals. These occasions thus permit a fairly accurate estimate of clan stocks of *palumtabu*. At three *matamatam* that I visited, from nineteen to twenty-six rolls were displayed, and the

[2] I never observed the coiling ceremony described by Parkinson (1887:105) and informants denied that any ceremony with religious implications was now performed. On the other hand, individuals knew with some precision when particular rolls were "tied" and what their contents were.

number of dances varied from nine to thirteen.[3] There was no
correlation between number of dances and number of rolls displayed, indicating that the differences in over-all wealth, as between *matamatam*-giving groups, are small and are not uniformly
expressed in displays or dancing.

Matamatam are given once every nine years by each major clan
in a village; small segments of a clan in other villages contribute
to *matamatam* given in a village where their's is a major clan. In
each village near Vunamami there are three major clans. Each
clan has an average of twenty rolls for funeral distributions (say
4,000 fathoms) stored for between zero and twenty-four years
(perhaps 12 years on the average). Amounts stored for *matamatam*
would fluctuate between zero and 3,000 fathoms over the nine-
year period, averaging about 1,500 fathoms at any one time. The
total *palumtabu* owned in a village thus averages 17,500 fathoms,
or roughly eighty rolls. A sample survey of ownership in Vunamami village confirms this figure. Vunamami itself has one-
eightieth part of the total Tolai population, yielding an estimate
for the whole Tolai area of 1,400,000 fathoms of *palumtabu*.

Tabu in circulation takes two forms—small change and large
sums. Small change is carried by every adult in amounts up to
three fathoms. Spot checks in the field confirm this figure, which
is also quoted for the 1880's by Parkinson (1887:104). An average
of one and a half fathoms per adult yields a figure of 30,000
fathoms total stock for the Tolai area. Small change is held in
units (or multiples of units): a length of about three inches (i.e.,
about twelve shells) is called a *palatabu*; about eight inches is
a *pidik*; about three feet is *a peapar*; and about six feet is *a pokono*.[4]
The length called by each of these terms may vary between five

---

[3] A joint *matamatam* which I could not attend was given in November
1961 for 350 victims of the 1937 eruption at Mount Kalamanaganan.
Twenty-six dances were performed, presumably simultaneously. I exclude
this ceremony as an extraordinary one.

[4] Variant and additional terms for the various units are given by Bley
(1897:96), Bürger (1913:19), Kleintitschen (1906:182), Parkinson (1907:87),
and Powell (1884:55). Some of the variants are regional forms (e.g., *gogo*
and *loloi* for rolls). Some misunderstanding of methods of measurement
is also involved, but that described by Powell of units equalling distances
from finger-tip to wrist, elbow, arm-pit, centre of the body, and the
finger-tip of the opposite hand accords with my own experience of New
Guinea measures, both among the Tolai and elsewhere. I quote only those
lengths currently used in trade in Vunamami, however.

and ten inches for *a pidik*, and between eight and thirteen shells
for *a palatabu*. How this inexactness is tolerated will be discussed
later; for the moment, what is significant is that a person with a
fathom and five *pidik* in his bag may have any amount from
one and a half to two fathoms. Totals of small change must
involve this degree of inexactness.

There are other reasons why estimates of larger sums held are
also subject to error. This kind of *tabu* circulates rapidly, and
although amounts may be extremely large, owners describe their
holdings only in vague round numbers. The *tabu* is usually stored
in skeins (*a rip*) of five or ten fathoms, hung on pegs in the
owner's *tabu* storeroom. But some is kept as loose shells in lemonade bottles or kerosene drums, labelled as to contents, with certain amounts in odd heaps awaiting restringing as *a rip*. The
range in amounts held is immense; one man in Vunamami had
over a thousand fathoms unrolled, six other rich men had between
25 and 150 fathoms; five poor men had between one skein and
20 fathoms. With these qualifications I estimate a total of about
3,000 fathoms in skeins in Vunamami. The wartime destruction
of *tabu* in Vunamami means that inland areas are probably somewhat richer (as T. S. Epstein's estimates for Rapitok n.d. would
also suggest) and a Tolai average of thirty fathoms per adult male
or 300,000 over all seems reasonable.

Totalling these estimates gives a grand total of 1,730,000 fathoms
for the whole area.

TABU PRODUCTION

The *nassa callosa* shell is not scarce in New Guinea waters. On
my first visit to Ela Beach in Port Moresby I picked up five shells
in a few minutes while paddling with my children. On several
beaches near Rabaul, *nassa* are found, although the exact location
of colonies is concealed by the women who find them (see Meier
1909:95). In the 1870's beaches opposite Massikonapuka Island,
fifty miles away, were a main source, with a few expeditions for
shell going further west. In the last few decades shell has been
brought from the east and south coasts of New Britain. But since
the 1880's the largest source of Tolai *tabu* has been the eastern
Nakanai coast of New Britain. Reports from around 1900 speak
as if it were the only source.

Tolai informants and Europeans from Nakanai agree that most

shells come from seven villages (see Kleintitschen 1906:91)—five
Methodist ones of which Matililiu is the most important, and two
Catholic villages further west. In recent times, but especially
since 1950, the Nakanai people have collected the shell for themselves and have even brought it into Rabaul for sale. But the most
common way of obtaining shell (and what appears to have been
the traditional way) is for parties of Tolai to travel to Nakanai.
Most parties are of four or five individuals; occasionally they are
as large as twenty. They take with them the amounts that they
wish to convert to shell, usually in the form of trade goods, worth
between two and five pounds per person, and also contributions
from others in the village. The trip is made by Government or
Mission trawler at a cost of thirty-five shillings (thirty without
food) per person. On arrival at Nakanai the party is welcomed
by the friend (*a talai*) of the leader, who looks after them during
their stay in return for gifts (*a wapuak*). The relationships between leaders and Nakanai friends are long-standing: one Vunamami man had visited his friend in Nakanai three times between
1950 and 1961, another had met a Nakanai prisoner at Rabaul
gaol and the following year had gone to stay with him for six
months. By giving additional presents to the friend, the party may
build a shelter at the beach from which to wade for shells (*di
gumu ra tabu*), or they may give all the trade goods to the friend.
Nakanai people then gather shells to repay the advance, at a
standard rate: a package (*a pulu*) in a betel leaf was worth one
shilling, and an empty fifteen-ounce salmon tin (*a pal a tin*)
equalled five shillings in trade goods. These rates remained stable
from at least 1920 to 1950, when the rate abruptly doubled. South
coast areas in 1961 were asking one pound per salmon tin.

It may take several months for enough shells to be collected to
repay the advance, during which time the party is the guest of the
leader's friend. Two women collecting for two months from a
nassa colony on a Tolai beach in 1961, going every morning when
the sea was calm and the bottom was clear, gathered two and six
salmon tins full, respectively. A collecting party may have to return home before repayment is complete and leave the goods as a
deposit. A large party in from three to six months may collect
enough shell to fill four four-gallon kerosene drums.

But the work of making *tabu* has barely begun. The longest and
most painful part is to cut the whorl of the shell away from the lips
(*a binabar*) and then to string the lips together (*a niuk*) on lengths

of rattan. Women do this work, but in short spells only and as a favour, for it gives "a pain in the back" (*a kinadik na muruna*). One who returns from Nakanai must seek out all his female friends and persuade each one to accept a tin of shell for cutting. It takes a month or two to get them all cut and threaded on to rattan,[5] and for this work he must give a large present. These presents are not standard (*wakir ta toto*), as are most prices, but they usually are a pound or thirty shillings. Alternatively, two or three of the five fathoms of *tabu* made from a tin may be given to the woman who cuts and threads it.

With these figures it is possible to consider the economics of *tabu* production in 1961. A man going to Nakanai with £25 in trade goods subscribed by several villagers would bring back sufficient shell for 250 fathoms. He would spend a further £3 for his travel, and three to six months of his time. On his return, another £50–£75 (or 100–150 fathoms) would go on preparing the shell, making an average cost per fathom of about seven shillings,[6] plus half a day of his time. *Tabu* production would be profitable only if the exchange rate were above ten shillings per fathom, if a man had female dependents who would prepare the shell more cheaply, or if a man had no more profitable use for his time. Men with time tend not to have the necessary capital, however, and are financed by wealthier villagers. This means a risk for suppliers of capital. As can be expected, when the 1961 exchange rate was ten shillings the amount of *tabu* production was not large, and the Vunamami men who went to Nakanai were either older, conservative, but poor men without large plantings, or youths who had not yet a settled job or plantings and who regarded their three months as a holiday "to see the world."

A Tolai missionary who had been in Nakanai for fifteen years in the 1930's and 1940's told me that the number of parties at the Methodist villages in any one year ranged from one or two to six

[5] Evon Hesse-Wartegg (1902:184, *Monatshefte* 1901:440) reports that a woman can prepare 100 shells a day working full time. He is wrong, however, in saying that a fathom has several thousand shells; it has somewhat over 300 by actual counts.

[6] T. S. Epstein (1964:57) talks of "the price of a fathom (of *tabu*) at Nakanai." My evidence is that there is no such thing. My evidence conflicts with Epstein's report at almost all points. She largely relies on 1900 missionary evidence which is unreliable as a guide to general practice. My analysis of why the 1900 observers reported what they did invalidates secondary analyses based on their descriptions.

or seven. Visits continued during the war years. There was usually
an alternation of villages; if a Raluana party came one year, a Vunamami party came the following year. If an average of five parties
a year is assumed for all seven villages together, and each party
returned with shell for a thousand fathoms, the average increment
to Tolai stocks would be of the order of 5,000 fathoms per annum.
This represents about 0.3 percent of total stocks. Even if this estimate is only half the real figure, the increase would still not keep
pace with an increase in Tolai population of over 3 percent per
annum.

On the other hand, this low average resulted from a precarious
balance of economic factors. If the exchange rate of *tabu* against
cash increased, or if alternative employment became scarce, *tabu*
production would have become more profitable. This appears to
have been the case in 1950–1951 and in 1899–1901 (Bley 1900:
104), when there was an unusually large number of voyages to
Nakanai.[7] Direct testimony is unavailable, but I believe there was
a similar increase between 1875 and 1878, when the advent of
traders and peace produced similar economic conditions.

Considerable stocks of *tabu* were destroyed during the Second
World War. People would point out places where *tabu* stores of
up to four thousand fathoms were destroyed in Vunamami by
bombs or fire. They disagreed on how much the Japanese had
destroyed deliberately; rich men talked of searches, and of hiding
rolls of *tabu* to avoid confiscation; poor men said the Japanese were
not interested in *tabu* but only in Australian coins. They did not
pay for requisitioned food and therefore had no use for "native
money." I should interpret this to mean that if the Japanese sus-
pected an important man of wrongdoing they punished him by
confiscating his *tabu*, but they had no use for *tabu* as such. Whatever the reason, *tabu* was scarce after the war.

By 1950, owing to War Damage payments and a lack of consumer goods, the Tolai had built up supplies of cash. At the same
time, the intense work of rebuilding was over, and the new labour
demands of cocoa planting had hardly begun. Men had time to
spare, and the *tabu* exchange rate had risen sharply. Voyages to

[7] I found no actual reports of Nakanai voyages between 1884 and about
1900, although Bley gives the text of a native account in 1897. Kleintitschen,
on whose account many subsequent writers rely, arrived in 1900 and describes the boom period that he saw. It is not clear to what period Parkinson's classic account of 1907 refers.

Nakanai increased so much that the Nakanai arbitrarily doubled the price of a tin of shells from five to ten shillings.[8] This added another shilling to the cost per fathom, but the subsequent slowing of the trade was probably more the result of the cocoa-planting boom and the increase in agricultural wage rates.

The situation in 1899–1901 was more far-reaching in its consequences. European plantations were then in a phase of expansion, employing much non-local labour and buying local produce, but they were still largely reliant for their profits on the processing of native-grown nuts. Coastal natives had planted much of their land to coconuts and were receiving a satisfactory income of trade goods from the sale of nuts, without expending much labour on processing. Inland areas had not begun planting. Labour was available for voyages to Nakanai. At the same time the satiation of coastal demand for trade goods meant that the Europeans had to pay for nuts or services in *tabu*—which they could acquire only by purchase from the Tolai. Whereas since the 1870's two marks' worth of trade goods had been equivalent to one fathom of *tabu*, the exchange rate now rose to three or four marks (*Monatshefte* 1902:540, Kleintitschen 1906:95). The price demanded by Tolai for food was "growing year by year" (Methodist Minutes 1900), and traders were fearful that the Tolai, after buying trade goods at low *tabu* prices, would turn round and demand higher *tabu* prices for their nuts. At the same time it had also become easier to travel to Nakanai. AhTam had set up a shipyard at Matupit in 1895, and by 1900 Tolai were buying his sailing boats at prices of three to five hundred fathoms of *tabu*, and after 1899 were using them to go to Nakanai (Kleintitschen 1906:116, Bley 1900:104). The results were described by Bürger (1913:19) from the testimony of Fathers Bley and Kleintitschen. Expeditions involving a hundred to a hundred and fifty men went out, bringing back a minimum of fifty fathoms a man, and sometimes up to two hundred fathoms. Ten thousand fathoms a year, or an increment to stocks of 2 percent per annum, came in during boom times.

But Tolai control of the currency was intolerable to the German administration, for it meant that profits went to natives rather than to planters, and the government ordinances of 18 October 1900 and 26 July 1901 forbade the use of *tabu* in trade. The ordinances were not entirely successful. Natives still bought boats from AhTam

[8] I am indebted for this information to Mr. J. Page, who was A.D.O. Talasea at this period and had a long association with the Tolai.

with *tabu*, and in 1961 spoke protectively of him as being someone whom they had kept going in business by buying his boats for *tabu*, so giving him an (illegal) advantage in other trade. The site of AhTam's old store is still referred to as *pire AhTam*, and the present store owner benefits from old loyalties. But the increase in traffic with Nakanai was self-limiting: within a few years the value of *tabu* dropped to its former standard (Kleintitschen 1906: 95). In the first tussle between Tolai and German financiers the Germans won, but only at the cost of repressive political action.

With this detail of 1899–1902, it is possible to re-evaluate the history of 1870–1880. Vunamami informants insist that before 1870 the only outrigger canoes on the coast were those obtained in trade from the Duke of York Islands. Fishing was done from bamboo rafts. How could they carve with only stone axes? On the islands they had received steel axes from Europeans. Meier (1909:99–105) relates a myth from near Raluana that places the first voyages to Nakanai as coinciding with the introduction of the outrigger canoe. Previously, *nassa* shell had been collected on local beaches, but by 1870 it had virtually disappeared. Together, Carteret's report of outrigger canoes on the west coast of New Ireland in 1767 and the Duperrey expedition report of 1823 (1826: I, 98), that only canoes without outriggers were seen near New Britain, suggest that long-distance voyaging for *tabu* dates from about 1800 only.[9] It had not spread to any easterly groups by 1875 (Parkinson 1887:106). Extensive changes were under way in 1870 Tolai society, but they were held back by a shortage of *tabu* shell and inadequate means of sea transportation.

The effect on such a growing economy of the arrival of mis-

---

[9] I was told a little-known myth in Vunamami in 1961 about a culture hero, ToMarnakut But, who was white-skinned, who left his people and later returned in a boat with a white sail bringing new foods, outrigger canoes, and so on. He departed mysteriously and the later arrival of Europeans was welcomed as his return. This may be a reference to early sailings along the coast by Dampier or Carteret, or to some other "stimulus diffusion" introducing new culture elements between 1750 and 1800. Some such change may well have been behind the accounts of ritual, weapons, and foodstuff changes that German theorists interpreted as stories of an immigration from New Ireland some 150 years before 1900 (see Chap. 3 n. 3). Clearly an absence of *tabu* would have implied that Tolai culture was very different before 1750. But Vunamami people insisted there were Tolai-speakers on the Gazelle Peninsula practising agriculture and hunting before ToMarnakut But oriented them seawards. The Tolais are not recent immigrants.

sionaries and traders may be imagined. Within a few years both Methodist and Catholic missions were talking as though in July the whole male population left for Nakanai, wasting months when they could be productively employed, and leaving their families destitute. There were even some attempts by Europeans to cash in on this potential source of wealth. Powell (1884:184–245) describes one of the earliest efforts in 1877 which had to turn back, as there were no facilities beyond Massikonapuka; Danks, with the traders Holmes and Lyttleton (Danks 1933:107–122), went to Nakanai in August 1880 and reported that there were "rest houses at intervals on the way," even though, despite the trading, there were still no steel tools in Nakanai. I have consulted all available firsthand records for reports of later European traders voyaging to Nakanai and have found none, although some secondary sources talk of Europeans buying lengths of *tabu* in Nakanai. Since the major part of the cost of *tabu* lengths is labour by Tolai, it would seem more likely that the first few European voyages in the early 1880's found this out, and that few voyages occurred thereafter.

THE USES OF TABU

(a) Marketing and Small Change

The primary use of *tabu*, as described already, is its accumulation in rolls to be carved at the owner's funeral, and so to gain his admittance into the land of the dead. We may discount the present-day force of the religious motive, while still accepting that hoarding *tabu* for funerals is a major economic incentive for Tolai. It is easy to assume from this that the most observable use of *tabu*—to pay for goods in the market place—is the main means of accumulating it. Detailed consideration of the market use of *tabu* leads to a different conclusion, however: that it is almost impossible to accumulate *tabu* in small quantities, and that the belief that it is indeed possible to do so is a sort of Tolai Horatio Alger myth, motivating the poor to save their pennies wisely, but to lose their pounds foolishly, while the rich get richer through extravagance and financial manipulations.

The detailed description of markets in the Tolai area given in Chapter 5 analysed the rigid standards of exchange between *tabu* and native foodstuffs as contrasted to the variable prices in cash terms. In eighty-five years, *tabu* value has depreciated only 50 percent, whereas the value of cash has depreciated perhaps 90 percent in the same period. In the discussion of the operation of fixed equivalence and delayed barter, two issues were left for discussion in the present context: how far the units of *tabu* accounting are variable, and how far the flows of *tabu* from coast to inland and vice versa are in balance.

In terms of the number of shells in a length of *tabu* or of the length itself (which can be increased by spacing shells on the cane), there is considerable variation in the size of a *pidik*, for example. It may range from twenty-five to thirty-five shells and between five and ten inches. A customer may carry several units in his bag; when he buys a bag of lime he spends as little time selecting which unit he will use for payment as a European does in selecting one coin from a pocketful of coins of similar value. The seller accepts the *pidik* in the same way, not usually even looking at it as he tosses it on his pile of *pidik*. I should assume that a very short *pidik* might be challenged, if the seller herself would be unable to use it for purchasing, but I have never seen this occur. If someone else will accept a length in exchange there is no point in challenging or testing each unit.

I did, however, observe one incident which would indicate that people are not unaware of the implications of variable standards, and that, in contexts where the *pidik* are not to be used in delayed barter, actual length is considered. One seller of lime packets with whom I was sitting had a customer return a packet for a refund. She picked out the shortest *pidik* in her heap to give him, and confirmed under questioning that she had done so deliberately. She was marketing lime for the IaMinat group and the *tabu* she obtained was to be restrung in long lengths, so that absolute length was important to her. But otherwise in normal trade she accepted *pidik* varying as much as 25 percent in length. Gresham's Law would seem to be operating, with short money tending to replace long money, but to an extent that is limited by the rarity with which minute gains can be converted into an appreciable profit.

The question of the coastal-inland balance of trade cannot be settled entirely by a study of market places. As an informant said at the arranged market (pp. 198–200), sales of fish by coastal Tolai at the *motonoi* counterbalance their purchases of taro at the markets. The north coast of the Kokopo Sub-district may be treated generally as a unit, selling fish to all villages inland of its *motonoi* and trading with them for other products in Kokopo market. I have estimated the total annual catch on this coast at 7,500 large mackerel, worth 7,500 fathoms of *tabu*. If only one-third of this is regularly sold to inland villagers, it would mean an average of fifty fathoms weekly coming to the coast. The demand for fresh fish for ceremonials alone would be about the same again. Forty-five such fish were eaten (along with quantities of canned meat and fish, since not enough fresh fish were available) during part of one initiation ceremony in 1961; smaller quantities are needed for smaller ceremonies all the time. Wealthy individuals, both inland and on the coast, also buy fish for private consumption or for political gifts, and altogether take about another third of the production. The fishermen themselves and their relatives in coastal villages consume the other third.

This conservative figure for the flow of *tabu* to the coast can be compared with the purchases of taro from inland areas. On four Saturdays in April and May at Kokopo an average of 150 bunches of taro were brought in, and 30 were unsold at noon. In August and September the average of 30 bunches brought in were all sold, but much of the *tigapu* bought as a substitute was paid for in cash rather than by *tabu*. An average over the year of 80 bunches a week, worth 40 fathoms, would seem reasonable. It would yield a net flow from inland to the coast of ten fathoms a week in the taro-fish trade. These Sub-district figures would have to be divided by a factor of about eight to give figures per village.

To them would be added an amount for the lime sold—some fifty packets a week at Kokopo year in and year out, or about five fathoms' worth. Much of this income came from non-Tolai workers, but the absolute size of net flows is so small as to be of little significance. Outside events, such as the arranged market, could more than redress any regular net balances for several months. In fact, in view of the 10–20 percent margin of error of my measurements, the net flows may well be non-existent.

But if the over-all flow is negligible, there is still extreme variability from week to week. During the period in which taro was in short supply, it would have been expected that its price would rise (if it was governed by immediate supply and demand) much more than the 25 percent that resulted from decreasing the size of bunches from eight to six pounds. It would also be expected to fall much more during times of plenty. The fish supply likewise is highly seasonal and randomly variable during the season. Even under normal conditions fish sell out quickly. When a ceremony is

in prospect, buyers tour the coast in the evening and deposit *tabu*
with agents in the fishing crews so that they can have first claim
on any fish caught the next morning. Obviously, buyers would be
at the mercy of the sellers if the system were one of variable
pricing.

But even within a variable price system these seasonal and random swings would do little to alter the net profits of either coastals
or inlanders. With a free market, the selling side would make large
profits at one moment, but would then be forced to pay out those
profits when it came time for it to switch roles and become the
buyer. Mutual accusations of profiteering would be bound to
arise; uncertainties over the market would mean an inability to
plan, and probably abstention from consumption and restriction
of production. It is difficult to imagine exchange starting under
such conditions. Fixed-equivalence trade avoids these uncertainties,
and it enables good relations to be preserved between villages and
individuals, while permitting the same (or greater) flow of goods
as would a system that allowed a few individuals to make short-term
profits. The degree of flexibility permitted within such fixed equivalences allows some profit making, but without great risk to the
system itself.

So far, however, we have looked only at the over-all balances
between villages and areas, ignoring the individuals who actually
make the transactions. In practice within Vunamami, most women
are net spenders of *tabu*, collecting small amounts for the lime
they produce but paying out more for the taro they bring home.
The *tabu* they pay goes to inland women; what they receive comes
from inland men, and immigrant workers. For their sales of European vegetables they receive cash. A few female entrepreneurs
who sell lime in bulk amass more *tabu* than they spend on meals
for their family, but the aggregate market for lime indicates how
small any individual profits must be. By contrast, Vunamami men
are net *tabu* earners. Thirty-two (or one-third of the labour force)
earned *tabu* from fishing in 1961. The twenty relatively poor men
obtained an average of sixty fathoms each in return for 150 days of
work; the twelve rich men obtained an average of fifty fathoms
for seventy work days and larger capital investments. As indicated, only about a third of these sums came from sales inland;
much of the poor men's income came from sales to richer coastal
non-fishermen. The poorer men used *tabu* for subsistence purchases, including contributions to their wives' marketing; richer

men saved much of their earnings. It will be realized that fluctuations in exchange rates would also wreak havoc with the power positions of husbands and wives, and rich and poor within villages, and make impossible some of the informal mechanisms which now compensate for inequalities—the contributions by husbands to their wives' food purchases, for example.

On the other hand, the size of the aggregate flows for some eight villages indicate how infinitesimal the profits to be obtained from marketing are for the individual seller. Even the fisherman earning sixty fathoms a year would have to work for fifty years and never spend a *pidik* if he wanted to amass the amount given away at one *matamatam*. We must look elsewhere for the sources of *tabu* for accumulations.

(b) Tabu as Services and Contributions

Liquid *tabu*, both skeins and small change, also circulates as payments for admission fees, as contributions to ceremonies, and for specialist services. Many of the specialist fees have been described in Chapter 4 as ranging between five and one hundred fathoms. The scale of contributions (*a nidok*) and admission fees (*a warwaruk*), although nominally one *pidik* on each occasion, may be judged from one wedding in Vunabalbal. There were four occasions on which contributions were called for: first as a gift to the host (*a warlapang*), then for a gift to the bride (*a nidok*), then for a gift to the groom (*a warwaruk*), and finally for a gift to the children of the marriage (*a tabarbul*). For each, the guests of the appropriate category walked to the centre and threw *pidik* onto a pile. Most guests contributed two or three times, receiving nothing except some betel nut on arrival. The contributions from one hundred and twenty guests totalled sixty-two fathoms of *tabu*. Another wedding at Rainau involved the Vunamami guests in hiring a truck, while the total contributions by about the same number of people came to seventy-two and a half fathoms plus £2 14s. for the *tabarbul*. These contributions, it should be noted, are quite distinct from the bride price, which is paid by the groom alone or by his closest relatives.

Weddings are the most formal *nidok* occasions, but others occur constantly. A party to raise funds for the village choir to participate in a competition, *tabu* thrown at the masked *tubuan* figure as it enters the village,[10] offerings at the opening of a new church, a col-

[10] See n. 17 below for a discussion of *tubuan* contributions.

lection for a popular government official on his departure, the coming-of-age ceremony called *a warkinim*, eating herbal medicines to speed the learning of new dances, or the clan accumulation of funds for an eventual *matamatam*—all involve a collection of small sums of *tabu* from those present, not to mention contributions of food or betel.

I was made aware of the financial drain involved by my own attendance at ceremonies. I had no *tabu* at first and could not buy any for cash. The wealthy men whom I usually accompanied surreptitiously supplied me with *pidik* when it came to my turn to contribute, and I naturally kept accounts of what I owed. Eventually I obtained long lengths of *tabu* and could repay my debts, but I was shocked at the speed with which it disappeared. I wondered how poor people could afford to attend ceremonies, and realized how many find excuses for not attending weddings, say, but how many make a point of contributing with everyone else when they do attend.

Over a year, a rich family may contribute some forty fathoms to collections of one sort or another. An important political figure attends even more ceremonies and parties than I did, and possibly three times as many as a poor man. He is also likely to bring his children, and they are given *tabu* to contribute too. His *pidik* tend to be twice as long as those of other contributors, and this, like his quiet assistance to others who lack *tabu*, does not pass unnoticed, though no one comments audibly. Members of a poor family, on the other hand, may contribute about ten fathoms in a year.

But contributing is not a one-way process for a rich man. He is often a host and may receive contributions at perhaps one in ten of his attendances. A poor man receives a collection probably once in a lifetime. Important men are also often given special gifts on public occasions as an appreciation for their presence; giving such gifts and the accompanying speech-making are parts of any Tolai ceremony. My own initial *tabu* stocks came in both ways—a collection for me when I agreed to act in the Ravalien purchase, and two fathoms given to me when I witnessed a friend's purchase of a dance copyright. Such gifts are not a new phenomenon. Parkinson reports (1887:124) that in the 1880's the importance of a man could be judged by the type of club he carried; the bearer of a black club (*a bangat*) could expect a two-fathom gift, the man with an ordinary wooden club (*a leplep*) could expect only one

fathom.[11] The net result is that a rich man, from my own experience and calculations, is slightly *in* pocket as a result of the various
small contributions; a poor man is almost always *out of* pocket.

The picture is even more one-sided if one considers the amounts
of skein *tabu* paid for specialist services, and the individual exchanges of *tabu* that occur after a *matamatam*. The payment to a
specialist—an amount ranging from five to one hundred fathoms—
is always an occasion for a small ceremony, at which the buyer of
the services—a dance copyright, for example—entertains a group
who pay *nidok*, and then hands skein *tabu* to the specialists and to
important guests. The *nidok* contributions rarely balance the
purchaser's expenses, as we shall see, but part of what flows through
his hands or into the stores of the wealthy, the important men who
invent dances or are otherwise creative, and those who witness their
purchase, comes from the *nidok* of the poor.

The most extravagant "throwing away" of money, by rich and
poor alike, comes in the evening after the dances of a *matamatam*.
The fun starts with the sponsor of the day's ceremony virtually
challenging three or four important men to sponsor a ceremony in
their turn. He picks up *tanget* branches, decorated with a five-
fathom skein of *tabu* (*a tatar vuai*), and publicly gives one to
each man whom he challenges. Then, followed by many of his
poorer clan mates, he starts out to honour the other big men.
Carrying *tanget* branches, decorated, but not with *tabu* (*a balbal*),
he circulates in the crowd with his entourage. When he meets a big
man he plants a *balbal* in front of him and throws down a fathom
of *tabu;* his followers each throw a *pidik* on the pile. Other important men start "honouring" others in the same way, accompanied
by their followers. "Honouring" is a way of repaying earlier
gifts, or of ingratiating oneself with up-and-coming men, or of
making peace with old enemies, or (for by nightfall much alcohol
has been consumed) of simply having a good time. With thirty
or more big men rushing about in the twilight followed by supporters, all throwing down *tabu*, the scene is one of conviviality
and unrestrained extravagance. With my very limited capital I
gave (and received) over five fathoms of *tabu* in half an hour. A
rich Tolai who was prepared to accumulate obligations could have
saved similar sums; one wishing to establish credit could have

[11] Parkinson interpreted these clubs—wrongly, I believe—as the staffs
of office of particular ranks in Tolai society.

distributed as much, but accumulation by rich men would have been much easier, since they receive but do not reciprocate the contributions of "followers."

(c) Distributions of Tabu

But if the *tabu* payments for services, or as contributions, result in a net flow into the hands of the wealthy, the question arises of how the less wealthy obtain their *tabu* in the first place. The simple answer is through the distributions—the "carving" of rolls —at funerals and *matamatam*. Poor people explicitly recognize that these are occasions for earning *tabu*. Thus when a *matamatam* was in prospect in Vunabalbal in 1961, neighbours encouraged my wife and me to dance. Where important men stressed the honour we would pay the *matamatam* sponsor and the village, poorer people stressed only the *tabu* we would receive.

The techniques of distribution illustrate how this interest can be overtly concealed, however. Thus for a dance the performers, perhaps sixty, arrange themselves facing the front in a long column of parallel rows (*a papal*) of two, three, or four individuals. Each individual in a back row follows the steps of the person who leads (*i olo*) his file as he backs, fills, turns, and waves his feather dancing sticks. The last movement of any dance is called "alternating the lead" (*di olo olo*). The leading row dances a sequence of steps; then the row furthest back comes to the front and goes through the sequence, being relieved by the last row again, until all rows in turn have led. The movement finishes when the original leaders are once again in the front. During the early movements of the dance a roll of *tabu* is brought out and stripped of its covers; long lengths of *tabu* and lighted cigarettes are given to the leading row and in the *olo olo* movement each row receives a gift in succession as it comes into the lead. The lengths of *tabu* broken off vary greatly, partly because the cane is apt to be brittle with age; many helpers hand it out, thrusting it into moving hands holding dancing sticks, and often giving two or three shares; there is confusion over lighting cigarettes and pushing them into the mouths of moving dancers. No dancer can look at what he has received, and any *tabu* that falls on the ground is ignored, except by small boys in the front of the spectators.

At a funeral the rolls of *tabu* are brought out for display as soon as the mourners have all arrived and are seated on mats in front of the makeshift "death house" where the dead body sits in state. The *garamut* (slit-gong) sounds the death call, and the rolls are carved and handed out, again by many helpers. They throw handfuls at the feet of mourners, giving varied lengths and often two or three shares to each individual. No one looks down to examine what he receives, for that is considered bad form. One is supposed to behave as though *tabu* did not matter and giving were indiscriminate.

But a pattern does exist. My wife, when dancing, received three fathoms; I received over two fathoms at funerals; less wealthy dancers, and my neighbours at funerals, received between a fathom and a fathom and a half; children rarely got as much as a fathom; lead dancers and other important men received up to five fathoms. After all the dancers have been given shares, what is left of *mata-matam tabu* goes to the important men who organized the dances; after the distribution at a funeral (*a minamai*) come the formal payments to the relatives of the dead man's widow and to others who have performed services for the deceased (*a rara na ubu*). Yet of the total amount distributed something like half, perhaps more, goes to the much more numerous poor. They flock to participate in dances, being held back mainly by the necessity of finding congenial partners to form a row, and of attending nightly rehearsals. At funerals, more poor people would attend to get *tabu*, if it were not the case that gate-crashers receive almost nothing.

The volume of *tabu* distributed annually can be estimated. The amount per *matamatam* is between 2,500 and 3,000 fathoms. Between 1937 and 1961 there were nine *matamatam* in Vunamami village, or an average of one every three years; a possibly incomplete count of eleven *matamatam* between 1947 and 1961 in the three villages of Vunabalbal, Bitarebarebe, and Balanataman villages confirms this frequency. The aggregate amount distributed by wealthy Vunamami men averages 1,000 fathoms a year. It goes largely to people from surrounding villages, but Vunamami dancers receive distributions in other villages. The best assumption would be that the flows are in balance,[12] and that Vunamami people receive 1,000 fathoms at *matamatam*.

[12] This would imply, first, that all villages give the same number of *matamatam* (the figure cited and the "challenging" to give *matamatam* would suggest that this is the case) and, second, that all villages dance as often at other villages; variations might be expected here in view of different village skills, and different degrees of full employment, but the variation would not be great, since there are also pressures to reciprocity by dancing groups.

The average frequency of funerals can be estimated from population figures and death rates. (There were no deaths in Vunamami in 1961.) Six would be expectable from Vunamami's population, but only one of these would be of an important man involving a distribution of the order of a thousand fathoms; the remainder would involve about a hundred fathoms each, to give a total figure of about 1,500 fathoms at funerals. Again it is to be assumed that Vunamami villagers would receive as much as they gave.

The combined total received by the village in distributions would thus be about 2,500 fathoms, with half going to wealthy families and half to poorer ones—an average of over twenty fathoms for each poorer family, and about sixty for wealthy families. This would mean that *tabu* received from distributions[13] provides two or three times as much income to poorer families as does marketplace trade. No one can get rich by trade; relying on distributions is preferable, and, for the select few, being a skilled provider of services is even better.

(d) Tabu-palumtabu *and Accumulation*

Against this picture of a hand-to-mouth budgeting in *tabu* and the difficulty of saving unless one is a skilled worker, the scale of distributions by the wealthy and their apparent readiness to amass and tie up immense quantities in unprofitable rolls seems a gross extravagence. When one sees that these people are not frugal savers, but eat larger amounts of the luxury foods of fish and taro, and casually contribute many times as much to collections, the question of how they can do it becomes insistent.

In the first place it must be recognized that publicly rolling up a coil is a claim not just to owning that amount of *tabu* but to having a constant supply of it. Parkinson (1887:105–106) described the ceremony of coiling thus: "When a man has collected more [than his daily needs] it is a matter of pride for him to place a roll of 50 or more fathoms in the *tabu*-house. Drums are beaten and the neighbours called to watch enviously as the lucky man opens the well-barred door and carries in his roll. Perhaps it is the first roll he has

[13] Although the analysis shows a net flow from the rich in one village to the poor in that village, it should be pointed out that this does not follow channels of "redistribution" (Polanyi *et al.* 1957). The rich of one village distribute widely to many villages, essentially paying people to witness their ceremony. It is only the aggregate of many such "open market" transactions that results in the net flow from rich to poor.

deposited. If so he must stand up to the mocking talk of the audience. 'Wait till tomorrow' says one, 'you may be hungry, and now you have no *tabu* to buy food'; or another shouts 'Hurry everyone, look in our huts, to see whether it is our *tabu* that he has stolen.' " To break up a roll after such public boasting would be the ultimate shame; ostentatiously foregoing consumption uses of *tabu*, and claiming that one can always earn more, is the way to claim prestige.

In the second place there seems to be a ceiling on the amounts so held, of about two thousand fathoms in savings for one's funeral, and another thousand or so in preparation for a *matamatam*. One's prestige cannot be enhanced by amassing more; distributing it not only converts prestige into political support but also asserts that the individual will earn more.

Before considering how an individual can enter these realms of high finance, let us consider how the sponsor of a *matamatam* can give away such large sums with the assurance that more will return to him. The first step, some two years in advance of the *matamatam*, is for the sponsor to announce his intention of honouring his clan dead (or the dead of his father's clan). He holds a ceremony which gains the support of the clan. I witnessed one such ceremony in 1961, for a 1963 *matamatam* of Galiur clan. I was told in advance merely that it was "selling a pig" (*a kunukul na boroi*) and that fifty-three people would come and pay two fathoms each for a piece of pork, all of them either of Galiur clan or the children of Galiur fathers. The sponsor welcomed everyone with a meal of rice, corned beef, and tea; a clan elder made a speech stressing that the ceremony was in honour of the clan dead, that cash would be needed for the concrete stones of remembrance (*wat na im*), and that *tabu* should be "ready for the blood of your father" (*i waninara ra gapui kai tamam*); other clan elders nodded approvingly. There followed three rounds of contributions: sons of the clan threw in two *pidik* each (*a waroi*); then two large slabs of pork were displayed, and in front of them each person in turn laid down two or more fathoms of *tabu* while his name was recorded in a book and absentees' names were called out; finally, names were read out again and each contributor exchanged an additional two or more fathoms for about four pounds of pork. All those who gave more than two fathoms were clan elders who had already sponsored *matamatam*; the clan *lualua* contributed twenty fathoms. Three persons gave a pound note instead of two fathoms.

The grand total of the collection was announced as 275 fathoms for one pig and 318 for the other, counting 192 fathoms from absentees. I estimated the actual attendance at over one hundred persons, though estimating was difficult because the ceremony was held from eleven-thirty to one-thirty on a dark, rainy night.

The cost to the sponsor for this announcement was about £15 for the food, and two pigs worth some £20 in the open market. By gaining the support of clan elders, thus ensuring that his *matamatam* would bring honour to the entire clan, he had raised some £296 in *tabu* as capital for the *matamatam*.

For details of the next stages of preparations I rely largely on observing what happened when John ToMarangrang of ToMomoi clan, Vunabalbal village, staged his *matamatam* in August 1961. It was held in honour of his mother, IaPiritila, who had died in 1906, shortly after his birth. He first enlisted the help of four other ToMomoi men as co-sponsors, and secured the help of important men in other villages who would bring teams to dance at the ceremony. He arranged with the owner of a *tubuan* in his own village to stage a *tabaran* dance (which also involved an initiation into the *tubuan* religion) for the ceremony. He built himself a new house of European design costing over £300, and moved his copra drier to a new site to make an arena for the dancing. He left the buying of food for entertaining and distribution and of cement for memorials until later, but he made sure his *tabu* and cash supplies were adequate.

John himself engaged a composer for two songs and dances to be performed by Vunabalbal village. The revelation (*a waba tabaran*) of these two dances was the public announcement of the *matamatam* four weeks later. John's expenses with one of these will indicate the expenses of other dance producers. Before the dance was performed by the composer, John made portions of *a maliu* magic available (basically ochre and ginger on leaves) to help prospective performers to learn quickly; each dancer paid a *pidik* for the privilege, making some four fathoms received. Then the dance was played through once by the composing team to the accompaniment of beating on lengths of bamboo. It was then played on hour-glass-shaped *kudu* drums, and the audience joined in. After several rehearsals a feast was held, costing some ten fathoms of *tabu*, at the end of which John paid the composing team 30 fathoms, and a fathom to each of the nine men who lent *kudu*. The total net cost thus came to 45 fathoms for each dance.

Four other co-sponsors of the *matamatam* from ToMomoi clan organized dance teams, at a cost of about 180 fathoms, and six men from other villages organized another six, costing about 270 fathoms. The owner of Tagatagal clan *tubuan*, who resided in Vunabalbal village, organized a *tabaran* dance, the finance of which will be considered later. The non-sponsoring organizers from other villages later received portions of the *tabu* rolls that were carved at the final performance and probably made a net profit on the transaction. It will be noted how the preparatory financing of the dances was widely spread.

John financed another ceremony two weeks later, fixing the final date of the ceremony (*di bubut ra bung*). A large feast costing 30 fathoms preceded the sounding fourteen times of a slit-gong (*garamut*), the fee for *garamut* use being three fathoms. The *garamut* was sounded again each evening thereafter, once less each time counting down from the original fourteen beats, until Dance Day.

Final preparations, including buying bananas, taro, wild herbs, and *tanget* leaves, was now a full-time job for John, who drove all over the Kokopo Sub-district in his Land-Rover and saw a constant stream of visitors. I estimate that he spent two fathoms daily for entertainment and that he bought more than 100 fathoms' worth of food, including over one hundred bunches of taro (many at the arranged market described in Chap. 5) and eighty stalks of bananas for distribution at the *matamatam*. Several other men also contributed banana stalks, each one of which had a fathom of *tabu* hung on it. At the *matamatam*, 167 such stalks were displayed. I estimate that John provided another 100 fathoms for distribution with the bananas and the *balbal*.

During the ceremony John himself cut up four rolls of *tabu*, totalling 1,100 fathoms while his co-sponsors each cut up smaller amounts totalling about 1,800 fathoms. John also met many cash costs on the day of the ceremony. Every dancer received a cigarette—or 800 Rothmans at three shillings for twenty, making £6; many louvres in his house were broken, and his garden and copra drier were trampled on, causing damage of about £5; cement for the memorial stones cost about £30, but its purchase was delayed until after November. And for Land-Rover travel during preparations, costs must have been more than £20.

John's total expenses, not including the building of his house and other lasting capital improvements, amounted to the large sum of 1,510 fathoms (1,100 of it in rolls and 410 in shorter lengths), and £61. His four co-sponsors each spent about 500 fathoms. John had, however, received something like 600 fathoms from "selling a pig" two years earlier. In other words, his out-of-pocket expenses may have been only of the order of 900 fathoms and £61. But to organize a ceremony of this kind took years of preparation and several months of full-time work. It was smoothly produced and an eminent success, thanks to John. The early clan approval at the pig sale had essentially been a vote of confidence in John's organizing ability, providing him with clan capital to supplement a rather modest expenditure on his own part. It is such approval that makes it possible for a public figure to *seem* to be extravagantly throwing away sums of the order of 3,000 fathoms.

There was good reason to support John. He had been the *luluai* of Vunabalbal from 1939 to 1952, and had given a *matamatam* in honour of his father, Abram ToBobo, in 1941. He jokingly remarked that his *matamatam* improved each time he gave one. In 1950 he had been elected Vunabalbal councillor, but had retired in 1952 to concentrate on business. Late in 1961 he again stood for election and was returned overwhelmingly.

Enos Teve, the richest man in Vunamami and former Paramount Lulai and Council president, whose life history will be detailed in Chapter 9, had given seven *balaguan*, the generic term for any ceremony like a *matamatam*. His first in Vunamami village before the Second World War had been in honour of his father, Levi ToLingling, who had fed him; it had come soon after he was appointed Paramount. His second, immediately after the war, was given on plantation land and was co-sponsored by the owners of Ravalien plantation as a way of mobilizing the people of Vunamami into moving from the beach and rebuilding. His third, in 1947, was given in Vunamami village to celebrate his son's initiation, and his fourth, in 1949, was in honour of his son's coming of age for marriage (*a warkinim*). His fifth was in Balanataman, the *madapai* of his own clan, also in 1949, to celebrate the reopening of Vunakabi *motonoi* which had been disused during the war, and the launching of a large canoe. His sixth, in 1955, celebrated the opening of Balanataman church. His seventh, in 1958, was a *matamatam* for the dead of his own clan. For my own departure Enos staged what may be counted as his eighth *balaguan*, a *kinawai* ceremony, in which *tubuan* land from canoes and dance through the village. It may be noted that Enos' Balanataman *balaguan* came at a time when, after making considerable profits from fishing, he became actively engaged in planting his own clan lands in that village to coconuts and cocoa, while his sixth and seventh marked his reinvolvement in Vunamami village affairs.

From both John's and Enos' point of view the *tabu* and the time expended on *matamatam* were at once effective in gaining political support. From the people's point of view their contributions at the early stages were well repaid by the eventual ceremonies.

But gaining political support does not necessarily yield a return in *tabu*. To show how the financer of ceremonies can profit from his supporters, I shall generalize from the *tubuan* ceremonies in preparation for John's *matamatam*, during which I was initiated. I do not wish to imply thereby that *tubuan* owners are solely motivated by profit considerations; my experience is that they are not only hard-headed businessmen but also conscientious theologians who are concerned about the inward and spiritual meanings of the outward and visible ceremonies which they organize. Being practical about organizing ceremonies almost necessarily involves casualness about the material trappings of religion, but with the practicality there may be a deeper awareness of the symbolism involved. With that understanding I shall discuss *tubuan* ownership as a business.

A *tubuan* owner has already made a large capital investment. He has paid initiation fees into each of the three grades of the society. He must then pay for the copyright of a mask, of knowledge of its meaning, and of its spell. A new mask that was invented following a vision in 1961, and displayed at the *tabaran* dance, could be bought for fifty fathoms; an already established *tubuan* was sold for one hundred fathoms in 1925. The clan of the *tubuan* owner then meets to approve the purchase, and to contribute to a second payment. Further payments of twenty or thirty fathoms may be given later if the inventor or seller supervises the buyer's ceremonies to ensure accuracy.

When an owner wishes to perform a dance he must "raise" (*watut*) the *tubuan*, first obtaining the permission of the man who "controls" (*kure*) the *tubuan*. The latter is the son of a man of his own clan, and is usually in his fifties or sixties. He guards the *tubuan* stores of *tabu*. My own *tubuan* had six hundred fathoms in two rolls, laid down before 1942, when I saw its treasure in

1961. A payment of a few fathoms must be given to the controller each time he is approached.

No raising is complete without an initiation (*a babat*). This involves secluding the participants in the bush for about two weeks, where they are fed by the *tubuan* owner; at this stage he is said to *be* the *tubuan*.[14] At least three feasts, demanding numbers of fish, are needed; skilled dancers, mask-makers, ceremonial advisers, drummers, and even general assistants are handsomely rewarded for their services; secret herbs and medicines must be used lavishly at all stages. At my own initiation cycle, seclusion was not strict, but an average of twenty men were in the bush every day, eating well. It was said that in the old days, they could take any food they wished from gardens, since it was the *tubuan* that took it, but in 1961 all food was bought for *tabu*. I estimate one-quarter *tabu* per head per day for regular food, or seventy fathoms needed for keep, plus sixty taro bunches, forty-five fish, and large quantities of coconut, betel, and so on for the two final ceremonial feasts (*a warwakak* and *a warkong*); as a non-initiate I could not witness the preparation of the first feast (*a punuongo*) and have no figures for it, but I should estimate one hundred fathoms' worth of food for the three. The total outlay for food was 170 fathoms.

The return came in initiation fees. Novices paid half a fathom to go through the first stage (*di vuolo*), five fathoms for the second stage (*di guboro*), and ten fathoms for the third stage (*di dukduk*). Relatively few went through the early stages, but twenty-three paid ten fathoms, yielding a total of 247 fathoms for the *tubuan*.

The preparation of the costumes and the dance rehearsal meant supporting twenty-four dancers for twelve days, and another twenty-six dancers for a shorter period (members of other *tubuan* which had been "raised" elsewhere, who came together at the time of performing), together with six costume-makers and instructors. Food cost an estimated 45 fathoms. The feast when the costumes were taken over by their wearers (*a wartak*) cost 25 fathoms for

[14] This symbolic incarnation of the *tubuan* occurs at an "eruption" (*ra punuongo*). It is interesting to note how this verbal usage parallels that for businesses, described earlier, in its clear distinction between when an individual is acting for himself and when he is acting as an incorporated person, "the business," "the car," "the *tubuan*," etc. *Tubuan* profits go into the *tubuan* treasury, supervised by the "controller," and presumably pass intact to the new owner, if the *tubuan* is transferred. But it is the *tubuan* owner who gains power and renown from ceremonies and who makes personal profits from ancillary activities.

taro, and should have cost 25 more for fish. None being available, fifty tins of corned beef at 3s. 6d. per tin—worth 175s. in all— were used instead. Thirty fathoms were then given to the mask-makers, making a total of 125 fathoms.

In return the *tubuan* received a payment from each viewer of the costumes, at their "ceremonial landing place" (*a balilai*), of half a fathom from non-dancers and a fathom from dancers. Sixty-eight fathoms were collected.

I have not included above the costs of obtaining the materials for the costumes and medicines. I include these as costs of staging the performance. Feather ornaments and the wooden face of the single *tabaran* mask are kept from one performance to another; all other parts are burned after the performance. Nothing is paid for materials gathered in the bush, but on the three occasions when I was secretly called out with my car to collect materials from distant areas, the *tubuan* insisted that it should pay for the petrol. Mosquito netting, cloth, ginger and lime cost a pound at the most, but probably five fathoms' worth of ochre was used. Ten fathoms would cover these costs (though not the beer consumed in the bush by foragers).

Each of the fifty dancers received a fathom from the *tubuan* when "leading" at the *matamatam*, and 29 fathoms were paid to the dance instructors a week later when the *tubuan* was given its ceremonial farewell (*a warbaiai*). If the *tubuan* had had to use the secret place (*a taraiu*) of a different *tubuan* in order to stage the dance, a gift called "the leaf of a bird" (*a mapina beo*) would have had to be paid. The *matamatam* sponsor undertook to re-imburse the *tubuan*'s costs of staging the dance, with 100 fathoms of *tabu*.

My total estimates are thus that the *tubuan* owner paid out the equivalent of 384 fathoms, and received 415 fathoms. He did not himself keep detailed accounts, but said his total outlay "for the dance" had been £46 15s. in cash and 163 fathoms of *tabu*. I assume that he ignored food costs and initiation fees, for he felt that the *wartak* contributions and the payment by the sponsor balanced his *tabu* expenses. The cash, he thought, was his own contribution to the village *matamatam*. In other words, the initiation was an affair of the *tubuan* and it returned a profit of 77 fathoms on an outlay of 170 fathoms.

Generalizing from this single instance is somewhat risky, but the initiation profits I saw may have been on the low side. Parkinson (1907:588) reports payments of from 20 to 100 fathoms[15] as initiation fees, which would make profits astronomical, given constant costs. This is likely, for I do not see how more food could have been consumed. What I saw lived up to the boast that "the *tubuan* is the food store of the people" (*ra tubuan a pal na nian kai ra tarai*). Similar profits were also obtained, not only by the *tubuan* staging the dance, but by the other *tubuan* which were raised at the same time and which contributed dancers only. These *tubuan*, however, did not incur the "production" losses of staging the dance.

When a *tubuan* is raised it also receives many incidental payments: fines from non-members who come too near, contributions when it enters a village, payments for settling disputes, or thank-offerings when a member has good fortune. These could bring the profits for an average "raising" to more than 100 fathoms, and it is clear that an unscrupulous owner, charging high initiation fees and demanding other payments, could double or treble this figure. He would obtain them on an initial investment of between fifty and 100 fathoms, and a short-term investment of about 200 fathoms for each "raising." *Tubuan*-owning is good business, even if the staging of dances is a non-profit public service.

Tubuan ownership also leads into other business activities. Much of the *tabu* that I saw paid by initiates was not their own but came from the stocks of the *tubuan* owner and five other big men, who measured out the lengths and tied them (*di bibiu*) in the correct ceremonial way. These loans to younger men are repayable in *tabu* and services later on. Some are wiped out voluntarily (see Parkinson 1907:588), especially if the *tubuan* owner considers the recipient an up-and-coming young man, worthy of patronage. It is this sort of young man that can complete the three stages of initiation in three years, while other men may take twenty-five years to go through. Such a man may eventually be given ownership of a *tubuan* for a nominal fee, by a patron wishing to retire.

CONCLUSIONS: TABU AND POLITICS

This review of the many uses of *tabu* makes it clear that there is a hierarchy. The petty exchanges of *tabu* in the market place make

[15] I suspect he may have been confusing them with the fees for buying a new *tubuan* copyright. I hope later to publish a fuller account of the *tubuan* religion, amplifying and clarifying some of the confusions in Parkinson's generally excellent summary.

everyone familiar with *tabu* and give all Tolai the feeling that they could one day be rich and powerful. In practice the sums that can be amassed are small, and they are overshadowed by the sums paid in contributions by the ordinary man in the street and by what he receives at distributions. Somewhat larger sums go to pay for specialist services, especially to the most important specialists who conduct ceremonies, compose dances, or carve canoes. These tend at the upper limits to be the same men who are important in other spheres, who organize the ceremonies or commission dances and canoes. These men, the organizers, are those who control the flow of the largest volumes of *tabu*; into their hands comes the major part of the contributions of the ordinary people. Much of this *tabu* is circulated rapidly, paying for specialist services of all kinds or buying the foods for ceremonials, but a portion goes into their personal stores. This returns to circulation only when the big men make distributions at *matamatam* or at their funerals. Even on these occasions, the capstone of the *tabu* economy, a major flow of *tabu* is that from one rich man to the others.

The conclusion is unmistakable, that although the free circulation of *tabu* at all levels gives the appearance of equality, power is in fact concentrated in the hands of those who give the important ceremonies—the *matamatam* givers and *tubuan* owners. Enough has already been said regarding the status of *matamatam* givers and the importance of ceremonies for gaining political support. The two individual givers already described account for almost half of all the *matamatam* given over a twenty-year period in several villages.[16] Here I shall concentrate on political power and *tubuan* ownership.

Informants talking generally about the *tubuan* always said "the *tubuan* is the government of the people" (*ra tubuan a matanitu kai ra tarai*). It hated theft, incest, adultery, and lying. A *tubuan* initiate whose wife was unfaithful could in the old days get the *tubuan* to kill the adulterer. The adulterer would disappear. The plaintiff's *tubuan* would have sent *tabu* to another *tubuan*, saying that the adulterer could be captured at a certain place, killed, and eaten. Later the plaintiff's *tubuan* would obtain/kill a victim in return, the reciprocal process being called *dir kul tule* (two reciprocally buy and sell). Less fatally, a *tubuan* could with impunity beat people who stole, lied, or beat their spouses within

---

[16] Statistics on *matamatam*-giving are cited in Salisbury (1967).

its home village, or could exact fines as commutation for a beating.
This power of the *tubuan* is still symbolized whenever a masked
tubuan figure enters a village, by its beating the most important
men present (albeit with fragile clubs). The *tubuan* provided physical support for the decisions of its owner, and because the actions of the *tubuan* were those of a supernatural being, they could
not be questioned (*pata warkurai tana*).[17]

A good deal of consultation between *tubuan* owners is implied
by the custom of *dir kul tule*, particularly when inter-village hos-
tilities usually meant killing foreigners on sight. In 1961 I observed
a similar pattern, of consulting specialists attending ceremonial
preparations in foreign *taraiu*, to ensure that ceremonials were correctly performed. Parkinson reports the same for 1890 (1907:559).
Collaboration in synchronizing initiations makes good economic
sense. Further *tubuan* links appear from Parkinson's (1907:578)
list of *tubuan* owned in the Raluana area around 1890, citing the
areas from which they were bought. They came from all over the
Tolai area, from the Duke of Yorks to the Warangoi. In short,
tubuan owners formed a small intercommunicating élite, even before 1875.[18]

In 1961 I collected the names of sixteen *tubuan* in the Kokopo
area, belonging to ten clans. Three had co-owners, and for three
I could find no owner's name (possibly because these *tubuan* were
alternative manifestations of differently named ones). This list is
not complete, but I should guess that the total number for these
villages does not exceed twenty-five, with perhaps thirty owners.
The number of *tubuan* controllers is less, since a single man may
control several *tubuan* owned by a single clan. The names of controllers are not publicly known, but the two whom I met both

[17] How readily people accepted the *tubuan*'s powers is debatable. Mission
and government competitors for those powers used terms like "extortion"
and "tyranny" to describe them. Informants in 1961 (and Hahl and Parkinson) stressed the way in which the *tubuan* protected its members, provided
the means of obtaining redress, and kept the peace. They stressed that *nidok*
to the *tubuan* was a form of taxation, and a way of thanking the *tubuan*
for visiting the village. Women complained of the riotous behavior of men
in the bush and of *tubuan* violence or disregard for non-initiates.

[18] It should not be thought that the intercommunication of this élite
meant that it was composed of friends or was solidary. It provided the
arena for some of the most intense rivalries among the Tolai, and at least
two major factions were evident to me. Some of my best information came
when rivals were trying to demonstrate how little other élite members
knew.

owned their own *tubuan* as well, and I daresay this is normal. My estimate would be one *tubuan* owner per 250 population.

Again Parkinson (1907:578) gives some confirmation of this ratio. He lists the six *tubuan* which co-operated under the *lualua* of Raluana in sending dancers to the Berlin Colonial Exhibition of 1896; two with Vunamami links overlap my list, and one is a double *tubuan*, both manifestations of which were owned by the same owner in 1896, although there are now two owners. He would appear to be exhaustive for villages close to his own plantation of Kuradui, suggesting again that *tubuan* owners form less than 0.5 percent of the population.

All 1961 owners were men in their fifties or sixties, and all those personally known to me had been *luluai* or *tultul* before 1950. All of them were regarded as well informed in land matters, and most attended meetings to codify Tolai land law and custom (Smith and Salisbury 1961). None were Local Government Councillors in 1960, though one had been a leader in the anti-Council Raluana incident of 1953 and others had been councillors earlier. This may well be merely a function of their age, however. Though all were literate, none was highly educated or English-speaking, their education having come before teaching in English. All were successful businessmen, not merely in *tabu* finance but as owners of stores, plantations, copra driers, and copra-buying stations. Most of them were also active in the Co-operative movement and in the affairs of the Tolai Cocoa Project.

They did not include all important political figures, however—notably not the councillors and Council presidents. Nor were all businessmen *tubuan* owners: the two largest trucking and store businesses were run by non-initiates. Briefly, *tubuan* owners are the most widely influential people, although the men most successful in a single field are those who are single-minded about it.

The question then arises of how men become *tubuan* owners, and achieve the level of *tabu* financing which this entails. In the next chapter we shall follow the life histories of some political leaders and their paths of social mobility in the past. Here I shall describe only current achievement patterns.

First, there is the influence of birth. The son of a *tubuan* owner cannot inherit his father's *tubuan*, because it is linked with the matrilineal clan of its owner. But the three *tubuan* owners whom I knew closely had financed all three stages of their sons' initiations into their own *tubuan*, before the sons were twenty. They gave their sons important parts in the dancing, carefully taught them ritual information and involved them in ceremonial organization. If the sons had ability and acquired further wealth as adults, they would be well prepared to buy their own *tubuan* when in their forties.

A second group of potential *tubuan* owners were people of the type of the co-sponsors of John's *matamatam*. They are solid citizens with much traditional knowledge, and considerable stocks of *tabu* acquired mainly from specialist skills, and from investing in such things as canoes, copra driers, and dance ornaments. They attend all ceremonies. My impression was, however, that they were unlikely to take such a dramatic step as buying a *tubuan*. One of them, for example, had undergone the first stage of initiation before the Japanese invasion, but only in 1961 did he finally complete the third stage. If they were to buy a *tubuan*, my prediction would be that they would take up a newly invented one, which would rarely perform dances, but would initiate a few youths and act as a satellite of a major *tubuan*. They were not expansionist entrepreneurs.

The third group of possible owners evident in 1961 were the lieutenants of the existing owners—those who led the dances, who did many of the organizational jobs, and who gave speeches at feasts. The three whom I knew well were all aged about thirty and had had some post-primary education in English. None was a close relative of his sponsor, the *tubuan* owner, but each was of his clan. All had spent some years at work away from their village soon after leaving school and had returned to take up responsible administrative jobs in the villages. ToUraliu, the manager of Talimut fermentery, has already been mentioned. All were becoming wealthy in *tabu* and cash, though how much was due to their sponsors' pushing and how much to their own efforts was hard to disentangle.

If, as I should predict, it is from the third group that the future financier-politicians are to emerge, the answer to the original question of how one can acquire wealth in *tabu* is clear. It comes to the man with organizing abilities, who can attract the attention of an already wealthy man of the same clan. The returns to the man who is merely a hard worker are small; the returns to the man with skill are higher, as are the returns to the man who acquires wealth, perhaps by inheriting it from his father; the highest returns go to the man with organizing skills, who has some capital behind him. Patronage may single him out from other candidates. It is the system of *tabu* finance that trains him for his organizing, political role.

Part Three

Politics and Development

Economic development in Vunamami, as it has been described so far, has never been a matter of single individuals innovating, creating businesses on their own, and getting independently wealthy. Though single individuals have innovated, their personal success, and the development of the society at large, have depended on the ability of innovative individuals to recruit followings. In some instances, as with cocoa growing, the followers have been merely imitators; in others the followers have been active supporters who have combined in collaborative enterprises. In all cases, in recruiting followings, the leaders have been able to use channels available in "traditional" society. Often the groupings they have used, as with "clan businesses," have nominally been traditional groupings. Development, the inference would be, requires the creative organizing of *people* to do tasks that unorganized people, or people in rigid organizations, could not do.

In such a formulation the importance of *tabu* finance and ceremonial entrepreneurship becomes even greater. While such a system is active in a society, new organizers are constantly being trained, the avenues of social mobility are clearly marked and kept open, incentives are provided for organizing on an everincreasing scale both to successful "big men" and to small household heads.

Yet so far in the analysis the emphasis has been on how economic activities can be viewed as interconnected, and on how economic magnitudes can be seen to have changed on the aggregate village level. Individuals have been mentioned, some of them frequently, primarily as examples, or

as names in historical events. When one wishes to analyse
the part that organization of people plays in economic development a different approach is required. Each important
organizing individual, each leader in development, emerged
from a distinctive background, which trained him, and gave
him the range of organizational channels that he later uti-
lized. The total range of channels open to all Vunamami
individuals can be visualized as a structure, available for
use in mobilizing people to realize goals—in short, as a
political structure. The channels have changed with time,
and so one may talk of a changing political structure, providing different opportunities for organizers.

This part will thus continue directly from the discussion
in Chapter 8 of ceremonial entrepreneurship in Vunamami
to a consideration of the individual political entrepreneurs
in Vunamami since the 1870's. After they have been discussed as individuals, their place in the changing political
structure will be considered, as well as the relationship between that structure and the concomitant economic changes.

IX

Vunamami Leaders

Every economic innovation in Vunamami history has been associated, in local accounts as well as in written documents, with the emergence of a dynamic leader. Ilaita ToGimamara is associated with the welcoming of missionaries and traders in the 1870's; ToInia with the acceptance of German control in 1891; Abram ToBobo, the *lualua* under Dr. Hahl, with the first planting of cash crops and the construction of roads; Enos Teve, the Paramount Luluai and first Council president, with the initial large-scale processing of copra in the 1930's, with the growing of cocoa around 1950, and with the search for new land after 1953; Vin ToBaining, Enos' successor as Council president, and the representative in the national Legislative Council, with the development of the Cocoa Project and of Council works, with land purchases from plantations and with involvement in pan-New Guinea politics. Of these, ToBobo, Enos, and ToBaining have been outstanding and innovative.

At the same time they are all cited as examples of highly traditional leaders. From casual talk in Vunamami one gets the impression that they *always* occupied positions of importance—that they had traditional status within their clans; that they were important in *tubuan* rituals and sponsored *matamatam* for clan ancestors; that they were knowledgeable in land matters and were *lualua*; that they were foci of residential groups of clansmen and were upholders of clan traditions. Ordinary people speak of their achievements with pride, and describe them as the traditional acts of "big men." Innovators appear as staunch traditionalists.

Behind this picture, ignored in general talk though widely known and not hidden when specific incidents are discussed, is the reality that most leaders achieved their positions on their own initiative. None was born poor, but equally none inherited clan headship.

This generalization is true even if one defines "leaders" more widely to include less important leaders. Other reasons are needed to explain, not merely why individuals became leaders, but why certain ones became outstanding and effected dramatic social changes. To illustrate factors common to all leaders, and also to illustrate how outstanding innovators differ from run-of-the-mill leaders, six vignettes will be presented here. These will include ToBobo, Enos, and ToBaining as outstanding innovators, plus ToInia and two less outstanding living leaders. Unfortunately no history could be obtained for Ilaita ToGimamara. The vignettes will be presented in chronological order.

CASE 1.—TOINIA AND THE ACCEPTANCE
OF GERMAN CONTROL

The story of ToInia, who achieved renown in the 1880's and was still alive in 1921, is based mainly on the testimony of his son, Alwas ToMatinur, who was born in 1891. Alwas was the first Tolai to work as a government clerk in the 1920's, and in 1961 he was the active chairman of the Kalamanagunan School Committee, which served three villages near Vunamami. An educated and learned man, in both Tolai and European knowledge, he was reputedly wealthy in both *tabu* and money, and was undoubtedly a *bon viveur* who spared nothing to attend social occasions over the whole Tolai area. Yet he dressed modestly, and he worked hard rounding up truants, helping build new classrooms, and collecting funds for projects, despite his seventy years. His memory was almost photographic and could be widely checked from other evidence (including Mission records).

ToInia was born about 1866, the younger son of a man of Tetegete clan, the major landowning clan of Vunamami. His own clan, Vunaibu, has its *madapai* in Ulaulatava, five miles inland. With limited prospects there, ToInia chose to stay with his father in Vunamami, and his father allocated him a plot of Tetegete land, named Bitaingita, to cultivate. In 1890 ToInia, long active in the Methodist Mission, went to live near the church while training as a preacher. He had recently married—grounds for his having to leave Tetegete land—and Alwas was born on Mission land. On 28 March 1890 occurred the murder of the overseer Moses, and the uprising and attack on Ralum under the leadership of To-Ruruk, who was the head of Vunaibu clan in Ulaulatava and an "elder brother" of ToInia. After military defeat ToRuruk went into hiding, and was captured only when ToInia revealed his presence, after ToRuruk attempted to seduce his wife. How this affected ToInia's relations with Vunaibu clan in Ulaulatava was not elaborated upon in the accounts I was told, but I assume he could not return there.

But in 1892 ToInia's father and other Tetegete men planned a *matamatam* for their clan ancestors. ToInia and a younger brother of Vunaibu clan immediately gave a *warap*—a thank-offering by a man to repay his father for the food given during childhood—of six hundred fathoms of *tabu*, which defrayed many of the *matamatam* costs. In return, Tetegete clan gave ToInia the acre of Bitaingita "for himself, his sisters' sons, and his lineage," that is, with clear title as clan land. It should be noted that six hundred fathoms is far more than the economic price for an acre planted to cocoa, even today. ToInia became an honoured land-owner in Vunamami, active in politics on the side of good relations with the government, and the founding ancestor of a large section of Vunaibu clan which lives on Bitaingita and nearby land acquired later. Jointly with a distantly related clan brother who also came to live in Vunamami, a man named Levi ToLingling, he obtained ownership of a Vunaibu *tubuan*, and gave *matamatam* in Vunamami for his clan ancestors.

CASE 2.—TOBOBO: COCONUT PLANTING AND POLITICAL UNITY

Abram ToBobo, who was born about 1865 and lived to 1937, is mentioned in many historical sources. About him miraculous stories are told, such as when, one Sunday, he prophesied to a congregation that he would die next day. He prayed for a sign from God that he would go to heaven, and immediately a lamp nearby shattered. He sang loud hymns of praise that he would die next day, and he died. To the very last his eyes "were clear, like those of a young man."

He was not strictly a resident of Vunamami but his early life was spent in Vunamami and he was later influential there. He was a member of Vunabalbal clan and lived much of his adult life on the clan *madapai* in Vunabalbal village. He was only the younger son of his family, and not the clan head by seniority. As a youth in 1875 he was one of the first converts to Method-

ism in Vunamami, and though he was not baptized until 1894, he
actively proselytized for the church, while pursuing a secular
career of achieving both wealth and renown as a warrior. In 1894
he jumped into prominence after the long war when Vunamami
and the inland villages united and twice nearly evicted all Europeans from Kokopo, thanks to the inspiration of a magic ointment
that supposedly repelled bullets. ToBobo, as the most active pro-
tagonist of peace, was later selected by Dr. Hahl as his direct agent
for contacts with the villages surrounding Vunamami. The exact
status of this position is not clear, but informants say that the Germans used for it the pidgin title *nambawan*, which the Tolai translated as *lualua*. Informants also say that at first four *nambawan*
were appointed, for Raluana, Davaon, Birara, and Vunamami,
and subsequently two more for Toma and Paparatava. ToBobo's
jurisdiction is also unclear; it definitely covered Vunamami, Vunabalbal, and Bitarebarebe but his efforts to extend it to other villages may well have been illegal, as when he was fined in 1896 for
dictating what mission Takabur village would adhere to.

ToBobo's appointment to this position, like the success of To-
Inia, was not a straightforward reward for public service. The
leader of the Vunamami confederacy, and the original purchaser
of magic ointment for it, was ToBobo's elder brother, the heir
apparent to the headship of Vunabalbal clan. The man who ensured the defeat of the confederacy by obtaining magic ointment
for the Buka troops of the government was ToBobo himself. With
the death of his brother he became the head of Vunabalbal clan.
But informants always assert that he opposed the confederacy because of his desire for peace and prosperity along the new lines
of church, government, and company. When he became *nambawan* it was essentially the confederacy, which his dead brother had
unified, that he administered.

He took his duties seriously, managing to carry out Dr. Hahl's
wishes but to represent Tolai interests at the same time. It was
undoubtedly his arguments that persuaded Dr. Hahl to make the
initial decision to set up Ralum Reserve, and he himself convinced
the Vunamami people that it was the only way to preserve their
land against encroachment. It was his own idea to lower bride
prices by fiat, as a way of lowering the age of marriage and thus
raising the birth rate in order to populate the land. Even so, many
people stress his motives as those of pity for the number of men
compelled to celibacy by high bride prices, and they describe his

order as the act of a generous father of his people. He was in-
defatigable in planting coconuts—the last one he planted fell in
1960—"in order to teach his people" say informants, ignoring the
fact that he became wealthy also. He supervised for the Germans
the construction of the Toma Road, but he did not hesitate to
complain to Dr. Hahl, and obtain the erection of concrete markers,
when Europeans encroached on Reserve land. He was, from 1894
on, a preacher in the Methodist Church.

In 1922 when Australian civil administration took over, his position was no longer recognized. Yet he continued to wear the
dress he had worn under the Germans, of a shirt and long trousers,
and was not prosecuted under the Native Regulation forbidding
the wearing of shirts. Men who were small boys after the 1937
eruption remember being taken to see him, a semi-regal figure before his death.

CASE 3.—ENOS TEVE: COPRA DRIERS,
COUNCILS, AND COCOA

Enos is still alive and active, a polished white-haired gentleman,
modestly dressed and living in an undistinguished house, yet respected by government officials and Tolai alike as one of the prime
movers in Tolai modernization from the 1930's to the present.
But, as in other success stories, the benefits he has brought to the
whole of Tolai society have in many cases involved setbacks for
other individuals. The present history makes no attempt to conceal these negative aspects, but not as a means of detracting from
Enos' reputation. It is hoped that by documenting both sides, a
fuller appreciation of the nature of his leadership can be obtained.

Born in 1900, Enos was the son of Levi ToLingling. His mother
was of Vunamerom clan, most of whose land is in Balanataman
village to the west, but which is also allied to Takaptar clan of
Vunamami village and to other clans in villages to the east. Collectively the name Tuluai is applied to all these clans. Levi, of
Vunaibu clan and from Tokokok village, had settled in Vunamami
village on land claimed through his wife, in Lumluvur ward. He
became wealthy. His unrelated clan brother ToInia was his
friendly rival in Kunakunai ward.

Enos' mother died soon after his birth, and Levi remarried a
woman of Vunaruga clan by whom he had three sons. Levi now
had a claim to the use of Takaptar land only through Enos, his

son, yet he continued living, working, and prospering in Vunamami. By 1921 he was co-owner of the Vunaibu *tubuan* with
ToInia, and managed to politick so well that Enos was initiated
before ToInia's son Alwas. Levi trained Enos in fishing and in
business techniques, and together in about 1927 they began negotiating to purchase land in Lumluvur to which they would have
clear title, instead of living on sufferance on Takaptar land. This
land belonged to Matupit clan, whose *lualua* was Pero ToKinkin,
a former Vunamami resident who had been Parkinson's confidant
and the *lualua* of Raluana. One hundred and fifty fathoms of *tabu*
were handed to Pero.

Almost immediately, while Judge Phillips' inquiry into the tenure of Ralum Estate was in progress, Mr. Rowe of Ravalien plantation claimed the plot, and transfer was held up until boundary
markers were erected, leaving the plot in the Reserve. At this
point Levi died, leaving Enos as the guardian of his stepmother and
three half-brothers, and the centre of a major dispute.

Vunaibu clan claimed that Levi had bought Pero's land with
Vunaibu *tabu*, and that the meagre stocks of *tabu* found in Levi's
store were the result of depredations by Enos. His half-brothers
and stepmother felt that they were entitled to shares of whatever
Enos had obtained from Levi. The case was brought before the
Paramount Luluai of the area for arbitration, a man named Amos
ToKauba, from Tingenavudu village. The latter decreed that the
land sale was invalid and null, and that, of the 150 fathoms paid,
fifty had belonged to Enos and should be returned to him. Enos
did not receive his *tabu*.

During the next few years Enos brought himself to public attention in many ways. He financed the possession of seine nets
and organized a successful Takaptar clan association for net fishing. He continued a fight with Mr. Rowe, when the latter erected
a bamboo barrier across a right of way leading to a fishing site.
Enos claimed it was illegal and erected to spite Vunamami people
who sold coconuts to Chinese traders and not to Mr. Rowe, while
Mr. Rowe maintained it was needed to keep his cattle from stray-
ing. The District Officer supported Mr. Rowe, but then Enos
barred a plantation road that made a short cut across Reserve land,
and Mr. Rowe agreed to compromise. Both barriers were removed.
When the office of *luluai* of Vunamami fell vacant, the District
Officer appointed Enos to it in May 1935.

In 1936 the police, acting on information they had received, discovered Amos, the Paramount Luluai, drunk, and he was removed from office. Tingenavudu villagers, who subsequently have a history of non-cooperation with Paramountcy and Council enterprises, still talk ruefully about who gave the information, but other villages show no interest. Immediately afterwards, Enos took Amos to court for misappropriating the fifty fathoms paid into court in connection with his land case, and Amos was gaoled for six months. Vunamami villagers praised the way he had exposed a corrupt Paramount Luluai. In 1937 Enos was appointed to the vacant office.

As Paramount he energetically organized all villages. Soon after the 1937 Rabaul eruption he went to Salamaua (probably on an Administration programme to show leaders the native councils developing there), and from each migrant labourer from Vunamami Paramountcy he collected five shillings to start a fund for building community facilities and schools. The £300 in this fund was eventually paid to the Vunamami Council account in 1950. He initiated the co-operative clearing and planting of land at Talimut, which had lain idle since Judge Phillips had decreed it was part of the Reserve: no village had dared antagonize another by moving in first. He actively encouraged the erection of copra driers, along the lines of the Vunamami village drier which had been built on land he had donated, following his organization of a *kivung* on becoming *luluai*.

Under Japanese occupation Enos carried on as usual, organizing when told to do so but also standing up for native rights when possible. He has a missing big toe to show for one act of defiance. When the major Japanese bomb dump at Ravalien was blown up by a grass fire set by Tolai working for the Coastwatchers, Enos won clemency for the Vunamami villagers who had been forced to dig a mass grave for their own execution. He argued stubbornly despite interrogation that a Japanese truck had passed near the place where the fire broke out shortly beforehand, and that a carelessly thrown cigarette end had probably caused both the fire and the explosion.

After the war he was on hand to preside over organizing the "Committees" which anticipated the eventual Village Councils, while he was also actively seeking new economic opportunities for the Tolai people (and for himself). During the period of residence on the beach he organized another Takaptar clan fishing *kivung*, and on return to Vunamami village he used the *kivung* funds to rebuild the pre-war drier. He sponsored an unofficial school in Vunamami. He formed a copra-buying group to sell the copra to P.C.B., bought a truck, and started a co-operative store. Most important, in 1949, he was (with Napitalai of Ngatur, and Elison of Balanataman) the first Tolai to be approached by the Agricultural Officer about planting cocoa. He immediately planted his own clan lands in Balanataman, and had the abortive coconut plantation at Talimut replanted to cocoa. In 1952 he was the prime mover in the building of the Vunamami Council co-operative cocoa fermentery at Ngatur, from which the Tolai Cocoa Project developed.

When councils were inaugurated in 1950, Enos was such an outstanding candidate for president that the ordinance was specially written to allow Vunamami Council to elect anyone as president, not merely a councillor elected popularly. For Enos to have to stand for election "would be an indignity" (Australian Public Service Institute 1955:103). The Council, according to its records, started life with a fund of over £2,500,[1] thanks to Enos. Its first act was to "put aside money for higher education . . . to plan for a school" (New Guinea 1954:6). Efforts were made to secure land and to erect buildings and get teachers, but the national shortage meant that no accredited teachers would be available until 1952. Nonetheless Enos ordered all young men whose educations had been cut short by the war to attend classes under native teachers in Vunamami village. In 1961 these men were the backbone of the local bureaucracy—storekeepers, medical assistants, Co-operative representatives, and the local councillor. In 1952 Enos retired as president, and Vin ToBaining, his classificatory son-in-law, was elected to the office, though Enos continued to attend meetings as an adviser.

Enos did not retire into inactivity. He became a director of the Tolai Cocoa Project, and a director of the New Britain Co-operative Association. His cocoa plantations steadily came into bearing, and his land-buying ventures became more and more important. In 1961, when the possibility of the Council's purchasing Ravalien plantation became imminent, Enos stood for councillor and was elected handily by secret ballot.

The kind of controversy that surrounded Enos' inheritance and his appointment as *luluai* has recurred. His post-war land acqui-

[1] It was the only council in New Guinea to have funds from its inception. Many observers attribute Vunamami Council's success to this factor.

sitions started in about 1946, when, while Paramount Luluai, he arranged with the *lualua* of Kabakaul clan, a youth of sixteen, to buy a large plot of flat kunai land. This bordered Rapopo airstrip and had been devastated by bombing. Transfer of the *tabu* payment was not completed, but Enos used the land for gardens and began planting it to coconuts. In 1958 the area of which it was part was surveyed by the Native Lands Commission (Kokopo case 4) and recorded as belonging to Kabakaul clan. In 1959 Enos suggested completing the transfer, but the *lualua* objected that he had originally agreed under duress, that he had meant to let the land be used only for gardens and not for permanent crops, and that Enos had planted an area outside what had been agreed upon. Finally Kabakaul agreed to sell two and a half acres, and Enos accepted, though it meant losing many of the coconuts he had planted. This case aroused numerous complaints that the sixty acres in the same general area, purchased by Vunamami and Vunabalbal villagers between 1947 and 1955, had also been sold under duress. But the Lands Commission had legally registered the transfers and no real action could be taken. Vunamami village remembers only Enos' example in searching out new land to buy.

But controversy in Vunamami village does centre around Enos' businesses. With eight other men of various clans associated with Takaptar, many of them immigrants to Vunamami, he formed the seine-net *kivung* in the late 1940's, everyone subscribing £10 each. In one year they earned £300 and 200 fathoms of *tabu*. Enos used £200 of this to rebuild his pre-war copra drier, even though two men of the *kivung* owned small driers of drums and scrap iron, located less than two hundred yards away. The two driers were torn down by their owners to "shame" Enos, and Enos' drier was boycotted. The *kivung* became inactive, and the whereabouts of its assets were lost track of. Despite the controversy, it may be noted that the two men who tore down their driers both told me that they voted for Enos in the secret ballot of 1961.

Enos is a staunch traditionalist. He has given seven *balaguan*, three of them *matamatam* for his own clan, one for his father's clan, one to celebrate a church building, and two to celebrate and motivate Vunamami and Balanataman's post-war reconstruction. For the last-named ceremony he commissioned the carving of the largest canoe on the coast, involving the reactivation of skills and ceremonies not practised for fifty years, and making possible the performance of *kinawai* ceremonies and the easier launching of large fishing traps. The canoe, of course, returns regular profits, though less than do many of Enos' other ventures. He "controls" the *tubuan* of his father's clan, which includes guarding the *tubuan*'s treasury. He seems to be an affectionate father and there have always been young children in his household. Orphans from many branches of Tuluai phratry have found a home with Enos, and have grown up either to assume successful positions in the government or to settle near to Enos and help him with his farming. He has had few children of his own, but whenever a wife had died—as has happened four times—he has remarried a young and good-looking girl to bear him children. To see Enos, sitting quietly gossiping with other older men at the market, while dandling his infant daughter on his lap, is to see the paradigm of Tolai paternal affection.

CASE 4.—BENIONA TOKARAI: SCHOOLS AND CO-OPERATIVES

Beniona was born in 1909, of Vunagigi clan, whose lands lay in Tokokok. He was, however, the son of a man of Papakan clan who had received a portion of Bitaingita from ToInia in return for political support. Beniona went to mission school in Vunamami and was one of the first pupils at the government school opened in Kokopo in 1923. He ran away after a few weeks, but fondly remembered the principal, W. C. Groves, when the latter returned to inspect the new Vunamami Council Area School at Nganalaka in 1954 to which Beniona was attached. This meeting set a seal on Beniona's career.

From Kokopo he went to Raluana Circuit Training Institution, and when George Brown College was moved to Vunairima in 1929 he was again a first pupil. Much of the pupils' time was spent in construction and planting the magnificent trees that now grace the area, but Beniona learned enough to remain as a teacher when he finished school in 1932. He stresses his loyalty to the headmaster, for he did not like Vunairima as a place. He married in 1934, and spent a happy year teaching at Raluana C.T.I. After a return to Vunairima, where his son Esau was born in 1937, he was posted permanently to Raluana. To many of the emerging élite of today Beniona is remembered as a sort of Mr. Chips.

He was in Raluana when the Japanese attacked, and he helped the last defender, a Mr. Smith, through the Japanese troop concentrations when resistance ceased next morning. He was enlisted as an interpreter by the Japanese, but he led a double life, organizing illegal church services, publishing a monthly church calendar using an old typewriter given him at Vunairima, and sheltering Allied flyers shot down in the area. When his typewriter was discovered he was nearly shot as a spy sending information to the Allies, but his *kempe tai* chief, Masimoto San, himself once a schoolteacher in the United States, believed his story. In 1944 Masimoto began a military and technical school for boys near Raluana. Beniona and two other teachers, under a Japanese named Yamata San, taught courses in the Japanese language, rice-paper manufacture, machining scrap aluminium, carpentry, and sake distilling.

With peace, Beniona returned to his father's village of Vunamami. When Vunamami left the beach he began the school, built on Enos' land, for those whose education had been interrupted. Starting with seven pupils, he built up the school, recruiting teachers from among his pre-war pupils, even though, by post-war standards, he was an untrained teacher, literate only in Tolai, not in English. By 1950 he had become a crusader on behalf of the Vunamami Council Area School, making long speeches on the benefits of education, the need for technical knowledge, and the value of co-operation. When Nganalaka school opened in March 1952, Beniona was specially asked by the District Education Officer to take over the "outside" teaching of crafts and agricultural work, while one of Beniona's former friends at Raluana named Darius ToMamua, a fully certificated teacher, taught "inside."

As the curriculum gradually became more academic, Beniona transferred his enthusiasm to councils and co-operatives. He was closely involved in the early unregistered co-operative efforts by Raluana. With ToMamua he was highly disturbed when Raluana rejected entry into the Council scheme with Vunamami. The two men actively fought on the minority side of the ensuing riots, and were both threatened with assassination. Beniona with his Raluana ties was active in the Co-operative restaurant, Unaruk, and at the first meeting of the New Britain Co-operative Association in 1954, he was the Bitatali representative. He became the Vunamami Council area representative later, and actively campaigned for

maintaining ties with Raluana through the Co-operative movement. He remains active in Co-operative Association affairs, though
not in the daily running of the Bitatali store.

Unlike the other leaders in our survey, Beniona's career has not
been financially successful. He owns only a small plot of land in
Vunamami village, and while working as a teacher he did not extend his holdings. Contracting as a carpenter still provides his
main cash income, but in 1953 he joined Enos in acquiring lands
to the east of Kokopo for coconut and cocoa planting. His wife
being of Papakan clan, he was able to get some land from Davara
clan (which is linked to Papakan), nominally for the use of his
son, even though the latter was employed as a schoolteacher outside the area. He was involved in the 1955 riots at Taui over land
purchases, and in 1961 had further difficulties when his wife, who
had divorced him, claimed guardianship of the land for her son
and her clan. Beniona worked constantly on the newly acquired
land, when not carpentering or making public speeches, yet by
1961 his plantings were not yet bearing, and the only return from
his land was the political support of Vunamami residents allowed
to plant gardens under his growing palms. He had not yet found
time to complete the modern house he had planned. The force
of his hortatory speeches was undermined by his apparent lack of
economic success.

CASE 5.—VIN TOBAINING, M.B.E.: "SOLIDARITY
IN COUNCILS, COOPERATIVES, AND COCOA PROJECT"—
"A TINUR WARARUNG TARA KAUNSIL, TARA
KOOPERATIV MA TARA POMENTARI."

Vin ToBaining of Ineinau clan was born in 1914. Ineinau, like
Vunagigi, was a Tokokok clan and its lands had been confiscated.
Vin's father, however, was Wili ToDik, a Methodist teacher of
Takaptar clan, normally residing in Vunamami but appointed to
the Bainings at the time of his son's birth. He was a rich man, one
of those who had his own horse and trap, and he saw that his
son got a good education. Vin went to Raluana C.T.I. and later
to Vunairima as a boarding student, and on completing his education (in Tolai, not in English) was taken on as a typesetter at the
Mission press in Vunairima. He married IaNuk, a niece of ToBobo,
and of Takaptar clan like his father, in 1938.

Not until 1942 when the Japanese occupation dispersed the

staff at Vunairima did he become involved in Vunamami village life, and even then he was not a distinguished resident, but one living on his wife's (and his father's) clan land. When the Australians returned and Enos was re-creating the lower echelons of village administration, he was appointed *tultul* of the village and subsequently a *Komiti,* in both of which capacities he performed efficiently. In the first election for councillor in 1950 he (literally) stood against several candidates, the election being determined by the length of the line of supporters who stood behind each candidate. Beniona, despite having the longest line, withdrew and told his supporters to support Vin, who then became councillor for Vunamami village. With his background he proved adept in parliamentary procedure, an effective speaker in debate, and an efficient workhorse to carry out all the administrative and supervisory tasks that devolved on the councillor living closest to the Council chambers. When Enos decided to retire as Council president he felt that Vin, his classificatory son, was the ideal person to carry on his work—the most educated man of the up-and-coming generation in the Council, rather than one of the more flamboyant, older "big men" of the outlying villages.

This proved an effective arrangement. The "big men" became absorbed in the construction and running of Nganalaka school and Ngatur fermentery; Vin, assisted by an efficient council clerk, set up a central bureaucracy, negotiated with the District Office, and supervised the highly successful construction and opening of the council chambers in Vunamami. From a command of the intricacies of budgeting, and of the committee procedures needed for ensuring co-operation, Vin moved into the fields of long-range planning and obtaining public support.

In December 1952 he (and the Native Affairs Officer) began modifying the Vunamami Cacao Marketing Account with the aim of turning it into a co-operative, using paid full-time workers, and he got the A.D.O. to approve rules making it compulsory for all Vunamami cocoa growers to use the fermentery. He pushed for Council land purchases along the lines of the Rabaul Council purchases at Vudal, and he worked for the eviction of Chinese living on Ralum Reserve and for the clarification of the land situation generally. He was overwhelmingly re-elected president by secret ballot in 1953, and has continued to be re-elected ever since.

At the same time he had to remedy his deficient involvement in village life. He began planting cocoa on his wife's land in 1951 only, but, hiring labour to help him, expanded his plantings faster than almost anyone in the area, so that by 1959, when the plantings were fully bearing, his cocoa income was second only to Enos', within Vunamami village. He also took two months off to be secluded in the bush and to learn the secrets needed for initiation into the *tubuan* religion, which his Mission education had kept from him. Initiation in its turn made it possible for him in 1959 to give a *matamatam* in honour of his dead father and in that way cement his ties to Takaptar clan.

Vin's massive build, and his forceful rhetoric, make him an impressive figure. He is normally quiet and unassuming in manner—I have watched him stand patiently in line at the post office counter while the assistant chatted with friends—yet in public speeches he works up passionate enthusiasm. His household is now replete with adopted children and dependent male relatives. He is the epitome of the traditional Tolai big man.

In 1958, while Vin was raising the question of Native Reserves in the New Britain District Advisory Council, the government at last made some Warangoi land available to Vunamami Council. The outstanding success of the Vunamami scheme, until difficulties arose because of the Administration's insistence on individual land tenure, was largely due to Vin. He personally supervised many operations, and himself accepted title to a block, in trust for Vunamami village, when jealousies arose and no individual would take over title. At the same time Vin was stumping the non-Council areas of Kokopo Sub-district, to persuade them to enter the Council—as he had done in Raluana in 1953 and 1954. This time he was successful, and by 1960 almost all of the Birara area and the Duke of York Islands had joined Vunamami Council. The 1961 elections to the Territorial Legislative Council, conducted by the electoral college method with votes assigned to Local Government Councils as blocks, found Vin the most dynamic of the Tolai Council presidents with the largest block of votes (see Salisbury 1964). He was elected the member for New Guinea Islands. Vunamami Council began building him a presidential residence on his wife's land, maintaining that they would keep him as president for his lifetime.[2]

[2] As a postscript on Vin ToBaining's career it may be noted that despite his lack of English, he was one of the most effective native members of the legislature, after John Guise. He took a prominent part in the Select

CASE 6.—POLOS: THE RISING GENERATION

This case must necessarily be an incomplete case; it may be no case, for Polos may be superseded as a coming leader, but because he is a likely candidate it seems worth presenting his history to show how the pattern is being repeated.

Born in 1925, of Tagatagal clan, he went to the Mission school in Vunamami, but then was one of the first boys from Vunamami to go on to Malaguna Technical College in 1939. Unfortunately the war cut short his education, although he had already acquired considerable fluency in English. When the war finished he was sufficiently advanced in his education to act as a junior teacher, under Beniona, at the school that was then started. Shortly after, as the government administration settled down, he was offered a post and served as clerk and interpreter at hospitals in Rabaul and Kokopo.

Although his clan owned only one small plot in Vunamami he came back to the village when an uncle who had been a major cocoa planter in Ngatur turned over some acreage to him to work. Not content with becoming a large cocoa grower from scratch, he immediately fell in with the land-buying schemes to the east of Kokopo, and bought for himself alone a plot of almost fifteen acres. At the time of the riots over these purchases, his close acquaintanceship with District officials proved of value in presenting the Vunamami case. At the following elections he was made councillor, but he served only two terms before declining re-election.

Committee which worked out the constitution of the subsequent House of Assembly in which an indigenous multiracial majority was ensured in open roll voting. Vin was not elected to the House of Assembly in 1964, the Tolai electorate being split in two, and the smaller part in Kokopo Sub-district (i.e., Vunamami Council) being attached to the numerically much larger Baining groups to the south. A non-Tolai was returned for this East Gazelle (Kokopo) seat. Vin received an M.B.E. for his service in the legislature, in the 1965 New Year's Honours List. He was active in the movement that led to the amalgamation of all the Tolai Local Government Councils into one council in 1963, subsequently becoming its president. Its deliberations have become a major forum for independent, non-Administration discussion of policy in New Guinea. It is perhaps the most effective, as well as the wealthiest and most powerful, grass-roots constituency organization behind its local member (ToMattias ToLiman, M.H.A., Undersecretary to the Department of the Administrator) in the whole of Papua/New Guinea.

He nevertheless remained active in village affairs, perhaps more active than before. His clan, although numerically unimportant in Vunamami, has ritual pre-eminence from owning a *taraiu* in the bush on the Vunabalbal–Vunamami boundary. Polos, a slim athlete, is a fine dancer especially in the *tubuan* dances when a ceremony is held based on that *taraiu*. He also proclaims *bagil* or prohibitions on the gathering of coconuts, collecting the fines for infractions and keeping accounts of them. His bookkeeping skills are widely used in other ways. Vunamami residents paying tithes to the Methodist Church account by delivering copra to the Co-operative, do so by paying into an account listed in Polos' name. He represents Vunamami at Co-operative Association meetings. He was an initiator of a revolving credit association of thirty men, designed to facilitate house-construction, and also its treasurer. By 1962 two European-style houses had been built, thanks to Association funds; one of them was Polos'. When land questions arose, especially in connection with the purchase of Ravalien plantation, and the making of claims to modify Judge Phillips' judgement, Polos was there, and was looked up to as an expert on law and procedures. Yet in his personal life, despite his wealth, he lived quietly and could be seen early most mornings, pedalling his bicycle to his distant plantations. Although he had no village land on which to house dependants in 1961, he provided housing temporarily for friends and relatives working in government offices, one of whom commuted from Vunamami to Rabaul, and in return the latter helped him with plantation work on week-ends. He had also "adopted" an immigrant from the Sepik District of New Guinea, a man who is a skilled fisherman, and provided him with board and lodging while he performed expert tasks at the village *motonoi*.

THE PATTERN OF LEADERS

The descriptions by ethnographers and by informants of Tolai "traditional leaders"—*ngala*—are unanimous in describing the despotic nature of their control—their ability to give whimsical orders and to have them carried out, and the way in which their control was based on the ownership of land, *tabu*, and *tubuan*. By controlling land the big man was able to reward followers and to attract dependants to live near him, thus providing him with a labour force. As a wealthy man he could finance the ceremonial needs of his followers, making marriage possible for them by providing bride prices, and it was advantageous for followers to deposit *tabu* with the big man for safe keeping. *Tubuan* ownership was partly dependent on land ownership and on wealth in *tabu*, which permitted the purchase of a *tubuan*. But ownership in turn gave political control of a quasi-military force, and a source of further revenue. *Tubuan* ownership, like land ownership, was closely connected with clan membership, so that big men tended also to be the *lualua* of clans. It is easy to make the assumption that leadership was an ascribed characteristic, devolving upon the heir—the sister's son—of the clan *lualua* by virtue of his birth.

The assumption is simplistic, if not entirely false, for the traditional view of clan origins is that a leader *without* land clears an area of forest (or otherwise obtains "new" land as *pia na bartamana*) and attracts dependants to come and live with him, and all their descendants become a clan known by the name of the plot of land, the clan *madapai*. Clearing virgin forest may not have been common by 1870, but setting up new clans (or new segments of larger phratries) by buying land and attracting dependants was clearly recognized as an avenue of mobility to big man status in the 1870's. So too was the pattern of currying favour with an existing big man, who then would confer the attributes necessary for achieving success on an intelligent and active sycophant, rather than on a less suitable and perhaps rebellious sister's son. Particularly did this occur when the big man was the father of a son whose career he could encourage (as Malinowski has described for the Trobriands, though he mistakenly took one case as a universally applicable norm). In short, although many pre-1870 clan *lualua* did owe their positions to heredity, most of the big men had achieved that position through demonstrating political and business skills, and had subsequently consolidated their position by becoming clan *lualua*. Hereditary position was no bar to big man status, but only a minority of hereditary *lualua* had the ability that was also required.

Against this background it will be realized that all six Vunamami emergent leaders show the pattern of "traditional leaders." Except for Beniona, all, at their prime, were rich men, landowners, with a coterie of dependants of closely related clans, and with high positions in the religious hierarchy both of Methodism and of the *tubuan*. Beniona's lack of financial success undoubtedly weighs heavily against his future reputation as a leader. When Vunamami people express pride in these leaders it is their "traditional" nature that is stressed—their knowledge of land affairs, their ability to look after the interests of dependants, their financial success, their continuing involvement in village affairs with no appearance of being stand-offish, their concern with clanship and religion.

But whereas the non-hereditary character of traditional big men must be inferred from ideal accounts, it can be traced in detail in these six histories. First, none was the heir to headship of an important Vunamami clan. ToBobo was a member of the most important Vunabalbal clan, but he depended at first on a Vunamami base of support; the clans of ToInia, Enos, and Polos were important outside Vunamami but unimportant there; Vin's and Beniona's clans were landless after the Tokokok expropriation. Yet most had a dormant claim to clan status: ToBobo and ToInia were younger brothers of clan *lualua;* Enos' clan is allied to one of the major founding Vunamami clans, and Polos' clan has ceremonial rights in Vunamami. As the leaders became successful, so these dormant claims could be stressed, and the lack of hereditary status underplayed.

All the leaders in their early careers were dependent on sponsors or patrons. For ToInia, Enos, Beniona, and Vin their fathers were their first sponsors—not by giving them hereditary status, but by giving them material gifts of *tabu* or land at crucial points of their careers, and by actively educating them in the abilities needed for success. ToBobo and ToInia as youths attached themselves to the Methodist Mission; Beniona and Vin went to Mission school, and Polos went to Malaguna Technical. Yet none of the early sponsors ensured the success of their protégés; at some point in each leader's career the early sponsor was rejected, either actively or because of circumstances, and a new sponsor was found. For Beniona, Vin, and Polos the war provided the disruption of their early mission or technical school sponsorship; for ToInia and ToBobo the rejection was dramatic, involving what would seem to have been acts of treachery (though no one remembers them as such); for Enos the death of his father set in train the sequence of disputes with his father's clan and his half-brothers that eventually led to his being recognized by the Administration.

In all cases a second sponsor was then sought out. ToInia became the favourite of the German administration; it is quite possible that it was a reward paid for betraying his clan brother that enabled him to pay the large sum of six hundred fathoms to his father's clan, for land and for adopted status in Vunamami. ToBobo's career as *lualua* followed the career of Dr. Hahl, and, like it, was eclipsed with Australian administration. Enos, too, came to government attention, first as a "troublemaker" against the planters and the conservative landowners, but then as a progressive innovator who would make an effective Paramount Luluai. Beniona, Vin, and Polos all began the second stage of their careers as the protégés of Enos in his post-war reorganization ventures. Success in those later careers has accompanied the success of the innovations which they, as leaders, suggested, and which their intelligence and managerial and diplomatic skills made practicable.

To an outsider, all the careers could be interpreted cynically in terms of unprincipled exploitation of others in pursuit of personal gain. A minority of Tolai who have been the objects of exploitation make the same judgement. But the majority of Tolai stress how the innovations of the leaders have been motivated by and have produced welfare for everyone.[3] The mark of the successful leader is that he can convince others that they are not followers but partners in an enterprise. In Vunamami this has been possible, for each leader has spoken of his activities as being those of an entire group—associations conducting businesses are "*clan* associations," planting of coconuts is done to save *ra tarai* ("the people") from German encroachment, private land purchases are to enlarge *village* holdings, co-operatives and fermenteries should be supported for the benefit of all members of Vunamami *council*. By living unpretentiously and without aloofness, the leader demonstrates that he is himself only one of the group. What he must have, however, are groupings towards which he can express loyalty and which he can convince others are worthy groupings to be loyal to. Even the "traditional leader" setting up a new clan segment on a "new" plot of land had to convince others that the segment was worth working for. When the groupings already exist, all the leader has to do is to activate existing loyalties and convince others that sup-

[3] I should add that close personal acquaintance with all four living Vunamami leaders, and with numerous other leading Tolai, convinces me of the sincerity of their own aims of educating and leading all Tolai to a better way of life. They are highly intelligent men who are aware of the short-run hardships their actions may entail, but they have made their own calculations of the courses which would produce the greatest long-range good for most people. For a novelistic treatment of how long-run sincerity in a political leader may appear inconsistent with short-run ruthlessness, the reader is referred to Joyce Cary's *Prisoner of Grace*.

port for him is beneficial for the entire grouping. His task is relatively easy. As the leader of an existing group he can easily become
a "traditional leader," especially if his techniques for reaching that
position are traditional ones. All Vunamami's successful leaders are
thus remembered as "traditional leaders" using traditional channels
of mobility and leading traditional groupings.

Yet a distinction can be made between the main leaders and the
lesser ones. The main leaders are those whose reputation goes
beyond their own grouping; this is the criterion an observer uses to
establish who is a "main leader." In terms of loyalties this implies
that no member of the leader's grouping will express disloyalty to
him in the presence of outsiders, for the leader and the grouping
are so identified that disloyalty to the leader is felt to be disloyalty
to the group. ToInia did not become the personification of Vunaibu
clan, for his following of dependants on Bitaingita comprised men
of too many non-Vunaibu clans; he had to share clan pre-eminence
with Levi. He is remembered for his clever land deals, but many
people see them as self-motivated rather than as altruistic on behalf of his clan. Beniona, without the wealth or official position
that would make his ex-pupils dependent on him, is remembered
fondly by them but is not identified with a grouping. With little
land in Vunamami, and his new land acquisitions not yet yielding
wealth or available for settling dependants, he is not yet identified
with a clan. His son's clan, from which support would have been
most likely, was divided in its attitudes to him by the divorce of
his wife. Polos, too, has yet to demonstrate that his land purchases
are motivated by public spirit and not by desire for personal gain.
A leader who is only partly successful is remembered publicly as
self-motivated and is a rebel against tradition; a leader who is
fully successful may have incidents of self-motivation remembered in private, but in public he is remembered as altruistic and
a supporter of the traditions.

In short, the question for which this chapter provides the most
answers, is not that of how individuals achieve success, but that of
how individuals active in economic and political change achieve
the public recognition that confers on them the role of a historical
figure. Much of the aura surrounding historical figures, the stories
of their dynamism, the listing of their "traditional" attributes, and
the associating of their names with every important event during
their period of office is, in fact, the halo effect of local historical
memory. Certain advantages of wealth and education, taken in

the broad sense to include training in organization, especially during adolescence, can help many able people to success. A demonstration that they are not merely the creature of an early sponsor is needed to make it clear that they are successful in their own right. Their success is consolidated by wealth, by building a coterie of permanent supporters, and by associating a whole social grouping with the success. The "historical figure" does something more: he happens to be on the spot, and to remain in charge of the situation, when a technological innovation occurs, and confers major benefits more widely than on a single social grouping. In the next chapter we shall consider the political changes that accompany major technological advances and permit benefits to spread more widely.

X

Political Consolidation
and Economic Development

Four main themes have run through this book. Here I shall try to bring them together in relation to the central underlying aim of the work—the understanding of the meaning of economic development.

Two of the themes have been primarily ethnographic. First, in describing how economic change looks from a village point of view, I have tried to analyse for each activity the economic concepts used by the local people in making their allocational choices. The result has been, I believe, to show that in each activity there is economic rationality, not always in the short term but in the long run, and bearing in mind the "costs" of operating in a small-scale society. Thus "delayed barter" may seem inexplicable to an observer accustomed to short-term profit-making in highly complex and diversified markets; it becomes entirely rational when viewed in a context of highly variable supplies in a market where there are essentially only two groups which alternate the roles of buyers and sellers. The indigenous concepts provide a vocabulary for understanding bilateral negotiated trade, though not open-market trade. Or in the case of copra production methods, the peasant producers appear rational in terms of output per man-day—their major cost—while at the same time plantations, calculating in terms of output per acre of land, can maintain that *they* are rationally organized, only because a distorted wage structure exists.

The second ethnographic theme has been to show how differently a change process looks from the inside and from the outside. In seeking to establish this point I have, perhaps, made too sharp a distinction between the two views. It is not in fact necessary to regard one as true and the other as false, but rather to recognize that the truth lies in a combination of both views. Outside observers too readily assume that their view of change is right, and that the inside view is distorted. I have stressed the reverse position to redress the balance somewhat. The balanced view, with which I should hope to conclude, is that change is a complex process. Without stimuli, usually from outside, and without a spread of knowledge from the vast reservoir that exists in the world as a whole, a local society is unlikely to develop. Yet the mere giving of stimuli, "encouraging development" or "teaching new crops," is as inadequate for producing development as is the mere availability of knowledge. The process by which such developments are accepted and then adapted to local conditions, and, in turn, bring about a reinterpretation of existing practices, is at least as important for the success of development. Yet understanding the local view of economic change is possible only if one is prepared to accept the earlier conclusion—that the local economy has a rationality that needs detailed analysis and a use of indigenous economic concepts.

These two ethnographic themes are so fundamental that they will not be further discussed here. Instead I shall concentrate on the two analytic themes: the relationship between a continuity of tradition and successful economic change, and the nature of the social reorganization that economic change requires. The two are closely interwoven. Thus, to take one change as a specific example, that of cocoa growing and processing, the *content* of the change was entirely introduced from outside—the crop itself, the techniques of fermenting, the bank that gave the loan, the registration of the Tolai Cocoa Project with the national government. Yet the attitudes and concepts brought to bear on this content were all long-standing ones—"traditional," from the short-term perspective of both Europeans and New Guineans, for whom what happened five years ago is ancient. Cocoa in the local context was another cash crop like the "traditional" copra crop. The highly flexible matrilineal system of land ownership meant that it was easy to get rapid planting of large areas, using "traditional" means of labour recruitment such as the granting of rights to garden use of land while shade coconuts were being established. Crop processing, though more complicated, was still a variation of the kind of processing used "traditionally" for copra. Subscribing for a jointly owned *kivung* drier was already "traditional," although the composition of *kivung* had changed markedly since 1875 when they were exclusively clan-based. Accepting a loan to finance a project was also traditional, and the traditional attitudes (of desiring to pay off a loan as quickly as possible so that the material assets would become the property of the subscribers themselves, and also of removing the stigma of indebtedness) were also originally applied to the bank loan. Cocoa fitted easily into patterns of local thought. People could more easily learn new techniques with a familiar model to work from.

Another aspect of the importance of familiarity was that the people could evaluate the likely profitability of the new crop in the same way that they evaluated copra. The delay in obtaining returns was not an important disadvantage, as it would have been in a subsistence cropping area; in fact, the shorter establishment period for cocoa may have been an attraction for copra growers. The possibility of building up lasting assets for the benefit of future generations by planting cocoa would seem to have been in growers' minds from the start, to judge by the way in which they registered their trees. This is a traditional way of judging how successful a business enterprise is likely to be. Although labour requirements for harvesting could not be accurately foreseen, wealthy landowners could afford to take a risk on them, even if smaller landowners held back until the yields were clear.

Many writers have commented on how readily technical innovations are adopted when they are seen to have a clear and immediate advantage: the advantage of steel axes over stone, or of penicillin over herbs. Yet these are only simpler examples of my general point, that when an innovation retains some continuity with the past, people can compare it with a known standard and to that extent are better able to judge its likely profitability. Only if it is likely to be profitable will it be accepted. An understanding of pre-existing means of estimating profitability—the underlying structure of local costs—is needed before one can predict local reaction to an innovation.

Yet another element of continuity is the role played by leaders in ensuring the acceptance of change. Most people do not go through all the calculations implied above, but they assume that respected individuals who accept the change have calculated. They copy leaders. Rogers (1962) has referred to this as the two-stage process in the adoption of innovations. But it implies that some structure of leadership exists prior to the change, although the relationship between the first-stage leaders—the innovators—and their followers—the accepters—may well not be one of formal authority. Some studies of innovation stress that innovators communicate best through informal channels. A pre-existing structure of leadership where people with recognized positions (but not necessarily formal authority) readily communicate informally throughout the society, would seem to favour the rapid spread of behaviours adopted by leaders. A readiness by such leaders to make changes would seem to provide the ideal condition for the adoption of innovations.

Even so, to continue with the example of Vunamami cocoa adoption, the long-term profitability of cocoa growing could not be accurately foreseen in advance. Returns now obviously depend on world market prices, and on climatic and disease conditions. Yet even within these unpredictable limits, the return to the peasant grower could still be greatly increased if less time were wasted in numbers of people individually bringing beans to centralized fermenteries. In other words, reorganization of the process of production continues long after the adoption of an innovation, and may not be completed for many years. For productive organization to change, there must be a degree of flexibility in other social groupings; and in this case it would seem that rigidity has begun to set in, following Administration control of the Project, with great pressure from the top for further centralization. This would make the crop even less profitable for the peasant grower, unless some channel for the expression of grower opinion emerges. It could well kill the cocoa industry entirely while curing inefficiencies in marketing and fermenting. Adoption of innovations without the accompaniment of social organizational change can be self-limiting; the appropriate changes do not necessarily follow automatically.

Yet in Vunamami the important technological changes up to 1950 have all been followed by social reorganizations that have successfully institutionalized the innovations or made them profitable. The central problem of this work is to try and explain why.

The first reason is that the statement contains a tautology. Only those technological changes that have been followed by social reorganization are ones that have been "important." Numerous changes have been introduced that have not been economical or have not been followed by the requisite social changes, and they have either remained unimportant or have disappeared entirely. Kapok trees were introduced by the Germans; without the marketing arrangements to use the product in local upholstery, they remain unimportant trees. Rice, repeatedly introduced by Agricultural Officers and by the Japanese, is an uneconomic crop in New Guinea because of its high labour requirements unless machinery can be used; problems of milling and marketing have ensured its failure except at times of extreme starvation or depression. Centralized village copra driers in the 1930's proved uneconomic because of the costs of transport, although village feelings of patriotism got them started; social reorganization in the late 1940's and 1950's ensured the success of small copra driers, however, although reforms in the transport system are now making larger driers profitable for store owners living along the main roads. Whether any of the unsuccessful crops might have been successful if the necessary social changes had also occurred is a meaningless speculation. All that can be said is that a certain number of the plethora of innovations that are constantly occurring are not successful, are not adopted over wide areas, and are unimportant. They occasion or involve no social changes. They must be considered different from those where economic profitability was present, given the cost structure of peasant society, and where social changes occurred. The calculations of economic profitability, and its principal dependence on the labour inputs needed by peasant farmers, have already been discussed. Let us now turn to the social and political processes involved in successful economic changes.

As described in the Introduction, four such changes can be isolated: the development of trading in coconuts, the planting of coconuts, the development of copra processing, and the development of the more complicated cocoa growing and marketing organization. Dates for each change can be given: 1878 for the first reign of King Copra; 1897 for the start of coconut planting on a large scale following the adoption of the Reserve policy; 1948 as the beginning of successful copra processing, after a false start in the 1930's; and 1953, the year of the Vunamami Cacao Marketing Account, as the start of cocoa processing and marketing.

A first point to note is that each of these economic changes *followed* fairly closely a preceding political change. By 1878 the pre-contact situation, in which the effective political units had been the small hamlets of about thirty persons, had changed dramatically in Vunamami on the coast. Before 1875 these hamlets had often fought one another, even within the boundaries of the same larger unit, the village, that periodically combined under a strong fighting leader (*a luluai na winarubu*). The hamlet leaders, rich men and clan *lualua*, were the significant politicians. During 1875–1876 the presence of both missionaries and traders served to bring the village units into greater prominence, and to concentrate power in the hands of village heads. Churchbuilding could be done only on a basis of units of two hundred individuals—that is, villages—and the hamlet head who sponsored the church became, for church purposes, the village head. The several big men of a coastal village tended to monopolize trade with Europeans, and with their increasing wealth they acquired the guns that established them as village leaders. Guns were used against inland villages, and the fighting was organized and conducted by village units rather than being the petty ambushing and killing practised between hamlets. The infrequently activated "crisis" form of indigenous organization came to be the regular form for everyday action, under a single leader.

A similar political change took place before 1897. Both the war of 1890 and that of 1893 had involved *ad hoc* alliances of several villages, numbering up to two thousand men, against the Europeans. These had emerged, during the years preceding, as groupings allied by a large degree of intermarriage, by common links along a chain of trade running inland, and presumably by the alliances of *tubuan* owners, but with no formal political unity aside from that provided by the needs of the moment and by the energy of the man who organized the alliance. But in 1893 the defeat of the alliance and the killing of its leader did not destroy it, as had been the case heretofore. The alliance was established as a permanent grouping under the recognized leadership of a *lualua* or *nambawan*, ToBobo, when Judge Hahl arrived in 1896. A new level of lasting political unity had emerged.

The Mandate of 1921 marked a political retrogression for the local people, until an office of Paramount Luluai was reinstituted in place of the *lualua* in 1929. The Paramountcies may have been somewhat larger than the jurisdictions of the *lualua* before 1921, but this is not entirely clear. There were, in the Kokopo Sub-district, exactly the same number of each, and they were based on the same villages, Vunamami, Birara, Raluana, Toma, and so on—though now the populations were larger, ranging up to four thousand. The units of the 1893 alliance persisted as the largest effective local units, though it was not until 1937, the beginning of "Village Councils" as local courts in Rabaul District, and the appointment of an effective Paramount in Vunamami, that the units began to take over new activities.

In 1950, with the establishment of Local Government Councils, the area advanced again in political organization. The councils were in many ways a continuation of the Paramountcies, but their jurisdictions were enlarged. Vunadidir, Toma, and Nangananga Paracountcies combined to form one council; Vunamami was joined by a few villages from outside, and over the next ten years most of Birara Paramountcy joined it, though Raluana remained aloof. Six thousand became an average council size. In their powers, too, particularly that of collecting tax money, the councils continued a practice that had been under way for the preceding thirteen years under the Paramounts and the village *Komiti*, but this *ad hoc* informal arrangement became formally recognized. And where the Paramount had occasionally been able to force his own decisions through unofficially but without any question, as a result of his own personal drive, now the authority of the Council president was validated by an election, and was universally accepted. With the emergence in 1952 of a new president, raised within the system, this wider political consolidation was further stabilized.

Further consolidation occurred in 1964, during the writing of this book, in which all the councils throughout the Gazelle Peninsula combined to form a Gazelle Council embracing 40,000 people. What economic change is presaged by this political consolidation will have to be the subject of a later study, as will the eventual consolidation of Papua and New Guinea into a single unified country. Enough has been said to make a *prima facie* case for linking wider political consolidation and economic change.

A third element of each political change must also be recalled from chapter 9: both the political consolidation and the subsequent economic innovations are, in local thinking at least if not exactly in fact, identified with a single dynamic leader.

Are these four cases to be dismissed as just coincidence? Or even if the interaction of political consolidation and economic change is accepted as one of cause and effect, are they to be viewed as resulting from the fortuitous emergence of a rare dynamic leader at a particular stage of history? I do not believe such a coincidence could occur four times within a single village, especially when four other coincidences would also have to be explained—namely, the availability of the external stimuli of knowledge, of traders, of administrative policies, and of agricultural extension at exactly the same time that the leaders emerged.

I prefer to try and connect the various observed events common to each of the four cycles, to show how they could be seen as part of a single logically related process, all interrelated with no one element as primary cause. I shall attempt to describe this process in generalized terms, as a hypothetical model of successful economic change in a wealthy agricultural society (i.e., one with more land and more jobs available than people to fill them). I shall refer back to Vunamami as a concrete example of the working of the model.

In the first place the elements of such a model must fit a society that was never stagnant and unchanging, though at any one time the dynamic forces that could provide movement might have been in balance, so that no over-all movement might be visible from the outside. I should thus postulate a continual flow of innovations as occurring, but virtually all of them proving uneconomic. I should also postulate a political system in which, at any one time, many persons are competing for the limited number of political and organizational offices available within any politically sovereign or quasi-autonomous unit. I shall refer to such individuals, in accordance with a terminology described in Salisbury (1964), as "executives." At the same time, the individuals who obtain the headships of each unit—"directors" in my 1964 terminology—are continually trying to expand their jurisdictions by influencing other groups, making alliances, and so on. A local "director" may be successful in combining units for a short time, but the larger units that he controls usually tend to fall apart when he dies, or when the emergency that called them into being declines. Politically there is a dynamic equilibrium.

I thus see the competition between "directors" (including aspirants to directorship) as the impetus towards political consolidation. In a situation of crisis, consolidation can be realized, taking a form very like those that have arisen in similar crisis situations in the past. But when the crisis is greater than usual, or lasts longer, the larger political unit of consolidation does not immediately fall apart, and allow the system to return to a low-level equilibrium.

The leader of such a successful consolidation has extremely wide powers. As I have shown (Salisbury 1964),[1] directors tend

[1] This article presents descriptive material in support of the present characterization of Melanesian leadership, and reconciles the practical despotism commonly found with the universal democratic ideology which is most commonly described and analysed. The article is based on Tolai experience but uses Highland materials to confirm the picture. Subsequent

to have a different order of power from that exercised by their executives. The latter are seeking promotion by trying to please their superiors and their supporters, and their actions are bound by the rules or customary expectations and sanctions of both sides. A director is to some degree limited in power by the need to placate his followers, but the best way of satisfying his followers is for him to gain material benefits and prestige for them by his leadership. If he can do that, then he is granted a wide freedom to ignore normal canons of behaviour and to act as he sees fit. He can, in other words, be despotic; he can act according to his own wishes. These may not involve oppression of followers, though success in some of his actions may lead to the acceptance of a degree of oppression in others. Over a long period of time, however, the limits of acceptance and the spheres of potential autonomous action by a director come to be more closely defined. He is more and more bound by the precedents of his own behaviour and that of his predecessors. There develop expectations regarding the director role.

But the director who emerges at the head of a newly (if temporarily) consolidated political unit is not so limited. There are few, if any, pre-existing expectations about his position; even oppression by him is tolerated in the light of anticipated benefits that will accrue from the actions of a wider unit, under his leadership, and, for a short time at least, people suspend judgement about the wisdom of many of his actions. The crucial issue is whether the crisis that brought him to power is resolved. If it is, he will be remembered as a successful leader, who unified his people and brought lasting benefits. If it is not, he will either be largely forgotten, or he will be remembered as a self-seeking aspirant to power, whom the people rejected as a despot—though he may at the same time anticipate successful unification of society under another leader.

But if it is a successful political consolidation that makes a man remembered as a leader, rather than any extraordinary inherent personal abilities, we need to consider what makes for political success. One aspect has been indicated in chapter 9—the need to be able to mobilize some loyalty to or pride in the consolidated larger unit. A second attempt to consolidate a unit is thus more

---

studies have tended to confirm the existence of despotism indigenously but at the same time to question whether all directors were despotic.

likely to succeed than the first, since the first attempt is likely to have produced some awareness of the possibility of the wider unit's existing. It is likely to have thrown up a name or slogan expressing loyalty to the wider unit that a politician can use to gain support at the second attempt.

A second aspect, one that is most central to this book, is that if an economically profitable technological innovation is introduced concurrently with a successful political consolidation, the material benefits accruing are likely to be attributed to the consolidation. Its disadvantages are more likely to be forgotten, and only its advantages remembered. Reciprocally, the fact of political consolidation makes the success of a technological innovation more likely.

In the first place, the leader in a unification has all the ideal characteristics of an economic innovator: he is personally respected as more than merely the occupant of a defined political position; in order to have effected the unification he must have a wide network of informal communication links; his judgements of what is the right course to be taken are likely to be accepted on trust by followers, at least for a trial period. Initial costs, such as the cost of new tools to replace those rendered obsolete by the change, may be ignored in a flush of enthusiasm for following such a leader, when, without that enthusiasm, these costs might be felt to make a desirable long-term change unprofitable in the short run.

This does not mean that the political leader must be an inventor, or even the first to recognize the merits of an innovation brought from outside. As with the acceptance of copra driers in Vunamami in the late 1930's, he may merely advocate something that has been invented elsewhere, or, as with the growing of cocoa, the merits of the innovation may already have been widely recognized. But giving his approval to the innovation transforms it: instead of being known but impractical, it becomes popular and possible. In popular thought at least, the name of the politician becomes identified with the technological innovation.

In the second place, the fact of unification provides the degree of social organizational flexibility that is desirable if the most efficient means of arranging production is to emerge. Thus the new Vunamami Local Government Council was ready to experiment with running its own fermentery at Ngatur, but when an improved organization for financing and marketing was suggested in the form of the Tolai Cocoa Project, no rigid commitment to the Vunamami Cacao Marketing Account had developed. Further experimentation was still acceptable, and in many ways people were interested in explicitly trying out new organizational forms —committees, co-operatives, budgeting—as a result of the success of the political change.

On a third, more material, level we can also see that wider political unity tends to make profitable economic enterprises that would not have been profitable within smaller political units. This is not simply a matter of economies of scale, although these do enter in. Many of the innovations, such as the small copra driers, required neither larger work forces nor a mass-marketing system for their success. They would have been technically possible before the political consolidations of the 1930's. Even the central fermenteries of the Tolai Cocoa Project could have been paid for (though not so rapidly) out of growers' revenues. My own calculations of the labour and capital requirements for running Ravalien plantation and its fermentery showed that they were all technically within the capabilities of Vunamami village in 1961.

But with wider political unity the market for raising capital is less restricted; a village would not have to devote its entire resources to a single project if it had access to support from a Council. For Vunamami village to buy and operate Ravalien plantation would have meant that all other projects would have had to be ignored, and that if that one project had failed (perhaps for extraneous or petty reasons like the dishonesty of one man) then the village would have suffered immeasurably. The village's capital resources could not justify the risk; for such a major purchase the capital market provided by a Council, and its reserve funds, was the minimal one that could finance it.

The form of the capital holding corporation is also important, as the discussion of businesses in chapter 7 showed. In establishing public support for such corporations, whether co-operative or private, it is of utmost importance that the people should feel that they have some control over the leaders, or some participation in planning the future use of the resources of the corporation. People should feel that if their interests are ignored, there is a superior authority to which they can appeal. The suspicion of businesses run by important political figures, who may with impunity exploit the ordinary public, has been noted. By their political connections these men can get away with exploitation. In a colonial situation there is little faith that the foreign administering power will support an ordinary person against politically powerful figures; only at levels of grouping at which political decisions are made by New Guineans is there a feeling that such support will be guaranteed. Within a politically autonomous village, the lineage may remain the largest important capital-holding unit (see Plotnicov and Befu 1961), with the village providing sanctions in case of disputes. Within the framework of a regional political structure village enterprises may be possible. With supra-village political groupings, *kivung* recruiting from several clans develop. The size of the largest economic grouping in a society tends, in short, to be somewhat below the size of the largest political grouping. Unification permits larger capital-holding units.[2]

A fourth contribution of political unification to economic success may be generally described as being in the field of communications. By this I do not mean simply the building of roads or bridges or other items that are listed in the capital requirements budgets for developing countries under the heading "communications." Rather, I include communication in the broad sense, that is, the development of group unity by bringing people together who formerly were isolated. We have seen how eliminating inter-hamlet feuding and consolidating the powers of village leaders combined with the presence of missions and traders to open the way for copra trading inland. The changing emphasis of trading, from inter-village delayed barter to open-market cash trading with bargaining, was a consequence of political consolidation. Political consolidation made it possible for individuals to roam widely and to meet from the supply side the opportunities which the presence of traders presented in providing a mass demand. So, too, the expansion of possibilities for recruiting workers and acquiring new knowledge are a matter of communications. The presence of large teams of workers was vital in resettlement schemes that involved clearing virgin forest. The recruitment and support of teams of village workers for the Council scheme was as dependent on the development of better and more extensive communications as was

[2] When, as sometimes happens, a single business is as great as the country in which it is located, the situation is unstable and fraught with suspicions of exploitation. The existence of international corporations that are often larger than the national unit within which they are operating poses one of the most urgent problems of political control in developing countries today.

the hiring of workers from western New Britain and the New Guinea Highlands to work on the individual landlord schemes promoted by the Department of Agriculture. Yet another aspect of widened communications with political consolidation was the way in which new political bodies or offices provided channels for disseminating information about innovations. ToBobo, as representative of an enlarged social grouping, had direct contacts with higher levels of the German administration than his predecessors who had led only villages. These channels of communication permitted the land situation to be clarified and information about coconut planting to be disseminated. In 1950 the use by the Agricultural Extension Officer of the forum provided by the new council was an important way of acquainting the people with the details of the new crop, cocoa.

A final and perhaps most fundamental connection between the success of moves for political consolidation and the success of technological innovations lies in the area of education and the provision of skilled managerial manpower. First let us take the situation before unification, at, for example, the time when villages consolidated under ToBobo or into Paramountcies. As managers each village had its own "director" in the form of a *luluai* or big man; there may have been in each village a single contender for his directorship. There may also have been another eight executives at various levels, men who were active organizers but who were unlikely to lead their villages or to give *matamatam*. Each village had perhaps ten politically active men in its population of two hundred (or 5 percent), with only one percent being top-level directors. After unification, it would not be necessary for the new single director of the emergent Paramountcy to remove any of the existing leaders of village units from their positions, because all the former tasks would still have to be performed. His position would be an additional one, while a whole new range of executive positions would be opened up—the people working directly under the newly emerged director, co-ordinating activities throughout the Paramountcy, most of which had not existed under the previous system of independent villages. If as many jobs were created for each director as previously existed in the villages, it would mean an addition of eight central bureaucrats plus the director (and one rival). For the population of 2,000 the number of politically active persons would rise from 100 to 110. The overhead "organizational" costs of running a political grouping of this size would increase, but not so fast as its effectiveness in facilitating economic productivity. Provided an appropriate economic innovation was in prospect, similar gains could be expected at each unification.

The opening up of this type of position would have a double importance, however. These positions are ones that would likely be available for patronage gift by the new director. To them he would presumably appoint individuals representing several key areas. Some of them would be progressive former directors of villages whom he could rely on to support his economic and political innovations. Their promotion would then leave vacancies for the mobility of younger executives to lead villages. At the same time, if the pattern of patronage appointments described in chapters 8 and 9 were followed, still other young men would be selected out for direct appointment to assist the director, to be trained to succeed him. In this way political unification would open up opportunities for social mobility at all levels.

Yet if there were economic prosperity at the same time, the less successful village headmen who had not been promoted but who had not lost their jobs would not feel slighted, for additional work of organization would devolve on them. They would be better off financially and would not at first realize that they were now executives and not directors. They would not be an inevitable nucleus of a dissatisfied "conservative" wing, especially if the new leader could, as Vunamami leaders all did, maintain that he had a claim to being a "traditional" leader. Conservatives could see the new leader as the defender of tradition against overwhelming modern corruption, and could ascribe the success of his actions to the way in which he preserved continuity with the past. "Radicals" might, at the same time, praise him for his innovations. The result would be an upsurge of patriotism throughout the wider group, a recognition that "we," a newly unified single body, achieved success together. Each social segment would be satisfied, and all would focus their satisfaction on the political leader who would be seen as the cause of prosperity. Increased efficiency in local management by existing leaders could be accompanied by the emergence of new managers at the wider group level.

Such managers would need training. Traditional activities like those connected with shell money and the *tubuan*, if continued, would still train many organizational entrepreneurs. The new political positions would offer comparable training, and the same motivation for success, in both financial and prestige terms. It would be at a somewhat higher level, however. Thus when Vunamami Council was formed there was a group of young men whom Enos had previously patronized and organized to run a volunteer school. These men he appointed as the junior Council executives right at the start; they became skilled in the new organizational techniques along with the old, presiding over meetings, organizing committees, writing minutes, preparing budgets, handling complaints, getting formal Administration approval of decisions, and so on.

But when the technological innovations began to require organizational changes and flexible new-style managers, a small supply of appropriately trained people would be at hand. As happened in Vunamami, some of the original political appointees could transfer to the new enterprises, taking their training with them and retaining personal ties with their old colleagues. Their departure would open up further vacancies in the political hierarchy, with possibilities of more rapid promotion all round. Economic expansion would continue the general satisfaction and keep the same leader in power.

Expansion may not continue indefinitely and the model's course may break down. The supply of trained managers may be inadequate, although the Vunamami experience suggests that a gap of three years between the commencement of managerial training through politics, and the need for reform of the productive organization may be enough to start the flow. This assumes the presence, however, of a pool of generally educated young men. The number trained in three years can provide the cadre to train more in a steady flow for the future. Expansion may also slow down for economic reasons—declining world market prices for copra and cocoa are examples for Vunamami—but some slowing down may not negate all support for the leader and the new régime. As long as there are still some rungs free on the executive ladder and the leader can promote more of his supporters without demoting other people, opposition will be negligible. But as soon as the ladder is full, and the only alternative to waiting for a senior person to die or retire is to depose him (or get his superior to dismiss him), unrest is likely to occur. The leader will depart (or become oppressive). The political structure will become rigidified and politics will become a jockeying for limited positions, not a struggle to create imaginative policy.

But the process of self-sustained growth is the one that most concerns us here. The picture of this process that has emerged in this final discussion is one that includes far more than merely economic factors such as the availability of capital or an increase in gross national product. Technological innovation is seen as perhaps the most basic factor in producing growth. But if an innovation is not economically feasible or justified in terms of the local cost structure (which may include high interest rates because of a shortage of locally generated capital), then it will not produce results. Economic factors are thus vital as providing the *possibility* for self-sustained growth. They may more often provide the *barrier* to it.

But the main precipitant cause, triggering off the growth made potential by technological innovations in societies which, like Vunamami, are relatively affluent and not agriculturally involuted (Geertz 1963*b*) is, I maintain, one of organization. By this term I mean much more than merely economic entrepreneurship. True, individuals must be free to take risks and exploit economic opportunities as they see them, but this is a minor aspect of what is needed. A society attempting to grow by individual entrepreneurs acting alone would not get far. Growth requires that individuals must be able to invent organizational forms, or to adapt them creatively, both to get production going efficiently and to provide the supporting institutions ensuring that contracts are kept, that information can be communicated, and that training can take place. In a word, growth requires political development.

On the broad level this may well be a matter of the consolidation of small, quasi-autonomous political units into larger wholes —a process which, when viewed from the village level of Vunamami, appears to offer possibilities into the distant future. Consolidation of an already unified nation-state could imply the involvement of a greater number of people in the policy decisions of that society, by means of an improvement in the administrative structure. In either case political activity provides the improved security and communications that are required for economic development. It is also vital in providing the spur of leadership, the opportunities for mobility, and the managers to cope with organizing economic production.

On the village level, by contrast, the implications of organizational change appear dramatically in the tables given in chapters 3 and 4 of the proportions of manpower employed in various activities. Under the pre-1875 non-expanding economy, 70 percent of people's time was spent in production and distribution, 10 percent in sickness, and 20 percent in "organizational" activity. (I have included 2 percent of the trading category as being *tabu* trading and hence a political organizational activity.) Slight increases in political activity followed each consolidation, but since productive activities also subsequently increased, there was not much cumulative change. The major changes have come since the 1940's as more people have gone into paid labour, until the time expenditure is now 52 percent in production and distribution, 6 percent in sickness, and 42 percent in other activities. Most of these other activities have not been work for European primary producers, but work within the village as providers of administrative services. Self-sustained growth will mean the continuance of this trend. What "development" means for the village is the provision of the services of education, justice, communications, entertainment, religion, and family life on a steadily increasing scale, and by individuals who are paid to specialize in providing those services more efficiently than before. This has meant an increase in the proportion of incomes paid in taxation—directly to the Council, indirectly to the Central Administration, and in the form of church collections and offerings and *nidok* contributions to the *tubuan*. I have estimated annual *tubuan* contributions (Salisbury 1966) as 35 percent of *tabu* incomes. I estimate the "taxes" paid in cash as about the same proportion of cash receipts.

But those who provide services in turn buy food and housing from the primary producers. Incomes have risen all around, so that after-tax incomes may well be no less than they were ten years earlier, while the services received have increased many times. The proportion of non-primary producers that can be supported (hence also the level of services that primary producers can expect) clearly depends on the level of productivity of primary production. Yet the availability of employment outside primary production has helped directly in raising the efficiency of that production. Though the absolute size of the primary productive labour force has not declined, the availability of a variety of jobs has meant a highly mobile labour force, and much switching from less rewarding forms of primary production to those giving a higher return per man-day. Thus the increase in service personnel within the society has had the multiplier effect of raising the incomes of primary producers while also improving the efficiency of production.

In short, at the local level, the process of economic development can be seen as involving both technological improvement and the desire by the people to provide increased services for themselves. Only with technological improvement can a larger proportion of the people be "freed from the productive process." Only if there is a positive pressure for more services, however, will that liberation occur. Only if there is full employment will the service providers not be seen as exploiting the "producers." Only if the people are prepared and able to provide those services for themselves will there be a cumulative increase in the flow of benefits from those services. The people of Vunamami can look back with nostalgia to the days when the *tubuan* was *a matanitu kai ra tarai* —when the people provided the services of government for themselves. They can appropriately feel that their traditions are worth preserving because they strengthen them in their adoption of sustained economic change. They appreciate the interdependence of political consolidation and economic development.

Appendices

Appendix

A

Land Use and Productivity

Acreages under various crops cultivated by Vunamami people were estimated on the basis of surveys of a limited number of plots, and inquiries about the crops on all other plots, average sizes of which were taken as three-quarters of an acre for house sites and three and a half acres for cultivated plots. These figures are consistent with both the total village area and the sample surveyed.

ACREAGES OWNED BY VUNAMAMI RESIDENTS,
IN USE FOR VARIOUS PURPOSES

Location	House Sites	Sole Coco-nuts	Mixed Nuts, Cocoa	Sole Cocoa	Food Gardens	Public Use	Bush
Within Vunamami	18	94.5	178.5	35	14	14	—
In walking range	—	49	101.5	5	1.5	—	7
Out of walking range	—	7	28	—	—	—	—
New distant areas	—	—	90	15	—	—	—
Total	18	150.5	398	55	15.5	14	7

To permit yield figures to be compiled, I make the following adjustments to allow for areas not yet in full bearing, and for areas under mixed cropping, to give a figure of "effective acreage" equivalent to full-bearing acreage under a sole crop. I take an acre of house site to yield half an effective acre of coconuts, and an acre of mixed coconuts and cocoa to equal half an acre of coconuts, plus two-thirds of an acre of cocoa. Seventy acres of coconuts were immature (mainly in distant areas); 70 acres of cocoa were in full bearing, 45 were bearing at half-volume, 20 were just coming into bearing, and the rest were

355

immature. This gives an effective acreage of coconuts of 269 acres and of cocoa of 92.5 acres of bearing trees.

Yields were calculated from the figures of total sales of copra to Bitatali Co-operative by residents of Vunamami, and of sales of wet

YIELDS PER ACRE UNDER PEASANT
AND PLANTATION CULTIVATION

	Effective Acreage	*Total Yield*	*Yield per Acre*	*Plantation Yields**
Copra	269	51 tons	3.8 cwt.	5.7 cwt.
Cocoa	92.5	10.5 tons	2.3 cwt.	6.7 cwt.

* Figures for plantation yields are taken for copra from Australia (1953*a*:34) and for cocoa from Henderson (1954:31).

cocoa beans to Talimut fermentery by Vunamami residents (divided by 2.5 to give a figure for dry beans). Owners of a few plots outside walking range did not sell produce at these agencies, but the amounts omitted are small—perhaps a ton of copra sold directly to the C.M.B. and 400 lbs. of cocoa sold to Ngatur fermentery. The majority of distant plots had not come into bearing in 1961.

Appendix

B

Time Budgets

All operations of work in Vunamami were extensively observed and timed between April and September 1961. An assistant was then given the names of four individuals each week whose activities he recorded from 4 September to 20 November 1961. Different names were selected each week from a panel of 27 names, providing a stratified sample of the 75 Vunamami men not employed in regular wage labour. They included the following categories:

(1) 4 wealthy landowing men aged between 45 and 60
(2) 4 wealthy landowning men aged between 30 and 45
(3) 8 poorer men aged between 40 and 60
(4) 5 poorer men aged between 20 and 40
(5) 6 men with little land but skilled in crafts or business.

These categories are used in the table below.

The assistant recorded activities in the vernacular. He did not ask about Sunday work, for it would be an insult in Vunamami to suggest that one did not observe the Sabbath. Detail was sufficient to permit direct classification of the work as shown except for three cases. (*a*) When a site of new planting was listed and both coconuts and cocoa were being planted at that site, I have allocated half the work of owners to planting coconuts and half to planting cocoa. Non-owners' work at the same sites was for the planting of gardens under immature trees. (*b*) A listing of "*kana uma*" (his garden) was taken to mean subsistence gardening, although the word can be used for a coconut planting. (*c*) A report of "his coconuts" or "weeding his coconuts" was taken to mean coconut planting (or maintenance), unless it was

TIME ALLOCATION OF VUNAMAMI NON-WAGE WORKERS, 1961

Activity	(1)	(2)	(3)	(4)	(5)	All
	*Percentage of Time Spent by each Category of Worker**					
(a) Sickness	—	4 (1)	—	—	2 (1½)	1 (2½)
(b) Ceremonies, meetings, etc.	10 (4½)	4 (1)	4 (2)	3 (1)	6 (4)	6 (12½)
(c) Trading, etc.; Co-op meetings	16 (7)	—	7 (4)	11 (4)	7 (4½)	9 (19½)
(d) Businesses, pigs, carpentry	5 (2)	—	—	—	24 (15½)	8 (17½)
(e) Fishing	—	6 (½)	25 (14)	26 (9)	12 (7½)	14 (32)
(f) Gardening	11 (5)	8 (2)	14 (8)	10 (3½)	7 (4½)	10 (23)
(g) Coconut planting	1 (½)	20 (5)	2 (1)	6 (2)	6 (4)	6 (12½)
(h) Copra	41 (18)	—	5 (3)	3 (1)	6 (4)	12 (26)
(i) Cocoa planting	1 (½)	18 (4½)	9 (5)	6 (2)	6 (4)	7 (16)
(j) Cocoa production	2 (1)	27 (6½)	14 (8)	11 (4)	8 (5)	11 (24½)
(k) Houses, crafts	6 (2½)	8 (2)	6 (3½)	7 (2½)	6 (4)	6 (14½)
(l) Casual labour	1 (1½)	2 (½)	5 (2½)	7 (2½)	1 (½)	3 (6½)
(m) Idle, visits	6 (2½)	2 (½)	9 (5)	9 (3)	7 (4½)	7 (15½)
	100 (44)	100 (24½)	100 (56)	100 (34½)	100 (63½)	100 (222½)

* Categories of worker are listed in the text. Figures of man-days are given in parentheses.

followed next afternoon or day by a report of "splits/dries coconuts," when it was classed as copra production.

The three months surveyed (September–November) are probably close to yearly averages, since they include two months of the dry trade-wind season and one month of the wet northwesterly monsoon, with the following qualifications: (i) fishing activity is high, with traps being made so as to be ready for the monsoon period; (ii) cocoa production involved one month of secondary flush and two months of low production and therefore may be slightly low; (iii) ceremonial activities were few following a hectic month in August; (iv) sickness figures are lower than those indicated by aid-post attendances.

The established coconut plantings of the older landed men and the men's involvement in ceremonies, politics, and finance are clearly reflected. So too are the investments by younger landed men in planting coconuts and cocoa. Men with little land show little variation by age. They spend much time in fishing—a marginally productive activity—for this is the season for it, and the remainder of their time is spread in small amounts over a variety of tasks. They show the most underemployment. The non-landed craftsmen show an intermediate pattern; they do a variety of jobs to fill in time when not using their skills, but they also have political and financial interests. It should be noted that most idle time is in half-day units, when one task has been completed and there is not sufficient time to warrant travelling to another distant work site.

A smaller sample of time budgets was obtained for men from the inland villages of Vunabalbal and Bitarebarebe, for comparison with the Vunamami figures. The percentages are listed below:

TIME ALLOCATION OF VUNABALBAL AND
BITAREBAREBE NON-WAGE WORKERS, 1961

	Percentage of Time Spent by each Category of Worker*					
Activity	(1)	(2)	(3)	(4)	(5)	All
(a) Sickness	8	6	—	—	3	5
(b) Ceremonies, etc.	2	2	—	—	—	1
(c) Trading, etc.	7	8	—	—	—	4
(d) Businesses, etc.	3	2	—	—	47	10
(e) Fishing	—	—	7	—	—	1
(f) Gardening	9	6	17	30	—	9
(g) Coconut planting	3	8	23	10	6	9
(h) Copra production	19	8	—	—	—	8
(i) Cocoa planting	—	27	27	10	13	15
(j) Cocoa production	24	16	17	10	22	20
(k) Houses, crafts	3	2	—	—	6	3
(l) Casual labour	17	10	3	40	3	12
(m) Idle, etc.	3	4	7	—	—	3
	100	100	100	100	100	100
	(29)	(24½)	(15)	(5)	(16)	(89½)

* Categories of workers are listed in the text. Figures in parentheses are of man-days. The sample was small and this table must be viewed as highly approximate.

Over-all trends appear despite the smallness of the sample: The time-allocation pattern repeats the Vunamami pattern of older landed men involved in cash cropping, younger landed men in planting tree crops, and landless men in varied activities. The contrast in time use resulting from more land being available, less early in-

involvement in coconuts, and more involvement in cocoa is also evident. Men with only a little land spend time planting cocoa and not
fishing; underemployment is lower; casual labour is much used for
road clearing in the bush; greater wealth in these villages results in a
fuller employment of tradesmen.

Neither table includes wage workers, who were discussed in chapter 4, and were included (with migrants) in the calculations to give
the final column of Table 4. In Table 4 activities $a + m$, $b + l$, and
$d +$ wage labour have been combined, and seasonal adjustments made.

Appendix

C

Household Incomes

For each Vunamami household a gross income was computed, based on records of cocoa sold to Talimut fermentery, and of copra to Bitatali Co-op; on known and estimated salaries of those employed; on estimates of drier usage or volume of contract work; on average yields from fishing; and on a few business records kept by individuals. No attempt was made to compute subsistence income, marketplace sales of food, yield from traditional business or skills, or yield from businesses where no records were kept. Resulting figures are thus conservative, but not exceedingly so. Seven households have been omitted from the tabulation because they could not be positively identified in the records. They were mainly small households of youngish cash croppers with two dependents.

The table on page 362 shows the households with various types of composition.

For households with only one male worker the average incomes for various sized households were as follows: one or two persons, £66.8; three persons, £107.3; four persons, £87.1; five persons, £133.1; six persons, £55.9; seven persons, £140.2; eight or more persons, £286.2.

Over all, the ranges in incomes were as follows: o–£20, thirteen households; £21–£50, ten households; £51–£100, nineteen households; £101–£200, nineteen households; £201–£300, eight households; £301–£400, two households; £401–£500, four households; £501 and up, four households.

HOUSEHOLD COMPOSITION AND INCOMES IN VUNAMAMI

Number of Members in Household	Number of Males of Working Age				Total
	0	1	2	3&4	
1	3	1	—	—	4
2	2	3	1	—	6
3	1	6	—	—	7
4	—	10	—	—	10
5	—	12	2	—	14
6	1	7	2	—	10
7	1	6	3	—	10
8	—	3	—	—	3
9	—	6	3	—	9
10–14	—	3	1	2	6
	8	57	12	2	79
Average income in £'s	10.6	136.7	283.2	307.5	150.5

The sources of income (fees to contractors being counted as a wage income, and fishing returns as business income) were:

from cash cropping	£ 4,995
from wage income	£ 5,790
from businesses	£ 1,082
Total	£11,867

It will be realized that households with no male worker are those of widows or aged men; six of them had less than £20 income, and the other two had between £21 and £50. They will be omitted in tabulations classifying households in relation to the characteristics of household heads.

(a) *Income by Age of Household Head*

Birthdate of Household Head	Number of Males of Working Age	
	1	2, 3, or 4
Before 1920	£ 88.7 (20)	£348.2 (6)
1921–1930	£173.5 (30)	£273.5 (5)
1931 and after	£121.5 (7)	£178.9 (3)

Figures in parentheses are the number of households on which averages are based.

The modal household pattern is of a single family, headed by a man in his thirties, with possibly an aged father as a dependent. Such families receive closest to the modal income. Single family households with older heads receive markedly less income, being almost exclusively cash croppers or fishermen. Those with younger heads have not yet reached their peak of earnings. The highest incomes are received by households where the older household head has been successful either as a white-collar worker or as a businessman, and has one or more dependent adult males living in his household. Multiple-family households with young heads usually have a relatively unsuccessful father living with a son who heads the household. The father still cash crops or fishes.

(b) Income by Occupation of Household Head

When households are classified in terms of the major source of income of the household head, the pattern becomes clearer. For six households where fishing was the major source of income the average income was £32.3. For 37 households of cash croppers the average income was £129.6. For 24 where the household head was a wage earner, the average was £239, and for five where he was predominantly a businessman the average was £266.7. The very highest incomes were obtained by those who earned salaries but also owned businesses and employed workers to grow cash crops.

I wish to thank Miss Katharine Roback for help with these tabulations.

Appendix

D

Expenditures

No attempt was made to obtain comprehensive household budgets, in view of the problems of extended sampling over a period of time, of great inter-family variation, and the difficulties of ensuring correct record-keeping. The following reconstructions of average expenditures for three "family types" are based on small sample data, or on aggregate figures as explained below. The three type families are those of (A) a cash cropper in his thirties with a wife and three children; (B) a wage-earner with a wife, five children, and an aged father and mother; and (C) an older businessman, with a wife, a twenty-five-year-old son and his wife, a widowed sister, and two teen-aged children.

(*1*) *Food costs.*—Six families, two of cash croppers with three and four members, two of wage earners with six and seven members, and two of businessmen, also with six and seven members, were each studied for one week regarding their food consumption. There was a consistent pattern of meals throughout; breakfast was of carbohydrate plus tea; lunch was either not taken or was a small amount of carbohydrate; evening meals included carbohydrate, a green vegetable, and usually some protein—tinned fish or meat. On Saturday and Sunday breakfasts included a tidbit, and both midday and evening meals contained protein. Richer families differed from the poorer ones in many ways. At breakfast their tea had milk in it, and the carbohydrate was biscuits or bread rather than bananas or sweet potato; children in poorer families always had carbohydrate, but the adults sometimes went without. At midday the richer families, though not eating heavily, often had a green vegetable or a tin of fish shared among six or seven persons as a relish; poorer families often did not eat, especially if they were working in the fields. For evening meals a green vege-

Item	Expenditures in £'s for Households		
	A	B	C
Food for cash	29	62.4	80.8
Household goods and mainte-nance	2	15	20
Clothing	4	10	11
Housing repairs	—	6	10
Luxuries: tobacco	5	20	20
travel	1	15	20
parties, etc.	1	10	20
Taxes: Council	5	10	11
church	5	20	25
Total recurrent expenditures	£ 52	£168.4	£217.4
Increased household goods	2	25	20
New housing	20	40	30
Co-op subscriptions	5	10	15
Fermentery equity	5	1	20
Ravalien purchase	4	5	5
Church rebuilding	2	8	10
Total capital expenditures	£ 38	£ 89	£100
Average income	£110	£286	£307
Balance for saving or optional expenses	£ 20	£ 28.6	−£10.8

table was almost universal, but poorer families tended to have rice and tinned fish, whereas the richer ones ate sweet potatoes or taro (perhaps with coconut cream) and fresh fish, pork, or corned beef. Cash expenditures, including market purchases, averaged 11s. 1½d. for cash croppers (8s. 3d. + 14s.), 24s. for wage earners (24s. + 24s.), and 33s. for businessmen (37s. + 29s.). These weekly averages have been multiplied by 52 to give the figures in the table.

All households also ate home-produced foods. The proportion can be calculated from the estimates on page 366 of the source of food for particular meals. If one weights the importance of the three meals as 2:1:4, it indicates that wage-earner households produce 61 percent of their food, businessmen households 63 percent, and cash croppers about 72 percent.

(2) *Household goods.*—An indication of the scale of purchases can be gained from a census of major items owned by 67 male-headed

households. Forty-five owned one or more bicycles (worth about £20 each when new), 53 used mosquito nets (worth £1 10s. each) with an average of about two per household, 26 owned sewing machines (about £35 new) with several being purchased in 1961 at prices up to £51, 15 had Tilley or Coleman lamps in working condition (cost about £7 10s.), and three had radios (then costing £25).

SOURCE OF FOOD FOR MEALS OF SIX VUNAMAMI HOUSEHOLDS*

	Breakfast		Source of Food Lunch		Dinner	
	Cash	Home	Cash	Home	Cash	Home
Cash croppers	7	7	$1\frac{1}{2}$	$5\frac{1}{2}$	$2\frac{1}{2}$	$11\frac{1}{2}$
Wage earners	10	4	3	10	$3\frac{1}{2}$	$10\frac{1}{2}$
Businessmen	8	6	$3\frac{1}{2}$	$8\frac{1}{2}$	4	10

* Figures are of numbers of meals bought for cash or composed of home-produced food.

Manufactured furniture was rare, although a few families had one or two metal beds, and many had a set of shelves, with or without a door, which served as bookcase, china cabinet, display case, etc. Most had one or two chairs and a screened food safe. Many had a homemade table/writing desk. All had cooking pots, plates and utensils, cups, dishes, mirrors, mats, hurricane lamps, flashlights, blankets, and numerous wooden or attaché cases containing clothes and valuables. About one-third of all households owned an iron, though only a few irons were heated by kerosene pressure pumps.

During 1961 ownership of consumer durables obviously increased. At least three cameras were bought during my stay, and many people were talking of buying radios; purchases of new sewing machines were compared at the newly formed Women's Club, where the monopoly of what in pidgin is called *singa* was being challenged. Stocks listed would be valued at £2,563 new, requiring an annual replacement of about one-sixth, or £427 worth. For 1961 I estimate that total expenditure was double that.

Additional expenditures on household maintenance—for soap, kerosene, flashlight batteries, or homemade coconut midrib brooms—I estimate from the total purchases at Bitatali Co-operative as being worth £250 per annum for Vunamami.

All these expenses are disproportionately incurred by the richer families; owning a kerosene lamp means one must buy kerosene, while flashlights need batteries. Older household heads own more and have higher maintenance expenses; younger wage-earning families tend to buy more new equipment. My household estimates reflect these trends, within the estimates of total Vunamami expenditure.

(3) *Clothing.*—Clothing in Vunamami, though always neat, was well-worn, carefully mended and washed. Women and children's clothes were homemade, and often elaborately embroidered. Everyone owned a white Sunday outfit, as well as two or more weekday sets of *laplap,* and shirt or blouse. Most men also wore shorts underneath. Wealthier men usually wore drip-dry white shirts, and they owned ties and plastic sandals; their laplaps were tailored. But annual replacement demands for everyone would be for two sets of clothing per person or £2 for a male, £1 for a female, and 10s. for a child, with a little more for a wealthy family. There was some increase in wardrobes in 1961: new outfits were bought for both the *matamatam* and the choir festival in August, and plastic sandals came into fashion. I have not attempted to allow for this small expenditure.

(4) *Housing.*—Of the 67 households surveyed, 52 had corrugated iron over at least part of the roof. A full roof cost about £200; a small half-roof might cost £60. Twenty-four houses had at least one water tank, costing £50, and ten had used sawn timbers for the frame, averaging about £20. Nails for any house cost over £5. Exclusive of any costs of hiring carpenters, paying for one's own labour, acquiring or transporting local materials, and so on, the total cash investment in housing in Vunamami was thus about £8,500. Local materials depreciate rapidly because of termites and rot, but European materials are re-used in later structures. Many houses had improvements or repairs made in 1961, and more than ten houses were in various stages of construction, with owners buying new materials and incorporating them into the structures whenever cash was available. I estimate a total outlay of about £1,400 for materials, of which about £200 would have been for repairs and minor improvements. Although more repairs would be needed in the existing houses of richer people, all types of household were involved in the housing boom.

(5) *Luxuries.*—Only universal luxuries have been itemized, other expenses being lumped together in an "optional expense" category. Tobacco was the major universal luxury. Bitatali store sales indicate an aggregate Vunamami purchase of about £800 during 1961, or roughly two and a half packets a week per household. The avidity with which cigarettes were accepted when one offered them, and the frequency with which stick tobacco was smoked in private suggest

that this demand was highly income-elastic, however. Betel and lime, the other major stimulants, were usually obtained by home production. Cold soft drinks, especially when visiting Rabaul, were another universal. Travel was another, though disproportionately for richer men, and less for women. Many men went by passenger truck to Rabaul each week-end; perhaps two women went each Saturday to sell in Rabaul market, and a few wage-earners' wives went in on week-days to shop for special items. I estimate the cost of men's travel to Rabaul at about £375 per annum, of truck charters for special occasions at £100, and of women's travel at £100. "Business travel" costing perhaps £500 and using locally owned Land-Rovers has been excluded.

(6) *Taxation.*—The rate of Council tax in 1961 was £4 for an adult male, and £1 for a female. The numerous indirect taxes paid on imported goods, copra fund levies, licence fees, and so on are ignored in this computation, but combine to make a relatively high tax burden. Aggregate Council tax contributions were over £400 in 1961.

Contributions to the church are even higher than Council taxes in Vunamami. About £400 was given for general church purposes, and about £400 in offerings for the local minister and teachers.

(7) *Savings.*—It rapidly became apparent that any systematic formal questioning on savings would be highly unreliable, since it was a very delicate subject. Inquiries were limited to a few highly trustworthy individuals who were not also close friends. Supplemented by glimpses of friends' bank books, these occasioned an estimate of total Vunamami savings of £5,000, mostly in the Savings Bank, although some individuals kept stores of £100 in their houses. Bank accounts were paid into fairly regularly, and withdrawn from periodically for major purchases like buying roofing iron. All accounts that I saw increased in 1961, but the over-all increase would be small.

Virtually compulsory saving was involved in the Cocoa Project loan repayments, the Co-op share subscription, the Ravalien purchase fund, and the church building fund. For Vunamami villagers only, payments were £263, £485, £250, and about £300, respectively. The last two payments were made by nearly all households evenly; cocoa payments were made overwhelmingly by richer businessmen, and by cash croppers; Co-op subscriptions, being based on the volume of purchases, as well as of copra deliveries, included considerable sums from wage earners but otherwise followed the pattern of cocoa payments.

Residual balances are entirely hypothetical. They serve, however, to show how social obligations constitute a relatively high fixed cost for wage earners and businessmen, and may lead to hardship for those earning less than the median, whereas a relatively less wealthy cash-cropper with few obligations may have considerable disposable income. Businessmen with a *tabu* income (see chap. 8) may use it, rather than cash for many of the items listed.

Appendix

E

Investment

The various forms of investment in Vunamami will be considered separately. Where possible, a figure will be calculated for the total capital stock of that item, of the amount constituting replacement expenditure, of the expenditure made in 1961, and hence, by subtraction, of the net addition to capital in that year.

(*1*) *Tree crops.*—Three measures could be used for this investment: acreage, labour input, or cash equivalent. Since trees are not usually planted by paid labour, only the first two will be considered.

Land owned in 1961 included 150.5 acres of sole coconuts, 398 of interplanted cocoa and coconuts, and 55 of sole cocoa, or the equivalent of 351 acres of coconuts and 320.3 acres of cocoa. Of these, 70 acres of coconuts and 185 acres of cocoa were, by my estimate, not bearing. About 15 acres of coconuts and 50 acres of cocoa were planted in 1961, about 10 of them on land cleared of forest at the Warangoi. Vunamami coconuts are over-age, and I should estimate that 3.3 percent (rather than the usual 1.5 percent) would constitute replacement planting, or about 12 acres annually. Between 4 and 5 percent is the suggested depreciation rate for cocoa trees (Australia 1958:20); 16 acres would be needed annually for replacement in Vunamami. Net investment in 1961 was thus of 3 acres of coconuts, and 34 acres of cocoa, plus 10 acres of forest clearing.

Labour inputs for forest clearing and for establishing cocoa are given as 60 and 80 man-days an acre (Australia 1958:34). Coconut planting on cleared land probably takes about 25 man-days an acre. Total planting time in 1961 would thus be estimated at 600 (10 acres × 60) plus 4,000 (50 acres × 80) plus 375 (15 acres × 25), or 4,975 man-days. An estimate of total planting time based on time budgets

(Appendix B) would be 2,925 man-days, or 13 percent of 75 non-wage workers' time.

Two main sources of discrepancy in these two estimates appear likely. First, peasant planters work faster than the indentured labourers who form the basis for published estimates of labour inputs. Second, half of the costs of establishing cocoa come in the second and third years after planting; in the time budgets much of this work of weeding, thinning shade, and so on may have been reported as cocoa maintenance. This would also help to explain the low productivity reported in chapter 3. I should thus compromise and estimate the total labour of planting and establishment at about 3,500 man-days in 1961. About 1,200 of these represent replacement expenditure, leaving a net investment of 2,300 man-days. This is 10.2 percent of the non-wage labour output of Vunamami.

(2) *Social and infra-structure.*—New capital works by Vunamami Council comprise about 40 percent of annual tax receipts. The amount paid for by the taxes of Vunamami residents is thus about £160. The total amount invested during the ten years of the Council's existence has probably been twelve times that; assuming a twenty-five-year life for buildings, replacement expenditure amounts to about £80.

Vunamami church in 1961 was a fully depreciated structure of local materials, built by local labour. The investment of £300 in a new church was entirely new.

(3) *Businesses.*—Investments in major businesses during 1961 were £485 to expand Co-op working capital, £263 for Talimut fermentery loan repayment, and £250 for purchase of Ravalien plantation. The Co-op and fermentery accounts allow for depreciation, so that the sums contributed are net capital additions. Two village driers were constructed in 1961 at a cost of about £125, replacing dilapidated ones. The twelve driers within Vunamami and two owned elsewhere cost an estimated £50 each, or £700 altogether. An eight-year life would require £90 of replacements annually, leaving a net investment of £35 in 1961. Other businesses—pig fences, Land-Rovers, canoes, etc.—probably merely replaced their used assets in 1961. No Land-Rovers were bought, but profits from the IaMinat group set aside for replacement probably equalled the total replacement needs.

(4) *Consumer durables.*—Housing in Vunamami was worth £8,500 for European materials alone; total expenditure was about £1,400 in 1961. If twenty years is taken as the life of materials, replacement expenditure would be £425, and net investment £975.

My estimate of household equipment investments is that £2,563-

VUNAMAMI CAPITAL INVESTMENTS IN 1961*

		Total Stock	Value of Annual Replace-ment	Spent in 1961	Net Invest-ment	As % of Income
Tree crops	in acres	596	28	65	37	NA
	in man-days	?	1,200	3,500	2,300	10.2†
Infra-structure, in £s		1,920	80	460	380	3.4
Businesses:						
major, in £s		?	?	998+	998	8.5
driers, in £s		700	90	125	35	.3
Consumer durables:						
housing, in £s		8,500	425	1,500	975	8.3
equipment, in £s		2,563	427	854	427	3.6
Total in cash		?	?	£3,837+	£2,815	24.1%

* Figures are derived as explained in text and Appendix D.
† This is a percentage of the amount of non-wage labour performed in Vunamami.

worth are owned, that £427-worth need replacement annually, and
that 1961 expenditure was at twice that level, or £854.

The over-all proportion of income used for new capital investment
is extremely high in comparison both with developed countries and
with developing countries. It is well over the 5 percent level taken by
Rostow as an index of incipient take-off into sustained growth. Part of
the reason for this is that there is only a small amount of previous investment stock, and most of the gross investment expenditure is new.
On the other hand, one may question the wisdom of the allocation of
investment funds. High expenditures for consumer durables are perhaps typical of societies entering a phase of mass consumer demand,
and the low level of local infra-structure investment can be explained
by the investment by the central government using the Australian
subsidy. The large compulsory investment in major businesses with
somewhat low rates of profitability compares unfavourably, however,
with the small amount that can find investment openings in highly
profitable local businesses.

Appendix

F

Population

A house-to-house census of Vunamami was conducted between 1 and 8 May 1961 by Dale ToPin, including names of residents and of absent dependents. This census was checked against government village census books and Council vital statistics registers, especially for ages and names of absentees, although it was found that the Council registers were very incomplete, and the government census books, though listing all individuals, were inconsistent in listing individuals in the village of current residence, or of birth, or of residence at a former date. Genealogical and life-history data were then collected on all persons listed. A final check on the whereabouts of all listed persons and on the actual occupants of all houses was conducted on 17 June 1961. Final census figures refer to that date.

Persons were classified as (*a*) resident in Vunamami village; as (*b*) domiciled in Vunamami and either paying Council tax or the children of taxpayers, but residing elsewhere (i.e. migrants); or as (*c*) children of Vunamami residents attending boarding school. Dotted lines on the population pyramid indicate the hypothetical population, if there had been no drop in fertility during the war years and no great increase in infant and child mortality. It shows a child population loss of about 85. This figure takes no account of the much increased adult mortality during the same period.

Of the 99 wives domiciled in Vunamami, 62 had been born in Vunamami village, 24 in the neighbouring villages of Vunabalbal, Bitarebarebe, and Tingenavudu, and 13 elsewhere. Of 65 wives domiciled in Vunabalbal village, 35 had been born in that village, 14 in the villages of Vunamami, Bitarebarebe, or Tingenavudu, and 16 elsewhere. Although marriage is nominally viri-avunculocal, with brides and

POPULATION PYRAMID, VUNAMAMI VILLAGE

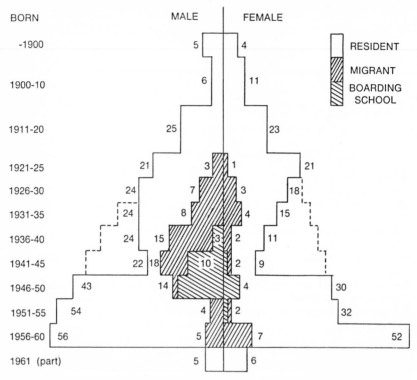

BORN	MALE	FEMALE	
			RESIDENT
-1900	5	4	MIGRANT
1900-10	6	11	BOARDING SCHOOL
1911-20	25	23	
1921-25	21	3 1	21
1926-30	24	7 3	18
1931-35	24	8 4	15
1936-40	24 15	3 2	11
1941-45	22 18	10 2	9
1946-50	43 14	4	30
1951-55	54	4 2	32
1956-60	56	5 7	52
1961 (part)	5	6	

grooms moving to take up residence on land owned by the groom's
clan, it will be appreciated that there is a high degree of intermarriage
within the four villages named, and that wives rarely move far at
marriage, often moving less than their husbands do.

There were no deaths in nine months of 1961, but there were 21
births. Part of this phenomenal natural increase rate of 5.2 percent per
annum was due to a high incidence of twinning. Seven living pairs of
twins were included in the census. A drop in the birth rate occurred
after 1961 as the war-depleted cohorts reached reproducing age.

Bibliography

A. PERIODICALS

Annual Reports. Various titles of Annual Reports of the Territory of New
Guinea. 1900–1913, *Jahresberichte über den Deutschen Schutzgebiete:*
1914–1921, *Report on German New Guinea under Australian Adminis-
tration:* 1922–1939, *Report to The League of Nations on the Mandated
Territory of New Guinea:* 1946——, *Report to the United Nations Trus-
teeship Council on Papua and New Guinea.*
Kolonialblatt. Deutsches Kolonialblatt. Official German Government Ga-
zette.
Kolonialzeitung. Deutsche Kolonialzeitung. Organ of the Deutsche Kolonial-
gesellschaft zu Berlin.
*Monatshefte. Monatshefte zur Ehren unserer Lieben Frau vom Heiligsten
Herzen Jesu.* (With title variations.) Journal of the Sacred Heart Mission
(M.S.C.). Hiltrup and Münster, Westfalen.
*Nachrichten. Nachrichten aus Kaiser Wilhelmsland und dem Bismarck
Archipel.* Organ of the Deutsche Neu-Guinea Compagnie, 1885–1898.
N.A.Z. Norddeutsche Allgemeine Zeitung.
P.I.M. Pacific Islands Monthly. Sydney.
Rabaul Times. Weekly. (Later incorporated in *New Guinea Times-
Courier.*)

B. PUBLISHED MATERIALS

Ainsworth, J.
   1924   *Report on Administrative Arrangements and Matters Affecting
          the Interests of Natives in the Territory of New Guinea.* Mel-
          bourne: The Government Printer.
Australia, Commonwealth of
   1920   *Interim and Final Reports of the Royal Commission on the Future
          Administration of Late German New Guinea.* Submitted to Par-
          liament 21 May 1920.
   1953a *An Economic and Cost Survey of the Copra Industry in the
          T.P.N.G.* Bureau of Agricultural Economics, Department of Com-
          merce, Canberra.
   1958   *Cocoa in Papua and New Guinea.* Report for the Department of
          Territories, by Bureau of Agricultural Economics, Canberra.

Banfield, E. B.
  1958 *The Moral Basis of a Backward Society*. Glencoe, Ill.: The Free Press.
Belshaw, C. S.
  1957 *The Great Village*. London: Routledge & Kegan Paul.
  1965 *Under the Ivi Tree*. Berkeley and Los Angeles: University of California Press.
Bley, B.
  1897 "Grundzüge der Grammatik der Neu-Pommerschen Sprache an der Nordküste der Gazellen Halbinsel," *Zeitschrift für Afrikanische und Ozeanische Sprachen*, 3:85–130.
  1900 "Lose Blätter," *Monatshefte*, 17:103–113, 152–164.
  1924 *Die Herz Jesu Mission in der Südsee*. Hiltrup: Herz Jesu Missionshaus.
Blum, H.
  1900 *Neu Guinea und der Bismarck Archipel*. Berlin: Schönfeldt.
Boserup, E.
  1965 *The Conditions of Agricultural Growth*. Chicago: Aldine Press.
Brown, G.
  1898 "Life History of a Savage," *Australasian Association for the Advancement of Science, Report of Meeting*, 7:778–790. Sydney.
  1901 "Some New Britain Customs," *Australian Association for the Advancement of Science, Report of Meeting*, 8:307–312. Melbourne.
  1908 *George Brown D.D. Pioneer, Missionary and Explorer*. London: Hodder & Stoughton.
Bürger, F.
  1913 *Die Küsten und Bergvölker der Gazelle Halbinsel*. Stuttgart: Strecker und Schröder.
Burry, B. P.
  1909 *In a German Colony*. London: Methuen.
Clark, C., and Haswell, M.
  1964 *The Economics of Subsistence Agriculture*. London: Macmillan.
Danks, B.
  1887 "On the Shell Money of New Britain," *Journal of the Anthropological Institute*, 17:305–317.
  1892 "New Britain and Its People," *Australasian Association for the Advancement of Science, Report of Meeting*, 4:614–620. Hobart.
  1899 *A Brief History of the New Britain Mission*. Sydney: Epworth Press.
  1933 *In Wild New Britain*. W. Deane, ed. Sydney: Angus & Robertson.
Dewey, A.
  1962 "Trade and Social Control in Java," *Journal of the Royal Anthropological Institute*, 92:177.
Duperrey, L. I.
  1826 *Voyage autour du Monde . . . sur "La Coquille", 1822–5*. 2 vols. Paris, Huzard-Courcier.
Epstein, A. L.
  1963 "The Economy of Modern Matupit," *Oceania* 33:182–215.

Epstein, T. S.
  1961 "A Study of Rabaul Market," *Australian Journal of Agricultural Economics*, 5:1–18.
  1963 "European Contact and Tolai Economic Development: A Schema of Economic Growth," *Economic Development and Cultural Change*, 11:289–307.
  1964 "Personal Capital Formation Among the Tolai of New Britain," in R. Firth and B. S. Yamey (eds.), *Capital, Saving and Credit in Peasant Societies* (London: Allen & Unwin).
  n.d. "Economic Change and Differentiation in New Britain." Mimeographed seminar paper, Australian National University.
Ewers, J. C.
  1955 *The Horse in Blackfoot Indian Culture*. Bureau of American Ethnology, Bulletin 159. Washington: Smithsonian Institution.
Finney, B. R.
  1965 "Polynesian Peasants and Proletarians," *Journal of the Polynesian Society*, 74:269–328.
Firth, R. W., Spate, O. H. K., and Davidson, J. W.
  1951 *Notes on New Guinea*. Mimeo Series P.S. 151, Australian National University, Canberra.
Fischer, J. L.
  1958 "The Classification of Residence in Censuses," *American Anthropologist*, 60:508–517.
Foster, G. M.
  1965 "Peasant Society and the Image of Limited Good," *American Anthropologist*, 67:293–315.
Geertz, C.
  1963*a* *Peddlers and Princes*. Chicago: University of Chicago Press.
  1963*b* *Agricultural Involution*. Berkeley and Los Angeles: University of California Press.
Goodenough, W. H.
  1956 "Residence Rules," *Southwestern Journal of Anthropology*, 12: 22–37.
Hagen, E. E.
  1961 *On the Theory of Social Change*. Homewood, Ill.: The Dorsey Press.
Hager, C.
  1886(?) *Kaiser Wilhelmsland und der Bismarck Archipel*. Leipzig: Gresser & Schramm.
Hahl, A.
  1897 "Über die Rechtsanschauungen der Eingeborenen . . . der Gazelle Halbinsel," *Nachrichten über Kaiserwilhelmsland, Beiheft*.
  1935 *Deutsch Neu Guinea*. Berlin: Dietrich Riemer.
Henderson, F. C.
  1954 "Cocoa as a Crop for the Owner-Manager in Papua and New Guinea," *P. & N.G. Agricultural Journal*, 9:45–74.
Hesse-Wartegg, E. von
  1902 *Samoa, Bismarckarchipel und Neuguinea*. Leipzig: Weber.

Hill, P.
1966 "A Plea for Indigenous Economics: The West African Example," *Economic Development and Cultural Change*, 15:10–20.

Hogbin, H. I., and C. H. Wedgwood
1953 "Local Grouping in Melanesia," *Oceania*, 23:241–276 and 24:58–76.

Hüskes, J., ed.
1932 *Pioniere der Südsee*. Hiltrup: Herz Jesu Missionshaus.

Jones, W. O.
1959 *Manioc in Africa*. Stanford, Calif.: Stanford University Press.

Keesing, F. M.
1952 "Research Opportunities in New Guinea," *Southwestern Journal of Anthropology*, 8:109–133.

Kleintitschen, A.
1906 *Die Küstenbewohner der Gazellehalbinsel*. Hiltrup: Herz Jesu Missionshaus.
1924 *Mythen und Erzählungen . . . aus Paparatava*. Vienna: Anthropos Bibliothek, Vol. 2.

Laufer, C.
1961 "Gebräuche bei der Herstellung einer Melanesischen Schlitztrommel," *Anthropos*, 56:459–468.

Linckens, H.
1921 *Streiflichter aus der Herz Jesu Mission*. Hiltrup: Herz Jesu Missionshaus.

Lyng, J. S.
1919 *Our New Possession, Late German New Guinea*. Melbourne: Melbourne Publishing Co.
1925 *Island Films*. Sydney: Cornstalk Publishing.

McCarthy, J. K.
1963 *Patrol into Yesterday*. Melbourne: F. W. Cheshire.

McClelland, D. C.
1961 *The Achieving Society*. Princeton, N. J.: D. Van Nostrand Co., Inc.

Mackenzie, S. S.
1938 *The Australians at Rabaul*. "Official History of Australia in the War of 1914–1918," Vol. 10. Sydney: Angus & Robertson.

Mair, L. P.
1948 *Australians in New Guinea*. London: Christopher's.

Mead, M.
1938 *The Mountain Arapesh: An Importing Culture*. Anthropological Papers of the American Museum of Natural History, Vol. 36.
1956 *New Lives for Old*. New York: William Morrow.
1960 "Weaver of the Border (New Britain)," in J. B. Casagrande (ed.), *In the Company of Man* (New York: Harper).

Meier, J.
1909 *Mythen und Erzählungen der Küstenbewohner der Gazellehalbinsel*. Vienna: Anthropos Bibliothek, Vol. 1.
1929 *Adoption Among the Gunantuna*. Publications of the Catholic Anthropological Conference, Vol. 1, No. 1.

Mintz, S. W.
    1961   "Standards of Value and Units of Measure in the Fond-des-Nègres Market Place, Haiti," *Journal of the Royal Anthropological Institute*, 91:23–38.
Moore, W. E.
    1966   *The Impact of Industry*. Englewood Cliffs, N. J.: Prentice-Hall, Inc.
Morison, S. E.
    1950   *Breaking the Bismarck's Barrier*. London: Oxford University Press,
Nag, M.
    1962   *Factors Affecting Fertility in Non-industrial Society*. Yale University Publications in Anthropology, No. 66.
Nash, M.
    1965   "Review of *From Stone to Steel*, by R. F. Salisbury," *Pacific Affairs*, 38:105.
New Guinea, Administration of
    1932   *Report of Director of Agriculture*. Rabaul.
    1954   *Rural Bias in Education*. Report to the Director of Education by F. Boisen and V. McNamara.
    1955   *Further Notes on a Rural Education Programme*. Report by F. Boisen to Director of Education.
Odgers, G.
    1957   *Air War Against Japan, 1943–1945*. Canberra: Australian War Memorial.
Overell, L.
    1923   *A Woman's Impressions of German New Guinea*. London: John Lane.
Parkinson, R.
    1887   *Im Bismarck-Archipel*. Leipzig: F. A. Brockhaus.
    1907   *Dreissig Jahre in der Südsee*. Stuttgart: Strecker und Schröder.
Pfeil, J. von.
    1899   *Studien und Beobachtungen aus der Südsee*. Brunswick: Vieweg.
Pitcairn, W. D.
    1891   *Two Years Among the Savages of New Guinea*. London: Ward & Downey.
Plotnicov, L., and Befu, H.
    1962   "Types of Corporate Unilineal Descent Groups," *American Anthropologist*, 64:313.
Polanyi, K.
    1966   *Dahomey and the Slave Trade*. Seattle: University of Washington Press.
Polanyi, K., Arensberg, C. M., and Pearson, H., eds.
    1957   *Trade and Market in the Early Empires*. Glencoe, Ill.: The Free Press.
Powell, W.
    1884   *Wanderings in a Wild Country*. London: Sampson Low.
Riesenfeld, A.
    1951   "Tobacco in New Guinea," *Journal of the Royal Anthropological Institute*, 81:69.

Rogers, E. M.
  1962   *The Diffusion of Innovations.* New York: The Free Press.
Rostow, W. W.
  1960   *The Stages of Economic Growth.* Cambridge: The University
         Press.
Rowley, C. D.
  1958   *The Australians in German New Guinea 1914–1921.* Melbourne:
         The University Press.
Salisbury, R. F.
  1957   *Economic Change Among the Siane Tribes of the New Guinea
         Highlands.* Doctoral dissertation, Australian National University,
         Canberra.
  1958   "An 'Indigenous' New Guinea Cult," *Kroeber Anthropological
         Papers,* 8:67–78.
  1959   "Social Factors in New Guinea Economic Development," in *Pro-
         posal for an Institute of International Studies Submitted to the
         Ford Foundation* (University of California, Berkeley).
  1962a *From Stone to Steel.* Melbourne and Cambridge: The University
         Presses.
  1962b "Early Stages of Economic Development in New Guinea," *Journal
         of the Polynesian Society,* 71:328–339.
  1962c "Matriliny and Economic Development." Paper presented at the
         American Anthropological Association Meetings, San Francisco.
  1964   "Despotism and Australian Administration in the New Guinea
         Highlands," *American Anthropologist,* Special Issue, 66(2):225–
         239.
  1966   "Politics and Shell-Money Finance in New Britain," in M. Schwartz
         and A. Tuden (eds.), *Political Anthropology* (Chicago: Aldine
         Press).
  1967   "ToNiri Buys a House," in W. T. Tucker (ed.), *Toward a
         Theory of Consumer Behavior* (New York: Holt, Rinehart &
         Winston).
  n.d.   *Fishing in Vunamami: A Buffer Industry in Economic Develop-
         ment.* Forthcoming.
Schnee, H.
  1904   *Bilder aus der Südsee.* Berlin: Riemer.
  1937   *Das Buch der Deutschen Kolonien.* Leipzig: W. Goldman.
Smith, S. S., and Salisbury, R. F., eds.
  1961   *Notes on Tolai Land Law and Custom.* Port Moresby: Native
         Lands Commission.
Stanner, W. E. H.
  1953   *The South Seas in Transition.* Sydney: Australasian Publishing.
United Nations
  1954   *Report to the Trusteeship Council of a Mission to Visit the Ter-
         ritory of New Guinea.*
Van der Veur, K., and Richardson, P.
  1966   *Education Through the Eyes of an Indigenous Elite.* New
         Guinea Research Unit Bulletin No. 12. Canberra: Australian Na-
         tional University.

Vogel-Hamburg, M.
 1911 *Eine Forschungsreise im Bismarck Archipel.* Hamburg: L. Fried-
   richsen.
Watson, J. B.
 1965 "From Hunting to Horticulture in the New Guinea Highlands,"
   Ethnology, 4:295–309.
Wawn, W. T.
 1893 *The South Sea Islanders and the Queensland Labour Trade.* Lon-
   don: Swan Sonnenschein.
Webster, H. C.
 1898 *Through New Guinea and the Cannibal Countries.* London: Fisher,
   Unwin.
Wegener, G.
 1903 *Deutschland im Stillen Ozean.* Land und Leute Monographien zur
   Erdkunde, Vol. XV. Bielefeld and Leipzig: Velhagen and Klaffing.
Weisser, J.
 1887 *Der Bismarck Archipel und das Kaiser Wilhelmsland.* Mitteilungen
   der Geographischen Gesellschaft in Hamburg, Heft 3. Hamburg:
   Friederichsen.
Wichmann, E.
 1917 *Nova Guinea.* Leiden: E. J. Brill.
Williamson, K. R.
 1958 "The Tolai Cocoa Project," *South Pacific*, 9:593–600.
Winthuis, P. J.
 1926 "Krankheit, Tod und Begräbnis bei den Gunantuna," in *Jahresbuch
   des Missionärztlichen Institute.* Katholische Ärztliche Fürsorge,
   Wurzburg.

C. MANUSCRIPT AND UNPUBLISHED SOURCES

Original documents were consulted principally at the Mitchell
Library in Sydney, the Department of Territories and Government Archives in Canberra, and in the office of the Hon.
Sec. New Britain Historical Society. Approval for publication
has been granted by those bodies and by Mrs. Louisa Miller.

Australia, Commonwealth of
 1923 Prime Minister's Department File A.1. 840/1/3.
 1933 Patrol Report K/1 1933–34 (Kokopo) by A.D.O. B. Calcutt, Ex-
   ternal Territories Dept File Q 386/3.
 1953b Notes on New Britain District. Prepared for the U.N. Visiting
   Mission.
Booth, A. S.
 Letter to General Secretary, M.O.M., 13 December 1910. Mitchell Li-
   brary Collection, Meth. Ch. O. M. 111.
Brown, G.
 Diary. Mitchell Library Collection, A 1686 11–14.
Danks, B.
 Diary. In Methodist Church Archives, Mitchell Library Collection, Meth.
   Ch. 616.

Letter to B. Chapman, 5 September 1880.
Letter to his cousins, 4 February 1881.
Letter to his wife, 28 October 1880.
—All in Mitchell Library Collection, Meth. Ch. 617.
Fellman, H.
 Letter to General Secretary, M.O.M., 1 July 1910. Mitchell Library Collection, Meth. Ch. O.M. 111.
Germany, Foreign Office
 Letter to General Secretary, M.O.M., 13 June 1891. Mitchell Library Collection, Meth. Ch. O.M. 167.
Methodist Minutes
 New Britain District Meetings, in *Minutes of Annual District Meetings,* Mitchell Library Collection, Meth. Ch. O.M. 5–26, 174–202. (After 1946, also in M.O.M. office, Rabaul.)
Miller, L.
 1958 Letter to Secretary, New Britain Historical Society, 13 April 1958.
 1964 Letter to Secretary, New Britain Historical Society, September 1964.
New Guinea, Administration of
 1956a Letter from Chief Justice to Chief of Native Lands Commission, No. R44/299/56, 14 July 1956.
 1956b Correspondence between Commissioner of Titles and Director of Native Affairs, File TC 3015, dated 18 January 1956.
Parkinson, R.
 1886 Letter to Sir George LeHunt, 20 March 1886. Mitchell Library, Parkinson Collection.
Public Service Institute
 1955 Notes on a course for Patrol Officers given at the Institute.

Index

Adoption: of employees, 156–157, 172, 328; of children, 161, 163, 322, 326
Adultery, 305–306
Agricultural Extension, 135–136, 140, 204, 254, 257, 259, 260, 346
AhTam, 242, 285–286
Alcohol, consumption of, 28, 134, 165, 170, 228, 247, 257, 293, 303
A.N.G.A.U. (Australian New Guinea Administrative Unit), 54
Axes: trade in, 22, 33, 76, 78; use of, 111, 113, 286

Bainings, 26, 30, 177, 324, 327
Balanataman village, 34, 76–77, 80–81, 95–96, 115, 135, 154, 158, 176, 192, 251, 300, 317, 320
Bargaining, in trade, 177, 180, 183
Barter, 178, 181, 182, 188
Beads, trade in, 22, 76, 113
Betel nut, 26, 158, 176, 200–201, 212, 368
Bicycles, 366
Big men, 23, 264, 271–272, 293–296, 305, 307, 328–329, 338–339, 346. See also *lualua*
Bitarebarebe village, 29, 76, 78, 176, 216, 222, 246, 258, 316, 359
Bitatali Cooperative Society, 62, 88–89, 127, 167, 216, 219–232, 235, 356
Bitaulagumgum Cooperative Society, 62, 167, 189, 216, 219, 222, 230, 235
Blood, and paternity, 73, 297
Brown, Dr. George, 21–24, 26, 74, 76–77, 111–113, 162, 185
Bush in ravines, 106–107, 110
Butuwin Hospital, 75, 78, 170

Cannibalism, 19, 24
Canoe: ownership, 152, 238–239, 331–332; production, 159, 286, 300
Capital: accumulating subscriptions,

105, 130, 253, 262–267, 265, 273, 275, 319, 344; creation by labour, 138, 370–371; for co-operatives 218–219, 230–232, 235; for businesses, 221–222, 244–245, 283; ownership 238–239, 269
Carpentry. *See* Skilled Craftsmen
Cash, 32, 37, 187, 283–285
Chickens, sale of, 122, 187–188, 212, 242, 248, 252
Chinese, 33, 40–41, 82, 87, 129, 173, 175, 184, 188, 190, 203–205, 212, 226, 275, 325
Church construction, 37, 42, 142, 243, 339. *See also* Mission, Methodist; Mission, Sacred Heart; Vunamami Church
Clans: formation of, 68, 70, 141, 329; and ceremonial payments, 69, 72, 86–87, 240; and land, 68–72, 88–89, 263; and businesses, 238, 270; ceremonial, 279–280, 297–301. *See also* Land, *Kivung*, and individual clan names
Clerical workers, 164, 166–168, 169, 170, 173, 202, 213, 220, 278
Clothing: introduction of, 22, 24, 30, 33, 36, 76–78, 161; purchases, 205, 216, 226–228, 365, 367
Cockatoos, 177, 192
Cocoa: introduction of, 36, 56–59, 135–145, 335–336; planting of, 97–99, 102–103, 320, 355–356, 370; yields, 259, 356; prices, 138, 258–259, 261–262. *See also* Fermenteries, Tolai Cocoa Project
Coconuts: Tolai planting, 43, 106, 108–109, 113–118, 124–126, 161, 355–356, 370; sales of, 112, 187, 214. *See also* Copra
Coffee, 29, 33, 36
Communications, expansion of, 345. *See also* Roads

383